Deregulating Property-Liability Insurance

Restoring Competition and Increasing Market Efficiency

J. David Cummins

Editor

D1231100

AEI-BROOKINGS JOINT CENTER
FOR REGULATORY STUDIES
Washington, D.C.

Deregulating Property Liability Insurance may be ordered from:
Brookings Institution Press
1775 Massachusetts Avenue, N.W.
Washington, D.C. 20036
Tel.: 1-800-275-1447 or (202) 797-6258
Fax: (202) 797-6004
www.brookings.edu

Library of Congress Cataloging-in-Publication data
Deregulating property-liability insurance : restoring competition and increasing market efficiency / J. David Cummins, editor
     p.   cm
Includes bibliographical references and index.
ISBN 0-8157-0243-4 (pbk. : alk. paper)
1. Insurance, Property—Deregulation—United States—Case Studies.
2. Insurance, Liability—Deregulation—United States—Case Studies.
I. Cummins, J. David
HG8531.D46 2001
368.1—dc21   2001004709

9 8 7 6 5 4 3 2 1

The paper used in this publication meets minimum requirements of the American National Standard for Information Sciences—Permanence of Paper for Printed Library Materials: ANSI Z39.48-1992.

Typeset in Adobe Garamond

Composition by Northeastern Graphic Services
Hackensack, New Jersey

Printed by R. R. Donnelley and Sons
Harrisonburg, Virginia

Deregulating Property-Liability Insurance

Foreword

The basic contribution of this book is to examine the potential impacts of deregulating prices in property-liability insurance markets. In general, the authors find that deregulation of prices will help restore competition and increase economic efficiency. For example, they argue that price regulation tends to reduce the availability of coverage and also reduces the quality and variety of products offered to consumers.

The findings on regulating prices in these markets are consistent with a broad literature in regulation that demonstrates conclusively that price regulation is generally bad for most consumers. This has certainly been the case in a number of industries studied in the United States, including airlines, trucking, railroads, and banking.

This book is one in a series commissioned by the AEI-Brookings Joint Center for Regulatory Studies to contribute to the continuing debate over regulatory reform. The series addresses several fundamental issues in regulation, including the design of effective reforms, the impact of proposed reforms on the public, and the political and institutional forces that affect reform. We hope that this series will help illuminate many of the complex issues involved in designing and implementing regulation and regulatory reforms at all levels of government.

ROBERT W. HAHN
ROBERT E. LITAN

AEI-Brookings Joint Center for Regulatory Studies

Contents

1 *Property-Liability Insurance Price Deregulation:
The Last Bastion?*   1
J. DAVID CUMMINS

2 *Automobile Insurance Regulation: The Massachusetts
Experience*   25
SHARON TENNYSON, MARY A. WEISS, AND
LAUREEN REGAN

3 *Private Passenger Auto Insurance in New Jersey:
A Three-Decade Advertisement for Reform*   81
JOHN D. WORRALL

   Comment on Chapters 2 and 3   135
RICHARD A. DERRIG

4 *Auto Insurance Reform: Salvation in South Carolina*   148
MARTIN F. GRACE, ROBERT W. KLEIN,
AND RICHARD D. PHILLIPS

5 *Regulation of Automobile Insurance in California*   195
DWIGHT M. JAFFEE AND THOMAS RUSSELL

   Comment on Chapter 5   237
DAVID APPEL

6 *Insurance Price Deregulation: The Illinois Experience*   248
STEPHEN P. D'ARCY

7 *Effects of Prior Approval Rate Regulation of Auto Insurance* 285
SCOTT E. HARRINGTON

   Comment on Chapter 7   315
   GEORGES DIONNE

8 *Form Regulation in Commercial Insurance*   321
   RICHARD J. BUTLER

9 *Insurance Regulation in Other Industrial Countries*   361
   GEORGES DIONNE

Contributors   397

Index   399

Deregulating Property-Liability Insurance

J. DAVID CUMMINS

1 Property-Liability Insurance Price Deregulation: The Last Bastion?

Over the past two decades, the United States has successfully deregulated prices and entry and exit restrictions, in whole or in part, for most industries that were once regulated: airlines, trucking, railroads, telecommunications, and banking.[1] Only a few industries stand as exceptions to this pattern, the largest being the property-liability insurance industry. It is perhaps not coincidental that this is the only such industry (of those mentioned here) still regulated at the state level for solvency, pricing, and entry and exit purposes, because deregulating at the state level requires action by all currently regulating jurisdictions rather than one decision at the national level.

In 1999 banking and insurance were allowed to combine as the result of sweeping financial modernization legislation (the Gramm-Leach-Bliley Act) passed in the United States. This change, as well as the 1994 deregulation of insurance prices and market entry in the European Union, makes it timely to examine the theoretical and empirical bases for continued regulation of rates and forms in the U.S. property-liability insurance market. Accordingly, the American Enterprise Institute–Brookings Institution Joint Center for Regulatory Studies sponsored a conference on insurance

The author thanks Herman Brandau, Richard Derrig, Georges Dionne, Robert Hahn, Dwight Jaffee, Robert Litan, Thomas Russell, and Sharon Tennyson for helpful comments on an earlier draft of this chapter.

1. The discussion of deregulation in this chapter applies primarily to pricing and entry-exit regulation. In the financial sector, both banks and insurers continue to be regulated for solvency as well as for other aspects of industry conduct and operations.

regulation in January 2001. This chapter synthesizes the principal findings of the papers presented at the conference and provides an analysis by the author of insurance price regulation, regulatory theory, and the welfare effects of regulation.

Potential Benefits from Deregulation: Overview

Insurance pricing is an important economic issue. Insurance plays a crucial role in enhancing economic welfare by permitting consumers and businesses to diversify risk. The property-liability insurance industry has annual premium revenues of about $300 billion, and insurance premiums account for a significant proportion of consumer expenditures, especially in states with high automobile accident costs. Consequently, even relatively small improvements in insurance market efficiency have the potential to substantially improve economic welfare.

Deregulation in other industries generally has had a favorable impact on consumer welfare, often reducing costs and prices, improving the quality and variety of services available to consumers, and providing incentives for firms to adopt new technologies and improve productivity.[2] Regulation has been shown to create inefficiencies, such as cross-subsidies among groups of consumers, that are reduced or eliminated under deregulation.

Because the insurance industry is competitive, deregulation is expected to bring benefits to insurance consumers similar to those realized in other deregulated industries. In addition, the better alignment of prices with costs that accompanies deregulation is expected to provide stronger incentives for safe driving, resulting in lower accident rates and reductions in insurance loss costs. Moreover, by suppressing prices below competitive levels, regulation leads to restricted availability of insurance coverage; such restrictions are significantly reduced in a competitive market. The remainder of this volume explores these and other regulatory distortions in more detail and analyzes the potential benefits from deregulation so that policymakers will have the information they need to redesign the insurance regulatory system.

Focus of the Conference

Insurance prices are substantially deregulated (de facto) for many commercial property-liability insurance markets, with the exception of

2. Winston (1993), Joskow and Noll (1994).

workers' compensation insurance where prices are still regulated by most states. However, workers' compensation markets and regulation are unique in many ways and have recently been analyzed.[3] Consequently, the present conference focused on the most important personal line of property-liability coverage—private passenger automobile insurance.[4] With annual premiums of about $120 billion that account for more than 40 percent of total industry revenues, private passenger automobile insurance is the most important business line for the property-liability insurance industry.

Automobile insurance prices are currently regulated in forty-nine states. In thirty-one states the regulation is of the *prior approval* variety, meaning that insurers must file rates with the state insurance commissioner and have them approved before they can be used in the market. In the other states, insurers can change prices without prior approval, usually with the proviso that they file the rates with the insurance commissioner, who can subsequently disapprove the rates. Only Illinois does not allow disapproval.

The conference centered around five state case studies. Academic experts analyzed the three most heavily regulated states—California, Massachusetts, and New Jersey—as well as Illinois, which has been deregulated for about 30 years, and South Carolina, which began to deregulate in 1997.[5] In addition, Scott Harrington conducted an econometric analysis based on all fifty states for the period 1974–98 to gauge the impact of regulation on insurance price levels, price volatility, and the proportion of automobiles insured in residual markets.[6] Georges Dionne analyzed insurance regulation in other industrialized countries. Because the primary regulatory constraint in the (non-workers'-compensation) commercial lines involves regulation

---

3. Danzon and Harrington (1997).

4. Homeowners' insurance is also price regulated in most states but was not discussed in detail at the conference in order to provide an in-depth analysis of automobile insurance. Most of the issues involving homeowners' insurance regulation parallel those in automobile insurance except that the former is more heavily affected by catastrophic risk in states with significant catastrophic exposure. Thus pressures for regulatory intervention in those states tend to be driven more by catastrophic risk exposure than by general inflation, as is the case with automobile and homeowners' insurance in states with limited exposure to catastrophic risk.

5. The California case study was conducted by Dwight Jaffee and Thomas Russell; the Massachusetts case study by Sharon Tennyson, Mary Weiss, and Laureen Regan; the New Jersey case study by John Worrall; the Illinois case study by Stephen D'Arcy; and the South Carolina case study by Martin Grace, Robert Klein, and Richard Phillips.

6. All states have laws stipulating that drivers who cannot obtain coverage from insurers on a voluntary basis can obtain insurance in the "residual market." The most common arrangement is the "assigned risk plan," where drivers entering the residual market are assigned to companies doing business in the state in proportion to their premiums written in the state.

of contract forms, Richard Butler analyzed the effects of form regulation on innovation and economic welfare in commercial lines markets.

Synopsis of Findings

This section provides a synopsis of the findings, which are explored in more detail in subsequent sections of this chapter. The findings can be summarized as follows: The market for private passenger automobile insurance is intensely competitive. If undisturbed by regulation, competitive market equilibrium will generate auto insurance prices that reflect an unbiased estimate of the expected costs of motor vehicle accidents as well as an appropriate profit for insurers, reflecting the risk they bear. There is no evidence that prices or profits in states that rely on markets to set rates are excessive or that insurers behave collusively.[7]

Automobile insurance price regulation tends to be imposed in response to rising premiums, which reflect rising claims costs. Because dissatisfaction with rising premiums is highest among drivers paying the highest premiums, regulation usually results in cross-subsidies flowing from low-cost drivers to high-cost drivers, increasing the premiums of the former and decreasing the premiums of the latter. Regulation also often results in rate suppression, where the total amount of premiums collected in a state is less than would be collected under competition.[8]

The amount of cross-subsidies and the degree of rate suppression vary by state and over time. Scott Harrington's findings (chapter 7), which confirm and extend those of a number of prior studies, indicate that on average prior approval regulation had little or no effect on rate levels over time. These results plus evidence presented in the state case studies suggest that periods of rate suppression in regulated states are followed by periods when insurers are able to earn higher than competitive profits, due to low inflation or declining loss costs. Insurers are often reluctant to reduce prices

7. See Cummins and Tennyson (1992). There is some evidence of cost inefficiency in the industry, paralleling similar findings in other industries such as banking. See Cummins and Weiss (1993) and Cummins, Weiss, and Zi (1999). Cost inefficiencies often develop in regulated industries because regulation blunts incentives to minimize costs and shelters inefficient insurers from competition. Thus deregulation of insurance prices can be expected to improve cost efficiency. Regulation sometimes may be appropriate to help ameliorate informational asymmetries between policyholders and insurers that can lead to cost inefficiencies. Regulators can do this by making prices and complaint statistics available to consumers over the Internet as is now done by states such as California and New York.

8. See Harrington (1992).

under these conditions for fear that they will be unable to raise premiums promptly and sufficiently if cost inflation accelerates.[9]

Cross-subsidization and rate suppression create additional economic inefficiencies. As Tennyson, Weiss, and Regan point out in chapter 2, subsidized rates reduce incentives for high-cost drivers to drive carefully, resulting in an increase in accident rates and insurance loss costs.[10] Harrington shows that regulation also results in reduced coverage availability in the voluntary insurance market, generally increasing the size of the residual market in regulated states. In addition, regulation leads to more premium volatility because price changes are less frequent and larger in regulated states than in competitive states (see chapters 2 and 6).

Thus, in the long run, rate regulation does not significantly reduce prices for consumers. However, it generally reduces availability of coverage, increases price volatility, and reduces the quality and variety of services available to consumers. The system also subsidizes high-cost drivers, sending adverse incentive signals and increasing accident costs. Regulation also increases cash flow volatility for insurers, raising the cost of capital. In essence, regulation creates material economic inefficiencies in order to provide cross-subsidies to the drivers who impose the highest costs on state automobile insurance systems.

Richard Butler's analysis of commercial lines policy forms regulation (chapter 8) shows that median times to market for new policies are about twice as high in prior approval states than in states that do not require forms approval. He also argues that forms approval is not needed in commercial lines markets because information asymmetries between buyers and sellers are minimal. Removal of commercial lines forms regulation would reduce insurance prices and increase market efficiency. Finally, in chapter 9 Georges Dionne argues that deregulation would enable the United States to keep pace with other industrialized nations in terms of

9. Recent increases in auto insurance costs in New York have prompted demands for more stringent rate regulation. Commenting on the crisis, New York's acting insurance commissioner said that many companies made mistakes in the late 1990s, underpricing their policies to gain bigger shares of the market. He also said that his department "*would not grant rate increases to bail out businesses that made poor decisions.*" (emphasis added). James C. McKinley Jr., "Facing Big Rise in Car Insurance, Albany Scrambles for a Solution," *New York Times*, May 3, 2001, pp. A1 and B2.

10. However, Jaffee and Russell's analysis of California price regulation suggests that this adverse incentive effect can be at least partially offset by safe driver insurance plans and other effective experience-rating programs. Subsidization also may reduce the number of uninsured drivers in a state, but it is doubtful that interfering with the competitive pricing process is the best way to provide premium relief to high-cost drivers.

enhancing competition in insurance markets and providing U.S. consumers with the full benefits of international financial services competition. However, he also points out that the deregulation of insurance markets must take into account the different information problems in these markets, including adverse selection and moral hazard.

Insurance Price Regulation and Regulatory Theory

The rationale for industrial regulation has received considerable attention in the economics literature. As with other industries, the earliest arguments for insurance price regulation were based on the view that regulation is needed to correct market failures. This *public interest* or *normative economic theory* rationale for regulation of insurance prices focused on two primary market failures: first, the tendency of insurers to engage in price wars that lead to widespread insurance insolvencies, and second, collusion among insurers that results in excessive prices and profits.[11] Prevention of price wars is a rationale that dates from the nineteenth century, when there were sporadic incidences of irresponsible price-cutting, primarily by fire insurance companies, followed by insurer insolvencies. Based on several recent decades of experience in states with competitive rating laws, there is no evidence that automobile insurers in competitive markets engage in destructive price wars. Rather, there is considerable evidence that prices in competitive insurance markets reflect expected claim costs and fair profits for insurers.

At one time concern over collusion in the insurance industry was well founded. As Stephen D'Arcy points out in chapter 6, the primary incidence of collusion in U.S. property-liability insurance occurred during the 1930s, when insurers operated as a cartel. This led to the *Southeastern Underwriters* case in 1944, where the U.S. Supreme Court ruled that insurers were subject to federal antitrust laws.[12] In 1945 Congress passed

11. As Georges Dionne and Jaffee and Russell point out, regulation also is sometimes used to modify the premium structure to provide incentives for safe driving. Regulation is occasionally motivated by the objective of controlling fraud and other dissipative expenses. However, *price* regulation is not the best way to address the fraud problem. Instead, creation of an industry-wide fraud bureau, such as the Massachusetts Insurance Fraud Bureau (see subsequent discussion), or other types of law enforcement mechanisms would attack fraud directly and more efficiently.

12. From 1869 until the *Southeastern Underwriters* case, federal law did not apply to the insurance industry, based on the U.S. Supreme Court ruling in the case of *Paul* vs. *Virginia*. The Court overturned this ruling in its *Southeastern Underwriters* decision.

the McCarran-Ferguson Act, allowing states to continue regulating and taxing insurers provided that they effectively administered antitrust laws to prevent collusive behavior. After passage of McCarran-Ferguson, most states adopted prior approval rate regulatory laws, many of which remain in effect to this day.

The concern that insurers will collude to fix prices at unreasonable levels is no longer well founded. The cartels of the 1930s are long gone, and rating bureaus, which formerly filed for rate changes representing hundreds of insurers, no longer engage in that practice.[13] Advances in computing and databases allow all but the smallest insurers to analyze data and conduct actuarial calculations with a speed and sophistication unheard of in the past, reducing the need to rely on rating bureaus with their potential for stifling competition.

Moreover, prior economic analyses, as well papers presented at the conference, support the conclusion that unregulated insurance markets are competitive and do not lead to excessive prices or profits.[14] Thus the collusion-antitrust rationale for price regulation is no longer credible.

If a compelling public interest rationale for insurance price regulation does not exist, how can the persistence of this type of regulation be explained? Economic theory offers some assistance in understanding this phenomenon. The predominant positive (non-normative) explanation for the existence and form of regulation is the *interest group* or *Chicago theory* of regulation.[15] Stated briefly, the interest group theory is based on the argument that regulation provides a mechanism through which organized interest groups can influence the distribution of economic rents in an industry. In this theory a utility-maximizing politician or regulator allocates "benefits across consumer and producer groups so that total political utility is maximized."[16] Whether regulation exists, the type of regulation adopted, and the distribution of rents at any given time are hypothesized

---

13. Rating bureaus now act primarily as statistical agents, pooling data so that insurers, especially smaller ones, can attain statistical credibility. The concept is that insurers use the pooled data to estimate expected loss costs and then add their own underwriting cost and profit charges. Controversy still arises over loss trending, that is, whether rating bureaus should be allowed to include estimates of future loss inflation in their statistical data or whether that step should be left to the individual insurers. An exception to the general rule about bureaus is the Automobile Insurer's Bureau of Massachusetts, which makes full price recommendations for all private passenger automobile insurers in the state, under the terms of its current laws and regulations.

14. See Joskow and McLaughlin (1991); Cummins and Weiss (1992); Harrington (2000).

15. See Stigler (1971); Peltzman (1976).

16. Peltzman (1989, p. 10).

to depend upon the relative costs and benefits of political influence activities among the existing interest groups. The groups receiving the largest economic rents are viewed as "winning" in the competition to influence the regulator. Two important predictions of the interest group theory seem particularly applicable to insurance price regulation: First, regulation will tend to create systematic cross-subsidization, creating price-to-marginal-cost ratios that differ across groups of consumers. Second, regulation will tend to offset to some degree the effects of competition on the division of rents between producers and consumers.

Several interest groups compete for economic rent distribution in the automobile insurance industry, including insurers (producers), classes of consumers with different underwriting characteristics, and insurance agents.[17] Producers fall into two primary categories whose interests do not necessarily coincide:

—*bureau insurers*, who traditionally set prices jointly through rating bureaus and tend to utilize the relatively high-cost independent agency system of product distribution, and
—*independent insurers*, who set prices more or less independently and tend to utilize relatively low-cost product distribution channels such as direct marketing, employee sales agents, or exclusive agents.[18]

Interest group theory helps explain why prior approval price regulation was adopted in most states after the breakup of the cartel and the passage of the McCarren-Ferguson Act in 1945. At the time the industry was heavily influenced by insurers that were members of rating bureaus, many of whom had been involved in the cartel. The adoption of prior approval

17. See Cummins, Phillips, and Tennyson (2001). As explained in Richard Derrig's commentary on chapter 2, the lawyers, chiropractors, and physicians who constitute the legal liability industry also are important interest groups that can affect the type of regulation that exists in a state, as well as the type of auto accident compensation system—tort versus no-fault. Because these groups benefit from payment of automobile liability claims, through contingent fees in the case of lawyers and fees for services in the case of doctors and chiropractors, they have a strong interest in maintaining the status quo. These groups also tend to favor cross-subsidization because it maximizes the number of drivers who purchase insurance by making liability insurance more affordable to high-cost drivers.

18. These categories oversimplify the structure of the market and are used here primarily for expositional convenience. The reader is cautioned that some companies do not naturally fit into either group and that there is considerable heterogeneity within the bureau and independent segments of the industry.

regulation can be viewed as favoring the interests of bureau insurers because they were allowed to file rates on behalf of all member companies, which at that time constituted the vast majority of the industry. The argument was that regulatory scrutiny of rate filings would prevent monopoly pricing. However, bureau rates tended to be set to facilitate survival of the least efficient bureau insurers, thus discouraging price competition. More efficient companies could compete by filing *deviations* from bureau rates or by paying dividends, but deviations could be costly for smaller firms and were discouraged by laws and regulations in some states. Thus for the most part price competition was very limited, and prices tended to be set above competitive levels.

The auto insurance market began to change dramatically in the 1950s when independent insurers such as State Farm and Allstate began more aggressive price competition.[19] These companies typically had lower expense ratios and used more refined risk classification systems than the bureau firms, enabling them to "skim the cream" by capturing drivers with the most desirable underwriting characteristics, who were overpriced at bureau rates. The result was a gradual decline in the auto insurance market share of the bureau companies and an accompanying decline in the economic rents generated for these firms through regulation.

Interest group theory predicts that changing market conditions, resulting in a shift in the balance of political influence among competing groups and a reduction in the economic rents of the incumbent interest group(s), should lead to regulatory change. In fact, pressure for deregulation and adoption of competitive rating began in a significant number of states by the early 1970s, and the National Association of Insurance Commissioners (NAIC) published a landmark study advocating competitive rating in 1974.[20]

Early movement toward price deregulation in automobile insurance also coincided with an upsurge in auto insurance loss costs in the late 1960s and early 1970s. The declining importance of bureau insurers, the market share gains of the generally more efficient independent insurers, and escalating inflation in loss costs and premiums shifted the balance of political influence in the insurance industry. The new power centers were the growing independent insurers and consumer interest groups. The for-

---

19. These firms also tended to utilize exclusive agents or company employees to distribute their products, giving them a lower cost structure than most bureau-affiliated firms, which tended to use independent agents for distribution.

20. NAIC (1974).

mer group favored deregulation because prior approval rate regulation impeded price competition and hence prevented efficient insurers from fully recognizing the benefits of their lower costs via price competition.[21] The interests of this segment of the industry coincided with the economic theory ideal of permitting competition to drive prices to the lowest possible level consistent with existing technology.

Emergence of consumers as an important interest group is less easy to explain using the interest group theory of regulation, which posits that *well-organized* interest groups tend to be most influential because their costs of organizing and exercising influence are lower than those of less well organized entities. Instead, this phenomenon is probably better explained by the *political entrepreneurship theory* of regulation.[22] According to this theory, regulatory change under some circumstances can be engineered by political entrepreneurs such as candidates for public office or consumer advocates. It is hypothesized that political entrepreneurs can tap into public dissatisfaction about market outcomes in specific industries and motivate consumers to express their policy preferences through the political process. For example, auto insurance prices have been a potent political issue in legislative and gubernatorial elections for decades in states such as New Jersey and Massachusetts. California's Proposition 103 referendum in 1988 can also be viewed as the outcome of opportunistic behavior by electoral candidates and consumer advocates, although the Proposition 103 battle had a grass-roots component as well. The objective of consumer interest groups generally has been to obtain lower prices, especially for high-cost drivers who are paying the highest premiums. Thus consumer movements have sought to reduce rates in general and to achieve cross-subsidies benefiting high-cost drivers.

In the early days of the deregulation movement in the 1970s, pro-competition insurers and consumer interest groups were sometimes on the same side of the deregulation issue. In these instances both groups argued for deregulation as a mechanism to limit the power of the bureau companies and bring rates down to competitive levels. However, during the past twenty-five years, these two groups usually have been at odds in their attempts to influence regulators, with the insurer group arguing for competitive rating and consumers arguing for regulation.

---

21. The bureau insurers continued to lose private passenger auto market share to the independent insurers during the 1970s and 1980s, with an attendant drop in their stake in the regulatory outcome. However, it was not until the mid-1980s that bureaus stopped filing rates on behalf of their members.

22. Joskow and Noll (1994).

Most of the chapters in this book show that in many states the consumer groups have been more influential than the pro-competition insurers (see especially chapters 2, 3, and 4). Thus one of the principal conclusions of this book is that the most common underlying reason for the current existence of property-liability insurance price regulation is consumer political pressure to reduce premiums and enforce cross-subsidies. Dwight Jaffee and Thomas Russell present an interesting example in California, where rising insurance premiums led to the passage of Proposition 103 in 1988, mandating a 20 percent rollback in insurance premiums and introducing prior approval rate regulation in a state where competitive pricing had been in effect for the previous 40 years (see chapter 5). Proposition 103 essentially pitted drivers in urban areas, where prices were highest, against drivers in suburban and rural areas, where prices were lower, and it passed by the narrowest of margins. Political pressures due to high premiums also have prompted stringent regulation in Massachusetts and New Jersey, again leading to cross-subsidies flowing from low-cost drivers to high-cost drivers.

Pressures for cross-subsidies and price control also tend to drive regulation in most other regulated states, although usually to a lesser degree than in California, Massachusetts, and New Jersey. The experiences described by Sharon Tennyson, Mary Weiss, and Laureen Regan (chapter 2), Jack Worrall (chapter 3), and Martin Grace, Robert Klein, and Richard Philips (chapter 4) suggest that the intensity of regulation tends to be directly proportional to the magnitude of the premiums charged in a state and to the variability of premiums among geographical areas and classes of drivers.

Regulating insurance prices is not a rational response to rising insurance premiums. Insurance premiums in a competitive market are driven by expected loss costs. Loss costs are determined by accident rates, the costs of auto repairs and medical care, and legal liability rules, none of which are under the direct control of insurers. Interest rates, another factor exogenous to the insurance industry, are also important because premiums reflect the present discounted value of loss cash flows.

At the present time, pro-competition insurers continue to press for deregulation to allow price-setting according to economics rather than politics. Whether deregulation will succeed depends upon convincing consumer interests and the regulators and politicians who depend upon their support that deregulation will have a net benefit to consumers as well as insurers. The chapters in this book are intended to provide information that can advance the debate over automobile insurance price deregulation.

Distortions from Insurance Price Regulation

As the foregoing discussion suggests, one adverse effect of regulation is to weaken the link between expected loss costs and premiums, creating cross-subsidies among classes of drivers. The Automobile Insurers Bureau of Massachusetts estimates that drivers in some Massachusetts rating classes and geographical territories receive cross-subsidies as high as 60 percent of the premium they would have paid if prices were strictly based on expected loss costs (reported in chapter 2). Drivers in other rating class or territory combinations had their premiums increase up to 11 percent in order to subsidize higher-cost drivers. On average, non-Boston territories pay a subsidy of 2 percent of premiums to support a 20 percent average premium reduction for drivers in Boston, and experienced drivers pay an average subsidy of 1.6 percent to support a premium reduction of 9 percent for inexperienced drivers. Cross-subsidies in most price-regulated states are not as high as in Massachusetts, which has a long history of rate "tempering"; but subsidies tend to be the rule rather than the exception when prices are regulated. In addition to cross-subsidies among classes of drivers in the voluntary market, in most regulated states drivers in the voluntary market subsidize drivers in the residual market.

As the authors of chapter 2 point out, cross-subsidization of insurance rates has a number of adverse consequences. Drivers decide how much and how safely they drive based on the marginal costs and benefits of driving. If high-cost drivers do not pay the full marginal costs they impose on the system, they will have an incentive to drive more and take less care; and if low-cost drivers pay more than their marginal costs, they will drive less than under competitive rating.[23] The net effect is likely to be an increase in accident rates and insurance loss costs, adding to the inflationary pressures on insurance premiums. Thus ill-advised attempts to lower premiums for some drivers through cross-subsidies have the effect of adding fuel to the inflationary fire.

Papers presented at the conference also provide evidence that regulation leads to rate suppression, defined as the situation where total insurance premiums collected in a state are not adequate to pay losses and provide a fair profit to insurers. For example, strong evidence presented chapters 2

---

23. See also Harrington and Doerpinghaus (1993). In their chapter on California rate regulation, Jaffee and Russell argue that the adoption of a more rigorous safe driver insurance plan under regulation tended to offset the adverse incentive effects of regulation on accident rates. Thus countervailing policy instruments may mitigate some of regulation's adverse effects.

through 4 suggests that rates were significantly suppressed in Massachusetts, New Jersey, and South Carolina. Tellingly, insurer losses due to rate suppression disappeared in South Carolina following deregulation.

The intensity of cross-subsidization and rate suppression varies by state and over time. From 1974 to 1998, on average across all jurisdictions, regulation had only a small, weakly significant downward effect on price (see chapter 7). This finding and evidence presented in chapters 2 and 4 suggest that periods of rate suppression in regulated states tend to be followed by periods when insurers are able to "catch up" to competitive rate levels, usually because inflation is low or costs are declining. This is partly because insurers are reluctant to reduce prices in regulated states, even when premiums are high relative to expected costs, out of concern that they will not be able to raise premiums again if cost inflation accelerates. There is evidence that premiums in California, for example, would have fallen significantly during the 1990s had California retained competitive rating rather than adopting prior approval.[24] As further demonstrated in chapter 7, such price stickiness in regulated states increases the volatility of average expenditures on automobile insurance, reducing the consumer welfare benefits of insurance coverage by partially offsetting the risk-reducing effects of insurance.

Insurers may or may not be able to recover the investment income deficiency caused by rate suppression during catch-up periods in regulated states, depending on the magnitude and timing of the rate suppression and catch-up period cash flows. However, this regulatory uncertainty increases the volatility of insurers' premium cash flows, leading to higher costs of capital in the industry. Higher costs of capital eventually translate into higher premiums, other things being equal.[25] Thus prices in regulated states are likely to include a charge for regulatory risk that is not present in competitive markets.

It is also clear that regulation generally increases the proportion of drivers who cannot obtain coverage in the voluntary market and instead must insure their vehicles in what is called the *residual market*. Generally speaking, most states assign policyholders in the residual market to insurers based on their market shares in the primary market. In some instances rate

24. See the discussant comments by David Appel in this volume.
25. Cummins and Sommer (1996) show that higher risk may induce insurers to hold more capital, which in a regulated financial institution is costly due to agency and regulatory expenses, corporate income taxes, and other dissipative expenses. Such costs must ultimately be borne by policyholders in order to retain capital in the industry. Thus higher risk is likely to translate into higher insurance prices.

suppression and subsidization can become so severe that the voluntary market fails, resulting in more than half the drivers being insured in the residual market and the exit of numerous insurers from the state. For example, the proportion of drivers insured through the residual market in Massachusetts hovered between 40 and 50 percent for most of the 1980s and reached a high of 72 percent in 1989. Even in states where cross-subsidies and rate suppression are less severe, regulation has a statistically and economically significant impact on the size of the residual market (chapter 7). The effect, of course, depends upon the stringency of regulation and the level of loss costs and inflation in a state. Post–Proposition 103 regulation in California did not significantly increase the size of the assigned risk plan in that state (see chapter 5). However, it is likely that the effects of California regulation were blunted by declining insurance loss costs during the 1990s.

A mild degree of rate suppression for a limited period of time does not lead significant numbers of insurers to withdraw from a state. This is primarily because regulated states usually impose exit restrictions, which do not allow insurers to withdraw from the automobile insurance market unless they surrender their licenses to write all other types of property-liability insurance in the state. The loss of potentially profitable commercial lines and homeowners' business thus often discourages insurers from exiting the auto insurance market. However, insurers tend to reduce product quality and take other steps in response to rate suppression as a way to cut their losses in regulated states. For example, insurers may stop writing new business or tighten underwriting standards to narrow the range of acceptable applicants. In addition, they are likely to scale back or abandon investments in new products or other innovations that would otherwise benefit consumers.

If rate suppression is severe or lasts for a considerable period of time, however, insurers do begin to exit the auto insurance market. This reduces the number of insurers providing auto insurance in the state, limiting consumer choice. For example, from 1990 through 1996, an average of 59 insurers were operating in South Carolina's regulated automobile insurance market, compared to an average of 197 insurers writing automobile insurance in the other southeastern states. After South Carolina deregulated, the number of companies nearly doubled within a year.[26]

---

26. Jaffee and Russell find that significant market exit did not occur in California after introduction of price regulation. Again, this is likely because rate suppression in California has been relatively mild and because regulation was implemented during a period when loss costs were generally declining.

A common pattern of market exit is the withdrawal of national insurers from a state, so that a higher proportion of the market is serviced by
single-state insurers. These are either independent firms or single-state
subsidiaries of national firms, formed to limit the exposure of the parent
firm to automobile insurance losses in the regulated market. In Massachusetts, for example, the top ten auto insurers in 1982 were all national writers, while only three of the top ten were national writers in 1998 (see
chapter 2). A similar pattern occurred in New Jersey (chapter 3).

To the extent that exiting insurers also withdraw from other lines
of insurance, rate suppression in the automobile insurance market can adversely affect markets for other types of property-liability insurance. To the
extent that economies of scale exist in the industry, the replacement of
larger, national firms with smaller regional and single-state firms drives up
the average costs of providing insurance. Financial quality also is reduced
because smaller insurers tend to have higher insolvency probabilities than
larger firms.[27]

Thus, on average, price regulation does not significantly reduce the
long-term cost of automobile insurance to consumers. However, it does
reduce the availability of coverage and increase price volatility. The system
subsidizes high-cost drivers, reducing incentives for careful driving and
increasing accident costs. Regulation also raises the cost of capital in the
industry by increasing cash flow volatility. Finally, regulation can cause
insurers to exit a state's insurance market, reducing consumer welfare by
limiting choice and increasing insurer default probabilities. In essence, regulation generally creates material economic inefficiencies, such as consumer welfare losses due to limited choice, insurance availability problems,
reduced product quality, and higher expected insolvency rates, in order to
provide cross-subsidies to the drivers who impose the highest costs on the
state automobile insurance systems.

Implications of Deregulation for Efficiency and Productivity

By limiting price competition, regulation protects inefficient opera-
tors and blunts incentives for insurers to minimize costs. The level of cost
efficiency in the U.S. property-liability insurance industry is about 68 percent, implying that on average firms in the industry could reduce their

27. Cummins, Grace, and Phillips (1999).

operating expenses by about 32 percent by becoming fully efficient.[28] The deregulation of insurance prices would result in a shift of business to efficient insurers and provide a strong incentive for inefficient firms to improve operating efficiency or exit the industry. Closing the efficiency gap would reduce industry operating costs and lead to lower prices for insurance consumers. Inefficiency in the industry is a pure deadweight cost that could be reduced by removing restrictions on price competition.

Moreover, studies of other industries have shown that deregulation often results in unexpected dynamic productivity benefits.[29] Regulation reduces incentives for firms to improve productivity and innovate in services and service technologies. For example, the development of hub-and-spoke systems in the airline industry is credited with significant reductions in industry operating costs, which have been largely passed on to consumers through lower prices.[30] This development was unforeseen at the time airline fares were deregulated. In the banking industry, deregulation is at least partially responsible for the adoption of technologies that reduce both bank and customer transaction costs as well as for the introduction of a wider range of financial services and products. Deregulation could have similar effects on the insurance industry via innovations in marketing, underwriting, policyholder services, and claims settlement that could reduce prices and increase product quality.

Commercial Lines Policy Form Regulation

In the (non-workers'-compensation) commercial lines of property-liability insurance, prices are de facto unregulated. Business firms and insurers are free to negotiate prices without significant regulatory interference, either directly or through insurance brokers, who shop the market for their clients' coverage. The result is a highly competitive market that is often considered commoditized because most business customers buy insurance based primarily on price, conditional on the insurer's having an adequate financial rating (usually an A.M. Best's rating of A or above).

Even though prices are not regulated, thirty-six states still have prior approval regulation for contract forms. This means that insurers must

---

28. Cummins, Weiss, and Zi (1999).
29. Winston (1993).
30. Joskow and Noll (1994).

file new contract forms with state insurance commissioners and wait for approval before using them. The time to bring a new contract to market varies widely among the states and is significantly higher on average in prior approval states than in those that do not require form approval (see chapter 8). The time to market ranges from 22 days in Michigan, which does not require prior approval of commercial lines policy forms, to 223 days in Louisiana, which requires prior approval. The median time to market in regulated states is 72 days versus 43 days in unregulated states.

The primary normative economic rationale for policy form regulation is buyer protection. This rationale is most likely to be valid when there are significant informational asymmetries between buyers and sellers. When sellers are well informed about the meaning and importance of insurance policy provisions and buyers are less well informed or uninformed, there is potential for consumer abuse and fraud. In such markets policy form regulation is likely to increase demand for insurance coverage if it reduces the possibility of insurer fraud and provides a type of "warranty" of the contract language. In chapter 8 Richard Butler presents empirical evidence that when such information asymmetries exist, there is a net benefit to consumers when auto and homeowners policy forms are regulated.

Conversely, in markets where both buyers and sellers are knowledgeable about contract language, regulation tends to increase the price of insurance and reduce the demand for coverage. When a new and innovative policy is introduced, the "first-mover" is likely to earn higher than competitive profits. Prices and profits will be reduced as competitors enter the market with comparable policy forms, and eventually a competitive equilibrium is reached where prices cover expected costs and a fair profit for insurers. By slowing down the introduction of competitors' policies, policy form regulation increases the amount of time between the introduction of a new policy and the entry of sufficient competitors into the market to drive prices to competitive levels. Thus in regulated states innovations will spread more slowly, and prices will tend to be higher than in states that do not regulate policy forms.

Considering the potential benefits of commercial lines form deregulation, it is curious that this type of regulation has survived over such a long period of time. Consistent with the interest group theory of regulation, the primary reason for the survival of form regulation seems to be the opposition of insurance agents to form liberalization. Thus form regulation serves a producer protection function for well-organized groups of agents who believe that freer competition in contractual language will weaken the link between agents and insurance buyers and ultimately reduce their profits. Therefore deregulation of policy forms will have to overcome the opposition of this and possibly other interest groups.

Aside from the welfare losses to buyers that result from commercial lines form regulation, policy form regulation also is problematic because of the emergence and rapid growth of the alternative risk transfer (ART) market. The ART market provides business firms with alternatives to traditional commercial lines insurance. Among the important ART mechanisms are self-insurance, captive insurance subsidiaries, and securitized financial instruments issued directly in the capital markets. The insurance brokers, reinsurers, and investment banks that serve as the supply side of the ART market have a significant competitive advantage over traditional commercial lines insurance companies: their contractual agreements are not subject to state prior approval regulation. Consequently, the time to market for new contracts in the ART market is comparable to the 22 days required in unregulated Michigan rather than the median 72 days in prior approval states.

By deregulating policy form approval, states can provide a "level playing field" for commercial insurers as they compete with the ART suppliers. This is important for reasons that go beyond mere "fairness." Specifically, if insurers and the ART suppliers are able to compete freely without regulatory restrictions, the insurance-ART market will provide the most efficient risk transfer at the minimum price to the business firms who are buying the protection. The reduced cost of risk transfer will at least partly be passed along to consumers in the prices of products they buy.

Thus, based on Butler's theoretical and empirical results, deregulation of commercial contract forms would be beneficial. However, personal lines form regulation seems to perform a significant consumer protection function and hence appears to be justified. Even in the personal lines market, however, insurance prices will be lower and demand for insurance higher if the time lag between form filing and form approval can be reduced.

Insurance Regulation in Other Industrialized Nations

As Georges Dionne points out in chapter 9, there is a worldwide trend toward less restrictive regulation of the financial services sector. In the United States, the passage of the Gramm-Leach-Bliley Act in 1999 significantly reduced restrictions on the variety of products and services that can be offered by financial services firms—for example, it is now permissible for financial holding companies to own both banks and insurers as well as other types of financial services firms. The Third Generation Directives of the European Union (EU), introduced in 1994, were designed to eliminate most types of regulation (including price regulation) in insurance markets and removed most restrictions on European insurers operating across national boundaries. The EU's objective is the creation of a single European market for insurance and other financial services. Japan also has initiated regulatory reform that eventually is expected to include deregulation of insurance prices. If U.S. consumers are to receive the full benefits of increasing worldwide financial services competition, it is important for the United States to join the trend toward insurance price deregulation.

However, the deregulation of insurance markets must take into account the different information problems in these markets: adverse selection, ex ante moral hazard and its effect on accidents rates, and ex post moral hazard, which is often associated with insurance fraud. This is consistent with the experience described below regarding the deregulation of savings and loans and airlines. That is, other policy changes may be needed to counteract any emerging problems triggered by the increase in competition following deregulation.

Does Regulation Have a Role in Competitive Insurance Markets?

The theme of the conference and of most recent economic research on insurance has been that deregulation generally will enhance insurance market efficiency. This raises the question of whether regulation has any role in competitive insurance markets. The answer is a qualified "yes," but generally only in situations where serious market imperfections exist.

One example where regulation is appropriate was discussed earlier: approval of personal lines policy forms. Regulation can also play a positive role by helping to increase the availability of information on market prices and quality. For example, several states, including California and New York, provide access to insurance price and consumer complaint data on their websites. This is helpful because it reduces search costs for consumers and enables them to make better decisions when shopping for insurance. Regulation of prices in the residual market also would seem to make sense because this market is inherently noncompetitive. However, any such regulation should allow rates to reflect expected costs and fair profits to avoid distorting the voluntary market due to cross-subsidization. If the residual market begins to grow after adoption of residual market rates in a competitively rated state, it is strong evidence that residual market prices have been set too low.

Solvency regulation also appears to provide a net benefit to insurance buyers and is another instance of an appropriate informational and bonding role for regulators. By providing information on insurer financial quality, regulators allow buyers to choose an insurer with low insolvency risk. Furthermore, by effectively monitoring insurers that experience deteriorating financial conditions, the regulator can help minimize the number of policyholders having claims settled by guaranty funds rather than by solvent insurers.[31] It has been argued that private monitoring firms can substitute for state regulators in the role of solvency monitors, but this would be more appropriate for business firms and those sophisticated consumers who know where to find and how to interpret private monitoring data. Moreover, such firms have no authority to intervene to minimize losses to policyholders and guaranty funds when an insurer's financial condition is deteriorating.

Government intervention also can play a role where programs that could reduce insurance costs do not arise naturally in competitive markets due to externalities and free-rider problems. One example is fraud prevention. One of the most important reasons for inflation in automobile insurance loss costs is consumer fraud, motivated by the availability of pain and suffering awards for bodily injuries. The quest for pain and suffering awards motivates claimants to fake bodily injuries or, more commonly, to "build up" a minor injury to appear more serious and thus qualify for a higher award.[32]

Individual insurers that fight insurance fraud do not receive the full marginal benefits of their expenditures because some of these benefits accrue to competing insurers. Thus insurers with active fraud-prevention programs create externalities that help their competitors, who can free ride

---

31. The unpaid losses of insolvent insurers are borne by insurance guaranty funds, which operate at the state level and obtain funds by assessing solvent insurers. Settlement of claims through guaranty funds is less desirable to claimants because claim payments are often delayed and are subject to upper limits that can leave some losses uncompensated.

32. Weisberg and Derrig (1991); Cummins and Tennyson (1992); Cummins and Tennyson (1996).

on the benefits of fraud prevention.[33] Under these circumstances the amount of fraud prevention actually implemented will be less than if fraud-prevention expenditures were expanded until the marginal costs equaled the marginal benefits marketwide.

An innovative program that attempts to capture the externalities of fraud resistance is the Massachusetts Insurance Fraud Bureau (MIFB). The MIFB was created by an act of the Massachusetts legislature in 1990 and is funded by the insurance industry. The mission of the MIFB is to prevent and investigate fraudulent insurance activity. It maintains a staff of fraud investigators and attorneys to track down and prepare cases for the prosecution of individuals involved in insurance fraud. The bureau has achieved more than 350 convictions to date and has been credited with saving millions of dollars for insurance companies and their policy-holders. The MIFB exemplifies the kind of innovative private sector–governmental partnership that has the potential to reduce insurance costs and premiums.[34]

Georges Dionne points out another way that regulation may play a positive role in insurance markets, based on experience in the insurance markets of France and Quebec. Recent theoretical research suggests that multiperiod contracts need some form of *commitment* from the insurer to provide a way to deal with moral hazard and adverse selection. Yet results presented in his chapter show that this is not necessary for adverse selection in either France or Quebec because private insurers efficiently manage this information problem with risk classification. However, the literature suggests that matters are less simple with moral hazard. Preliminary results indicate that some form of commitment by the insurers (or the industry) on the bonus-malus scheme is effective against this information problem.[35] Usually such a commitment is elicited by regulating the bonus-malus scheme, and the argument doing so is similar to that offered for insurance fraud, which is another form of moral hazard.

---

33. Insurers that vigorously resist fraud generate publicity about fraud convictions and raise the awareness of judges and juries about the fraud problem, thus providing a deterrent effect that bene-fits both fraud-fighting insurers and their competitors. The marginal benefit to competitors is an exter-nality that tends to result in suboptimal expenditures on fraud prevention.

34. Derrig and Krause (1994)

35. A bonus-malus plan is an experience rating formula that gives drivers rate credits and debits based on accident and conviction records. In most cases the driver's bonus-malus record is transferred to the new insurer if the driver switches companies.

Is There a Downside to Deregulation?

The experience with deregulation over the past thirty years in the United States has been generally beneficial.[36] However, there have been instances in other industries where deregulation has been followed by higher costs, reduced service quality, and other serious market problems. In most such cases, however, it was not deregulation per se but rather deregulation coupled with exogenous events and policy failures in other areas that were responsible for the problems. For example, although deregulation preceded the savings and loan (S&L) industry's widely publicized and very costly financial debacle during the 1980s, the S&L crisis was triggered by interest rate volatility and exacerbated by moral hazard stemming from the presence of federal deposit insurance. The resulting costs would have been much lower had prudent bank safety and soundness regulation been practiced rather than the regulatory forbearance that permitted financially vulnerable S&Ls to run up huge deficits before regulatory action was taken. Likewise, the congestion that often plagues the airline industry could have been avoided had policymakers appropriately increased airport and air traffic control capacity in response to the increased demand for air travel brought on by lower prices following deregulation.[37]

The message from these seeming examples of deregulatory failure is not that deregulation should be avoided but rather that it sometimes needs to be accompanied by other policy adjustments that respond to the changing market conditions brought about by deregulation. It is also worth emphasizing that the United States has conducted a "controlled experiment" in insurance deregulation over the past thirty years, whereby competitive pricing was permitted in some states and regulated pricing required in others. The results of the experiment, as reported in this book, show that price competition is superior to regulation and that unexpected ancillary problems, such as those affecting the S&Ls and airlines, have not arisen in states with competitive insurance pricing.

36. Winston (1993); Joskow and Noll (1994).

37. The problems resulting from electric utility "deregulation" in California have no particular implications for insurance deregulation. The California deregulation imposed a regulatory structure that is not true deregulation and is much more complicated than the straightforward removal of prior approval rate and form regulation and exit restrictions that would constitute price deregulation in insurance. Additionally, unlike electric utility firms, insurers are not saddled with the massive sunk costs of existing generating plants and lengthy build times to add new capacity. Insurance is primarily a variable cost industry that can, in the absence of restrictive regulation, respond quickly and efficiently to supply, demand, and loss shocks.

Conclusions

The time has come to deregulate prices in the personal lines of property-liability insurance. In the long run, price regulation does not result in lower prices for consumers, but it can create serious economic inefficiencies that destabilize insurance markets and ultimately increase the price of insurance. By deregulating insurance prices, the United States can keep pace with other industrialized nations and provide its consumers with the full benefits of international financial services competition. Deregulation of commercial lines policy forms also would correct a market inefficiency and lead to lower prices and enhanced welfare in the commercial lines market.

Although the chapters in this book provide extensive information on the effects of insurance price regulation, the policy debate would also benefit from a more explicit cost-benefit analysis of insurance regulation.[38] Such an analysis would provide econometric and other evidence to guide policymakers in reengineering their approach to insurance markets as well as baseline predictions that could be used to gauge the realized effects of deregulatory programs subsequently introduced.

References

Cummins, J. David, Martin F. Grace, and Richard D. Phillips. 1999. "Regulatory Solvency Prediction in Property-Liability Insurance: Risk-Based Capital, Audit Ratios, and Cash Flow Simulation." *Journal of Risk and Insurance* 66 (3): 417–58.

Cummins, J. David, Richard D. Phillips, and Sharon Tennyson. 2001. "Regulation, Political Influence, and the Price of Automobile Insurance." *Journal of Insurance Regulation* 20 (fall): 9–52.

Cummins, J. David, and David Sommer. 1996. "Capital and Risk in Property-Liability Insurance Markets." *Journal of Banking and Finance* 20 (6): 1069–92.

Cummins, J. David, and Sharon Tennyson. 1992. "Controlling Automobile Insurance Costs." *Journal of Economic Perspectives* 6 (2): 95–115.

———. 1996. "Moral Hazard in Insurance Claiming: Evidence from Automobile Insurance." *Journal of Risk and Uncertainty* 12 (1): 29–50.

Cummins, J. David, and Mary A. Weiss. 1992. "Structure, Conduct, and Performance in Property-Liability Insurance." In *Financial Condition and Regulation of Insurance Companies,* edited by Richard Kopcke and Richard Randall, 117–54. Federal Reserve Bank of Boston.

38. This analysis would be similar to the research discussed in Hahn and Hird (1991).

_____. 1993. "Measuring Cost Efficiency in the Property-Liability Insurance Industry." *Journal of Banking and Finance* 17 (2–3): 463–81.

Cummins, J. David, Mary A. Weiss, and Hongmin Zi. 1999. "Organizational Form and Efficiency: An Analysis of Stock and Mutual Property-Liability Insurers." *Management Science* 45 (9): 1254–69.

Danzon, Patricia M., and Scott E. Harrington. 1997. *Rate Regulation of Workers' Compensation Insurance.* American Enterprise Institute (AEI).

Derrig, Richard A., and Laura K. Krause. 1994. "First Steps to Fight Workers' Compensation Fraud." *Journal of Insurance Regulation* 12 (3): 390–415.

Hahn, Robert W., and John A. Hird. 1991. "The Costs and Benefits of Regulation: Review and Synthesis." *Yale Journal on Regulation* 8 (1): 233–78.

Harrington, Scott E. 1992. "Rate Suppression." *Journal of Risk and Insurance* 59: 185–202.

_____. 2000. *Insurance Deregulation and the Public Interest.* AEI–Brookings Joint Center for Regulatory Studies.

Harrington, Scott E., and Helen I. Doerpinghaus. 1993. "The Economics and Politics of Automobile Insurance Rate Classification." *Journal of Risk and Insurance* 60 (1): 59–84.

Joskow, Paul L., and Linda McLaughlin. 1991. "McCarran-Ferguson Act Reform: More Competition or More Regulation?" *Journal of Risk and Uncertainty* 4 (4): 373–401.

Joskow, Paul L., and Roger G. Noll. 1994. "Deregulation and Regulatory Reform During the 1980s." In *American Economic Policy in the 1980s,* edited by Martin Feldstein, 367–440. University of Chicago Press.

National Association of Insurance Commissioners. 1974. *Monitoring Competition: A Means of Regulating the Property and Liability Insurance Business.* Kansas City, Mo.

Peltzman, Sam. 1976. "Toward a More General Theory of Regulation." *Journal of Law and Economics* 19 (2): 211–40.

_____. 1989. "The Economic Theory of Regulation after a Decade of Deregulation." *Brookings Papers on Economic Activity: Microeconomics,* 1–41.

Stigler, George. 1971. "The Theory of Economic Regulation." *Bell Journal* 2 (1): 3–21.

Weisberg, Herbert I., and Richard A. Derrig. 1991. "Fraud and Automobile Insurance: A Report on the Baseline Study of Bodily Injury Claims in Massachusetts." *Journal of Insurance Regulation* 9 (4): 497–541.

Winston, Clifford. 1993. "Economic Deregulation: Days of Reckoning for Microeconomists." *Journal of Economic Literature* 31 (3): 1263–289.

SHARON TENNYSON
MARY A. WEISS
LAUREEN REGAN

2 | Automobile Insurance Regulation: The Massachusetts Experience

Compared to other states, Massachusetts has a uniquely interventionist automobile insurance regulatory system. Not only does the state set uniform rates to be charged by all companies, virtually all aspects of the market's operation are regulated. For example, the state

—determines driver-rating classes and territories, using an extensive system of cross-subsidies built into class and territory rates;
—approves vehicle risk ratings;
—sets the conditions for policy cancellation;
—evaluates the cost containment efforts of insurers;
—determines the terms under which an insurer can exit the market.

This regulatory system, with some modifications, has been in operation since the mid-1970s.

This chapter analyzes the impact of this regulatory system on the Massachusetts automobile insurance market. To anticipate the magnitude of its impact, one need only bear in mind two points: first, this system is imposed upon a nonmonopolistic market in which more than 100 firms

The authors acknowledge financial support from the AEI-Brookings Joint Center for Regulatory Studies and from USDA grant NYC-324306 (Tennyson). J. David Cummins and Richard Derrig generously provided data used in the analysis. Derrig also generously shared his knowledge of Massachusetts regulatory history and institutions. Byeongyong Choi provided valuable research assistance.

operated prior to regulation; second, individual consumers are free to choose whether and how much to drive, with no risk of insurance refusal and relatively weak links between the risks a driver imposes on the market and the insurance premium paid. As a consequence, the behavioral incentives of both firms and consumers are significantly distorted relative to the unregulated market.

The core philosophical underpinnings of the Massachusetts system have undeniable social merit. The objectives of the automobile insurance laws are to achieve universal insurance coverage and ensure reasonable rates for all drivers, while maintaining insurer solvency. At least for liability insurance, universal coverage is desirable because it reduces the negative externalities that drivers impose on others (in the form of accident losses). Lowering rates for liability insurance coverage, even if achieved through rate subsidies for some drivers, may increase insurance purchase or the amount of coverage and thereby enhance social well-being.[1]

Massachusetts has succeeded in achieving high levels of automobile insurance purchase: it is consistently ranked among the states with the lowest rates of uninsured motorists.[2] However, the cross-subsidies in place to achieve this appear to have gone beyond the level required to enhance social efficiency. The incentive distortions created by the system imply that both insured losses and insurer operating costs are likely to be much higher than under open competition. The overall effect is that reasonable insurance rates are less likely to be achieved under the current regulatory system than under alternatives.

The remainder of the chapter develops this argument and supports it with empirical evidence. First we describe the history and important features of the Massachusetts regulatory system and then examine insurer profitability under regulation. With this as institutional background, we analyze the incentives created by the regulations and look for empirical evidence of these effects in the market. We conclude with a discussion of implications for reforms.

The Massachusetts Regulatory System

Massachusetts was the first state in the country to legislate compulsory automobile insurance with specific minimum coverage limits.[3] The

---

1. Keeton and Kwerel (1984).
2. Insurance Research Council (1999).
3. This section draws heavily on Rottenberg (1989); Derrig (1993); Stone (1977, 1978).

law went into effect in 1927 and required the insurance commissioner to set uniform rates to be charged by all insurers for compulsory coverages. Rates for optional coverages were regulated via prior approval of the commissioner. In 1970 Massachusetts enacted no-fault automobile insurance (effective 1971). With this change uninsured motorist coverage and property damage liability coverage also became compulsory and thus were included in the uniform rate setting. A *mandatory offer* rule was also established in the law, under which no insurer could deny compulsory insurance coverage to a driver. In 1973 the mandatory offer rule was extended to optional coverages. By 1975 the regulatory system had been consolidated such that uniform rates for all coverages were set by the insurance commissioner. Firms were allowed to deviate from the state-set rates, but only in a downward direction and only with the prior approval of the commissioner.

In 1976 legislation was passed allowing for more competitive automobile insurance rate setting. The legislation provided for what is generally called a *file and use* system, under which large insurers (over 1 percent market share) could file their own rates at any time, provided there was a 45-day waiting period prior to the rates becoming effective in the market. A common set of rating territories was mandated, as well as a detailed set of filing forms. During the waiting period, the commissioner could disapprove the rates, based on standards written into the statute. Rates did not need to be specifically approved by the commissioner prior to their market introduction.

The legislation contained an additional provision, however, that has proven important in determining the actual process of rate setting. Section 5 of the law allowed a return (for one year at a time) to the traditional system of state-made rates if, after holding a hearing, the insurance commissioner determined that competition was "insufficient to assure that rates will not be excessive" or was "so conducted as to be destructive of competition or detrimental to the solvency of insurers."[4] That is, if competitive rating did not appear to meet the dual goals of insurance rates that were neither excessive nor inadequate, the commissioner could suspend competition and set uniform rates. Since the standards for this determination were not specified in the legislation, the commissioner was granted broad discretion in this regard.

The new law became effective in 1977, and the transition to price competition was not a smooth one. Partly due to territory changes, prices

4. Stone (1977).

for some risk classifications rose tremendously, and comparative price information was difficult for consumers to obtain. The number of consumer complaints to the Division of Insurance rose to a record high. As a result, Insurance Commissioner James Stone called for hearings under section 5 in May 1977, only a few months after the first competitive rates went into effect.

Based upon the hearings, Commissioner Stone reinstituted state-made rates for 1978. His opinion was that competition was not occurring in the marketplace because

—insurers were not providing consumers with price information to allow comparison shopping;

—insurers were not aggressively trying to increase market shares and raised rates greatly for some classes of risks;

—relatively few consumers switched companies despite large price differentials, while companies ceded a large number of drivers to the residual market facility.

The commissioner specifically rejected the companies' arguments that the problems were transitional in nature.

The actions of Commissioner Stone and of the Massachusetts state legislature in 1977 further weakened the environment for competitive rating. The legislature ordered rebates on 1977 premiums for many policyholders and passed legislation forbidding premium surcharges to policyholders insured through the residual market facility. In determining the 1978 rates, the commissioner rejected age, gender, and marital status as rate classification variables, arguing that they "failed to meet a minimum standard of social acceptability."[5] He further argued that all insurers should be required to utilize the same classification variables. These actions made it apparent that the state was little prepared to tolerate negative effects of competitive rating for any automobile insurance consumers.

In his written opinion on 1978 hearings to determine whether 1979 rates should be competitively set, Commissioner Stone acknowledged the tension between the social objectives written into Massachusetts auto insurance law and competitive rate setting. He concluded, however, that since only competitive rating was optional under the law, it must yield to the social objectives. In view of the severe constraints placed on competition,

5. Stone (1978).

even the state's insurers offered (weak) support for continuing the state-made rating system into 1979. Thus began the tradition of annual hearings to determine whether market conditions allow for competitive rate-setting. In each year to date, the decision has been made to continue state-set rates for one more year.

Regulatory Process

Once a hearing has been held to rule out the use of competitive rates for the upcoming year, the hearing process for determining the state-set rates is set into motion. The main parties to the hearings are the Massachusetts Automobile Insurers Bureau (AIB), which files recommendations on behalf of the automobile insurers; the State Rating Bureau, which presents the Division of Insurance's perspective on rates; and the Office of the Attorney General, which presents its own analysis of rates as part of its consumer protection role.[6] The hearings are public, and representatives of private industry and consumer organizations may also provide opinions and comment. The rates determined from this hearing process must be charged by all firms writing in the state, irrespective of differences in operating costs, unless an insurer offers a commissioner-approved discount below the state-set rate.

A host of inputs to the rate-setting process are also evaluated by the insurance commissioner in separate proceedings each year. The commissioner evaluates current financial and insurance market conditions and sets the underwriting profit provision in the rates. Additionally, since 1984 the commissioner has annually approved rate credits and surcharges to be applied under the Safe Driver Insurance Program (SDIP), which modifies premiums based upon a driver's recent accident experience. Since 1986 the commissioner has also been under legislative mandate to hold an annual review of insurers' cost containment efforts. The driver classes and territories and all other classifications used in setting rates for individual consumers are also determined by the commissioner.[7] Insurers may not innovate by changing class and territory definitions.

Driver classes have not been subject to much revision over time, but some additional rate classes were introduced in 1981. As noted earlier, age, gender, and marital status are not allowable rate classification variables.

6. Derrig (1993).
7. For example, multicar discounts and discounts for antitheft devices.

Table 2-1. *Massachusetts Driver Rating Classes, 1998*
Units as indicated

Class	Description	Number of exposures	Percent of market
10	Experienced operator	2,787,395	76.1
15	Senior citizen	528,203	14.4
17	Principal operator, 3–6 years driving experience	92,628	2.5
18	Occasional operator, 3–6 years driving experience	46,060	1.3
20	Principal operator, 0–3 years driving experience, no drivers training	18,373	0.5
21	Occasional operator, 0–3 years driving experience, no drivers training	11,504	0.3
25	Principal operator, 0–3 years driving experience, drivers training	44,164	1.2
26	Occasional operator, 0–3 years driving experience, drivers training	73,718	2.0
30	Business-use operator	61,813	1.7

Source: AIB (1999).

The class definitions used since 1981 group drivers into nine categories: experienced drivers, senior citizen drivers, business-use drivers, and six classes of inexperienced drivers. The inexperienced driver categories vary with the length of driving experience, whether the driver had formal drivers' training (for those with less than three years of driving experience), and whether the inexperienced driver is the principal operator of the vehicle. Table 2-1 illustrates the driver-rating classes and the percentage of insured exposures contained in each class for 1998.

Territory definitions are determined systematically and updated every two years based on an empirical evaluation of claims costs by town.[8] Territories are not determined by geographical proximity, except at the level of the town. Territories are defined by grouping together towns for which estimated mean losses per insured car are the most similar. This is accomplished by application of a grouping algorithm to estimated town loss costs (for five major coverages) based upon actuarial analysis of historical claim

8. This is the current schedule, which appears to have begun in 1989 when territories were updated for the first time in five years.

frequency and claim severity by town. The methodology appears not to have varied much over time, but the assignment process does produce changes in territory assignment for individual towns.[9] New territories have occasionally been created when large statistical differences in loss costs appeared for one or more towns. Until the mid-1980s, towns were grouped into twenty-five territories, ten of which represented individual subsections of Boston. The same basic territory framework exists today but with two additional territories added, for a total of twenty-seven. Table 2-2 reports the existing territory definitions and the insured exposures in each territory for 1999–2000.

Regulated Rates

Rates are determined by applying financial models to aggregate industry data to estimate a target underwriting profit margin, taking into account both expected investment income and insurance underwriting risk.[10] This target underwriting profit margin, in conjunction with projections of industry loss costs and expenses, yields an average statewide rate required to achieve that margin. The implied percentage rate change is then distributed by class and territory to determine specific rates for the 243 (9 classes times 27 territories) individual rating cells.

Rates are systematically leveled across classes and territories through restrictions known as tempering and capping. The leveling is accomplished according to procedures that have remained essentially unchanged since the early 1980s. Tempering requires that differences in rate relativities across the different class-territory cells be adjusted downward by a preset procedure; this reduces the differences in rate levels across the rating cells. Capping requires that the annual increase in rates for any single class-territory cell not exceed the average statewide rate increase by more than a predetermined percentage. Thus capping reduces the changes in rate levels for each rating cell across time.

A final set of interclass rate constraints is applied within each territory to ensure that the lower risk classes do not pay more than a given percentage of the rate paid by higher risks. For example, traditionally the experienced driver rate is set at no greater than 95 percent of the lowest inexperienced driver rate, the business-use rate is at least as great as the experienced

9. For 2000–01, for example, the AIB analysis resulted in recommended territory changes for 43.6 percent of towns, although for the vast majority of these by only one territory (AIB, 2000a).

10. For an in-depth discussion of the financial modeling, see Derrig (1987).

Table 2-2. *Massachusetts Automobile Rating Territories, 1999–2000*
Units as indicated

Territory	Number of towns	Location	Number of exposures	Percent of market
1	47	Non-Boston	197,452	5.4
2	47	Non-Boston	216,111	5.9
3	39	Non-Boston	330,468	9.0
4	29	Non-Boston	333,530	9.1
5	28	Non-Boston	343,784	9.4
6	27	Non-Boston	404,397	11.0
7	20	Non-Boston	237,570	6.5
8	12	Non-Boston	216,057	5.9
9	5	Non-Boston	138,982	3.8
10	8	Non-Boston	184,836	5.0
11	1	Non-Boston	16,856	0.5
12	6	Non-Boston	209,802	5.7
13	4	Non-Boston	121,789	3.3
14	5	Non-Boston	138,431	3.8
15	4	Non-Boston	164,425	4.5
16	2	Non-Boston	32,634	0.9
17	1	Boston	15,609	0.4
18	1	Boston	14,130	0.4
19	1	Boston	13,742	0.4
20	1	Boston	14,465	0.4
21	1	Boston	36,187	1.0
22	1	Boston	6,962	0.2
23	1	Boston	31,605	0.9
24	1	Boston	22,440	0.6
25	1	Boston	9,733	0.3
26	1	Boston	15,575	0.4
27	66	Non-Boston	196,284	5.4
Total	360		3,663,856	100.1[a]

Source: AIB (1999, 2000a).
a. Percentages do not add to 100 due to rounding.

driver rate, and so forth.[11] The application of these constraints introduces additional cross-subsidies across territories.

Insurance rates are further leveled by the way in which the expected residual market operating deficit is added into premiums. The expected total deficit amount is divided equally across insured exposures and

11. See AIB (1998).

included in each class-territory rate as a flat dollar amount (as opposed to loading in relation to that class-territory's contribution to the residual market, or to loading it as a percent of the rate). The procedure implies that low-rate cells pay a higher proportion of their rate as residual market subsidy than do high-rate cells.

This complex system of cross-subsidies produces significant variation in premium charges relative to premium charges based on costs alone.[12] The net effect of tempering, capping, interclass constraints, and residual market deficit loading is that some classes and territories receive significant rate subsidies, with the remaining classes and territories paying relatively smaller rate surcharges.[13] To demonstrate the complexity and magnitude of the rate cross-subsidies, table 2-3 displays insurer estimates of the subsidies contained in the rates for the compulsory package of coverage for selected classes in each territory cell for the year 2000. A negative number in the table indicates that the cell received a subsidy, whereas a positive number indicates the cell paid a surcharge.

The extent of cross-subsidies is large: 169 rating cells (70 percent) received a subsidy, while the remaining 74 cells (30 percent) paid a surcharge. The variation in cross-subsidies paid and received is also large. The smallest subsidy received was $0.70, a reduction of 0.1 percent in the rate (class 17, territory 3). The largest subsidy received was $1,951.30, yielding a rate 58.5 percent below the cost-based rate (class 20, territory 16). The smallest surcharge paid was $1.00, yielding a 0.1 percent increase in the rate (class 21, territory 3), and the largest surcharge paid was $38.20, a 12.9 percent increase in the rate (class 30, territory 27).[14]

Table 2-4 summarizes the general direction of rate subsidies for the year 2000 by reporting insurer estimates of the percentage subsidy received by major territory and class groups in two common packages of coverage. As in the previous table, a negative number indicates the group received a subsidy on average, and a positive number indicates the group paid a surcharge on average. The table demonstrates that inexperienced and urban drivers received significant cross-subsidies from other drivers (especially

---

12. Rate leveling is mitigated for individuals to some extent by the Safe Driver Insurance Program (SDIP), which allows for rate discounts and surcharges based on the insured's recent driving record. Rates are set, however, so that expected surcharges and credits balance out within each class-territory cell.

13. The system balances out to zero because of different rate levels and the different number of exposures in each class and territory cell.

14. These statistics represent values calculated across all rating classes, not just those shown in the table. Some classes were omitted from the table to increase readability.

Table 2-3. *Rate Subsidies for Compulsory Package of Coverages, Selected Rating Classes, 2000*[a]
Units as indicated

	Class									
	10		17		20		25		30	
Territory	Dollars	Percent[b]	Dollars	Percent	Dollars	Percent	Dollars	Percent	Dollars	Percent
1	20.10	6.5	5.30	0.8	−48.80	−3.8	−44.90	−3.9	24.90	7.6
2	34.10	10.6	3.60	0.5	−84.40	−5.9	−76.80	−6.0	36.40	10.5
3	22.80	6.4	−0.70	−0.1	−114.30	−7.6	−101.00	−7.5	24.50	6.9
4	24.80	6.8	−5.20	−0.7	−152.80	−9.8	−136.50	−9.7	24.40	6.1
5	16.60	4.3	−12.10	−1.4	−213.50	−12.8	−192.40	−12.8	21.90	4.9
6	14.70	3.6	−15.80	−1.7	−245.70	−14.2	−221.60	−14.2	21.20	4.5
7	28.00	6.6	−18.10	−1.9	−305.10	−16.6	−275.40	−16.7	19.00	3.8
8	12.10	2.7	−22.40	−2.3	−347.70	−18.5	−314.10	−18.6	17.80	3.5
9	19.10	3.9	−26.20	−2.6	−501.90	−24.8	−452.40	−24.9	20.60	4.3
10	11.40	2.2	−35.90	−3.2	−636.30	−29.7	−571.90	−29.6	14.40	2.6
11	15.30	2.7	−38.40	−3.3	−592.20	−28.1	−533.80	−28.1	11.40	2.0
12	6.30	1.1	−132.20	−10.6	−845.00	−36.3	−759.70	−36.2	6.70	1.1
13	6.30	1.0	−213.60	−15.4	−926.90	−38.5	−833.10	−38.4	6.80	1.1

14	−33.30	−4.6	−334.60	−22.6	−1,065.70	−42.1	−957.80	−42.0	−36.00	−5.5
15	1.50	0.2	−485.40	−29.7	−1,256.80	−46.5	−1,130.60	−46.4	1.60	0.2
16	−272.40	−23.9	−1,073.30	−49.6	−1,951.30	−58.5	−1,749.00	−58.2	−289.80	−32.3
17	4.30	0.8	−33.40	−3.0	−505.40	−25.1	−454.60	−25.1	4.60	0.9
18	−4.30	−0.5	−273.50	−19.9	−800.00	−35.4	−721.70	−35.5	−4.70	−0.8
19	−10.90	−1.2	−340.90	−23.4	−927.80	−39.4	−836.80	−39.5	−11.50	−1.8
20	−7.80	−0.8	−309.60	−21.2	−932.10	−39.1	−839.20	−39.1	−9.10	−1.4
21	−79.70	−6.0	−892.40	−43.4	−1,657.20	−54.4	−1,423.70	−51.9	−84.50	−9.7
22	−66.50	−4.7	−955.60	−44.9	−1,883.40	−57.9	−1,638.80	−55.9	−71.60	−7.7
23	2.60	0.4	−339.60	−23.6	−977.90	−40.7	−879.60	−40.6	2.00	0.3
24	−3.60	−0.5	−222.40	−17.4	−731.20	−33.5	−658.20	−33.5	−4.00	−0.7
25	−6.20	−0.9	−392.30	−26.3	−1,038.20	−41.7	−935.30	−41.7	−7.10	−1.0
26	−15.90	−1.8	−627.90	−36.7	−1,324.90	−47.8	−1,191.50	−47.7	−16.80	−2.3
27	36.20	13.0	7.10	1.1	−39.60	−3.2	−35.70	−3.2	38.20	12.9

Source: AIB (1999).
a. Subsidy is the difference between the average rates generated by the commissioner's decision and the cost-based rate.
b. Percentages are calculated as a proportion of the cost-based rate. Negative number, group received subsidy; positive number, group paid surcharge.

Table 2-4. *Cross-Subsidies in Automobile Insurance Rates,*
Summary for 2000
Percent

	Compulsory package of coverages	Standard package of coverages
By territories		
Boston	−20.10	−15.90
Non-Boston	2.00	1.50
By driver classes		
Experienced	1.60	0.90
Inexperienced	−9.00	−6.90
Business use	11.80	9.90

Source: AIB (1999).

business-use classes) in the state. This general pattern of cross-subsidies is observed in every year, with minor variations.

Other Regulatory Features

Several other features of the regulated Massachusetts automobile insurance market are important to understanding its characteristics and its dynamics. First, related to the objective of universal coverage, consumers receive extensive protection from policy cancellation. Once a policy is written, an insurer cannot refuse to renew it for reasons other than fraud, failure to pay a premium, or other technicalities. Since 1984 insurers may refuse to write a policy, but the insurers who act as residual market servicing carriers must accept all applicants. Undesirable policies can be ceded to the Commonwealth Automobile Reinsurers (CAR), the residual market facility, at the state-set rate.

CAR operates as an industry-run reinsurance pool. Premiums generated from a ceded policy are paid to CAR, minus a servicing fee to the ceding insurer. In part because there are no premium surcharges for policies insured through CAR, it operates at a significant deficit. The underwriting losses of CAR are shared by all automobile insurers in the state, according to a complex set of rules based on the insurer's market share and its share of policies ceded to CAR. These rules and the rule-setting process within CAR have generated controversy, lawsuits, and federal government investigation, due to charges that the residual market burden is unfairly allocated across insurers to the advantage of a select few.

Another important regulatory feature is the strong restriction placed on insurers' rights to exit the automobile insurance market. An insurer wishing to withdraw from the market must submit a written plan to the commissioner for approval. If the commissioner determines that the insurer is withdrawing for a reason other than to protect its solvency, then he or she has the right (by statute) to suspend the insurer's license to write in any other line of business. A withdrawing insurer must pay its share of losses on policies insured by CAR for three years after its exit. Prior to reforms in 1991, the rule was eight years of assessments.[15]

Reforms

Massachusetts's no-fault compensation system requires drivers to purchase first-party personal injury protection (PIP) insurance and restricts injured parties' ability to file bodily injury liability (BIL) claims. The threshold for claimant eligibility to file a BIL claim is based on the dollar value of medical expenses claimed. Initially this tort eligibility threshold was set at $500, and the maximum coverage limit for PIP was set at $2,000. As part of the Auto Insurance Reform Law of 1988, in 1989 the tort eligibility threshold was raised to $2,000, and the PIP coverage limit was raised to $8,000.

The Reform Law also modified the discounts and surcharges to insurance premiums under the SDIP to increase the responsiveness of premium differentials to recent accident experience. The new law also focused on cost containment of property damage insurance claims. It permitted insurers to make claim payments directly to claimants rather than to repair shops as an incentive to claimants to find low-cost repairs, and it allowed insurers to negotiate with repair shops for lower charges, such as for labor and parts.

Also with cost containment objectives in mind, the Insurance Fraud Bureau (IFB) of Massachusetts was created in 1990 and began operation in 1991. It was established by state statute and is funded and operated by insurers in the state.[16] The IFB has broad authority to investigate fraud in all lines of insurance but focuses primarily on fraud in automobile and workers' compensation insurance. A primary objective of forming the IFB

---

15. Yelen (1993).

16. The impetus for the IFB came from the auto insurance industry in the state, stimulated by an AIB study of fraud and buildup in auto injury claims (Weisberg and Derrig, 1991). The insurance commissioner and other public officials are members of the governing board.

was to increase the investigation and criminal prosecution of insurance fraud. To support this objective, insurers are required by law to report instances of suspected fraud to the IFB. The bureau has access to confidential information that might be required to prove fraud and receives prosecutorial support from the state attorney general's office. Since its inception the IFB has received over 16,000 referrals, about 20 percent of which it has investigated further. By early 2000 approximately 1,900 investigations had been completed, resulting in 502 cases referred for prosecution.[17]

Regulatory Stringency in Rate Setting

Much of the attention directed toward Massachusetts's automobile insurance regulation has focused on the average levels of rates set under regulation. It has been argued that periodically automobile insurance rates in Massachusetts are suppressed below market levels—not just for some classes and territories, but for the market as a whole. Although this is not a statutory feature of the regulations, if the system tends to suppress rates, this will have important implications for market operation and outcomes. Thus we investigate the overall stringency of the regulated rates prior to analyzing the impact of regulation on the market.

Automobile Underwriting Results

Figure 2-1 provides a rough indication of the regulatory trends over time by showing the annual average markup of premiums over losses as a percent of premiums in Massachusetts's automobile insurance versus that for the U.S. automobile insurance market as a whole. The time period illustrated is from 1980 to 1998. The markup percent is defined as earned premiums minus incurred losses (including loss adjustment expenses) as a percentage of earned premiums. This statistic is not a measure of underwriting profitability because underwriting expenses (for which we do not have data by line of insurance) are not included as costs.

Our interest is not in the absolute level of the markup but in comparing this markup in Massachusetts to that for the U.S. market as a whole. Comparisons across states can be interpreted to reflect differences in the

17. IFB (2000).

Figure 2-1. *Premium Markup over Losses, Private Passenger Auto, 1980–98*[a]

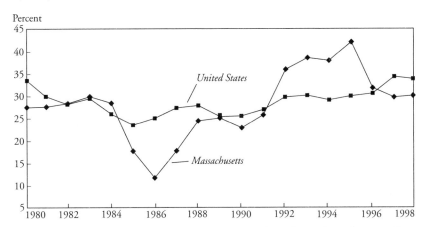

Percent

Source: Authors' calculations from A. M. Best Co. and NAIC databases of insurers' annual statement filings.
a. Markup percent = earned premiums − (incurred loss + loss adjustment expenses)]/earned premiums

profitability of insurance writings as long as insurer expenses, investment strategies, and claims payment delays do not vary significantly by state. Under this assumption figure 2-1 shows that for much of the sample period, the Massachusetts auto insurance market was less profitable than the U.S. auto insurance market overall. This was especially true during the latter half of the 1980s. In the early 1990s, the Massachusetts premium markups were greater than average, and since the mid-1990s, they have been more on a par with nationwide results.

Figure 2-2 attempts to relate these results to Massachusetts's regulatory stringency. The figure shows insurer projections of the automobile underwriting profit percent that could have been achieved at the rates set by the insurance commissioner, relative to the underwriting profit percent set as a target by the commissioner in determining the rates.[18] The time period illustrated is 1980–98.

The figure demonstrates that the target underwriting profit has been relatively constant over time, but for much of the 1980s, the underwriting profits achievable under the rates fell short of the target. This shortfall appears to have been due to overly optimistic estimates of losses in the

18. AIB (2000b). Actual premiums will differ from this projection due to variations in drivers' choices of coverage limits and deductibles and to discounts below the state-set rate that some insurers may offer in some years to some classes of drivers.

Figure 2-2. *Massachusetts Target and Projected Underwriting Profit, 1980–98*

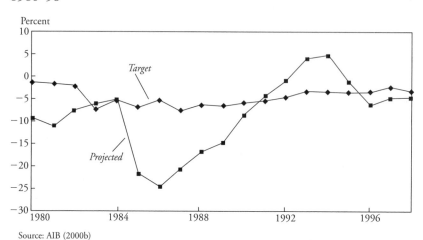

Source: AIB (2000b)

state-set rates. Derrig documented that from 1978 to 1990, the state-set rates were based upon loss cost projections that were too low by an average of 11 percent per year.[19] During the first half of the 1990s, there was a reversal as achievable underwriting profits exceeded the target embedded in the state-set rates. By 1995 many Massachusetts automobile insurers began discounting below the state-set rates.

An important difference between the automobile insurance market of the 1980s and the 1990s was the pace of cost and premium inflation. The 1980s were characterized by rapid growth in automobile insurance loss costs. For the market as a whole, the increase in premiums and investment income did not keep pace, and automobile insurance economic profits declined.[20] As a result of the stringent rate decisions, the Massachusetts market did much worse than average. The Massachusetts regulatory environment was extremely contentious during the period, and automobile insurers successfully sued to overturn the commissioner's rate decisions in 1980, 1987, and 1988. By the late 1980s, the climate had deteriorated to such an extent that insurers began withdrawing from the market.[21]

In contrast, the 1990s were characterized by only modest loss and pre-

19. Derrig (1993).
20. Cummins and Tennyson (1992).
21. Derrig (1993); Yelen (1993).

mium inflation, with premium rates for automobile insurance flat or falling in most states by 1995. State-set rates in Massachusetts have declined by nearly 25 percent since 1994.[22] The period of rate declines appears to be ending, however, and contentiousness has returned to the Massachusetts regulatory process in recent years. In 1999 the AIB unsuccessfully appealed the commissioner's rate increase of 0.7 percent, and it filed for a reconsideration of the 2001 decision to decrease rates by an average of 8.3 percent.[23]

This pattern of increased regulatory stringency during inflationary periods and decreased stringency during noninflationary periods suggests either the use of backward-looking loss cost prediction models or the influence of politics in rate determination.[24] Political models of regulatory behavior posit that interested parties invest resources to influence the outcome of regulation in their favor.[25] These models predict that consumers will be relatively more influential when the issues are both easily understood and directly meaningful to them.[26] Automobile insurance prices were certainly of concern to consumers in the 1970s, when competitive rating was first attempted, and again in the late 1980s, as auto insurance price inflation stimulated interest in regulation and other price-reducing initiatives.[27] Consumer concerns waned in the 1990s as prices stabilized and began to decline.

Several features of the automobile insurance environment in Massachusetts may make politicized rate setting more likely. Automobile insurance premiums in Massachusetts have traditionally been among the highest in the country, increasing the importance of the issue to consu-

22. Massachusetts Division of Insurance, "Division of Insurance Announces Cut in Personal Auto Insurance Rate," press release, Boston, 2000.

23. "AIB Files a Motion of Reconsideration with Commissioner of Insurance." December 20, 2000. (www.aib.org [October 2001]).

24. Cummins (1990) demonstrates that use of accounting profit measures in regulatory determinations can delay rate increases during periods of inflation. Weiss (1990) and Tennyson (1993) find evidence consistent with this effect in regulated auto insurance markets.

25. Early models of this type were developed by Peltzman (1976) and Becker (1983); more recent models include that of Grossman and Helpman (1994). Meier (1988, 1991) uses this theory to analyze many aspects of insurance industry regulation; Harrington (1994) applies it to states' passage of no-fault auto legislation; Carroll and Regan (1998) apply it to states' unfair claims settlement laws. Suponcic (1998) and Cummins, Phillips, and Tennyson (2001) apply the theory specifically to auto insurance rate regulation.

26. Meier (1988).

27. See, among others, Cummins and Tennyson (1992) and Jaffee and Russell (1998) for analysis of the economic and political environment for auto insurance in the 1980s.

mers. Moreover, when compared to those of other states, Massachusetts' regulatory system may more readily sustain media and consumer attention: the adversaries are clearly identifiable, the commissioner's decision generates a single percentage rate change effective January 1 each year, and the change is determined through a public hearing process. These features may increase the relative influence of consumer interests in rate-setting decisions.

Insurer Returns on Equity

While useful for comparative purposes, the markup of premiums over losses or underwriting profit ratios for individual insurance lines does not adequately portray the overall impact on the firm from writing various coverages. Return on equity (ROE), another measure of firm performance, does not suffer from this drawback. To further examine the impact of Massachusetts' regulation on insurer profitability, we analyze annual firm-level data on ROE over the time period 1990–98.

An insurer's ROE is determined by both the underwriting and investment activities of the firm. Most firms write more than one type of coverage, and underwriting results (and risk) vary by line of insurance, affecting ROE. Investment results depend on the allocation of funds into different investment classes, such as stocks and bonds, and therefore also affect ROE. Firm characteristics, such as marketing system, organizational form, market power, ability to minimize nonearning assets, and geographic dispersion of premium writings, may also affect ROE. Finally, market developments outside of the immediate control of the insurer, such as regulation and the underwriting cycle, will affect ROE.

To isolate the impact of an insurer's exposure in Massachusetts from these other influences, we estimate a multiple regression model of insurers' ROE. The starting point for sampling was the set of all U.S. insurers filing an annual statement with the National Association of Insurance Commissioners in any of the years from 1990 through 1998. To remove outliers from the data, we eliminated firms with

—zero or negative values for premiums, surplus, liabilities, assets or expenses;
—implausibly high or low values of premiums written relative to surplus, liabilities to equity, returns on equity or returns on assets;
—other obvious reporting errors in important financial variables.

Firms with missing values for any of the regression variables were also eliminated from the sample. The resulting sample used in the regression analysis consists of 17,275 observations, or about 1,900 insurers in each year over the period from 1990 to 1998.

Three variables are included in the regression model to capture the effect of different lines of coverage on ROE: the proportion of total premium writings in automobile insurance, workers' compensation insurance, and homeowners' multiperil insurance. Differing insurer investment portfolios are controlled for by including the proportion of the portfolio invested in stocks and in bonds as regression variables.

Other firm characteristics controlled for are organizational form (stock versus mutual insurer), the number of states in which the insurer writes business, and market power. The expense preference hypothesis indicates that mutual insurers may have a lower return on equity. Additionally, stock insurers write more complex, large risks, suggesting that they should earn a higher ROE than mutual insurers. The firm's market power is measured as the average market share (in all lines) of the insurer in the states in which it writes. We hypothesize that greater market power will lead to a higher ROE.

Our data do not include the marketing system(s) used by the insurer. Thus the relationship between ROE and marketing system is controlled for by including two marketing system proxies: the proportion of total expenses spent on advertising and on agents' commissions. Typically insurers are broadly classified as direct writers or independent agency insurers; however, a growing number of insurers distribute business using both independent agents and direct writing. The specification of marketing system proxies used here can accommodate this phenomenon.

Controls for the insurer's operating environment are also included in the model. Property-liability insurance is notorious for its underwriting cycles, alternating periods of rising then falling underwriting profit. Dummy variables for each year are used to control for this phenomenon. Finally, two state-specific controls are present in the model: one for the proportion of the insurer's writing in regulated states and one for the proportion of the insurer's writing in no-fault states. The variables included in the regression and their summary statistics for the combined period 1990–98 are listed in table 2-5.

Weighted least squares, with assets as the weighting variable, were used to estimate the regression model because ROE among small insurers is expected to be more volatile than among larger insurers. Table 2-6 reports

Table 2-5. *Return on Equity, Regression Variables and Summary Statistics, 1990–98*

Variable	Mean	Standard deviation
Net income/surplus	0.067	0.133
(Net income + unrealized capital gains(losses))/surplus	0.075	0.147
Proportion of insurer's total premiums written in Mass.	0.027	0.131
Auto liability in Massachusetts	0.008	0.065
Workers' compensation in Massachusetts	0.026	0.395
Homeowners' insurance in Massachusetts	0.020	0.108
Interaction of Mass. auto liability and homeowners' insurance	0.001	0.008
Proportion of invested assets in stocks	0.109	0.161
Proportion of invested assets in bonds	0.658	0.273
Invested assets/total assets	0.882	0.113
Proportion of insurer's total premiums		
In homeowners' insurance	0.095	0.187
In auto liability	0.189	0.253
In workers' compensation	0.096	0.239
Written in no-fault states	0.382	0.394
Written in regulated states	0.697	0.368
Number of states the insurer writes in	13.381	17.484
Average market share in states the insurer writes in	0.003	0.010
Stock dummy (= 1 if stock)	0.186	0.389
Proportion of total expenses spent on advertising	0.009	0.035
Proportion of total expenses spent on agents commissions	0.140	1.408

Source: Authors' calculations from sample of firms obtained from NAIC databases of insurers' annual statement filings.

the weighted least squares estimates of the regression model over the pooled time period 1990–98. Models with two alternative dependent variables are presented: in the first models ROE is measured as net income relative to surplus, excluding unrealized capital gains; in the second models ROE is measured as net income plus unrealized capital gains relative to surplus.

For each dependent variable three empirical models are estimated, differing only by the measure of the firm's exposure in Massachusetts. First, the relationship between ROE and an insurer's total premium writings in Massachusetts is examined. This analysis indicates very generally if an insurer's writings in Massachusetts significantly affect its ROE. We also examine the impact on an insurer's ROE from writing several specific types of coverage in Massachusetts, including automobile insurance. Finally, to determine whether any cross-subsidies among lines of insurance occur in Massachusetts, we examine the relationship between a firm's ROE and the interaction of its automobile and homeowners' insurance writings in the state. If rates are not suppressed, then insurers might share the wealth with policyholders by charging lower rates on homeowners' policies. Alternatively, suppression of rates may lead to higher homeowners' premium charges.[28]

The estimated impact of Massachusetts writings on a firm's ROE can be summarized simply. The coefficient estimate on the proportion of *total* insurer writings in Massachusetts is positive and significant, indicating that over the sample period insurers writing business in the state experienced higher ROE on average. However, when these premium proportions are broken down by line of business, the results show that insurers writing *automobile* insurance in Massachusetts experienced a lower ROE, and these results are significant at the 1 percent confidence level. In the models that include an interaction term between the proportion of Massachusetts premium writings in automobile insurance and in homeowners' insurance, the coefficient estimates for the interaction variable are positive and significant. This signifies that insurers writing both homeowners' and auto insurance in Massachusetts experienced somewhat higher ROEs than insurers writing auto insurance alone. Thus insurers may have benefited somewhat from cross-selling homeowners' insurance or from passing on losses in auto insurance to homeowners through larger homeowners' insurance premiums.

The findings in table 2-6 may partly reflect the effects of the discounting occurring in Massachusetts auto insurance during the latter part of the sample period. To examine this possibility, table 2-7 reports the estimates obtained from separate regression models for each year in the sample period. The models estimated use as a dependent variable ROE including unrealized capital gains as a component of income, and include per-line premium proportions rather than total premiums in Massachusetts. The results are similar to those in table 2-6, although with lower levels of significance, as expected, due to the smaller numbers of observations. In all years in the sample period except for 1996, the coefficients for Massachu-

---

28. Lower rates for homeowners might also occur if economies of scope between automobile and homeowners' insurance existed, so that insurers writing both coverages would have lower expenses than insurers selling either line alone. Under automobile insurance rate suppression, insurers might be able to cross-subsidize auto insurance if policyholders face substantial search costs or if substantial switching costs occur when policyholders change insurers.

Table 2-6. Regressions of Firm Return on Equity (ROE), Pooled Data, 1990–98[a]

Explanatory variable	Without capital gains[b]			With capital gains[c]		
Intercept	−0.1099*** (−9.315)	−0.1082*** (−9.045)	−0.1109*** (−9.267)	−0.2532*** (−18.293)	−0.2631*** (−18.808)	−0.2649*** (−18.918)
Proportion of insurer's total premiums written in Mass.	0.0458*** (5.181)	...	...	0.0357*** (3.447)	...	...
In Mass. auto liab.	...	−0.0281*** (−4.703)	−0.0444*** (−6.458)	...	−0.0659*** (−9.428)	−0.0767*** (−9.524)
In Mass. workers' compensation	...	−0.0006 (−0.401)	−0.0006 (−0.389)	...	−0.0014 (−0.784)	−0.0014 (−0.778)
In Mass. homeowners' insurance	...	0.0166*** (2.782)	−0.0138** (2.309)	...	0.0041 (0.588)	0.0023 (0.324)
Proportion of prems in Mass. auto liab. × proportion of prems in Mass. homeowners	...	...	0.3005*** (4.777)	...	...	0.1989*** (2.7)
Proportion of invested assets in stocks	−0.0258*** (−2.779)	−0.0275*** (−2.972)	−0.027*** (−2.92)	0.1697*** (15.616)	0.1709*** (15.784)	0.1712*** (15.817)
Proportion of invested assets in bonds	0.0579*** (7.017)	0.0562*** (6.807)	0.058*** (7.026)	0.1231*** (12.71)	0.1238*** (12.812)	0.125*** (12.926)
Invested assets/total assets	0.1873*** (17.955)	0.1817*** (17.416)	0.1818*** (17.439)	0.1995*** (16.312)	0.1976*** (16.187)	0.1977*** (16.197)
Proportion of insurer's total premiums						
In homeowners' insurance	−0.1334*** (−20.907)	−0.1518*** (−17.856)	−0.1589*** (−18.42)	−0.0787*** (−10.072)	−0.0918*** (−9.221)	−0.0964*** (−9.547)
In auto liability	−0.043*** (−10.551)	−0.0351*** (−8.02)	−0.0346*** (−7.919)	−0.0119** (−2.5)	−0.0061 (1.187)	−0.0064 (1.246)

In workers' compensation	−0.0237***	−0.0223***	−0.0222***	0.002	0.0055	0.0056
	(−6.024)	(−5.616)	(−5.59)	(0.429)	(1.188)	(1.205)
In no-fault states	0.0091***	0.0147***	0.0153***	0.0176***	0.0248***	0.0252***
	(2.622)	(4.328)	(4.515)	(4.309)	(6.251)	(6.353)
In regulated states	−0.0068*	−0.0031	−0.0033	−0.0138***	−0.009**	−0.0092**
	(−1.894)	(−0.874)	(−0.93)	(−3.299)	(−2.169)	(−2.2)
Number of states the insurer writes in	0.0002***	0.0002***	0.0002***	0.0004***	0.0006***	0.0006***
	(3.565)	(4.245)	(4.895)	(7.714)	(10.22)	(10.505)
Average market share in states the insurer writes in	−0.0764**	−0.0151	0.0601	0.0533	0.2292***	0.2789***
	(−2.105)	(−0.376)	(1.392)	(1.253)	(4.87)	(5.52)
Stock dummy (=1 if stock)	−0.0265***	−0.0191***	−0.0168***	−0.0225***	−0.0093***	−0.0077**
	(13.296)	(−7.462)	(−8.423)	(−8.099)	(−3.105)	(−2.536)
Proportion of total expenses spent on advertising	0.6316***	0.6053***	0.6064***	0.6092***	0.5623***	0.563***
	(13.296)	(12.698)	(12.73)	(10.937)	(10.082)	(10.096)
Proportion of total expenses spent on agents' commissions	0.0038**	0.0029	0.0034*	0.0059***	0.004***	0.0043**
	(2.129)	(1.635)	(1.867)	(2.809)	(1.912)	(2.042)
Year dummies	Yes**	Yes***	Yes***	Yes**	Yes**	Yes**
Summary statistic						
Adjusted R^2	0.1145	0.1148	0.1159	0.1885	0.1922	0.1925
N (sample size)	17,276	17,276	17,276	17,276	17,276	17,276

Source: See table 2-5.

*Significant at the 10 percent level.

**Significant at the 5 percent level.

*** Significant at the 1 percent level.

a. Regressions were estimated using weighted least squares; t statistics are shown in parentheses.

b. ROE without capital gains = (net income)/surplus.

c. ROE with capital gains = (net income + unrealized capital gains)/surplus.

Table 2-7. Regressions of Firm ROE, Yearly Data, 1990–98[a]

Explanatory variable	1990	1991	1992	1993	1994	1995	1996	1997	1998
Intercept	-0.0769***	-0.1138***	-0.0045	-0.2074***	-0.3469***	-0.2175	-0.1268	-0.3452***	-0.1966***
	(-2.4940)	(-3.7540)	(-0.0990)	(-4.8560)	(-7.1730)	(-5.2080)	(-3.0960)	(-8.2090)	(-5.2550)
Proportion of insurers total premiums written									
ln Mass. auto liability	-0.0852**	-0.0478***	-0.1300***	-0.0612***	-0.0414**	-0.0973***	-0.0403**	-0.1126***	-0.0701***
	(-4.01810)	(-2.7980)	(-4.9240)	(-3.4790)	(-2.0270)	(-4.7940)	(-2.0000)	(-4.9070)	(-3.4340)
ln Mass. workers' compensation	-0.0271*	-0.0120	-0.0028	-0.0050	-0.0076	-0.0024	-0.0436**	-0.0257	0.0034
	(-1.9380)	(-1.0000)	(-0.9330)	(-0.4010)	(-0.4250)	(-0.6160)	(-3.2570)	(-1.3700)	(1.1200)
ln Mass. homeowners' insurance	-0.0131	0.0324**	0.0218	-0.0150	0.0235	-0.0102	0.0480**	-0.0446*	0.0480**
	(-0.7470)	(1.9830)	(0.8080)	(-0.9690)	(1.1400)	(-0.5070)	(2.2600)	(-1.6780)	(2.1750)
Proportion of invested assets in stocks	-0.0831***	0.3510***	-0.0049	0.0488	0.632	0.01900***	0.1676***	0.3429***	0.2659***
	(-3.0680)	(11.8900)	(-0.1250)	(1.5410)	(1.5700)	(7.1450)	(5.4530)	(11.0570)	(9.1100)
Proportion of invested assets in bonds	0.0217	0.1179***	0.0561*	0.1065***	0.1077***	0.0986***	0.0940***	0.1525***	0.2150***
	(0.9480)	(4.9910)	(1.6510)	(4.0060)	(2.9150)	(4.2100)	(3.3230)	(5.2300)	(7.9830)
Invested assets/total assets	0.1931***	0.1642***	0.1113***	0.2182***	0.3443***	0.2413***	0.1829***	0.2884***	0.0842***
	(7.0470)	(5.9090)	(2.6390)	(5.8090)	(8.2760)	(6.2740)	(5.2710)	(7.7030)	(2.8040)
Proportion of insurer's total premiums									
ln homeowners' insurance	-0.1836***	-0.1990***	-0.1390***	-0.0406	-0.4307***	-0.0135	-0.1921***	0.1400***	-0.0601**
	(-6.6940)	(-7.8760)	(-3.5040)	(-1.5070)	(-14.1030)	(-0.4620)	(-6.7090)	(4.4650)	(-2.4810)
ln auto liability	-0.0950***	0.0033	0.0797***	0.0146	0.0455***	0.0655***	-0.0314*	0.0204	-0.0299**
	(-6.6810)	(0.2720)	(4.2080)	(1.0390)	(3.0780)	(4.5570)	(-2.1350)	(1.2000)	(-2.3520)
ln workers' compensation	-0.0759***	-0.0622***	0.0781***	0.0370***	0.1372***	-0.0027	-0.0563***	-0.0094	-0.0212*
	(-5.2170)	(-5.1420)	(4.5640)	(2.9010)	(9.5610)	(-0.1940)	(-4.3000)	(0.6740)	(-1.6870)

In no-fault states	0.0269***	0.0211**	−0.0983***	0.0055	0.0260**	0.0676***	0.0308***	0.0904***	0.0531***
	(2.6440)	(2.1620)	(−6.9860)	(0.5070)	(2.1710)	(5.8160)	(2.8780)	(7.6900)	(5.0080)
In regulated states	0.0164	−0.0321***	−0.0533	0.0097	0.0175	−0.0475***	−0.0008	−0.0191	0.0089
	(1.4900)	(−3.2140)	(−3.5460)	(0.8760)	(1.3680)	(−3.7850)	(−0.0740)	(1.5810)	(0.8620)
Number of states the insurer writes in	0.0000	0.0007***	−0.0002	0.0006***	−0.0003*	0.0014***	0.0003	0.0020***	0.0004**
	(0.1600)	(4.3030)	(−1.0700)	(3.8110)	(−1.7680)	(8.3910)	(1.4880)	(10.2640)	(2.2910)
Average market share in states the insurer writes in	−0.1435	−0.8737***	−0.2216	0.6733***	−0.5698***	0.7611***	0.3065***	0.5053***	0.4946****
	(−0.8200)	(−6.6960)	(−1.0330)	(5.7270)	(−4.5380)	(6.0070)	(2.5960)	(3.5100)	(3.8590)
Stock dummy (=1 if stock)	n.a.	−0.0045	−0.0141	n.a.	0.0187**	−0.0143*	−0.0319***	−0.0311***	−0.0212***
		(−0.6850)	(−1.4050)		(2.0360)	(−1.7210)	(−4.0790)	(−3.6100)	(−2.7350)
Proportion of total expenses spent on advertising	0.1255	0.7313***	1.4529***	0.8010***	0.5714***	0.6400***	0.4663***	0.1551	0.8123***
	(0.6880)	(3.7260)	(5.2460)	(4.6270)	(2.8720)	(3.5890)	(3.9560)	(1.0840)	(6.3170)
Proportion of total expenses spent on agents' commissions	−0.0246***	−0.0104*	−0.0033	0.0196***	−0.0412***	0.0105	0.0052	0.0093	−0.0005
	(−2.7420)	(−1.7590)	(−0.2420)	(2.7930)	(−3.7660)	(1.3120)	(1.3760)	(1.4010)	(−0.1040)
Summary Statistic									
Adjusted R^2	0.1641	0.2430	0.1390	0.0630	0.2650	0.1500	0.1190	0.2330	0.0990
N (sample size)	1884	1922	1875	1918	1920	1951	1929	1929	1948

Source: See table 2-5.

n.a. Not available.

*Significant at the 10 percent level.

**Significant at the 5 percent level.

***Significant at the 1 percent level.

a. Regressions were estimated using weighted least squares; t statistics are shown in parentheses. ROE = (net income + unrealized capital gains)/surplus.

setts auto insurance premium writings are negative and significant. More-over, there is no evidence that auto insurance premium writings in Massa-chusetts affected ROE more negatively during the latter 1990s than during the earlier years of the decade. The negative relationship between ROE and Massachusetts auto insurance writings does not appear to be driven solely by the price competition in recent years.

The ROE regressions demonstrate that firms with a higher share of their premium revenues obtained from sales of automobile insurance in Massachusetts earned lower rates of return on equity in the 1990s. This result could be attributable directly to rate regulation or to other features of the regulatory system, or indirectly to regulation through its effects on firms' decisions to write automobile insurance in Massachusetts. Whatever the precise causal mechanism, that the effect is significant is striking. This effect, in conjunction with the large historical variation in underwriting profits over time, the politically contentious regulatory environment, and uncertainty about rate adequacy, will affect insurers' decisions regarding entry, exit, and operations in the market and thus must be viewed as an important result of regulation.

Incentive Effects

A key feature of the Massachusetts regulatory system is the extensive cross-subsidies in the rates. As discussed previously, cross-subsidies arise from a variety of sources. Tempering and capping of rates introduces cross-subsidies from low-risk classes and territories to high-risk classes and territories. Restrictions on the use of age, gender, and marital status as rating factors also introduce cross-subsidization from low-risk to high-risk drivers within classes if risk actually does change with these variables. The lack of premium surcharges to policies insured through CAR introduces subsidies from the voluntary market to the residual market. The flat loading of residual market deficits by class-territory cell into voluntary market rates introduces yet further cross-subsidies across classes.

Cross-subsidies distort consumer decisions because the insurance premiums charged do not reflect the true costs of providing their insurance. If premiums reflect the expected marginal costs of coverage, consumers have appropriate information on which to base their decisions about insurance purchase as well as car purchase or even whether to drive.[29] Consu-

---

29. Harrington and Doerpinghaus (1993).

mers who receive rate subsidies face less than the true expected marginal cost of their decisions regarding insurance and driving. They will therefore be more likely to drive and to purchase more insurance than they otherwise would. Consumers who pay rate surcharges will demonstrate the opposite response, being both less likely to drive and likely to purchase less insurance. The combined effect of these incentive distortions is a greater relative participation of high risks in the driving and insuring populations, which in turn increases the average expected cost of insurance coverage relative to that under a cost-based system of rates.

If the expected marginal cost of insurance is partially under the control of the consumer, the incentive distortions of cross-subsidies will be even greater. Suppose, for example, that drivers make choices regarding the amounts and types of driving that they do, their driving behavior, and other actions that affect their expected accident frequency or severity. In this case the Massachusetts rate structure and the cross-subsidies built into the rates will increase the risky choices of all drivers, not just those currently receiving rate subsidies. This is because, at the margin, there is relatively less penalty for risk taking.[30]

In Massachusetts the rate categories are few and not based on loss or accident experience.[31] Policies cannot be cancelled based on loss or accident experience. Higher premium charges due to higher accident costs of any one driver will be shared across all members of the class-territory rating cell, dampening individual incentives to reduce costs. Risky choices may move a driver into the residual market but at no premium differential. These effects imply that accident rates will be higher, and expected accident losses higher, under the Massachusetts regulatory system than otherwise.

There may be an additional upward shift in *insured* claims and loss costs due to the greater incentives for claims filing introduced by the rate structure. Consumers will consider marginal costs and marginal benefits when deciding whether to file a claim. Restrictions on policy cancellation, relatively small premium penalties for high losses, and tempering of rate

---

30. There is some change in insurance rates based upon an individual driver's recent experience, through the SDIP program. In addition, vehicle choice determines rates for first party property damage coverages.

31. In most automobile insurance markets there are two or more risk tiers in the voluntary market, distinguished by different underwriting standards and different rates. "Preferred" risks pay the lowest rates, followed by "standard" and "non-standard" risks. See Bartlett, Klein, and Russell (1999) and Jaffee and Russell (1998).

increases across time all suggest that the future consequences of filing a claim—or of filing many claims—are lessened. This will increase consumer propensity to file claims.

These same arguments apply not just to legitimate claims, but also to fraudulent or exaggerated claims. Under Massachusetts law insurers can cancel a policy because of fraud, but proving fraud may be costly and difficult. This restriction and the cross-subsidies in the rates reduce the marginal cost of fraud to claimants. In addition, the no-fault compensation system increases the marginal benefits of exaggerating bodily injury claims. Injured parties may be eligible for compensation under bodily injury liability coverage if their medical expenses exceed $2,000. BIL claimants may be compensated for the full value of medical and wage losses and for noneconomic losses such as pain and suffering. The generous compensation provides significant incentives for BIL fraud, and the medical expense threshold for BIL eligibility provides significant incentives for PIP build-up.[32] These forces together imply that there may be a greater incidence of fraudulent claims, especially for bodily injuries, in Massachusetts.

In sum, rate cross-subsidies produce behavioral incentives that will lead to higher average costs than if premiums reflected the true expected costs of coverage. The extent to which these incentives increase average costs depends on how responsive driving, insuring, risk-taking, and claiming decisions are to insurance prices and on the degree to which cross-subsidies change prices. All else equal, larger cross-subsidies will produce larger incentive distortions and thus larger cost increases.

Residual Market Operation

Rate cross-subsidies are a big contributor to residual market size. The fixed classification system and lack of (upward) pricing freedom suggest that insurers may decide only to insure or to cede any particular risk. If drivers within each driver class and territory represented homogeneous risks, then cross-subsidies imply that all drivers in the rating cells that receive subsidies would be ceded to the residual market. With heterogeneity in rating cells, cross-subsidies occur across drivers within each rating cell. In this case only drivers with significantly higher than average expected losses in each cell should be ceded to the residual market. Cross-subsidies

32. Weisberg and Derrig (1991); Derrig, Weisberg, and Chen (1994); Cummins and Tennyson (1992, 1996).

imply that a higher proportion of drivers in subsidized rating cells will have higher than the average expected losses anticipated by the rate allowed for the class. Thus a higher proportion of drivers in subsidized classes and territories will be insured through the residual market.[33]

A large residual market may adversely affect insurer behavior. The cost of claims from residual market policies are paid out of CAR funds collected from premiums. However, any fund shortfalls are shared across insurers. Loss sharing and the fact that the insurers responsible for funding the shortfall are not all directly involved in claims settlement imply that the incentives to hold down claims costs may be lower for CAR claims.[34] This suggests that claims costs from residual market policies as well as the level of claims fraud may be higher than otherwise expected.

The size of the residual market may also affect consumer incentives. The operating deficit of the residual market is funded in Massachusetts by explicit increases in voluntary market rates. The method of flat loading the deficit into the class-territory rates increases the cross-subsidies in the rates, enhancing the incentive distortions discussed previously. If the residual market is a large percentage of the total cars insured, it will produce a large operating deficit, as well as a large operating deficit per car insured in the voluntary market. This will increase the premiums paid by all drivers, regardless of the actual risk they impose upon the insurance system. Thus when the residual market size is large, there is yet another portion of the premium charge that is not related to driver behaviors or choices at the margin. This may reinforce the aforementioned incentive distortions by weakening drivers' perceptions that their insurance rates respond to the decisions they make.

Rate Suppression

To the extent that insurance rates overall are held below the level that would be obtained in the absence of state-set rates, insurers' incentives to sell automobile insurance in the market will be reduced. Firms will respond to rate suppression by ceding more policies to the residual market, by reducing service quality, or in extreme cases by exiting the market.[35] Exit

33. In practice the decision is more complicated in Massachusetts because insurers receive credits toward their contribution to the residual market deficit for voluntarily writing certain subsidized classes and territories. Thus the ceding decision will be based on the expected profit or loss to the insurer after taking into account residual market credits.

34. Blackmon and Zeckhauser (1991).

35. Harrington (1992).

restrictions, in the form of lost business from other lines and the continued sharing of CAR losses, dramatically increase the cost of leaving Massachusetts' automobile insurance market. However, exit will still occur if losses from continued operation exceed the costs of exit.

Just as important, insurers will not want to enter a market in which rates are suppressed. Even if current rates are adequate, if the regulatory environment makes future rate suppression likely or possible, uncertainty about future rate adequacy will dampen entry. Entry will be further deterred if the state has exit restrictions in place. The combined effect of increased incentives to exit and decreased incentives to enter suggests that fewer firms will operate in a market subject to actual or potential rate suppression.

Additionally, the characteristics of firms operating in the market may be distorted by the potential for rate suppression. Single-state insurers may have appeal because of their accounting transparency with regard to profit reporting to regulators. They may implicitly constrain regulators regarding rate adequacy, since single-state firms in a regulated state are more likely to experience financial distress if regulated prices are set too low. However, when small, single-state insurers write a large share of the market, higher costs may result because small firms may have higher operating expenses.[36] Such insurers will also likely face higher insolvency risk due to their smaller capitalization and lower geographic diversification, resulting in higher costs of capital.[37] This will generate higher premium charges to consumers.

Implications

When considered in combination, the most striking feature of the incentive distortions created by Massachusetts' regulation is that most will lead to higher costs in automobile insurance. The primary effect is predicted to be on insurance loss costs, but average insurer operating costs may also be higher. Higher loss and expense costs will result in higher automobile insurance premiums, since premiums must cover costs.

Rigorous empirical measurement of the incentive distortions gener-

---

36. Consistent with this, Tennyson (1997) found that market-share-weighted, statewide average expense ratios were significantly higher in stringently regulated states than in other states.

37. Apart from a few widely publicized cases, insolvencies occur disproportionately among the smallest insurance firms. See Best (1991).

ated by regulation is beyond the scope of this study. Instead, we examine the effect of regulation on market aggregates to test whether the predicted outcomes from incentive distortions are evident. Our theoretical discussion has generated several predictions. First, the Massachusetts automobile insurance market structure will be distorted by regulation, with fewer firms operating and a higher proportion of single-state firms. Second, the residual market in Massachusetts will be larger than normal, with ceding patterns over time related to rate adequacy and cross-sectionally related to rate cross-subsidies between consumers. Third, Massachusetts will have higher claims costs than otherwise expected.

Impact of Regulation on Market Structure and Competition

Table 2-8 reports on the size and structure of the Massachusetts private passenger automobile insurance market. For comparison the table also shows the mean values over all states excluding Massachusetts and over all Northeast states excluding Massachusetts. States in the Northeast region are included because, like Massachusetts, they tend to be more urbanized and have a stronger historical tradition of selling by independent agents. The table reports the number of firms and measures of market concentration for the years 1980, 1989, and 1998 and calculates the percentage change in these variables for the period 1980–98 and for 1980–89 and 1989–98 separately. The data on firms and market shares were constructed by aggregating over insurance groups and independent single companies that reported positive direct premiums written in a state in a given year. The table reports the unweighted means by state.

There are several notable differences between the Massachusetts market and other states. First, although Massachusetts is not a small market as measured by either written car-years or direct premium volume, the number of firms in the market is significantly lower than the averages for all other states and for other states in the Northeast. In 1998, 38 firms operated in the Massachusetts private passenger automobile liability market, while the average over all other states was 76 and over all other Northeast states was 69. The number of direct writer firms is also significantly lower, with only 8 in Massachusetts versus an average of 20 in all other states and 16 in other Northeast states. Automobile insurance markets in all states have consolidated over time, and hence there are fewer firms writing in

Table 2-8. *State Automobile Insurance Market Structure, 1980–98, Selected Years*
Units as indicated

	Massachusetts			All other states			Other Northeast states		
Variable levels	1980	1989	1998	1980	1989	1998	1980	1989	1998
Written car-years (in thousands)	2.747	3.198	3.841	2.117	2.670	3.095	2.356	2.873	3.220
Direct premiums written (in thousands)	939.189	2,461.149	3,074.251	627.825	1,464.913	2,323.728	820.387	1,754.040	2,807.744
Number of firms[a]	62	58	38	98	91	76	89	81	69
Direct writer firms[a]	18	14	8	27	26	20	25	21	16
Direct writer share	0.301	0.250	0.210	0.591	0.64	0.654	0.453	0.505	0.52
Four-firm concentration	0.388	0.390	0.492	0.496	0.544	0.553	0.374	0.439	0.472
Herfindahl index	559	632	932	885	1043	1046	558	685	768
Percent change	1980–89	1989–98	1980–98	1980–89	1989–98	1980–98	1980–89	1989–98	1980–98
Written car-years	16.4	20.1	39.8	26.1	15.9	46.2	21.9	12.1	36.7
Direct premiums written	162.1	24.9	227.3	133.3	58.6	270.1	113.8	60.1	242.2
Number of firms[a]	-6.5	-34.5	-38.7	-7.1	-16.5	-22.4	-9.0	-14.8	-22.5
Direct writer firms[a]	-22.2	-42.9	-55.6	-3.7	-23.1	-25.9	-16.0	-23.8	-36.0
Direct writer share	-17.0	-15.8	-30.2	8.3	2.2	10.7	11.5	3.0	14.8
Four-firm concentration	0.6	26.1	26.8	9.7	1.7	11.5	17.4	7.5	26.2
Herfindahl index	13.1	47.5	66.7	17.9	0.3	18.2	22.8	12.1	37.6

Source: Authors' compilation from A. M. Best Co. and NAIC databases of insurers' annual statements.
a. These statistics are for firms writing private passenger automobile liability insurance. All other statistics are for all private passenger automobile coverages combined.

each state in 1998 than in 1980, but the decrease in firms in Massachusetts is larger than average. In 1980 Massachusetts had about two-thirds as
many auto insurance firms as other states on average, but by 1998 it had
only half as many.

The market share of direct writer firms, at only 21 percent, was also
significantly lower in Massachusetts in 1998; in other states direct writers
achieved on average a 65 percent market share, and in other Northeast
states direct writers held 52 percent of the market. The difference in the
direction of change over time is even more striking. Over the past three
decades, there has been a significant national trend toward growth in the
direct writer share of the private passenger auto insurance market.[38] In our
sample, from 1980 to 1998, direct writer market share increased from 59
to 65 percent in all other states on average, and from 45 to 52 percent in
other Northeast states. Yet over the same time period, direct writer market
share fell from 30 to 21 percent in Massachusetts.[39]

While compelling, these summary statistics fail to fully convey the
nature of the very distinctive shift in the Massachusetts automobile insurance market over the last two decades. There has been a pronounced shift
from the largest automobile writers toward firms that write only in Massachusetts. Table 2-9 lists the ten largest private passenger auto insurers, by
premium volume, in Massachusetts for the years 1982, 1990, and 1998.
In 1982 all of the Massachusetts market leaders were large national or
regional insurance groups. By 1990 only six of the ten were national writers, with the remaining four Massachusetts market leaders writing only in
that state. By 1998 fully seven of the ten largest auto insurance writers in
Massachusetts were single-state firms or very localized insurers.

This shift in market leadership is partly attributable to the voluntary
shrinking of market shares and the withdrawal of national insurers mentioned previously. Of the ten market leaders in 1982, only four continued
to write automobile insurance in Massachusetts in 1998. Three of these
remain among the top ten insurers, but two of these (Travelers and Commercial Union) have restructured their automobile insurance business to
be written by single-state subsidiaries.[40] More generally, twenty-four firms

---

38. For an in-depth discussion of this trend and the academic literature about it, see Regan and Tennyson (2000).

39. While not reported here, analysis of homeowners' insurance market structure revealed far less
difference between Massachusetts and other states.

40. Travelers formed Premier Insurance Company in 1993, and Commercial Union formed Commercial Union Homeland Insurance Company in 1989.

Table 2-9. *Market Leaders, Massachusetts Automobile Insurance, 1982–98, Selected Years*

1982		1990		1998	
Group Name	*Number of states*	*Group Name*	*Number of states*	*Group Name*	*Number of states*
1. Travelers Ins. Group	51	1. Travelers Ins. Group	51	1. Commerce Group	2
2. Liberty Mutual Ins. Group	51	2. Commerce Group	51	2. Arbella Ins. Group	1
3. Lumbermans Mutual (Kemper)	51	3. Liberty Mutual Ins. Group	51	3. Safety Group	1
4. Allstate Ins. Group	51	4. Arbella Ins. Group	1	4. Metropolitan Group	47
5. Allianz Ins. Group	51	5. Allmerica Finance Corp. (Hanover)	51	5. Liberty Mutual Ins. Group	51
6. Sentry Ins. Group	51	6. Commercial Union[a]	1	6. Allmerica Finance Corp. (Hanover)	51
7. Commercial Union Ins.	51	7. Safety Group	51	7. Commercial Union[a]	1
8. Hanover Ins. Companies	51	8. USF&G Group	51	8. Trust Ins. Group[b]	3
9. Netherlands Ins. Corp.	51	9. Metropolitan Group	48	9. Travelers Ins. Group[a]	1
10. Hartford Group	51	10. Sentry Ins. Group	51	10. Plymouth Rock Ins.	1

Source: AIB and authors' compilation from A. M. Best Co. data and NAIC data.

a. Travelers and Commercial Union writings are now conducted through single-state subsidiaries Premier Insurance Company and Commercial Union Homeland Insurance, respectively.

b. Trust Insurance Group was declared insolvent in 2000.

have voluntarily withdrawn from the state's market since 1988. Only six withdrew as part of an announced strategy to reduce their automobile insurance exposure nationally; the vast majority simply withdrew from Massachusetts.[41] Table 2-10 lists the insurance groups that have exited the Massachusetts automobile insurance market since 1988.

Table 2-10 also lists the market entrants since 1988. Consistent with the expected combined effect of stringent regulation and restrictions on firm exit, entry into the market has been less vigorous than exit. We were nonetheless able to identify ten entrants during the sample period, although three of these resulted from restructuring of preexisting groups. Interestingly, seven of the new entrants were new Massachusetts-only start-ups. Moreover, of the seven 1998 market leaders that were single-state firms, five had entered the market since 1985. Thus one very apparent trend in the market is the entry and expansion of new, single-state insurers. Figure 2-3 shows the growth in automobile insurance market share of single-state insurers over the period 1990–98.[42]

What explains this pattern of entry and growth? New entrants had a distinct advantage over older firms in the Massachusetts market prior to 1989 due to the allocation of residual market losses based on historical market shares. Prior to that time, market share in 1982 was used as the basis for loss sharing, and increases in new writings above a firm's 1982 level decreased the residual market share of the firm. CAR rules have since been modified but still have provisions that grant recent entrants more favorable loss share assessments. Entry into Massachusetts also has been facilitated by the exit of national insurers. Several of the new firms were formed by taking on the business of exiting insurers. For example, Pilgrim entered in 1987 as a CAR-servicing carrier that took on the high-risk policies of Fireman's Fund. Organizing as a servicing carrier makes entry easier since profits are earned from CAR fees and no underwriting risk need be taken on. Organizing as a single-state firm may also be preferred by insurers for the reasons discussed earlier, but there are no obvious operating advantages that accrue to a single-state firm.

Entry of new firms into the market and changes in the identity of market leaders are typically viewed as evidence of competition in a market.

41. Derrig (1993); Yelen (1993).

42. The large decline in single-state firms' market share in 1998 appears to be due to Commerce Insurance Company, which in that year had positive premium writings in California and Rhode Island as well as Massachusetts, thus technically dropping out of the single-state category. However, only 0.1 percent of its 1999 premiums were written in other states.

Table 2-10. *Entry and Exit in Massachusetts Automobile Insurance Market, 1988–2000*

Voluntary exits (by group)		Involuntary exits	Entrants
Aetna[a]	Hartford	American Mutual Ins. Co.	American Auto Ins. Co.[b]
AIG	Home	American Universal Ins. Co.	American States Ins.
Allstate	John Hancock[a]	American Hardware Mutual	Commercial Union Homeland[b]
Central Mutual	Kemper	New England Fidelity Ins.	Commonwealth Mutual[c]
Chubb	Nationwide	Providence Washington	Masswest Ins. Co.
Cigna[a]	Peerless	Trust Ins. Co.	New England Fidelity Ins.
Colonial Penn[a]	Reliance		Peoples Service Ins. Co.
Continental	Royal		Pilgrim Ins. Co.[d]
Crum and Forster[a]	St Paul		Premier Ins. Co of MA[b]
Fireman's Fund	Shelby		Trust Ins. Co.
General Accident	USF&G[a]		
General Motors Ins.	Utica National		

Source: Derrig (1993), Yelen (1993), and authors' compilations from NAIC data and A. M. Best Co. reports.
a. Exit was part of a more general strategy to reduce or withdraw from automobile or personal insurance lines.
b. Firm entry was part of a strategy to organize an existing group's business under a Massachusetts-only firm.
c. Merged with Arbella Insurance Group in 2000.
d. This firm is the residual market servicing carrier for Plymouth Rock Insurance.

Figure 2-3. *Market Share of Single-State Writers, Massachusetts Private Passenger Automobile Insurance, 1990–98*

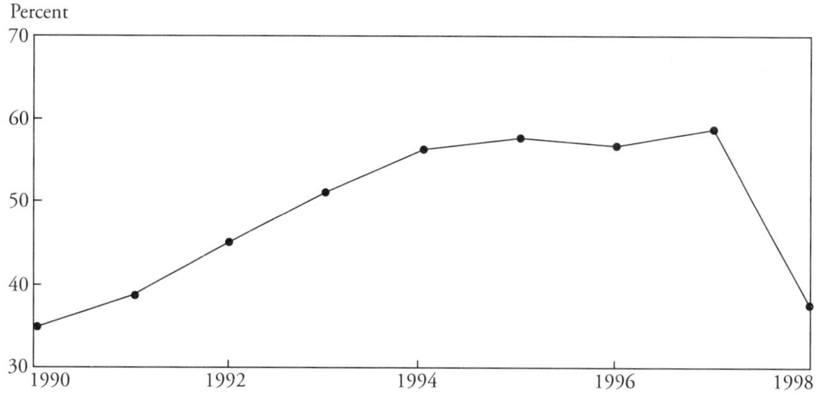

Percent

Source: Authors' calculations from A. M. Best Co. and NAIC databases of insurers' annual statement filings.

While the reasons for these changes in Massachusetts are considerably different than those observed under open competition, they nonetheless indicate that some forces of competition are at work in this market. The degree of competition is restricted, of course, and firms normally unable to compete may be able to enter and succeed in this market.

Price competition across firms is also apparent in the market, to the limited extent allowed under the law. Beginning in 1995 many Massachusetts automobile insurers have offered consumers rates that are discounted below the state-set rate. Many of the discounts have been offered as group discounts, but substantial discounts to individuals in certain safe driver categories (as classified by the SDIP) have also been offered.

The intense price competition may have contributed to the insolvencies of two single-state insurers, Trust and New England Fidelity, in 2000. These firms grew rapidly and suffered significant operating losses prior to their insolvency. The impact on the market is significant, as the two firms together accounted for nearly 5 percent of the auto insurance market in Massachusetts. Three other recent start-ups have also been merged into larger insurers due to financial troubles.[43] These developments highlight the risks associated with having small, single-state insurers constitute a significant portion of the market.

43. B. Mohl, "State Takes Control of Troubled New England Fidelity: Mass. Auto Insurers See Market Trend," *Boston Globe*, September 22, 2000, p. D3.

Residual Market

Residual markets operate in all states to provide automobile insurance to high-risk drivers that insurers are unwilling to accept in their normal risk pools. In a competitive insurance market in which risk classes and rates are freely determined, we would expect only a small percentage of drivers to fall into this uninsurable category. This is in fact what we observe in states with comparatively unregulated auto insurance markets. In states that regulate more heavily, the fraction of cars insured through the residual market is often greater. Figure 2-4 displays the annual percentage of cars insured through the residual market in Massachusetts compared to the averages in all other regulated states and in all unregulated states for the time period 1972–98.

A striking feature of the figure is the large size of the Massachusetts residual market, even in comparison to other regulated states. This is consistent with the predicted incentive effects of regulation. In this regard it is interesting to note that the size of the Massachusetts residual market was comparable to that in other states prior to 1974, but it began to grow dramatically just after the mandatory offer rule came into effect for both compulsory and optional insurance and about the time that all rates began to be set by the state. Being required to accept all applicants, without the flexibility to adjust prices to reflect risk, leaves insurers with a simple binary decision—insure in the voluntary market or cede to the residual market. This simple decision is reflected in the statistics on residual market size in Massachusetts.

Overall rate inadequacy also will lead to a larger residual market pool. If regulated rates are set below the expected costs of insuring a driver, then insurers will prefer to cede that policy to the residual market pool. The pattern of residual market size in Massachusetts over time follows that of regulatory stringency in rate setting and implies rate suppression in the latter 1980s.[44] The residual market size peaked in 1989, followed by a noticeable decline in both its absolute size and its size relative to other state pools over the 1990s. This may be due to easing of state rate-setting stringency, CAR reforms, SDIP reforms, or a combination of these factors.

44. There is a strong negative correlation between Massachusetts auto insurance underwriting profits and residual market size. The correlation coefficient between these two variables from 1980 to 1998 is -0.766. A simple regression of the percent of cars insured in the residual market in a given year on the automobile underwriting profit percent in the previous year achieves an R^2 of 64 percent over the time period 1981–98.

Figure 2-4. *Residual Market Shares, 1972–98*

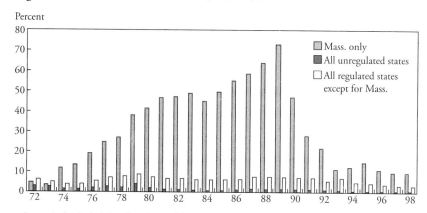

Source: Authors' calculations from Automobile Insurance Plans Service Office, *AIPSO Facts*, various years.

Due to the lack of premium surcharges to drivers insured in the resid-ual market, Commonwealth Automobile Reinsurers operates at a signifi-cant deficit. Table 2-11 shows CAR's annual operating deficit over the period 1974–95, both in the aggregate and per insured car. Not surpris-ingly, the trend in the operating deficit follows that of the percentage of cars insured in the market, with operating losses of over $500 million dol-lars a year in the latter part of the 1980s. Operating losses per car insured in the voluntary market peaked in 1989 at over $600 per car.[45]

The pattern of cessions across policyholder groups is also consistent with expectations. The strong restrictions on policy cancellation in com-bination with the inability to freely adjust rates over time should make insurers very reluctant to cover inexperienced drivers. This reluctance will be intensified by the fact that inexperienced driver classes in Massachusetts receive rate subsidies. This outcome is clearly manifested in table 2-12, which shows cessions to CAR by driver experience for 1985–98. In every year and all driver classes, the percentage of inexperienced drivers (those with less than 3 years driving experience) insured in the residual market has been much higher than that for experienced drivers. As the size of the residual market has declined in the 1990s, the relative fraction of inexpe-rienced drivers in the residual market has grown dramatically. This is

45. These statistics are measured with respect to car-years written, defined as one-twelfth the num-ber of exposure months of liability insurance on private passenger vehicles. Automobile Insurance Plans Service Office (1998).

Table 2-11. *Massachusetts Residual Market Operating Deficit, 1974–95*
Dollars, except as indicated

Year	Operating results (in millions)	Car-years written, voluntary market	Total car-years written	Loss per car-year	Loss per voluntary car-year
1974	−16.80	2,048,264	2,322,584	−7.23	−8.20
1975	−92.80	2,041,682	2,350,323	−39.48	−45.45
1976	−84.00	1,993,929	2,463,009	−34.10	−42.13
1977	−52.20	1,895,931	2,517,952	−20.73	−27.53
1978	−107.40	1,794,106	2,455,122	−43.75	−59.86
1979	−177.70	1,675,642	2,700,398	−65.81	−106.05
1980	−260.60	1,611,640	2,746,986	−94.87	−161.70
1981	−324.20	1,488,252	2,783,601	−116.47	−217.84
1982	−285.30	1,486,343	2,812,029	−101.46	−191.95
1983	−197.00	1,407,182	2,750,267	−71.63	−140.00
1984	−234.10	1,643,916	2,984,158	−78.45	−142.40
1985	−376.30	1,559,027	3,083,933	−122.02	−241.37
1986	−504.70	1,453,796	3,226,607	−156.42	−347.16
1987	−594.90	1,405,240	3,383,535	−175.82	−423.34
1988	−522.10	1,232,711	3,420,255	−152.65	−423.54
1989	−519.20	858,133	3,198,146	−162.34	−605.03
1990	−360.60	1,716,380	3,229,076	−111.67	−210.09
1991	−182.50	2,449,295	3,400,236	−53.67	−74.51
1992	−128.50	2,199,699	2,806,522	−45.79	−58.42
1993	−159.30	3,014,207	3,398,356	−46.88	−52.85
1994	−87.80	3,084,280	3,523,625	−24.92	−28.47
1995	−143.90	3,127,160	3,666,999	−39.24	−46.02

Source: Automobile Insurance Plans Service Office. *AIPSO Facts,* various years. New York.

attributable to a dramatic drop in the percent of experienced drivers ceded to CAR and is consistent with the more favorable underwriting environment of the 1990s.

Because the driver rate class definitions are extremely broad in Massachusetts, there exist not only cross-subsidies between classes but within classes as well. Table 2-13 demonstrates that within a given class, policyholders who receive rate subsidies are more likely to be ceded to the residual market. The table shows insurer estimates of the rate cross-subsidies within class 10 (experienced drivers) by driver age and gender characteristics for 1998. A positive number indicates that the driver group pays a premium surcharge, and a negative number indicates that the group receives

Table 2-12. *Exposures Insured in Residual Market, Adult and Youth Drivers Combined by Driver Experience, 1985–98*
Percent, except as indicated

Year	Insured in CAR	Drivers in CAR		Ratio of inexperienced to experienced
		Experienced	Inexperienced	
1985	50.3	48.0	74.9	1.56
1986	55.2	53.0	79.1	1.49
1987	59.5	57.5	82.0	1.43
1988	65.0	63.4	86.6	1.37
1989	68.7	67.4	85.8	1.27
1990	57.0	55.9	74.0	1.32
1991	36.2	35.3	50.6	1.43
1992	24.8	24.0	40.4	1.68
1993	13.8	12.8	33.7	2.63
1994	12.0	10.6	41.2	3.89
1995	13.3	11.7	47.5	4.06
1996	12.4	10.8	45.6	4.22
1997	10.9	9.5	40.3	4.24
1998	10.6	9.3	37.8	4.06

Source: AIB (1999).

a subsidy at the class rate. The table also shows the percentage of each driver group insured through CAR. Young drivers (especially young male drivers) within the class receive rate subsidies and are much more likely to be insured through the residual market.[46]

Loss Costs and Premiums

Average loss costs are defined as total insured losses divided by the total car-years insured. Loss costs can be decomposed into loss frequency (the number of claims per insured car) and loss severity (the amount of loss per each claim filed), with average loss costs equal to the product of loss frequency and loss severity. The major components of loss costs for which we have data stem from bodily injury liability (BIL) claims and

46. The patterns of cross-subsidies differ somewhat for different rating classes, but within all classes a higher fraction of drivers in groups that receive subsidies are insured through the residual market.

Table 2-13. *Cross-Subsidies and Residual Market Cessions, Experienced Driver Rating (Class 10), 1998*
Percent

| Driver characteristic | Rate subsidy | | Ceded |
	Compulsory package	Standard package	
Adult	4.2	5.0	8.5
Female youth	−25.5	−26.3	23.4
Male youth, principal operator	−46.3	−49.5	28.8
Male youth, occasional operator	−27.4	−29.4	24.7

Source: AIB (1998, 1999).

property damage liability (PDL) claims.[47] Table 2-14 reports loss frequency (as claims per 100 insured cars), loss severity, and average loss costs for BIL and PDL claims for Massachusetts and for the United States as a whole. The table displays both the 1998 levels and the mean levels over the time period 1980–98.

A number of factors unrelated to regulation imply that Massachusetts is expected to have higher than average loss costs for automobile insurance. In particular, Massachusetts is a relatively urban state with high traffic density, which increases traffic accidents. Massachusetts also has a relatively high level of per capita income and cost of living, which increases demand for insurance and claiming propensity. Consistent with this, table 2-14 demonstrates that Massachusetts loss costs are noticeably higher than the U.S. average for BIL and PDL, both in the latest year of our data and on average over time.[48]

Massachusetts BIL loss costs per car in 1998 were $206, 84 percent higher than the U.S. average of $112. The difference is created by greater frequency of claims in Massachusetts. Massachusetts claim frequency per 100 insured vehicles in 1998 was 2.29, but the U.S. average was only 1.17.

47. Data were obtained from the Insurance Research Council and were compiled from the Massachusetts AIB and from the National Automobile Insurance Institute (NAII) for states other than Massachusetts. NAII data on losses under collision and comprehensive coverages are available, but the insurers reporting data to the NAII represent a small percentage of the Massachusetts market.

48. To examine whether differences in average loss costs levels, frequency, and severity are systematic, small sample *t*-tests were conducted. The tests indicate that the differences between Massachusetts and nationwide loss costs are indeed systematic for both frequency and loss cost averages for bodily injury and property damage liability. However, for severity there is no significant difference between Massachusetts and the nation as a whole.

Table 2-14. *Massachusetts Loss Costs versus U.S. Average, 1998*
Dollars, except as indicated

	1998		Mean 1980–98	
	U.S.	Massachusetts	U.S.	Massachusetts
Bodily injury liability				
Loss frequency (no. of claims per 100 cars)	1.17	2.29	1.06	1.87
Loss severity per claim	9,585	9,016	8,355	8,481
Loss cost per car	112	206	91	164
Property damage liability				
Loss frequency (no. of claims per 100 cars)	4.09	7.06	4.38	7.46
Loss severity per claim	2,010	1,785	1,334	1,260
Loss cost per car	82	126	57	93

Source: Authors' compilations from Insurance Research Council (2000).

Over the entire time period, the U.S. average was 1.06 bodily injury claims per 100 insured vehicles, while the average for Massachusetts was 1.87, 76 percent higher. Average claim severity from 1980 through 1998 was higher in Massachusetts than in the rest of the nation, but not substantially: $8,481 versus $8,355, respectively, a difference of just 1.5 percent.

A similar pattern is evident in PDL losses. PDL loss costs in 1998 were $126 in Massachusetts, 53 percent higher than the $82 experienced for the country as a whole. As with BIL loss costs, the difference in PDL loss costs can be attributed to claims frequency rather than severity. The average number of property damage liability claims per 100 insured vehicles in the United States over the entire time period was 4.38, while Massachusetts PDL claims frequency averaged 70 percent higher at 7.46. PDL severity was comparable to the U.S. average, in fact slightly lower, in both 1998 and on average over the period 1980–98.

Of interest to our analysis is the effect of regulation, especially of the unique features of Massachusetts regulation, on loss costs in the state.[49] State-level data are used to perform a regression analysis of average loss costs to determine whether Massachusetts loss costs are higher because of its regulatory system. The regression model includes explanatory variables

49. As discussed previously, the cross-subsidies in the Massachusetts rates are expected to lead to higher loss costs than otherwise expected because of adverse incentive effects on driving, risk-taking, insuring, and claiming behaviors.

other than those influenced by regulation that might be expected to affect statewide average loss costs. A Massachusetts indicator variable is included, set to equal one for Massachusetts and zero for other states, to capture any cost differential in Massachusetts not explained by the other variables. A positive coefficient on this variable indicates that Massachusetts loss costs are significantly higher than those of other states, after controlling for the other factors.

Several control variables are included in the empirical model. Because no-fault automobile insurance systems should reduce the level of BIL losses, we include a dummy variable equal to one if a state has a no-fault auto law and equal to zero otherwise. There is an additional dummy variable for states that have no-fault laws with verbal tort thresholds, to allow for potential differences in the proportion of BIL claims eliminated under different no-fault laws.[50] We also include a dummy variable equal to one if a state regulates automobile insurance rates. If there are systematic effects on loss costs for regulated versus unregulated states, this indicator allows us to separate those from the Massachusetts effect.

The population density of the state, proportion of miles driven in urban areas, proportion of the population that is between the ages of 18 and 24, and per capita income in the state are also included as control variables. Population density should be positively related to accident frequency, but severity tends to be lower for densely populated areas (Miller, 1998). A similar relationship is expected for the urban miles variable. Since younger drivers tend to have more accidents, a state with a relatively younger population might have higher loss costs, all else being equal. However, it might also be the case that younger drivers experience lower severity per accident because income losses might be lower, injuries less severe, autos less expensive, or time to recovery shorter. States with higher per capita income levels might experience higher loss costs because cars are more expensive to repair, and lost income claims are higher. A variable is also included to measure the influence of medical care costs on claims costs across states. The variable is measured as the average cost of a hospital day in the state divided by 100.

To control for loss cost differences across geographic areas, we include dummy variables to indicate whether a state is located in the Northeast, Midwest, or West. This should control for any effect of location to the extent that Massachusetts loss costs are high because the state is located in

50. It has been traditionally held that verbal no-fault laws are more stringent than those with monetary thresholds. However, Cummins, Phillips, and Weiss (2001) find that some states' monetary threshold laws eliminate a greater proportion of BIL claims than the verbal threshold states.

Table 2-15. *Summary Statistics for Loss Cost Regressions, 1980–96*
Units as indicated

Variable	1980–96		1982–94	
	Mean	Standard deviation	Mean	Standard deviation
Population density (per square mile)	159.34	226.22	159.33	226.56
Proportion of population aged 18–24	0.13	0.03	0.13	0.03
Per capita income (dollars)	15,794.25	4,912.24	15,674.82	4,032.34
Proportion of miles driven in urban areas	0.50	0.17	0.51	0.17
Average cost of hospital stay (cost/100)			5.80	2.21
BIL loss cost per car (dollars)	79.63	43.75	81.27	43.15
PDL loss cost per car (dollars)	50.00	16.83	49.42	14.41
Average premium per car (dollars)	467.14	179.32	466.99	164.00
BIL/PDL claims frequency	22.49	10.22	22.64	10.28

Source: Data on claims frequency and claims costs from Insurance Research Council (2000); other data from Bureau of the Census, *Statistical Abstract of the United States,* various years (Government Printing Office).

the Northeast. Our omitted territory is the South. In addition, because loss costs increase over time, we include a series of year dummy variables, with the first year of the data period as the omitted year.

We estimate separate regression equations for state-wide BIL and PDL loss costs. The regression models for bodily injury and property damage liability loss costs differ in that the no-fault variables and the hospital cost variable are omitted from the analysis of property damage liability loss costs. We have demographic data only for 1980 through 1996, and so that is our period of analysis. However, as we have hospital cost data only for the 1982–94 period, we run two regression models for each dependent variable. The first model uses the full 1980–96 data set and omits hospital costs, while the second includes hospital costs but analyzes the 1982–94 period only. For comparison purposes, we estimate the model for both time periods for PDL costs as well as for BIL costs, even though the hospital cost variable does not appear in the PDL regression model. Table 2-15 shows the summary statistics for the variables used in the analysis. The left panel reports statistics for the period 1980–96, while the right panel reports for the 1982–94 period.

The estimation results are reported in table 2-16. The first two col-

Table 2-16. Regressions of Statewide Average Liability Loss Costs, 1980–96[a]

Explanatory variable	Bodily injury liability		Property damage liability	
	1980–96	1982–94	1980–96	1982–94
Intercept	−29.0927***	−15.7900	−10.2052***	7.1767**
	(−2.819)	(−1.363)	(−3.577)	(2.417)
Massachusetts dummy	27.5637***	21.1049***	22.5921***	24.3279***
	(4.923)	(3.342)	(14.822)	(13.839)
Population density	0.0228***	0.0409***	−0.0052***	−0.0089***
	(3.769)	(5.722)	(−3.312)	(−4.943)
Proportion of population age 18–24	−42.9162	−102.7150	89.3465***	−48.4193***
	(−0.753)	(−1.611)	(5.69)	(−3.215)
Per capita income	0.0034***	0.0024***	0.0010***	0.0024***
	(8.025)	(4.819)	(8.228)	(26.099)
Proportion of miles driven in urban areas	81.6433***	46.3403***	38.0531***	30.1879***
	(10.938)	(4.537)	(20.119)	(14.27)
Northeast region dummy	6.6282**	6.8688**	0.5298	−3.2977***
	(2.38)	(2.189)	(0.704)	(−3.987)
West region dummy	7.0501***	2.5124	−4.8868***	−6.5473***
	(3.299)	(0.993)	(−8.513)	(−10.021)
Midwest region dummy	−13.9868***	−12.7608***	−5.7120***	−7.4784***
	(−6.644)	(−5.393)	(−9.88)	(−11.386)
Hospital cost	...	7.3119***	...	...
		(7.749)		

	(1)	(2)	(3)	(4)
No-fault dummy	−16.2053***	−12.7450***	⋯	⋯
	(−8.694)	(−5.86)		
Verbal no-fault threshold	−6.8665*	−8.3487**	⋯	⋯
	(−1.942)	(−2.111)		
Rate regulation dummy	10.3824***	8.7698***	3.4353***	3.7682***
	(6.578)	(4.97)	(7.914)	(7.518)
Year dummy				
1981	1.1166	⋯	1.0415	⋯
	(0.268)		(0.903)	
1982	0.9704	⋯	2.9437**	⋯
	(0.231)		(2.534)	
1983	2.2817	−1.2567	3.4753***	−2.3284**
	(0.535)	(−0.306)	(2.949)	(−2.207)
1984	4.0210	−1.2354	6.7785***	−0.3430
	(0.923)	(−0.295)	(5.63)	(−0.327)
1985	6.7434	−1.3603	9.7209***	0.1911
	(1.485)	(−0.309)	(7.757)	(0.186)
1986	9.3707**	−1.2490	11.8875***	0.7401
	(1.989)	(−0.269)	(9.142)	(0.723)
1987	11.4094**	−1.2878	14.2032***	1.1185
	(2.304)	(−0.26)	(10.397)	(1.096)
1988	17.2802***	2.0141	17.1627***	2.1139**
	(3.306)	(0.376)	(11.906)	(2.072)
1989	20.7744***	1.1246	21.7695***	0.7430
	(3.291)	(0.167)	(12.514)	(0.673)

Table 2-16. *Continued*

Explanatory variable	Bodily injury liability		Property damage liability	
	1980–96	*1982–94*	*1980–96*	*1982–94*
1990	25.1484***	3.0236	22.8315***	0.1670
	(3.818)	(0.424)	(12.577)	(0.152)
1991	30.1373***	3.8805	20.1249***	−3.4103***
	(4.466)	(0.516)	(10.82)	(−3.083)
1992	30.8311***	0.9123	18.8357***	−5.9892***
	(4.412)	(0.114)	(9.786)	(−5.399)
1993	31.3589***	−1.6140	21.6042***	−4.6667***
	(4.322)	(−0.191)	(10.812)	(−4.195)
1994	28.1165***	−6.9786	25.7937***	−1.2727
	(3.81)	(−0.802)	(12.69)	(−1.16)
1995	22.1696***	...	29.1904***	...
	(2.855)		(13.646)	
1996	9.9753	...	36.0899***	...
	(1.22)		(16.027)	
Summary statistic				
Adjusted R^2	0.7794	0.7819	0.8861	0.8477
F statistic	111.449	97.484	263.514	224.661

Source: See table 2-5.
*Significant at the 10 percent level.
**Significant at the 5 percent level.
***Significant at the 1 percent level.
a. Regressions were performed using ordinary least squares; *t* statistics are shown in parentheses.

umns of the table show the results for BIL loss costs, and the second two columns report the results for PDL loss costs. The regression results strongly support the hypothesis that Massachusetts loss costs are higher than expected. Even after controlling for other factors, the coefficient on the Massachusetts variable is positive and significant at the 1 percent level in all models. Using the estimates for 1980 through1996, BIL loss costs average $27.56 higher and PDL loss costs average $22.59 higher than can be explained by the other variables in the model over the sample period.[51] If the entire coefficient value represents the incremental loss costs due to the unique features of Massachusetts regulation, then this is a significant increase.[52]

The regression results provide estimates of the average loss cost increment over the entire sample period. The trends over time in Massachusetts loss costs are also of interest because of the nationwide changes in auto insurance market conditions and the reforms enacted in Massachusetts in the late 1980s through early 1990s. To examine the trends in loss costs in comparison to other states, we plot Massachusetts loss costs for 1980 through 1998 against the unweighted mean for all states except Massachusetts and the unweighted mean for all other Northeast states.[53]

Figure 2-5 contains the graph of PDL loss costs over time. The figure shows that Massachusetts PDL loss costs have been higher than in all other states and all other Northeast states in all years of the sample period. Massachusetts PDL loss costs appear to dip down around 1989, and the rate of loss cost increase appears to have slowed in the 1990s. Recall that the Auto Insurance Reform Act of 1988 introduced cost containment measures for property damage losses and increased the sensitivity of insurance rates to recent accident experience. If effective, these reforms should have reduced the adverse incentive effects on driving and accident claims. The pattern of loss costs over time is consistent with a reform effect, yet the

51. These increments are in addition to the significantly higher loss costs for all regulated states, which average $10.38 for BIL and $3.44 for PDL.

52. Under certain assumptions we can construct a rough estimate of the overall impact of regulation on premiums. Nationwide, BIL plus PDL losses account for just under half of losses per insured car. If collision and comprehensive losses are affected by regulation similarly to BIL and PDL losses, our estimates would imply that losses per car are $100 higher than expected in Massachusetts. If premiums are 35 percent higher due to expense and profit loadings, this would suggest that on average Massachusetts drivers pay $135 more than they would otherwise, solely due to the impact of regulation on loss costs.

53. We also compared Massachusetts to all other no-fault states, with similar conclusions. The no-fault state averages were very similar to those for all other states and for the Northeast states.

Figure 2-5. *PDL Loss Costs per Car, 1980–98*

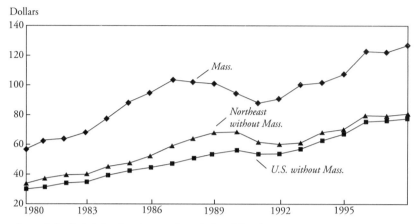

Source: Authors' calculations from Insurance Research Council (2000).

same effect is apparent in the data for other states and thus cannot be directly tied to the reforms.[54]

Figure 2-6 contains the graph of BIL loss costs over time. The graph reveals that Massachusetts BIL loss costs have been higher than in all other states and all other Northeast states in all years of the sample period. Massachusetts BIL loss costs were increasing at a high rate from the mid-1980s through 1993, after which time they fell and then flattened out. Beginning in 1994 the rate of change in BIL loss costs in Massachusetts began to mirror more closely that for other states. Recall that the Massachusetts Insurance Fraud Bureau (IFB) began operation in 1991, with particular concern for bodily injury fraud in auto insurance claiming. If effective, these reforms should have resulted in reduced BIL claims costs. The pattern of Massachusetts BIL loss costs over time suggests a significant reform effect, as no similar pattern is evident in the data for other states.

The primary impact of the 1989 increase in the tort threshold and the establishment of the IFB in 1991 should be in BIL claim frequency. Thus if the reduction in BIL loss costs is due to the reforms, we should observe

54. Of course, claims-handling reforms should have affected collision and comprehensive loss costs as well, for which we do not have data. Derrig (1997) estimates substantial cost savings from the reforms in these coverage areas.

Figure 2-6. *BIL Loss Costs per Car, 1980–98*

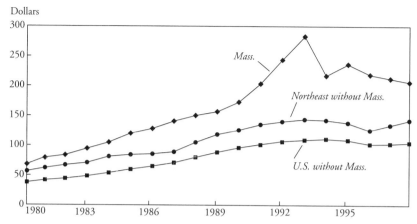

Source: Authors' calculations from Insurance Research Council (2000).

it in claims frequency as well. A measure of trends in BIL claims that controls for underlying trends in accident rates is the BIL claim frequency per 100 PDL claims (BIF/PDF). Figure 2.7 shows this statistic for Massachusetts, all other Northeast states, and all other states over the time period 1980–98. The Massachusetts BIL-to-PDL claim frequency in 1980 was below the average for all other states and for all other Northeast states. However, its rate of increase throughout that decade was noticeably greater than that of the other states, such that by 1990 Massachusetts' BIF/PDF was greater than average. Similar to the trend in BIL loss costs, by 1993 BIF/PDF began to flatten out and exhibit trends mirroring those in other states since that time. This pattern is consistent with the idea that the Massachusetts regulatory system encourages claiming and that the auto insurance reforms reduced this effect.

For consumers the ultimate impact of loss costs is seen in premium levels. Thus we also examine trends in the average premium per insured vehicle. Figure 2-8 shows the premiums per car-year over the period 1980–98 for Massachusetts, for all other states on average, and for all other Northeast states on average. The variable is defined as total premiums written in personal automobile insurance in the state divided by total car-years written, and it represents the average premium paid by each driver in the state. One problem with this variable is that it does not control for differences in coverage levels by state, nor for changes over time in coverage lev-

Figure 2-7. *BIF/PDF, 1980–98*

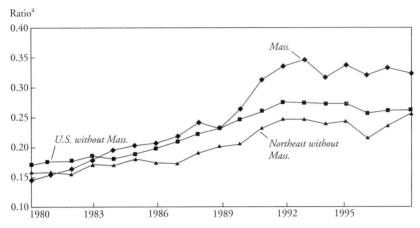

Source: Authors' calculations from Insurance Research Council (2000).
a. BIF/PDF = (BIL claim frequency) /100 PDL claims.

els or the composition of coverage. Nonetheless, it is a commonly used benchmark of premium levels across states.

Similar to loss costs, average premiums per car were higher in Massachusetts than in other states in all years of the sample period. Over the time period, Massachusetts premiums per car ranged from $341 in 1980 to $800 in 1998, reaching a peak in 1992 at just over $1,000. Average premiums have declined substantially in Massachusetts since 1992, while the averages for other states have remained relatively flat. This time trend of reductions is consistent with the pattern of actual rate declines over time in Massachusetts, and thus it is not likely to be driven solely by coverage reductions. While Massachusetts premiums remain relatively high, the differential between Massachusetts average premiums and other Northeast states was minimal by 1998.

While encouraging at first glance, the relative premium declines in Massachusetts have occurred simultaneously with a decline in the relative markup of Massachusetts premiums over losses (shown previously in figure 1-1). This is congruent with the steep decline in premiums in comparison to the modest decline in loss costs seen in figures 2-5 through 2-7. Given these comparisons and the fact that premium declines have occurred in part due to firms' discounting, it is not clear from the data that these premium decreases reflect a sustainable trend for the future.

Figure 2-8. *Premiums per Car-Year, 1980–98*

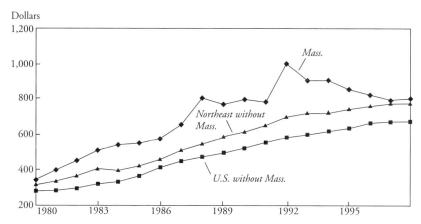

Source: Authors' calculations from Insurance Research Council (2000).

Conclusions

The Massachusetts regulatory system is extremely complex and appears to consist of numerous individually determined components. However, the various features of the system are logically linked when viewed from the perspective of pursuing social goals. A major objective of the auto insurance laws in the state is universal coverage of drivers at reasonable rates for all. The universal coverage aims are what lay behind the laws for mandatory insurance, mandatory offer rules, and limitations on policy cancellation. With mandatory insurance laws in place, affordability of coverage becomes important and provides the rationale for restrictions on rate class and territory definitions, rate subsidies, and lack of residual market premium surcharges. In periods of rising costs, suppression of overall rate levels is one way to protect insurance affordability, and individual insurer's losses are mitigated by the sharing of residual market losses. However, the possibility of rate suppression and the residual market sharing rules generate the need to place exit restrictions on insurers.

The complexity of this regulatory system thus reflects the difficulty of achieving its objectives within a market system. Access to insurance for any individual who chooses to become a driver is not compatible with ensuring that rates will be reasonable for all consumers. Weakening the link between actuarial risk determinations and prices will not only encourage high-risk drivers to enter the system but will reduce all drivers' incentives for safety and insurance loss control. This will result in higher insured losses and put upward pressure on insurance prices.

Our analysis of the impact of this system on the automobile insurance market shows that the number of insurance suppliers in the market is reduced and the character of suppliers is distorted toward smaller, single-state insurers. The residual market is larger than would be expected under competition, and insurance loss costs are higher than can be explained by market conditions alone. Simultaneously, insurer rates of return remain low under the regulatory system.

The market situation in the 1980s, a difficult period for automobile insurance markets nationally, was especially bleak in Massachusetts. A large majority of drivers were insured through the residual market, claims costs spiraled upward in double-digit inflation, and many large insurers left the market. In response, reforms were enacted at the end of the decade to reduce incentive distortions and to increase insurers' flexibility in claims handling. These reforms appear to have gone some way toward reducing the upward cost pressures manifested by the regulations, and insurance premiums have fallen in Massachusetts in recent years. However, these reductions have occurred during a period of cost and premium declines for the industry as a whole, and it is unclear whether current trends are sustainable over the longer term.

What is clear is that competition occurs in the Massachusetts auto insurance market to the extent allowed under regulation. This was demonstrated by the entry of new firms into the market after the withdrawal of national insurers, and it has been further demonstrated by the discounts insurers have offered to low-risk drivers in the latter 1990s. This competitive spirit should be encouraging to regulators concerned about the potential for competition in the market and should be encouraged by regulators through the relaxation of pricing restrictions. Prices that more closely reflect risk for all rate classes and territories will create the incentives needed to reduce the costs of automobile insurance for Massachusetts drivers.

References

A. M. Best Company. 1991. Best's Insolvency Study: Property-Casualty Insurers, 1969–1990. Oldwick, N.J.

Automobile Insurance Plans Service Office. 1998. *AIPSO Facts, 1998.* New York.

Automobile Insurers Bureau of Massachusetts (AIB). 1998. *Actuarial Notice 98-2: Subsidies in the 1998 Rates.* Boston.

_____. 1999. *Actuarial Notice 00-2: Subsidies in the 2000 Rates.*

_____. 2000a. *Recommended Territory Definitions, Docket R2000-08.*

_____. 2000b. *Underwriting Profit Filing, Section VI.*

Bartlett, D.K., III, R.W. Klein, and D.T. Russell. 1999. "Attempts to Socialize Costs in Voluntary Insurance Markets: The Historical Record." *Journal of Insurance Regulation*, 17: 478–511.

Becker, G.S. 1983. "A Theory of Competition among Pressure Groups for Political Influence." *Quarterly Journal of Economics* 48: 371–99.

Blackmon, B.G., Jr., and R. Zeckhauser. 1991. "Mispriced Equity: Regulated Rates for Auto Insurance in Massachusetts." *American Economic Review* 81: 65–69.

Carroll, A., and L. Regan. 1998. "Insurer Exposure to Extracontractual Liability under State Unfair Claims Settlement Practices Acts: An Empirical Examination." *Risk Management and Insurance Review* 2: 1–15.

Cummins, J.D. 1990. "Multiperiod Discounted Cash Flow Ratemaking Models in Property-Liability Insurance." *Journal of Risk and Insurance* 57: 79–109.

Cummins, J.D., R.D. Phillips, and S. Tennyson. 2001. "Regulation, Political Influence, and the Price of Automobile Insurance." *Journal of Insurance Regulation* 20: 9–50.

Cummins, J.D., R.D. Phillips, and M.A. Weiss. 2001. "The Incentive Effects of No Fault Automobile Insurance." *Journal of Law and Economics* (forthcoming).

Cummins, J.D., and S. Tennyson. 1992. "Controlling Automobile Insurance Costs." *Journal of Economic Perspectives* 6: 95–115.

_____. 1996. "Moral Hazard in Insurance Claiming: Evidence from Automobile Insurance." *Journal of Risk and Uncertainty* 12: 29–50.

Derrig, R.A. 1987. "The Use of Investment Income in Massachusetts Private Passenger Automobile and Workers' Compensation Ratemaking." In *Fair Rate of Return in Property-Liability Insurance*, edited by J. David Cummins and Scott E. Harrington, 119–46. Boston: Kluwer-Nihoff Publishing.

_____. 1993. "Price Regulation in US Automobile Insurance: A Case Study of Massachusetts Private Passenger Automobile Insurance 1978–1990. *Geneva Papers on Risk and Insurance* 18: 158–173.

_____. 1997. *Auto Property Damage Cost Containment: A Billion Dollar Decade of Progress in Massachusetts.* Boston: AIB.

Derrig, R.A., H.I. Weisberg, and X. Chen. 1994. "Behavioral Factors and Lotteries under No-Fault with a Monetary Threshold: A Study of Massachusetts Automobile Claims." *Journal of Risk and Insurance* 61: 245–75.

Grossman, G.M., and E. Helpman. 1994. "Protection for Sale." *American Economic Review* 84: 833–50.

Harrington, S.E. 1992. "Rate Suppression." *Journal of Risk and Insurance* 59: 185–202.

_____. 1994. "State Decisions to Limit Tort Liability: An Empirical Analysis of No-Fault Automobile Insurance Laws." *Journal of Risk and Insurance* 61: 276–94.

Harrington, S.E., and H.I. Doerpinghaus. 1993. "The Economics and Politics of Automobile Insurance Rate Classification." *Journal of Risk and Insurance* 60: 59–84.

Insurance Fraud Bureau of Massachusetts. 2000. *Prosecution Outcomes 1991 through 1999.* Boston.

Insurance Research Council. 1999. *Uninsured Motorists.* Malvern, Pa.

———. 2000. *Trends in Loss Costs.*

Jaffee, D.M., and T. Russell. 1998. "The Causes and Consequences of Rate Regulation in the Auto Insurance Industry." In *The Economics of Property-Casualty Insurance,* edited by David F. Bradford, 81–112. University of Chicago Press.

Keeton, W.R., and E. Kwerel. 1984. "Externalities in Automobile Insurance and the Underinsured Driver Problem." *Journal of Law and Economics* 27: 149–79.

Meier, K.J. 1988. *The Political Economy of Regulation: The Case of Insurance.* Albany: SUNY Press.

———. 1991. "The Politics of Insurance Regulation." *Journal of Risk and Insurance* 58: 700-13.

Miller, D. 1998. *Auto Choice: Impact on Cities and the Poor.* Report prepared for the Joint Economic Committee, 105th Cong. (July 1998).

Peltzman, Sam. 1976. "Toward a More General Theory of Regulation." *Journal of Law and Economics* 19 (August): 211–40.

Regan, L., and S. Tennyson. 2000. "Insurance Distribution Systems." In *Handbook of Insurance,* edited by G. Dionne, 709–48. Norwell, Mass.: Kluwer Academic.

Rottenberg, Simon. 1989. *The Cost of Regulation Pricing: A Critical Analysis of Auto Insurance Premium Rate-Setting in Massachusetts.* Boston: Pioneer Institute for Public Policy Research.

Stone, J.M. 1977. *Opinion, Findings and Decision on the Operation of Competition Among Motor Vehicle Insurers Rendered June 1977.* Boston: Massachusetts Division of Insurance.

———. 1978. *Opinion, Findings and Decision on the Operation of Competition among Motor Vehicle Insurers Rendered June 1978.* Boston: Massachusetts Division of Insurance.

Suponcic, Susan J. 1998. "The Politics and Economics of Rate Regulation." Ph.D. dissertation, University of Pennsylvania.

Tennyson, S. 1993. "Regulatory Lag in Automobile Insurance." *Journal of Risk and Insurance* 60: 36–58.

———. 1997. "The Impact of Rate Regulation on State Automobile Insurance Markets." *Journal of Insurance Regulation* 15: 502–23.

Weisberg, H.I., and R.A. Derrig. 1991. "Fraud and Automobile Insurance: A Report on the Baseline Study of Bodily Injury Claims in Massachusetts." *Journal of Insurance Regulation* 9: 497–541.

———. 1996. *Coping with the Influx of Sprain and Strain Claims.* Boston: AIB.

Weiss, M.A. 1990. "Productivity Growth and Regulation of Property-Liability Insurance: 1980–1984. *Journal of Productivity Analysis* 2: 15–38.

Yelen, S. 1993. "Withdrawal Restrictions in the Automobile Insurance Market." *Yale Law Journal* 102: 1431–55.

JOHN D. WORRALL

3

Private Passenger Auto Insurance in New Jersey: A Three-Decade Advertisement for Reform

In 1991 Marjorie M. Bertie gave the following overview of the New Jersey private passenger insurance market: "No discussion of failed political solutions to the auto insurance crisis is complete without a look at New Jersey, the state with the most tangled auto insurance mess in history. Even the Soviet Union would be hard pressed to match this economic disaster."[1]

New Jersey usually has the highest private passenger automobile insurance rates in the United States. Year after year state residents have listened to news reports, or read their local newspapers, and found that New Jersey, once again, was able to claim the dubious distinction of being the state with the highest average expenditure for auto insurance. The National Association of Insurance Commissioners (NAIC) annual expenditure calculations are dutifully reported, and state legislators and governors tremble. People who need their cars to drive to work, school, or church are not

Thanks go to Kevin Worrall for excellent research assistance and to Anita Lo for graciously answering my data questions. Bob Hartwig, Elizabeth Sprinkel, and staff at the Alliance of American Insurers, National Association of Independent Insurers, the Insurance Council of New Jersey, and the New Jersey Department of Banking and Insurance all took time to answer my questions. David Cummins provided the data and graciously helped with the nuances of both the convention blank and NAIC-BEDS data. He also made many helpful comments on earlier drafts of this chapter. Richard Derrig provided many useful suggestions. Discussions with my colleague, Emilio Venezian, have also been very helpful. Any errors and all opinions expressed in this chapter are mine.

1. Bertie (1991, p. 66).

concerned with the intricacies of insurance law or ratemaking. They simply want to know why they had to pay over $1,100 to insure a car in 1998 while folks in Iowa paid $460.

The answer to that question lies in the nature of the state itself and in the story of its regulatory history. For most of the 1980s and 1990s, New Jersey was the most expensive state in terms of average private passenger insurance.[2] Table 3-1 shows New Jersey and countrywide average expenditures for 1994 to 1998, the latest five years of data available for this study. New Jersey not only led the nation in average expenditure in each year, but its average expenditure grew faster than in the rest of the country. In 1994 New Jersey drivers spent 48 percent more than drivers elsewhere in the United States. In 1998 New Jerseyeans were spending 62 percent more, with a statewide average expenditure of $1,138 for private passenger auto insurance.

For the insurance economist, New Jersey is a dream. Its auto insurance system has offered a series of natural experiments in incentive response, regulatory lag, market failure, binding price constraints, "excess" profit law, barriers to exit, and cash flow residual market financing. The state is the most densely populated in the country, with 1,134 people per square mile as of 2000.[3] As of 1997 it had 695.66 registered motor vehicles per square mile.[4] It has metropolitan areas and cities that consistently rank at or near the top of the auto theft table, has been a haven for notorious fraud rings, and has had a "Cadillac" benefit system. New Jersey is a compulsory insurance state, which began the 1970s with a tort system. It introduced a no-fault choice with a low monetary threshold that was rapidly eroded by medical care price inflation and became a recipe for claim build-up and lawsuits. The state switched from an assigned risk plan to a "joint underwriting association" (JUA) with carrier fees based, in part, on loss payments, hence offering perverse incentives for larger claims payments.[5] After the JUA ran up a deficit of $3 billion, New Jersey switched to a state-run "market transition facility" (MTF), which managed to accumulate a deficit of $1 billion in two years. New Jersey is the state that gave the world the

2. Hawaii nosed New Jersey out for the most expensive state in 1992. See Joseph Donohue, "Car Rates Drop but Stay High," *Newark Star-Ledger*, February 14, 1994.

3. New Jersey has a land area of 7,418.84 square miles, and as of 2000 it had a population of 8,414,350. See Thomas Gallagher, "Census: Pa. Will Lose 2 House Seats," *Philadelphia Inquirer*, December 29, 2000.

4. Vehicle registrations by year are listed in table 3-13.

5. Browne and Wells (1999, p. 277).

Table 3-1. *Average Expenditures for Private Passenger Auto Insurance, New Jersey and Countrywide, 1994–98*
Dollars, except as indicated

| | Expenditures | | |
Year	N.J.	Countrywide	N.J. rank
1994	963	651	1[a]
1995	1,013	668	1
1996	1,099	691	1
1997	1,126	707	1
1998	1,138	704	1

Source: National Association of Insurance Commissioners (NAIC; 2000, table 2).
a. Most expensive.

"Remand Case" and the subsequent and infamous "Clifford formula," which is *still* being used as a ratemaking rationale in the state's rate cases, almost thirty years after its adoption.[6]

On May 19, 1998, Governor Christie Whitman signed the Automobile Insurance Cost Reduction Act and announced that the state finally had achieved auto insurance reform.[7] Although it is still early in the reform process, rates, like the Berlin Wall, may fall. The insurance commissioner has ordered a 15 percent rate reduction; however, some actuaries have priced the impact of the law changes and arrived at estimated cost savings well below 15 percent.[8] Insurers were reporting that expenditures on

6. For an example of a recent rate decision, see Tassini (2000). In 1969 the New Jersey Supreme Court ordered a "remand" of the 1967 Private Passenger Automobile Insurance rate case (see subsequent text). The remand resulted in a hearing before Insurance Commissioner Robert L. Clifford, who was himself to become a justice of the New Jersey Supreme Court. Commissioner Clifford basically ordered that investment income had to be explicitly considered in insurance ratemaking. He offered a formula that allowed a 6 percent return on "necessary" statutory surplus, which he defined as surplus necessary to write business at a two-to-one premium-to-surplus ratio. Any surplus in excess of necessary surplus was only entitled to earn a return of 1 percent. Any investment income earned on invested reserves could be used to reduce the allowed return on surplus. Modern financial economics would reject book and accounting measures of rates of return and call for market-based, discounted cash flow analyses. For a thorough discussion of appropriate techniques for the treatment of investment income, see Cummins (1990).

7. N.J.S.A. 39:6A–1.1 et seq. (*New Jersey Statutes Annotated*).

8. The actuarial firm of Miller, Rapp, Herbers, and Terry priced the bill for the American Insurance Association and estimated a 3 percent cost savings. Tillinghast, Towers, and Perrin did a study for State Farm and estimated that an earlier version of the bill would save 2 percent. See Victoria Sonshine Pasher, "Studies Seek to Steer N.J. Auto Reform," *National Underwriter Property-Casualty,* May 11, 1998, pp. 6, 56.

car insurance finally were decreasing in New Jersey, but this may be because of the mandatory 15 percent rate rollback, which took effect in March 1999. The true test of system reform is yet to come. It will be a few years before we see if claim costs fall, and the tort system will check the new law as it has all previous reform efforts. Meanwhile, some of the state's largest carriers have filed for hefty rate increases in late 2000 and early 2001.

The state still has strict prior approval rate regulation, with all of its attendant potential ills, but hope springs eternal. The New Jersey experience should provide an object lesson in how not to regulate rates and how to write bad insurance law. Surveys of economists and insurance professionals indicate that they have jaundiced views of price regulation. In 1995 Edward L. Lascher and Michael Powers surveyed members of the American Risk and Insurance Association (ARIA).[9] ARIA is the professional organization that sponsors the *Journal of Risk and Insurance,* the top-ranked academic insurance research publication. Its members are academic and industry-based scholars in finance, economics, law, actuarial science, and related disciplines with a primary interest in insurance research. Ninety-seven percent of those ARIA members surveyed agreed with the statement "Regulator imposed ceilings on rates are likely to cause firms to restrict coverage and/or withdraw from the market." Strong agreement was expressed by 70 percent. In New Jersey, firms have gone to court in attempts to exit the market. At times half of the insured drivers in the state have found themselves in the residual market. In other states many of those drivers would have been preferred risks. Lascher reported that 94 percent of ARIA members responding believed reductions in claim cost would lead to decreased premiums. Claim costs drive auto insurance cost. Lascher also reported that 90 percent of respondents believed that attorney involvement increased cost.[10] The trial bar in New Jersey has attempted to have "no-fault" repealed, and they have fought attempts to strengthen the limitation on lawsuits provision of New Jersey private passenger insurance law. Their view that an injured party should have the right to sue for recovery for pain and suffering may be utility maximizing for some, but it does not come without other costs to society.

In light of New Jersey's regulatory history and the aforementioned expert opinions, this chapter presents a brief overview of recent law changes

---

9. Lascher and Powers (1997).
10. Lascher (1999, p. 47).

and the concomitant 15 percent mandated rate rollback. It then lays out a framework for rate regulation of the private passenger business in New Jersey.

Automobile Insurance Cost Reduction Act and the 15 Percent Rate Rollback

The Whitman administration and the Republican-controlled legislature have passed a series of recent reforms to the private passenger insurance law. The first wave came in the summer of 1997: tier rating was adopted to provide pricing flexibility and deal with consumer anger over surcharges, and urban enterprise zones (UEZs) were formed to increase the availability of insurance and decrease the number of uninsured motorists in urban areas. The UEZs represent New Jersey's cities—some of the poorest areas in the United States—and constitute about 11.5 percent of private passenger automobile policies in force. The 1997 law change also repealed flex rates and adopted "expedited filings."[11] Although these changes may prove significant, it is the 1998 reform package known as the Automobile Insurance Cost Reduction Act (AICRA) that has generated the most publicity. This may largely be due to successful court cases defending the newly enacted law and to the rate rollback ordered after its passage.

AICRA introduced sweeping changes. The new law tried to strengthen the verbal threshold requirement for lawsuits. The law now requires that a claimant suffer a bodily injury "which results in death; dismemberment; significant disfigurement or significant scarring; displaced fractures; loss of a fetus; or a *permanent* [emphasis added] injury within a reasonable degree of medical probability, other than scarring or disfigurement. An injury will be considered permanent when a body part or organ, or both, has not healed to function normally and will not heal to function normally with further medical treatment."[12] This provision attempts to eliminate "soft tissue" suits and to focus on permanent injuries by requiring a physician to certify that injuries are permanent as defined by the law. Doubtless this pro-

11. Flex rating enables insurers to change rates within small percentage bands, 3 percent in New Jersey, without formal rate hearings, as long as the change would not result in rates that are inadequate, excessive, or unfairly discriminatory.

12. N.J.S.A. 39:6A-8(a).

vision of the law will be tested in the courts, and the definitions will be teased out through the legal system.

AICRA focused on reducing fraud, introducing a fraud prosecutor, and strengthening staff. It also made fraud a more serious crime. If you live in New Jersey or listen to the radio while driving through the state, you have probably heard the advertisement announcing that you will be caught if you engage in auto insurance fraud and that you can do jail time for the crime. A physician who certifies a fraudulent claim could lose his or her license to practice medicine.

The law called for revamping New Jersey's rating territories. A commission met from 1999 through 2000 to study the shape of new territories and prepared a draft report. Another provision changed the territorial rate cap system in an attempt to ensure equity, have more uniform territorial sizes, and focus rating on actuarially sound factors. (See subsequent section on caps.)

The reform introduced a new "basic policy" that offers drivers a chance to purchase minimal coverage and avoid driving uninsured. The policy has a $15,000 personal injury protection (PIP) medical expense limit and a $5,000 property damage liability (PDL) limit. It provides no bodily injury liability (BIL), but $10,000 of optional coverage may be purchased. It also carries no uninsured–underinsured motorist protection. The policy is clearly designed to give those who have been unable to drive legally in New Jersey's expensive market the opportunity to do so.[13]

The reform also introduced a "named-driver exclusion." The default under the old law charged high-risk drivers to the most expensive car on a policy. Families with teenage, inexperienced drivers saw their rates skyrocket as their newly licensed 17-year-old children were charged to mom or dad's new car. Now they can be excluded from using a specific car, and if they do drive it and have an accident, their carrier will not pay a comprehensive or collision claim.

AICRA provided choice in PIP in an attempt to control cost. The mandatory $250,000 coverage remains the default option, but consumers can now select PIP coverage at $15,000. The law change provided for tighter control of medical procedures and introduced an arbitration system for PIP claims. Obviously, this is designed to limit lawsuits and take cases away from tort and place them in the hands of arbitrators. The law

---

13. New Jersey Department of Banking and Insurance (1999a). See N.J.S.A. 39:6A–3.1(a) for a full description of the basic policy coverage.

established an ombudsman to investigate consumer complaints and also opened the door to intervention in rate hearings.

As a result of these reforms, on January 4, 1999, the commissioner ordered a 15 percent reduction in rates for all private passenger automobile insurance policies issued or renewed "processing on or after March 22, 1999." The reductions were to be distributed as follows: PIP, 27.25 percent; BIL with limitation on lawsuit, 24.33 percent; BIL with no lawsuit limitation, 3 percent; PDL, 3 percent; collision, 8.82 percent; and comprehensive (or other than collision), 3.0 percent.[14]

Notwithstanding the actuarial studies cited above, early results appear to indicate that policy expenditures have declined. Twelve member companies of the Insurance Research Council of New Jersey, with a combined market share of over 50 percent, reported that private passenger policies sold in the second quarter of 1999 had an average premium of $954, down from $1,138 in late 1997.[15] This 16.2 percent reduction comes as good news to New Jersey's long-suffering policyholders. However, by the end of 1999, the insurance council reported an average expenditure of $988.[16] The true test will be whether economic costs actually decline. New Jersey has a history of declaring war on costs, announcing that it has won the war, and pretending that deficits do not exist.

Private Passenger Auto Insurance Rate Regulation

New Jersey is a strict prior approval state. The insurance department's Office of Property and Casualty Insurance handles filings for rates, rules, and forms. They have a very heavy workload with 3,384 filings in 1998. Of that total, 714 were for personal lines, up from 483 personal lines filings in 1997. Elimination of flex rates and the introduction of expedited filings (see below) by 1997 law change plus the May 1998 passage of AICRA were probably major contributors to the increased filing activity. The department disapproved 16 filings and closed or withdrew another 789 in 1998; they approved 2,392.[17] All requests for rate increases

14. New Jersey Department of Banking and Insurance (1999d).

15. Joe Donohue, "Reforms Driving Down the Cost of Insuring Those Jersey Wheels," *Newark Star-Ledger*, September 29, 1999.

16. Joe Donohue, "Prudential Cuts Auto Rates 2.9 percent—However, New Jersey Re-Insurance Receives Permission to Boost Its Rates by 8.9 Percent," *Newark Star-Ledger*, June 17, 2000.

17. New Jersey Department of Banking and Insurance (2000a, p. 10).

must be filed with the Department of Banking and Insurance (hereafter, the Insurance Department). The commissioner makes a determination whether the rates are "unreasonably high, or inadequate, or unfairly discriminatory" and issues an order of approval or disapproval based on the determination.[18]

When a private passenger insurer files for a rate change, either the filer or the Insurance Department may request a hearing, which may be conducted by the commissioner, his or her designee, or by the Office of Administrative Law. The hearing is supposed to start within "30 days of the date of the request or decision that a hearing is to be held"(extensions are permitted), the findings and recommendation are to be presented to the commissioner within 30 days of close of the contested hearing, and the commissioner should render a decision within 60 days of receipt of the findings of fact and recommendations. The filer bears the cost of the hearing. The commissioner has the power to order temporary partial rates to be used until a hearing and determination can be made. These temporary rates can be subsequently adjusted by refunds, debits, or credits. No other rates, dividend plans, and the like can be used unless they are on file and approved by the commissioner. Filers are required to offer premium credits that must be a uniform percentage statewide for deductibles and exclusions under PIP and for tort limits under BIL. Insurers cannot vary the commission percentage they pay based on the policy options insureds choose.[19]

Recent Rate Cases

Table 3-2 shows the requests for rate changes filed with the New Jersey Insurance Department. Three determinations handed down by the department in the spring of 2000 were all for less than the amounts requested. After having one request for an increase denied, New Jersey Re-Insurance—a subsidiary of New Jersey Manufacturers, the third largest private passenger automobile insurer in the state—filed for a 22.7 percent rate increase in June 1999. The case was heard by an administrative law judge who ruled that New Jersey Re-Insurance should get an unspecified rate increase. On June 16, 2000, the commissioner announced that she had "modified the Administrative Law Judge's decision and found a rate

18. N.J.S.A. 17:29A-14(a).
19. For details about these provisions, see N.J.S.A. 17:29A-14(c and e), A-15, and A-15.1.

Table 3-2. *Disposition of Rate Filings, New Jersey Auto Insurance, 1998–2001*

Company	Date filed	Percent requested	Date decided	Percent granted
Decided[a]				
GSA	Sep 98	85.5	May 00	15.0
N.J. Re-Insurance	Jun 99	22.7	Jun 00	8.9
Prudential Group	Jan 99	−1.2	Jun 00	−2.9
Pending				
NJPAIP[b]	Sep 99	29.9		
Selective Group	Jul 00	18.9		
American International	Sep 00	20.1		
State Farm	Oct 00	16.8		
Colonial Penn	Oct 00	37.6		
Founders	Oct 00	14.5		
Proformance	Nov 00	7.5		
Liberty Mutual Fire	Nov 00	20.0		
Liberty Mutual	Dec 00	25.2		
Providence Washington	Jan 01	48.1		
CGU	Feb 01	7.3		

Source: Personal communication from the New Jersey Department of Banking and Insurance, January 4, 2001; Eugene Kiely, "N.J. Auto Insurers' Push Could Erase Cuts," *Philadelphia Inquirer,* April 12, 2001.

a. In private correspondence the Insurance Department informed me that twenty-nine requests for rate increases filed between January 1, 1998, and December 31, 2000, had been denied. The department supplied the information on cases decided after a hearing, but it did not list the names of the insurers or percent increase requested for those requests denied that did not go to a formal hearing before an administrative law judge.

b. New Jersey Personal Automobile Insurance Plan.

need of only 8.9 percent rather than the requested 22.7 percent."[20] It was one year from filing to the issue of the order.

The commissioner also ordered a 2.9 percent rate decrease for the Prudential Group that day. Prudential Group had filed for a 1.2 percent decrease in January. It took about five months for the decision. The department noted that "Prudential's last *prior approval* rate increase was 6.9 percent in *1990*." (Emphasis added.)

An interesting example of price regulation in New Jersey is the GSA

20. New Jersey Department of Banking and Insurance, "Prudential Group to Decrease Auto Rates 2.9 Percent; Smaller Company to See 8.9 Percent Increase," press release, June 16, 2000.

Insurance private passenger case. Maryland Casualty withdrew from the New Jersey market in 1997, with GSA assuming over 90 percent of Maryland Casualty's private passenger risks. Maryland Casualty had not had a prior approval rate increase since the late 1980s. GSA filed for an 85.5 percent rate increase on September 28, 1998. On October 8, 1998, GSA requested that the filing be sent to the Office of Administrative Law, which was done on December 24, 1998, and it was filed as a contested case. On February 10, 1999, the case was assigned to Administrative Law Judge John R. Tassini. After the proper notifications and prehearing motions, the plenary hearing was held on August 11, 13, and 19, 1999. Briefs were filed on November 15, 1999, and the record was closed on January 5, 2000. The initial decision was rendered on January 6, 2000: the Insurance Department's experts supported a 21.1 percent increase. On May 5, 2000, over a year and a half after GSA filed, the acting commissioner announced that she had "rejected an Administrative Law Judge's recommendation that GSA Insurance Company be granted a 34 percent rate increase for private passenger automobile insurance."[21] She granted a 15 percent rate increase. The Insurance Department's press release announcing her decision noted that GSA had lost more than $13 million in 1999.[22]

The three rate requests discussed above are counted by the department as "approved," even though the department approved an average of about 79 percent less than the rate request. From January 1, 1998, to December 31, 2000, the department made a final determination on thirty-two auto insurance rate filings. The department denied twenty-nine of those requests, and the insurers "accepted the denial," or at least they did not request a hearing. By the department's accounting method, the denial rate was approximately 90 percent.[23] However, by the author's assessment, all thirty-two rate requests were denied.

There are currently eleven rate requests pending (see table 3-2). These rate requests, filed after the law changed, do not bode well for the early success of the reforms of 1998. The combined market share of three of the insurers seeking rate hikes (State Farm, Liberty Mutual, and Selective Group) is 30 percent of the New Jersey market. An Insurance Department

21. For an excellent discussion of intended rate relief delay, see Tennyson (1993).

22. New Jersey Department of Banking and Insurance, "Acting Commissioner of Banking and Insurance Limits Rate Increase," press release, May 5, 2000. The department's release did not specify whether the loss was an underwriting or net income loss.

23. These rate-filing statistics were provided by the New Jersey Department of Banking and Insurance in private correspondence, January 4, 2001.

spokesperson has claimed the department will fight every one of these rate hikes, adding that the industry had "not demonstrated a need for these rate increases."[24] In April 2001 State Farm received permission to stop writing new private passenger automobile insurance policies after sustaining massive losses in the New Jersey market in 1999 and 2000.[25]

Qualified Persons

Someone designated as a "qualified person" can get copies of any filing and amendments and request that the commissioner hold a rate hearing on the filing. The designated "qualified person" is required to know New Jersey insurance law, have the ability to evaluate the technical aspects of a rate filing, have access to an actuary, have sufficient resources to undertake an evaluation of the filing, and represent the interests of consumers.[26] If the commissioner finds that the qualified person has made a substantial contribution to his determination, he can order that fees be paid to the qualified person. Although this appears to provide an opportunity for rent seeking, it may also offer a heavily burdened department the opportunity for expert input and advice. The Office of Property and Casualty handled 429 requests from insurers, law firms, and the public for records to review filings submitted to the public. As of December 2000, there do not appear to have been any hearings initiated by public intervention.

New Jersey had a public advocate who intervened in rate cases, but Governor Christie Whitman eliminated the position during her first year in office (1994). The Office of the Public Advocate was seen by some in the state as an entity that simply piled additional costs onto the regulatory system and by others as one that protected the consumer from price gouging by insurers. This issue was hot enough that in the 1997 gubernatorial race, Whitman's popular Democratic opponent, State Senator Jim McGreevey, the mayor of Woodbridge, proposed reinstituting the Office of the Public Advocate.[27] An exit poll the day of the election found that

24. Sandy McClure, "Legislator: No Car Insurance Rate Hikes," *Courier-Post*, April 12, 2001.

25. See Eugene Kiely, "N.J. Auto Insurers' Push Could Erase Rate Cuts," *Philadelphia Inquirer*, April 12, 2001. Mr. Kiely writes that state officials indicated State Farm lost $147 million in 1999 and $128 million in 2000. The article does not state if these are underwriting or total losses.

26. N.J.S.A. 17:29A–46.8. These potential interveners cannot engage in intervention in "expedited filings" (see subsequent discussion in text).

27. Joe Donohue and David Wald, "Car Rate Strategy Takes a Detour: Political Sidestep by McGreevey Camp," *Newark Star-Ledger*, September 4, 1997. McGreevey lost to Whitman in a very close and hotly contested race.

almost nine of ten voters reported that auto insurance was important in their decision on whether to vote for Whitman.[28]

Expedited Filing

New Jersey also has an expedited filing rule. A filer may use this option when requesting a rate increase of 3 percent or less or a decrease in its statewide base rate. The technical requirements include certification by a qualified actuary that the filing meets the requirements of the law and regulations set out by the Insurance Department, as well as generally accepted ratemaking principles. The filing cannot result in an increase over 5 percent for any single coverage, even if it meets the 3 percent average rate increase requirement. The commissioner should make the determination within forty-five days of receipt of the filing, which he or she can extend to sixty days. If a negative decision is not rendered or the rates are not modified within the time limit, the filing is considered approved.[29] This provision of Public Law (P.L.) 1997, chapter 151, section 34, seems similar to the "flex rating" that New Jersey had from 1988 to 1997, but the expedited filing comes with no guarantee. Under the flex-rating scheme, insurers were entitled to increases of 3 percent a year; however, the commissioner could grant larger increases.

State Farm took a case to the New Jersey Supreme Court, arguing that the state did not have the right to automatically limit flex increases to 3 percent. In a 1992 decision, the court held (6–1) in State Farm's favor.[30] There were flex increases of 5.2 percent in 1989, 6 percent in 1990, 6.5 percent in 1991, 5.18 percent in 1994, and 3.83 percent in 1995.[31] With the minimum 3 percent approved for 1992 and 1993, flex rates grew 37.6 percent over the 1989–1995 period. The medical care component of the consumer price index grew 46.9 percent over the same period.

Caps

There is subsidization in the New Jersey rates. Under AICRA an insured cannot be charged more than 2.5 times the territorial rate base nor more than 1.35 times the statewide average base rate. If the principle oper-

---

28. "New Jersey Race Ends with Undecided Results," *Daily Tar Heel*, November 5, 1997.

29. N.J.S.A. 17:29A–46.6.

30. Barrett Carter, "State Auto Insurers Gain a Split in Court," *Newark Star-Ledger*, July 30, 1992.

31. See Joe Donohue, "Car Insurance 'Flexes' with 5.18% Boost," *Newark Star-Ledger*, July 2, 1994, and "Auto Insurers Get 3.83 pct. 'Flex–rate' Hike," *Newark Star-Ledger*, June 20, 1995.

ator is sixty-five or older, the ratio is 1.25 times the statewide average.[32] Previous law had a simple 1.35 cap. These caps obviously fly in the face of actuarially sound pricing and generate poor price signals. Ostensibly rates under the New Jersey law should not be discriminatory, yet they are flattened for social purposes, and the cost burden is born by other policyholders.[33] These redistributions might be handled more efficiently through other, more explicit tax policy.

Rationales offered for private passenger caps range from avoidance of market disruption to social insurance aspects of private passenger insurance and minimization of the uninsured motorist problem. There are cap provisions for the basic policy, for example. The state has strong interest in urban areas, and, as insurance industry sources have reminded us, caps were introduced in 1983 to subsidize urban areas.[34] Auto insurance costs have figured prominently in New Jersey elections, and state politicians have had a delicate balancing act. Some may find their constituency in the cities and urban areas of the state, others in the suburbs.[35]

Urban Enterprise Zones

Governor Whitman signed P.L. 1997, chapter 151, on July 1. It established Urban Enterprise Zones (UEZs).[36] The scheme was designed to make insurance more available in New Jersey's urban areas, with twenty-seven New Jersey cities constituting the UEZs. It has been argued by some that insurers might practice price discrimination based on race. It would seem that the market could be sealed, and different elasticities of demand for coverage could exist. However, a careful econometric analysis of the question has shown that profit rates do not vary across racial groups. Differences in premiums, where found, were the result of differences in loss costs.[37]

Although the Insurance Department characterized the UEZ plan as "based on the expectation that various incentives could be used to encourage insurance companies to write more in the cities," insurers must insure risks in proportion to their writings in the voluntary market statewide. For

---

32. N.J.S.A. 17:29A–36(c). These caps are exclusive of surcharges and discounts.
33. Cummins and Weiss (1992); Bartlett, Klein, and Russell (1999).
34. Victoria Sonshine Pasher, "Studies Seek to Steer N.J. Auto Reform," *National Underwriter Property-Casualty,* May 11, 1998, pp. 6, 56.
35. Joe Donohue and David Wald, "Car Rate Strategy Takes a Detour: Political Sidestep by McGreevey Camp," *Newark Star-Ledger,* September 4, 1997.
36. N.J.S.A. 17:33C–2.
37. Harrington and Niehaus (1998).

example, if they insure 10 percent of the state's voluntary business, they must insure 10 percent of those who desire coverage and live in cities designated as UEZs. Insurance companies can use special agents to acquire the business. If an insurer is not within 95 percent of its assigned goal, the company will be assigned risks under a plan know as the Urban Zone Assigned Risk, which is not to be confused with the state's assigned risk plan described below.[38] In effect, the state has used its statutory and regulatory authorities to alter market shares and underwriting choices of private passenger insurers. The department noted that the UEZ market shares of thirty-six firms had increased, while those of ten had decreased.

The department believes the program is having the desired effect. Insured vehicles jumped from 487,618 in 1998 to 544,067 in 1999 in the UEZs. Total written exposures in the voluntary market, evaluated on December 31, 1999, increased from 4,509,675 in 1998 to 4,680,450 in 1999.[39] Although the growth of UEZ exposures was 12 percent over the time period and that of the voluntary market minus UEZs was only 4 percent, both UEZ provisions of the new law, good economic conditions, and other law changes, including the introduction of the new basic policy, may all have accounted for some of the growth in policyholders insured in UEZs.

Tier Rating

On July 1,1997, the state adopted a "tier rating system," with each insurer operating in the state required to notify the department by March 9, 1998, of its intent "to file a tier rating plan to replace an existing standard/non-standard rating system." Filings were due by April 1, 1998.[40] Under the tier rating plan, New Jersey's system of surcharging drivers for tickets and accidents came to an end. However, this plan, which required insurers to define a standard tier as drivers with six or fewer points, allowed for preferred and less preferred rating tiers. These preferred and less preferred tiers may be subdivided further. Insurers use different determinants in their risk classification schemes; hence price dispersion will be generated in the state and its rating territories.

---

38. New Jersey Department of Banking and Insurance (1999f). The urban zone assigned risk is managed by the New Jersey Personal Automobile Insurance Plan (see subsequent discussion). The state has a "take-all-comers" rule. Drivers with enough points for accidents, moving violations, and drunk-driving convictions can be refused coverage in the voluntary market. Such drivers find themselves in New Jersey's assigned risk plan (which should not be confused with urban zone assigned risk).

39. New Jersey Department of Banking and Insurance (1999b, 2000c).

40. New Jersey Department of Banking and Insurance (1998b).

During Governor Jim Florio's administration, a law passed in 1990 that eliminated place of residence, age, sex, and marital status as determinants.[41] Florio also proposed and was successful in passing a $2.8 billion tax increase. There was a voter revolt, and the Republican party took control of the state legislature in 1991. The legislature passed a bill to repeal the ban on residence, age, sex, and marital status as rating factors before they were due to be eliminated effective January 1, 1993. Governor Florio conditionally vetoed it, but the legislature overrode his veto.[42]

The traditional rating factors are allowed in New Jersey.[43] Use of these factors is barred in a few states, and there has been pressure to eliminate use of territories, largely due to political pressure for urban rate suppression.[44] P.L. 1998, chapter 22, amended the Automobile Insurance Cost Reduction Act and called for establishment of new territorial rating plans.[45] A commission was created to establish the factors for use in the design of the new territories. The state's twenty-seven territories have been in use for over fifty years, and the amendatory legislation offers guidelines on the redistricting of territories. It specifically calls for no schemes that "result in unfair inter-territorial subsidization among territories." Experience teaches that *unfair* covers a good deal of territory.

The tier rating scheme was designed to be revenue neutral, and a number of sources pointed out that the law change could result in increased rates for some risks and decreases for others.[46] The Insurance Department requires quarterly tier exposure reports and will have a data series to check market conditions in each territory.[47] Although a few companies have only one tier, by the end of 1998, the majority (thirty-four writers) had six or more tiers. The Insurance Services Office also filed six rating tiers. Six firms have ten or more tiers.[48]

41. See subsequent discussion on the FAIR Act.

42. Joe Donahue, "New Jersey Auto Insurance Market Nearing End of Road to Recovery," *Newark Star-Ledger*, February 21, 1993.

43. Joe Donohue and David Wald, "Car Rate Strategy Takes a Detour: Political Sidestep by McGreevey Camp," *Newark Star-Ledger*, September 4, 1997."

44. For an excellent discussion of rate compression and suppression, see Jaffee and Russell (1998).

45. N.J.S.A. 17:29A-48.

46. For example, see New Jersey Department of Banking and Insurance (2000a, p. 11) and Robert Schwaneberg, "For Jersey's Drivers, It's Shop til Insurance Drops," *Newark Star-Ledger*, August 2, 1998.

47. New Jersey Department of Banking and Insurance (1999e).

48. New Jersey Department of Banking and Insurance (1998a). The Insurance Services Office (see discussion of 1988 law changes) files only loss costs; its risk-rating method, however, can be adopted by companies, who must then use their own expense and profit provisions.

The Insurance Department provides consumers with a booklet explaining the tier rating system and giving a description of each insurer's criterion for tier assignment.[49] They also have made tier rating information, at the company and group level, available at their web site (www.njdobi.org). Because information makes markets function efficiently, this type of effort, together with the department's premium price comparisons within rating territory, should lead to more price searching. The Insurance Department facilitates that search by lowering the costs of information. They have established an 800 toll-free number and send consumers within-territory price comparisons for a number of typical policy options for drivers with different demographic and driving characteristics. In the program's first few months of operation, the department received 4,000 requests for such information.

In the early 1970s, survey research indicated that about half of auto insurance consumers never compared their auto insurance prices with those offered by other insurers.[50] The Insurance Research Council of New Jersey reported survey results that found that one in four drivers shopped for a new policy in the last six months (during 1999), 55 percent of movers found reduced rates, and 38 percent of those saved at least $400.[51] In 2000 the Insurance Council reported a 50 percent increase over the 1997–98 figures for consumers who switched their private passenger coverage to another insurer.[52] Since the price dispersion generated under tier rating can be great, Insurance Department efforts to disseminate pricing information should be encouraged.

Since price and quality can vary across policies, the Insurance Department sends both their *Shopping Guide* and the *Auto Insurance Complaint Ratios* for writers insuring 1,000 or more risks. This data is also provided at the department's website.[53]

Table 3-3 uses examples to illustrate the range and average premiums for coverage in a suburban New Jersey territory in 1999. Note that with the exception of the basic policy (example 7) and the single-car coverage for a married senior couple (example 4-A), the differential between the highest

49. New Jersey Department of Banking and Insurance (2000d).

50. Cummins and others (1974); Schlesinger and Schulenburg (1993).

51. Joe Donohue, "Reforms Driving Down the Cost of Insuring Those Jersey Wheels," *Newark Star-Ledger*, September 29, 1999.

52. Insurance Council of New Jersey, "Report Confirms 15% Rate Cut for Auto Insurance, Indicates NJ No Longer #1 in Nation for Now," press release, March 20, 2000.

53. New Jersey Department of Banking and Insurance (2000b). See also "NJ Auto Insurance Shopping Guide 2000" (www.naic.org/nj/filings.htm [July 2001]) and "Private Passenger Auto Insurance Complaint Ratios" (http://states.naic.org/nj/siteindex.htm [July 2001]).

Table 3-3. *High and Low Premiums, Private Passenger Auto Insurance, Territory 12, 1999*[a]

1999 dollars

Example	Premium			Differential
	Average	Highest	Lowest	
1-A[b]	1,155	2,537	661	1,876
2-A[c]	2,062	5,171	1,394	3,777
3-A[d]	1,785	3,744	1,167	2,577
4-A[e]	980	1,324	675	649
5-A[f]	1,129	1,978	712	1,266
6-A[g]	996	1,993	837	1,156
7[h]	262	569	204	365

Source: New Jersey Department of Banking and Insurance (2000b, 2000e).

a. Territory 12 is suburban Camden. Note: The Insurance Department *lists* premiums for all insurers writing business in the policy class. The highest and lowest premiums have been selected for illustrative purposes only. Companies exempt from the "take-all-comers" rule or those with membership requirements have not been included. All examples are for "verbal threshold."

b. Eighteen-year-old youthful male, unmarried principal operator, driver training, no good-student discount, no accidents or DMV violations past three years; pleasure use 12,000 miles; $250,000 standard PIP, $250 deductible, no qualifying discounts, liability-only policy, BIL and uninsured motorist liability (UI) $15/30 or combine single limit of $35,000 (PDL, $5,000); 98 Pontiac Grand Am SE, 4-door sedan, Insurance Services Office (ISO) rating 8.

c. Married couple, both 30–49 with newly licensed seventeen-year-old daughter, no driver training, no good-student discount, no accidents or DMV violations past three years, pleasure use 12,000 miles; $250,000 standard PIP, $250 deductible, no qualifying discounts, BIL and UI $100/*300* (PDL, $25,000) or combined limit of $300,000; 98 Pontiac Grand Am SE, 4-door sedan, $500 deductible for comprehensive and collision.

d. Married couple, both 30–49, two vehicles and no inexperienced operator, no accidents or DMV violations past three years, with same writer last fifteen years; car no. 1 husband to work 10 or more miles, 20,000 annual; car no. 2 wife to work less than 3 miles, 12,000 annual miles; no qualifying discounts, $250,000 standard PIP, $250 deductible, BIL and UI $100/300 (PDL, $25,000) or combined limit of $300,000. Car no. 1 98 Pontiac Grand Am *SE*, $500 deductible comprehensive and collision. Car no. 2 1997 Chevy Astro Van 4×2, ISO rating 6, $500 deductible comprehensive only.

e. Married couple, both 65–69, no accidents or DMV violations past three years, pleasure use 12,000 annual miles, $250,000 standard PIP, $250 deductible, no qualifying discounts, BIL and UI $100/300 (PDL, $25,000) or combined single limit of $300,000; 1998 Pontiac Grand Am SE, $500 deductible comprehensive and collision.

f. Twenty-six-year-old female, unmarried, no accidents or DMV violations past three years, pleasure use 12,000 miles annual, $250,000 standard PIP, $250 deductible, no qualifying discounts, BIL and UI $100/300 (PDL, $25,000) or combined single limit of $300,000; 1997 Saturn Coupe SC1, ISO rating 10, $500 deductible comprehensive and collision.

g. Thirty-year-old male, single-car policy, no accidents or DMV points past three years, drive to work less than 3 miles and 10,000 annual miles, $250,000 standard PIP, $250 deductible, no qualifying discounts, BIL and UI $15/30 (PDL, $5,000) or combined single limit of $35,000; 1998 Pontiac Grand Am *SE*, $500 deductibles comprehensive and collision.

h. Thirty-year-old male, single-car policy, no accidents or DMV points past three years, drive to work less than 3 miles and 10,000 annual miles, no qualifying discount, one year with company, *basic policy*, PDL $5,000, PIP $15,000, no physical damage coverage, no optional BIL coverage.

and lowest premiums exceeded $1,000 in the territory. A married couple with a newly licensed seventeen-year-old daughter (example 2-A) could save as much as $3,777 by shopping around. Although the case is not illustrated here, savings can be as great for a family with a newly licensed son.

Excess Profits Law

Without belaboring the fundamentals of price theory, those who put their capital at risk should have the expectation that they will earn the opportunity cost of that capital on a risk-adjusted basis. In general, expectations and outcomes do not always match. There may be "bad" years and there may be "good" years, but if returns, for example, show a log-normal distribution, one's best expectation would be the mean of the distribution. To the extent that outcomes are not entirely deterministic, a scenario where insurance is not necessary, luck plays a role in profit and loss. Excess profit laws, if binding, eliminate the upper tail of the distribution and reduce the expected return on capital.

In general, excess profit laws are bad. In cases where markets function relatively efficiently, and entry is not very costly, the inexorable forces of competition will erode any "excess profits." In states where price ceilings are set and binding, not only will the assigned risk pool blossom, but the excess profit rule could prove superfluous. Rates are set ex ante and in the face of considerable uncertainty about future outcomes. Mandatory rate rollbacks, before losses are incurred and developed, may not be efficient. For example, the passage of an insurance law with an *estimated* savings of 10 percent does not guarantee such savings. If actual losses exceed expected losses, revenues collected will be less than those required to attract and retain capital. If rates prove to be too high, cash flow timing can be changed and dividends paid, for example, to arrive at competitive rates.

The excess profit provision requires that private passenger insurers file annual excess profit reports. They are required for each company, including those in a group, and for each group for the major liability and property damage coverages. The law is designed to limit the ratio of total "actuarial gain" plus "excess investment income" to earned premiums to 2.5 percent over three calendar-accident years. Abstracting for simplicity, actuarial gain is defined as underwriting income minus any allowance for profit and contingency. Underwriting income is earned premium minus developed losses and loss adjustment expense, with other minor adjustments defined in the law. Excess investment income is defined as "actual investment income" minus "anticipated investment income." The former is the portion of income generated by investing policyholder-supplied funds. The latter is the percent that represents investment income and is used in the insurer's "approved rate filings."[54] This attempt by the excess profit law to allocate income on the basis of policyholder-supplied funds implies that insurers are simply holding money for people who sell them a cash flow. Unfortunately for insurers, they stand to lose the policy limits, and the sellers of the cash flow (insureds) do not have to contribute to "insurer supplied funds."

As measured by written premiums, the actual size of excess profits has been small relative to the size of the market. For example, on April 3, 1998, the commissioner announced that "since 1994, New Jersey consumers received a total of $4.15 million in excess profit refunds and $364.9 million in dividends from auto insurance companies." The total of $4.15 million over the 1994–97 period was less than 0.01 percent of direct written premiums. Liberty Mutual Fire Insurance Company refunded $1.5 million on business through 1997; they paid dividends of $26 million on 1997 New Jersey private passenger business. Electric Insurance Company paid $204,625 on the three calendar-accident years through 1997.[55]

In 1998 the Office of Property and Casualty Insurance evaluated sixty-three excess profit reports. State Farm Indemnity ($38 million), Hartford Group ($2.5 million), and Harleysville-Garden State ($3 million) were those that had to provide refunds under the law.[56] These 1998 excess profits constituted less than 1 percent of direct written premiums.[57] In 1999 the Hartford Group ($3.2 million) was again required to pay excess profit refunds, commencing by January 1, 2000.[58] Although these excess profits are large in absolute terms, they are much smaller than dividends and constitute a small percentage of written premiums. Table 3-4 lists the dividends paid and the percent of direct written premium they represent. It is instructive to examine the ebb and flow of dividends, as well as the market share of the residual market, as they both can provide information about the state of

54. See N.J.S.A. 17:29A5.6 to 5.13 for more gory details.

55. New Jersey Department of Banking and Insurance, "Two Auto Insurance Companies Must Return Excess Profit to Consumers," press release, April 3, 1998.

56. New Jersey Department of Banking and Insurance (2000a, p. 11).

57. Direct written premium is the total amount charged a policyholder less return and additional premium. Return and additional premium could be generated by additional insurance purchased during the year, or by changes to the coverage purchased. Direct written premium does not include reinsurance assumed or ceded.

58. New Jersey Department of Banking and Insurance (1999c).

Table 3-4. *Agency and Direct Writer Dividends, Private Passenger Auto Insurance, 1980–98*

Units as indicated

Year	Agency dividends		Direct writer dividends		Total dividends	
	Amount (dollars)	As percent of direct premiums[a]	Amount (dollars)	As percent of direct premiums[b]	Amount (dollars)	As percent of direct premiums[c]
1980	246,877	0.04	17,430,008	1.9	17,676,885	1.2
1981	230,590	0.03	19,298,473	1.9	19,529,063	1.1
1982	245,221	0.03	22,538,833	1.8	22,784,054	1.2
1983	376,001	0.04	26,149,609	1.9	26,525,610	1.2
1984	644,135	0.13	44,705,844	5.5	45,349,979	3.4
1985	923,174	0.19	49,743,602	5.8	50,666,776	3.8
1986	1,028,908	0.21	50,408,990	5.6	51,437,898	3.7
1987	3,831,666	0.80	82,085,010	8.6	85,916,676	6.0
1988	2,992,365	0.58	57,880,486	5.7	60,872,851	4.0
1989	1,782,962	0.30	56,054,309	5.3	57,837,271	3.5
1990	1,071,525	0.15	54,575,282	4.4	55,646,807	2.9
1991	1,654,420	0.20	42,486,281	2.9	44,140,701	1.9
1992	1,972,029	0.15	38,453,784	2.0	40,425,813	1.2
1993	887,889	0.05	16,351,020	0.6	17,238,909	0.4
1994	3,482,395	0.21	46,893,987	1.8	50,376,382	1.2
1995	986,475	0.06	84,403,148	2.9	85,389,623	1.8
1996	709,625	0.04	78,349,932	2.4	79,059,557	1.6
1997	468,842	0.03	175,790,748	5.1	176,259,590	3.4
1998	2,923,619	0.18	253,516,681	7.1	256,440,300	5.0

Source: Calculated from NAIC page 14 data (compiled annual reports) and Best's Executive Data Service.

a. Total agency dividends (PIP, BIL, and PDL) divided by total agency direct premium written.

a. Total direct writer dividends divided by total direct writer direct written premium.

b. Total dividends divided by total premiums.

market conditions. Some dividends paid may reflect the "threat effect" of excess profit law, but competition for good risks and differences in marketing and expenses are more likely to influence dividends.

Private passenger automobile insurance is sold by independent insurance agents (the independent agency system) who can represent a number of insurance companies or by insurance companies that sell policies directly to consumers (direct writers). Consumers who use the independent agency system will typically expect their agent to recommend the best coverage and price available. Consumers may also expect and be willing to pay higher prices for other services provided by independent agents. Direct writers typically market their product without an intermediary, for example, through direct mail or the Internet. They also use their company employees or agents who work exclusively for them. Their goals are to capture the expense economies available to their marketing approach and to pass the savings on to consumers. Independent agency business in New Jersey has never paid a dividend of 1 percent, although it came close in 1987, but direct writers paid between 5 and 8.6 percent of direct written premiums in the form of dividends between 1984 and 1989. They paid their highest dividends *before* the excess profit law was passed in 1988. They paid dividends even through the Joint Underwriting Association years, but dividends dropped during the Market Transition Facility period of 1990–93.[59] (See below.) For the 1997 and 1998 period, direct writers averaged a 6 percent dividend.

New Jersey's loss ratio has typically been larger than that of states with competitive rating laws. There can be a host of reasons why this is the case.[60] Table 3-5 lists loss ratios for private passenger automobile insurance in the New Jersey voluntary market and in groups of states that had either a competitive rating or prior approval law over the entire period from 1980 to 1998. Note that for seventeen of the nineteen years, the New Jersey loss ratio was higher than the average ratio for the ten states that maintained competitive rating laws over the entire sample period. These competitive rating states are those that provide the most pricing flexibility and the least rate regulation.[61] New Jersey also had a higher loss ratio than the average of the twenty prior approval states in sixteen of the nineteen years. (Two of the most strictly regulated prior approval states, Massachusetts and South Carolina, were excluded from the calculations.)

The loss ratios presented in table 3-5 are direct losses incurred divided by direct written premium net of dividends paid. Comparing loss ratios in cross-section may give some information about insurer profitability, but loss payouts, expense, dividend and tax flows, premium collection, and other cash flows can vary from state to state. Profitability can and does vary over time, as investment yields and cash flows change. The revenues col-

59. The Market Transition Facility stopped issuing policies in October of 1992. Those policies expired in October 1993. The Joint Underwriting Association and the MTF will be discussed below.

60. See the chapter by Scott Harrington where he uses multivariate analysis to examine the impact of rate regulation on insurance prices and volatility.

61. See the chapter by Scott Harrington for a taxonomy of prior approval and competitive rating laws.

Table 3-5. *Private Auto Insurance Loss Ratios, New Jersey versus Other States, 1980–98*

Millions of dollars, except as indicated

	New Jersey			Loss ratios[a]		
Year	Direct losses[b]	Direct premium[c]	Dividends[d]	New Jersey	Competitive rating[e]	Prior approval[f]
1980	1,138.6	1,498.3	17.7	76.9	62.0	65.3
1981	1,378.6	1,701.8	19.5	81.9	64.4	66.6
1982	1,459.4	1,979.1	22.8	74.6	68.8	68.1
1983	1,548.6	2,275.3	26.5	68.9	68.1	67.1
1984	1,208.0	1,320.3	45.3	94.8	76.2	71.4
1985	879.0	1,350.3	50.7	67.6	75.3	74.3
1986	1,026.8	1,385.7	51.4	77.0	68.2	72.9
1987	1,062.8	1,434.0	85.9	78.8	65.2	70.0
1988	1,198.3	1,533.8	60.9	81.4	66.5	71.6
1989	1,288.9	1,642.6	57.8	81.3	71.0	75.3
1990	1,496.0	1,939.2	55.6	79.4	72.8	74.4
1991	1,771.3	2,289.3	44.1	78.9	68.4	70.9
1992	2,113.8	3,242.3	40.4	66.0	62.8	66.5
1993	2,963.4	4,165.5	17.2	71.4	64.6	64.9
1994	3,291.5	4,253.9	50.4	78.3	66.5	65.5
1995	3,291.6	4,629.3	85.4	72.4	66.5	68.1
1996	3,537.7	4,942.0	79.1	72.7	66.2	67.3
1997	3,513.5	5,114.3	176.3	71.1	63.4	64.4
1998	3,178.2	5,165.4	256.4	64.7	65.6	65.9

Source: See table 3-4.

a. Direct losses incurred, PIP, liability, and physical damage, independent agency and direct writers combined.

b. Direct written premium, PIP, liability, and physical damage, independent agency and direct writers combined.

c. Independent agency and direct writers combined in millions of dollars.

d. Loss ratio = direct losses incurred/(direct written premium − dividends).

e. The ten states that had competitive rating laws over the entire sample period were Colorado, Idaho, Illinois, Indiana, Minnesota, Missouri, Montana, Ohio, Oregon, and Wisconsin. See chapter 7 by Scott Harrington for additional details.

f. The twenty states that had prior approval rating laws over the entire sample period were Alabama, Alaska, Delaware, Hawaii, Kansas, Louisiana, Mississippi, Nebraska, New Hampshire, North Carolina, North Dakota, Oklahoma, Pennsylvania, Rhode Island, South Carolina, Tennessee, Texas, Washington, and West Virginia. Two strict prior approval states, Massachusetts and South Carolina, were excluded. See chapter 7 by Scott Harrington for additional details.

lected in the voluntary market in New Jersey were reduced by the industry's funding of the deficits run up by the Joint Underwriting Association–Market Transition Facility schemes, described below. These revenue reductions *are not* reflected in the New Jersey loss ratios presented in table 3-5; hence those loss ratios are *understated*.

Between 1988 and 1993, expenditures for policies were down, dividends were up, and the residual market share—as will be shown—fell from roughly half of New Jersey's drivers to 2.5 percent. Table 3-5 shows that loss ratios fell in New Jersey in 1998, a year when the state's ratio was lower than the average for the competitive rating and prior approval set. Before the recent spate of requests for rate increases, the market appeared to be improving. At this point it is useful to examine the factors that shaped New Jersey's private passenger automobile insurance market into an example of failure.[62]

Laws, Regulations, and Problems

The principle determinant of insurance premiums is claim costs generated by the frequency and severity of claims and by the benefit system and its regulation in a state. These costs can be high due to factors beyond the control of the insurance industry: population density; personal income levels of the state's inhabitants and the age, value, and nature of the vehicles they purchase and insure; the nature of the law and regulation; and the propensity to engage in fraud and file claims (frequency and severity). High costs can also be partly attributable to actions of insurers themselves.[63]

In New Jersey, a segment of the public has focused its attention on insurance companies and accused them of "cooking the books" and "price gouging." The fact that those same insurance companies were trying to *exit* the market and attempting to refuse to write risks may have been lost on consumers. Policyholders wanted to know why they could buy full coverage in 1973 for $225 and have an average expenditure of $957 in 1992. The trial bar in New Jersey has blamed the high costs on "no-fault."[64]

62. Cummins and Weiss (1992) have pointed to the collapse of the voluntary market in New Jersey. See also Herb Jaffe, "Still an Assigned Risk Auto Rates Fall . . . but Face a Crossroad," *Newark Star-Ledger*, September 20, 1992.

63. For a discussion of costs, pricing rules, and the need for appropriate incentives for cost containment, see Cummins and Weiss (1991).

64. Joe Donohue, "Lawyer Lobby Targets No-Fault Auto Insurance," *Newark Star-Ledger*, December 15, 1994.

No-Fault in New Jersey: The 1972 Law

New Jersey is one of three states that offer elective no-fault as a choice. Motorists in the state can adopt a limitation on lawsuits option, or they can retain their right to sue. No-fault is the default option in New Jersey, and it is "selected" by almost 90 percent of insureds in the state. This seems to be a framing effect, since neighboring Pennsylvania offers choice with tort as the default, and only half of its drivers adopt no-fault. New Jersey's first no-fault law was the New Jersey Automobile Reparation Reform Act (P.L. 1972, chapter 70), which became effective January 1, 1973, after much study, debate, and rancor. Table 3-6 lists some of the major provisions of law changes for New Jersey private passenger automobile insurance over the last 30 years.

New Jersey was a financial responsibility and contributory negligence state prior to the New Jersey Automobile Reparation Reform Act. Between 1956 and 1969, the "cost of bodily injury liability coverage [was] up 237.4 percent, and property damage liability up 195.5 percent."[65] Insurers, through the National Bureau of Casualty Underwriters, filed for eight major rate increases over the twelve-year period, including three years in a row. In 1967, for the first time, a public rate hearing was called to consider a request for a 19.6 percent hike in bodily injury liability and a 22.7 percent increase in property damage liability. The industry and the Insurance Department brought in expert witnesses, and that rate hearing spawned the famous New Jersey Remand Case and the Clifford formula.[66] Claim frequency was high and, not surprisingly given the law, so was the propensity to file suits. In 1964, for example, claims frequency for bodily injury liability was 2.84 per 100; for property damage liability, 8.44 per 100. Note that one-third of property damage liability claims had bodily injury liability claims as well.[67] There was a fifteen-month delay on liability claims payment.[68] The market appeared to be tightening, and insurers did not want to take new policyholders. Risks assigned to the pool paid 20 percent more than the rate charged in the voluntary market; there were also potential surcharges for bad drivers. Insurers were accused of bullying tactics as "consent

65. Beale, Shambon and Hogan (1970, p. 24).

66. For a discussion of the rate hearing, see Beale, Shambon, and Hogan (1970, pp. 24–27). The New Jersey Remand Case and the Clifford formula mark the onset of an explicit recognition of investment income in insurance rate regulation.

67. Keeton and O'Connell (1967).

68. Beale, Shambon and Hogan (1970, p. 46).

Table 3-6. *Timetable for Selected Law Changes in New Jersey Private Passenger Auto Insurance*

Year	Law	Provisions
1972	N.J. Automobile Reparation Reform Act	Introduced elective no-fault
		Unlimited PIP medical benefits
		$200 monetary threshold
1983	N.J. Automobile Full Insurance	Joint Underwriting Association
		Caps on rates
1988	Insurance Reform Act	Flex rating
		Excess profit law
		Introduced verbal threshold
		PIP co-pays
		Mandatory comprehensive deductible
		Allowed 2 percent nonrenewal of policies, and one nonrenewal for every two new policies
		No filing "in concert" (no full bureau rates)
1990	Fair Automobile Insurance Reform Act of 1990 (FAIR Act)	Market Transition Facility (ended the Joint Underwriting Association)
		Reintroduced the assigned risk plan effective Oct. 1, 1992
		Introduced "take-all-comers" rule
		Eliminated unlimited PIP medical benefit (set $250,000 mandatory benefit)
		Required license surrender (all lines) for market exit
		Preinsurance physical damage inspection
1997	Public Law 1997, chapter 151	Tier rating
		Urban Enterprise Zones (UEZs)
		Introduced expedited filings (repealed flex rates)
1998	Automobile Insurance Cost Reduction Act	Strengthen verbal threshold
		Fraud prosecutor
		Revamp rating territories
		Introduce basic policy
		Named-driver exclusion
		PIP choice (eliminated mandatory $250,000 PIP medical)
		PIP arbitration system
		Medical cost controls
		Insurance ombudsman (investigate consumer complaints)
		Qualified-person rule

to rate" applications rose from 16,769 in 1966 to 20,041 in 1967 and to 22,326 in the first six months of 1968.[69] These requests to sell policies at above approved rates were accompanied by an increasing residual market share. By 1972, the year the law passed, the New Jersey Automobile Insurance Plan (the residual market) was insuring 407,471 vehicles; it would soon insure over 1 million. In the three years from 1970 to 1972, automobile negligence cases handled in superior and county district courts numbered 41,171, 41,695, and 38,967, respectively.[70]

The 1972 law introduced a $200 monetary threshold and provided *unlimited* medical benefits. Ten years after its effective date (January 1, 1973), medical price inflation had eroded the threshold to $77.62 in real terms. It was a simple matter to exceed the lawsuit threshold. The New Jersey Insurance Department sounded the alarm and called for legislative reform of the monetary threshold to reduce litigation and costs and to ensure availability. The department pointed out that from 1973 to 1982, *mandated* premium costs for PIP, BIL, and PDL increased 248 percent, and *Best's Insurance Management Reports* listed New Jersey as the state with the highest premium per car in the nation.[71] Average claim costs rose 119 percent, 96 percent, and 65 percent for PIP, BIL, and PDL, respectively, in the first five years after passage of the law.[72] The assistant commissioner warned the world that the New Jersey private passenger market was in disarray and nearly shouted that the residual market size and growth was a signal of the market's distressed condition.

> Availability of insurance protection mandated by New Jersey's No-fault bears an inverse relationship with the assignments made under the New Jersey Automobile Insurance Plan (NJAIP). . . . A large number of risks placed by assignment would indicate that the automobile insurance market is experiencing serious difficulties. This is the situation in New Jersey today. . . . the No-Fault Automobile Reparations system has not been addressed by the Legislature. Without meaningful tort reform legislation there is very little hope that insurance companies will once again voluntarily seek out automobile risks in New Jersey. To do so under the present circumstances would only increase the insurer's share of automobiles assigned to it by NJAIP, a risk most companies are unwilling to take.[73]

69. Beale, Shambon and Hogan (1970, p. 51).
70. Hansler (1982).
71. Hansler (1982, p. 21).
72. Hansler (1982, table VIII, p. 47).
73. Hansler (1982, p. 5).

Table 3-7. *Vehicles in NJAIP versus Total Vehicles Registered, Total Insured, and Estimated Total Uninsured, 1972–81*

Year	Personal passenger auto liability vehicles covered (pool)	Registered vehicles	Insured car-years[a]	Estimated vehicles uninsured[b]
1972	407,471	n.a.	n.a.	n.a.
1973	412,254	3,560,445	2,911,932	648,513
1974	303,338	3,629,502	3,129,816	499,686
1975	356,598	3,614,126	3,196,443	417,683
1976	561,904	3,692,661	3,319,742	372,919
1977	846,556	3,809,742	3,397,995	411,747
1978	1,039,524	3,900,605	3,411,268	489,337
1979	1,102,907	4,017,764	3,519,641	498,123
1980	1,190,647	3,994,171	3,454,975	539,196
1981	1,370,000	n.a.	n.a.	n.a.

Source: Hansler (1982, tables III and IV, pp. 42–43). Hansler used NJAIP data.

n.a. Not available.

a. These are for mandated coverage: PIP and liability.

b. The Insurance Department used the difference between registered vehicles and insured car-years for a rough indication of the uninsured motorist problem.

Escalation in the number of drivers insured through the residual market mechanism was well underway. Table 3-7 reveals that by 1978, over a million vehicles were insured through the pool, and by the end of the decade, one third of private passenger vehicles were covered in the residual market. Increasing frequency, severity, and cost, coupled with escalating premiums for New Jersey drivers, raised not only the issue of coverage availability but also the question of the uninsured motorist. The Insurance Department used the difference between registered vehicles (New Jersey was a mandatory liability state) and insured car-years to give a rough indication of the uninsured motorist problem. The differential hovered around a half-million vehicles from passage of the new law to the end of the decade. This differential averaged around 12 percent from 1973 to 1980 (table 3-7, last column).

Although the law was designed to speed up payment and limit lawsuits, the low monetary threshold proved no barrier to bodily injury claims. PIP claims from 1975 to 1981 increased from 64,696 to 119,239, up 84.3 percent. Over the same period, bodily injury claims rose from 45,726 to 86,841, an increase of 89.9 percent. The ratio of bodily injury claims to PIP claims was in the 70 percent range over that time period, but the ratio of bodily injury claims paid to PIP claims paid fell from 37.1 percent to 31.4 percent, a sure indication of increasing severity and costs.[74]

Although insurers are usually reluctant to abandon a market, Geico (in 1976), Safeco (1977), Nationwide (1981), and Progressive (1983) pulled out of the New Jersey market by the early 1980s. Losing two of the four largest private passenger insurers was a portent of things to come. They got out before the state slammed the door on exit and before the subsequent spate of suits filed by firms in the early 1990s, during the JUA debacle, seeking to bail out of the New Jersey private passenger insurance business. The pressure was clearly on the legislature to reform the private passenger law and do something about availability.

New Jersey Automobile Full Insurance Underwriting Association (NJAFIUA): The 1983 Law Change

Prior to 1983 New Jersey's residual market mechanism had been an assigned risk plan: drivers unable to secure coverage in the voluntary market had been apportioned according to an insurer's share of the voluntary market. Each insurer serviced its own assigned risks and was responsible for claims payment on all of its own policies; since its profits depended in part on its diligence, it had an incentive to economize on claims cost. The 1983 law change brought the Joint Underwriting Association to New Jersey.[75] The JUA would cover residual market drivers for policies effective from January 1, 1984, to September 30, 1992.[76] It proved to be an unmitigated disaster.

The Full Automobile Insurance Underwriting Association severely weakened the incentive to economize on claims cost because JUA schemes have servicing companies (some of which may not even be insurance companies). Drivers who cannot secure coverage in the voluntary market submit applications for coverage that are processed by the servicing companies. The results for all drivers insured in the JUA are shared by all insurance companies writing private passenger automobile insurance in the state. The insurance company's share of the financial responsibility is apportioned by its share of the voluntary business it writes in the state. If the JUA ran up deficits, an insurance company with 10 percent of the voluntary market would

74. Hansler (1982, table VI, p. 45).
75. P.L. 1983, chap. 362.
76. AIPSO (1992, p. 12).

be responsible for making up 10 percent of the pool deficit. Since the insurer was not actually servicing the policy or monitoring the activities of individual risks in the pool, it would have little control over the costs it was assigned to pay. The legislation creating the JUA provided for a residual market equalization charge (RMEC). The RMEC would have been charged to each policyholder, with the total revenue generated by the charge set so that the JUA would run on a break-even basis. If that scheme had been enforced, the pool would not have been able to run up the huge deficits that it did.

The JUA had fifteen servicing insurers: Aetna, Allstate, Cigna, CNA, Continental, Fireman's Fund, Hanover, Royal, Selective, Keystone, Liberty Mutual, Penn National, Prudential, State Farm, and Travelers. The JUA was supposed to have been funded with a policy constant (a component of premium that is charged on a per-policy basis) and an RMEC; the former was a thinly veiled subsidization scheme. It was not broken out as a separate charge on policyholder bills; hence many policyholders would not realize that they were paying it. Since drivers in both the voluntary and residual market had to pay this charge, bad drivers in the pool were receiving transfers from good drivers. Rates in the pool were artificially low, and nearly half of New Jersey's drivers ended up in the residual market.

In a 1997 New Jersey Senate Commerce Committee hearing, State Senator Raymond J. Lesniak characterized the JUA as "going on a cash flow basis and not reserving."[77] He was referring to the consequences of the decision to ignore unfunded liabilities. In 1985, not long after formation of the JUA, the commissioner did not allow an RMEC because the JUA was generating a positive cash flow. In discussing the incident, the Insurance Information Institute noted that the JUA began running up huge deficits from its inception, and after the commissioner's decision, they continued to increase in size.[78]

The JUA ran a deficit that ultimately exceeded $3 billion. To appreciate the magnitude of this deficit, one need only realize that the total private passenger automobile insurance direct written premium for the voluntary market in 1989, the last full year of the JUA, was only $1.6 billion (see table 3-5).[79] To enable future claims payments, most drivers in the state received a surcharge, some up to $222 a year. This surcharge created political havoc in the state. In addition, according to the insurance com-

---

77. New Jersey State Senate (1997).

78. Insurance Information Institute (1989).

79. The $1.6 billion in table 3-5 represents only direct written premium for independent agencies and direct writers.

missioner, insurers—who were not supposed to bear the cost burden of any deficits under the original law—paid out almost $800 million in JUA surcharges and taxes between 1990 and 1992. Insurers were to pay about $1.5 billion of the deficit, and the rest was to be paid through temporary charges to drivers and annual fees on professionals—doctors, lawyers, and others—working in the system.[80] The drivers' share was $1 billion, to be paid through higher registration fees and bad-driver surcharges.[81]

In 1990 the former manager of the JUA was indicted on charges of "theft by deception."[82] This came on the heels of Insurance Department charges that mismanagement led to $908 million in overcharges and to the pool's huge deficit. Insurers were charged with "ripping off the consumers." The servicing companies agreed to a settlement, negotiated under the auspices of Rutgers University Professor Sanford Jaffe, of $231.3 million, with $54.5 million going to the JUA and $176.9 million going to its successor, the Market Transition Facility. The insurers admitted no wrongdoing.[83]

1988 Insurance Reform Act and Verbal Threshold

By 1988 the JUA accounted for 43 percent of insured car-years and 50 percent of auto insurance premiums in the state. Between 1980 and 1988, claim severity had doubled: bodily injury liability from $7,592 to $14,484, property damage liability from $748 to $1,503, and PIP from $1,496 to $3,594; the ratio of BIL to 100 PDL claims increased from 17.5 to 21.0.[84] Medical care price inflation had eroded the $200 monetary threshold introduced in 1973 to $56. The market was in disarray.

In an attempt to stem rising claim cost and litigation, the 1988 Insurance Reform Act eliminated the $200 monetary threshold and replaced it with a "verbal threshold."[85] The verbal threshold would be sorely tested in the courts of New Jersey (and those tests would result in a "stricter" verbal threshold in the 1998 Automobile Insurance Cost Reduction Act). Incen-

---

80. Joe Donohue, "Auto Insurance Out of the Political Hotseat," *Newark Star-Ledger*, October 19, 1993.

81. Joe Donohue, "Auto Insurers Admit Rates Are Lower but Say the Figures Are an Illusion," *Newark Star-Ledger*, March 31, 1993.

82. Vincent R. Zarate, "SCI Launches In-depth Probe of Auto Insurance Companies," *Newark Star-Ledger*, May 20, 1990.

83. Joe Donohue, "Settlement to Reduce Losses from JUA Pool," *Newark Star-Ledger*, January 7, 1994.

84. Insurance Research Council (2000, table A-32). The 1988 estimates are probably conservative since they are based on voluntary market data.

85. P.L. 1988, chap. 119.

tives to end excessive medical utilization through PIP co-pays were also included in the 1988 law, as was a required comprehensive deductible.

As discussed earlier, the law change also brought "flex rating" to New Jersey. Insurers could file once a year. They were allowed to drop up to 2 percent of their policyholders in a territory when their insurance policies came up for renewal, and insurers could also drop one policyholder for every two new customers they wrote. These changes provided some political cover for easing some of the general rate suppression in the state, but the law still asserted that any rate increase granted could not result in "excessive rates," a point strongly made by State Senator Gerald Cardinale, chairman of the Senate Commerce Committee, in his summary of the law changes.[86] An excess profit provision was also included in the 1988 law change: insurers had to file reports annually and meet the 2.5 percent of earned premium test set out in the chapter law.[87]

The 1988 law forbade filing of full rates in concert; thus as of July 1, 1989, insurers had to make their own rate filings. At that time most New Jersey private passenger insurers were members of the Insurance Services Office (ISO). ISO, which was filing loss costs or pure premiums in other lines and states, announced that it was going to exit the property casualty rate advisory business altogether. Although large writers filed their own rates, most of the smaller insurers used ISO rates, some revising them, some adopting them as approved by the Insurance Department.[88] It was believed that prohibiting ISO rates would foster competition.

Whatever the belief, the JUA, its deficit ever growing, was still alive and not well. As the reform package took effect in the summer of 1989, the race for the governor's office began, and automobile insurance prices and reform were on the lips and minds of the candidates and the voters. Governor Jim Florio won the race, and auto insurance reform was at the top of his agenda when he took office in January of 1990.

Fair Automobile Insurance Reform Act of 1990 and the Market Transition Facility

When Governor Florio took office in 1990, he was confronted with a host of problems, not the least of which was a $600 million deficit that he inherited from his predecessor. But even before he proposed the $2.8 bil-

---

86. New Jersey State Senate (1997).

87. P.L. 1988, chap. 119, secs. 2 and .3.

88. See Alexander Milch, "July 1 to be More Than a New Month for Insurance Concerns in the State," *Newark Star-Ledger*, June 21, 1989.

lion tax increase that contributed to his losing his 1993 reelection race, his first official act was to introduce his auto reform package, the Fair Automobile Insurance Reform (FAIR) Act of 1990.[89] The law finally eliminated unlimited PIP medical benefits, reducing them to a mandatory $250,000. It also set up an inspection system for physical damage coverage, with cars being photographed before they were insured to help reduce fraud. The law also blocked exit, requiring insurers to give up their license to write other lines. Perhaps the most important aspect of the law was elimination of the JUA and establishment of the Market Transition Facility.[90]

Florio wanted to get the residual market under control, and he introduced the MTF to replace the JUA as the insurer of last resort for the private passenger market. The goal was to have the state out of the private passenger automobile insurance business in three years. The MTF was to issue policies with effective inception dates between October 1, 1990, and September 30, 1992. It would then be replaced by the New Jersey Personal Automobile Insurance Plan, a standard assigned risk arrangement. The MTF policies were to be serviced by four companies: Computer Sciences Corporation, Warner Insurance Services, Policy Management Services Corporation, and AMGRO. The complaint ratio for policies insured through the MTF and serviced by these four firms was almost 400 percent higher than those serviced by insurers in the voluntary market.[91] There is a general belief that service in the residual market is poorer than in the voluntary market and that rate suppression might account for this difference. The complaint ratio in New Jersey lends support to that general belief.[92]

The law ended the $222 surcharges mentioned earlier, but it introduced assessments on insurers. Insurers were required to pay 5 percent per year surtaxes, which were to run from 1990 through 1992, and separate 2.7 percent assessments from 1990 to 1997 for the JUA deficit. Insurers were prohibited from passing the cost on to policyholders, despite rate inadequacy. In fact, they were subsequently denied permission, by a 4–2 vote of the New Jersey State Supreme Court, to even deduct the cost of JUA charges from their excess profit reports.[93]

89. Editorial, "Unfinished Business," *Newark Star-Ledger*, December 26, 1994.

90. See P.L. 1990, chap. 8.

91. Joe Donohue, "Survey Finds Insurance Pool Firms Have Most Customer Gripes by Far," *Newark Star-Ledger*, April 1, 1993.

92. Pauly, Kunreuther, and Kleindorfer (1986).

93. Kathy Barrett Carter, "Justices Slam Car Door on JUA Cost 'End Run'," *Newark Star-Ledger*, June 15, 1995.

Drivers with bad driving records could be surcharged for up to three years under the law change, but from the outset, actuaries warned that rates were too low and that MTF deficits would be massive. Special Deputy Commissioner Len Freifelder warned *on the second day* of the MTF's operations that he estimated the pool would lose between $200 and $500 million *a year*. The actuaries Milliman and Robertson and William M. Mercer predicted a deficit of over $1 billion and recommended massive rate hikes. The commissioner claimed he was unaware that the MTF would run a deficit, but the industry took him to court in an attempt to avoid bearing the cost burden imposed by grossly inadequate rates.[94] The industry eventually settled and swallowed a half-billion dollars of the deficit. The New Jersey Economic Development Authority issued $750 million of bonds to help pay the rest, to be funded by surcharges on motorists with six or more points on their record.[95] Despite the warnings of Fellows of the Casualty Actuarial Society, the MTF Advisory Board was not listening. Ten insurers left the state between 1990 and 1993, and others wanted to do so. (See subsequent discussion on "Entry and Exit.")

As the MTF deficit mounted, the pool was gradually being depopulated. Between 1990 and 1993, the number of insured vehicle-years in the pool dropped from 1,336,325 to 97,317, or from 33.6 percent of total insured car-years to 2.2 percent. The principle reason for pool depopulation was the "take-all-comers" rule within the FAIR Act: insurers could not refuse to take any risk with less than nine motor vehicle points. Insurers were not having much success with attempts to get prior approval rate increases for their "voluntary business" either. Allstate and Aetna sued the commissioner for failing to respond to rate requests within the time stipulated in the law (thirty days), and 11 insurers filed for rate increases within one year of the inception of the FAIR Act.[96] From January 1990 through March 1993, only three prior approval rate filings were approved.[97]

Although the tenure of the MTF ended with policies expiring on September 30, 1993, it is still paying claims and defending suits. The New Jersey Insurance Department reported that the MTF paid $70 million to

94. Joe Donohue, "Insurance Firms Charge Fortunato Deliberately Ran Up MTF Deficit," *Newark Star-Ledger*, May 14, 1994.

95. Joe Donohue, "Whitman Backs Bonds for Auto Pool Deficit," *Newark Star-Ledger*, July 1, 1994.

96. Tom Hester, "Court Faults Fortunato on His Slow Response to Two Rate Hike Requests. Appeals Panel Orders Hearings on Bid by Allstate and Aetna," *Newark Star-Ledger*, May 15, 1991.

97. Joe Donohue, "Auto Insurers Admit Rates Are Lower but Say the Figures Are an Illusion," *Newark Star-Ledger*, March 31, 1993.

lawyers in 1995 and $40 million to lawyers in the year ending September 1996.[98] In 1998 the insurance commissioner announced that 7,013 claims payments, many of which had been delayed for up to eighteen months, were mailed in February. There were still 4,500 claims outstanding, but payments were finally being made on time.[99] Governor Whitman had won reelection, and her reform package (AICRA) was about to be adopted.

Concentration in the New Jersey Market

Although one might be tempted to question the need for an analysis of market structure in a state where the behavior of firms and of the residual market sends strong signals that market power is *highly* unlikely to result in excess profits, the data set out in table 3-8 for the New Jersey private passenger automobile insurance business demonstrate that concentration is low. There is research indicating that strict prior approval can lead to fewer insurers and affect the shares by distribution system.[100] However, both the concentration ratios and Herfindahl indices found in table 3-8 are lower than those usually seen in concentrated industries. Although the three Herfindahl indices are low, they have increased over the nineteen sample observations for PIP and liability coverages and fallen slightly for physical damage. However, each is still lower than the nationwide median state Herfindahl values reported by Cummins, and even with the slight increases noted, none are even in the "mildly concentrated" category.[101] It has been argued that market power measures can be misleading in that firms may have greater local market power than revealed in aggregations at the state level. The data available for this study do not allow for territorial disaggregation, but the Insurance Department, as noted above, is now collecting such data. Casual empiricism suggests that the argument has less power in a state as small as New Jersey.

It is worth noting that the four-firm concentration ratios have increased for each of the three coverages displayed in table 3-8. However,

---

98. Robert Schwaneberg, "Legislators Can Represent Insurance Pool. Ethics Panel Votes to Let Lawyer-Lawmakers Defend Auto-Policy Cases for Defunct Group," *Newark Star-Ledger*, February 14, 1997.

99. Robert Schwaneberg, "State Insurance Pool Begins On-Time Payments to Victims," *Newark Star-Ledger*, February 18, 1998.

100. Suponcic and Tennyson (1998, pp. 127 and 135).

101. Cummins and Tennyson (1992, p. 98).

Table 3-8. *Herfindahl Indices and Four-Firm Concentration Ratios,*
New Jersey Private Passenger Auto by Line, 1980–98
Units as indicated

	Herfindahl			Concentration ratio (percent)		
Year	PIP	Liability	Physical damage	PIP	Liability	Physical damage
1980	738	769	815	44.0	46.5	47.0
1981	705	712	773	43.6	44.8	46.5
1982	773	780	775	45.8	47.0	46.7
1983	734	727	691	46.2	46.6	45.2
1984	706	745	715	45.8	47.7	46.4
1985	757	759	740	48.1	48.7	47.9
1986	746	772	741	48.9	50.1	48.8
1987	806	822	765	51.6	52.7	49.5
1988	823	832	748	52.6	53.4	49.3
1989	866	815	697	53.5	52.4	48.0
1990	951	875	724	56.0	55.0	49.1
1991	942	866	737	56.3	54.8	49.3
1992	827	784	694	51.9	50.6	45.8
1993	826	778	716	50.9	49.0	47.0
1994	805	759	710	50.1	48.9	46.5
1995	856	786	751	51.3	50.3	48.3
1996	948	868	784	54.8	53.8	49.7
1997	965	883	810	55.2	54.0	50.0
1998	946	865	806	53.7	52.8	49.3

Source: See table 3-4.

the four-firm concentration ratios are in the 50 percent range, below the state median reported by Cummins in his nationwide study.[102] They have been generated by insurers with shares in the 10 to 15 percent range (Allstate, 16.2 percent; State Farm, 15.8 percent; New Jersey Manufacturers, 11.9 percent; and Prudential, 10.7 percent) and not by one firm with a 47 percent share.[103] Under different circumstances, one might argue that firms in a market suffer high costs to discourage entry, but such an argument applied to New Jersey, in the face of years of evidence of rate suppression, would be farcical.

102. Cummins and Tennyson (1992, p. 98).
103. New Jersey Department of Banking and Insurance (1998d).

Direct Writer Market Share

The data set available for this study does not permit examination of the stock-mutual market and expense shares over time, but it does provide a time series for direct writers and independent agency business. There were also five years of data available for brokerage and other business, but they constitute less than three percent of the writings in the New Jersey private passenger business. Table 3-9 reveals that between 1980 and 1998, the market share of direct writers, as a percentage of direct and independent agency business, grew from 58.4 to 70.3 percent for PIP, from 60.1 to 70.0 percent for liability (bodily injury and property damage), and from 61.9 to 68.2 percent for physical damage. It is quite striking, however, that direct writers have increased their shares relative to independent agency business since the demise of the JUA-MTF regime. From 1980 to 1992, the direct writers' shares increased 3.5 and 1.8 percentage points for PIP and liability, respectively, and *fell* 4.4 percentage points for physical damage. But from 1992 to 1998, they increased: 8.4 percentage points for PIP, 8.1 percentage points for liability, and 10.7 percentage points for physical damage. These translate into 13.6, 13.1, and 18.6 percent increases in PIP, liability, and physical damages, respectively—huge increases in just a six-year period.

Sharon Tennyson studied structure in the private passenger automobile insurance business in 1997 and found that the share of both the direct writers and the four largest private passenger insurers in the country were lower in New Jersey than in unregulated states, which is not inconsistent with the current data.[104] (In 1992 the share of direct writers was even lower.) Two of the largest insurers do not write in New Jersey; hence one would expect the market share of the four largest firms to be lower than in other states. The reason why they have not written in a state with a market of over 5 million registered private passenger vehicles (see table 3-13) is obvious: rates have been too low, and the regulatory climate, too uncertain.

Entry and Exit

If rates are too low, and quality cannot be reduced enough, one should see firms exiting the market.[105] New Jersey is an interesting case both

---

104. Tennyson (1997).
105. Pauly, Kunreuther, and Kleindorfer (1986).

Table 3-9. *Share of Direct Written Premium, New Jersey Private Passenger Auto by Line, 1980–98*

	Direct writers as percent of direct and agency business			Direct writers as percent of direct, agency, broker, and other business		
Year	PIP	Liability	Physical damage	PIP	Liability	Physical damage
80	58.4	60.1	61.9	n.a.	n.a.	n.a.
81	59.3	60.3	62.7	n.a.	n.a.	n.a.
82	61.2	61.9	62.5	n.a.	n.a.	n.a.
83	62.0	61.5	61.1	n.a.	n.a.	n.a.
84	60.6	61.9	61.7	n.a.	n.a.	n.a.
85	62.0	63.8	63.5	n.a.	n.a.	n.a.
86	64.0	64.6	64.5	n.a.	n.a.	n.a.
87	66.4	67.5	65.6	n.a.	n.a.	n.a.
88	67.3	67.7	65.1	n.a.	n.a.	n.a.
89	66.5	65.8	61.5	n.a.	n.a.	n.a.
90	66.2	66.0	61.1	n.a.	n.a.	n.a.
91	66.3	66.3	61.6	n.a.	n.a.	n.a.
92	61.9	61.9	57.5	n.a.	n.a.	n.a.
93	62.5	61.4	59.9	62.1	60.6	59.4
94	62.2	61.5	60.0	61.8	60.6	59.4
95	63.8	62.9	62.3	63.4	62.1	61.7
96	68.0	66.4	64.4	66.9	66.0	63.9
97	69.4	68.6	66.6	69.0	67.8	66.0
98	70.3	70.0	68.2	68.8	67.5	66.7

Source: See table 3-4.
n.a. Not available.

because there has been exit, which has clustered, in part, around law change, and also because the state has fought exit. Rate compression and suppression can lead to "beggar thy neighbor schemes."[106] Rate regulation and allowed rates of return based on a "whole firm" theory enable cross-line subsidy, not just subsidy within a line and across coverages within that line. If each activity is not allowed to stand on its own merits, with its price reflecting its value at the margin, capital will not be allocated to its most

106. If a company is unable to increase inadequate rates in a strictly regulated state, it may be able to increase rates in other states or lines of insurance to offset losses in the strictly regulated line.

appropriate uses. States that continually suppress rates may hope that their neighbors in other states will subsidize rates or that they can pursue social policy within their own state by redistributing income by cross-line subsidies. Cummins and Weiss have pointed out that entry is relatively easy in property-liability markets, and they have drawn attention to states' schemes to require license surrender in all lines and continued participation in pool deficits for a number of years after market withdrawal.[107] The New Jersey private passenger automobile insurance business epitomizes their analysis.

New Jersey not only forbade exit without license surrender, but it also granted exit only after an "agreed" waiting period of up to five years. For example, Atlantic Employers got permission in 1990 to *start* withdrawing in January 1996. In 1994 it petitioned to leave earlier, after filing for a 104 percent prior approval rate increase. It had a 2 percent market share, more than half that of the new entrants listed in table 3-10 below.[108] In 1990 Twin City Fire Insurance sued the Insurance Department, claiming that the requirement to surrender its other lines in order to exit the private passenger automobile insurance business was an "unlawful taking." The New Jersey Supreme Court unanimously upheld this FAIR Act provision, and a significant barrier to exit was sustained. Between the passage of the FAIR Act in March of 1990 and the state supreme court's decision on July 29, 1992, 40 percent of firms (thirty-two firms) writing private passenger automobile insurance had applied to withdraw from the New Jersey market.[109] Table 3-10 lists the firms that have exited the market and those that have entered, together with an estimate of the share of in-force policies they had in late 1997.

Of the new entrants, one has already folded, and another has a Weiss rating of E (very weak). One, Metropolitan, had a license in New Jersey, but it refused to write any business. It entered with the proviso that it could exit if the market was sour.[110] On August 27, 1997, the commissioner of insurance petitioned the state superior court for an order of liquidation for Home State Insurance. At that time they had approximately 40,000 private

---

107. Cummins and Weiss (1991, pp. 132–35).

108. Joe Donohue, "Three Auto Insurers Seek Approval to Drop Policies Due to Big Losses," *Newark Star-Ledger*, July 20, 1994.

109. Barrett Carter, "State Auto Insurers Gain a Split in Court," *Newark Star-Ledger*, July 30, 1992. This measure is calculated as a fraction of firms at the group level.

110. Joe Donohue, "Market Perks Up for Auto Insurers. Jersey Companies See Gains, or at Least, Hope," *Newark Star-Ledger*, December 7, 1997.

Table 3-10. *Exit and Entry, New Jersey Private Passenger Business, Selected Years, 1976–97*
Percent

		Entering	
Year	Exiting	Company	Market share[a]
1976	GEICO, UNIGARD		
1977	SAFECO		
1978	Warchester Mutual, Peerless		
1979	National Grange		
1981	Nationwide, Security of Hartford		
1983	Progressive		
1989		Home State Insurance	Insolvent
1990	Crum & Forster, John Hancock	N.J.CURE	0.320
1991	Horace Mann		
1992	Commercial Union,	Palisades Insurance	1.100
1992	Interboro Mutual,		
1992	Reliance, Wausau		
1993	American Reliance Indemnity,	National Consumer	0.730
1993	CUNA Mutual, St. Paul	Insurance	
1994	Atlantic Employers (CIGNA),	Proformance	0.442
1994	Property & Casualty of MCA,		
1994	Home Insurance,		
1994	Motors Insurance		
1996		Lanser Insurance[b]	0.136
		Metropolitan Property & Casualty	0.401
1997		American International Insurance Company of New Jersey (AIIG)	0.720

Source: New Jersey Department of Banking and Insurance data, received from the Insurance Council of New Jersey, January 4, 2001.

a. Market share is percent of *total policies in force.* Data is from the 1999 UEZ quotas. *National Consumer Insurance Company* (NCIC) is now part of the Robert Plan. Tier filing information was used for NCIC and AIIG to estimate their market shares. The UEZ data was as of September 30, 1998, and the tier filing data was as of November 17, 1998.

b. Insures teachers only.

passenger and 1,000 commercial policies in force.[111] New Jersey has a guarantee fund, the Property-Liability Insurance Guaranty Association, that will pay the claims of Home State Insurance. Association members are sur-

111. New Jersey Department of Banking and Insurance, "Home State Insurance Company Placed in Liquidation," press release, August 28, 1997.

charged one-third of one percent of direct net written premium, but they can charge their policyholders to recover the assessment.[112]

The remaining new entrants had about 3.85 percent of the policies in force in late 1998. For comparison purposes, the national market shares of SAFECO, Nationwide, and Progressive total about 10 percent. They exited the market during the erosion of the $200 threshold (see table 3-6) and the run-up to the formation of the Joint Underwriting Association. As seen in table 3-10, fourteen firms left the market from 1990 to 1994, a period that roughly coincides with the passage of the FAIR Act (March 1990) and the expiration of the last Market Transition Facility policy (September 30, 1993). Many of those who left are major property-liability and private passenger writers.

Table 3-11 shows that the number of firms writing private passenger automobile insurance has declined from 1980 to 1998. Firms writing physical damage dropped from 104 in 1980 to 64 in 1998, a decrease of 38.5 percent. Among direct writers there was a 50 percent decrease in the number of firms writing physical damage over the sample period. The number of firms writing private passenger automobile insurance did not decrease significantly nationwide over the same period.

The change in the distribution of firms in New Jersey can be attributable to mergers and acquisitions as well as entry and exit. The net result is that there are fifteen fewer direct writers and twenty-five fewer independent agency companies doing private passenger physical damage business in New Jersey. It is worth noting that since the Market Transition Facility ended, the net loss of direct writers is only one for each line—PIP, liability (BIL and PDL), and physical damage; however, the net loss among independent agency firms is 13 for PIP, 10 for liability, and 12 for physical damage. Thus direct writers have captured larger market shares, and the number of independent agency firms has declined much more rapidly than direct writers.

New Jersey has also seen the formation of New Jersey–only, wholly owned subsidiaries to shield the assets of the parent company from the negative effects of the state's market. Note the sudden increase in New Jersey–only firms coinciding with the Florio administration and the inception of the FAIR Act (1990) and the Market Transition Facility, which started with policy inceptions in October 1990. (See table 3-6.) Not only were firms applying to leave the market, some were also transferring mas-

112. New Jersey Department of Banking and Insurance (1998c).

Table 3-11. *Number and Type of Firms Writing Private Passenger Business in New Jersey by Line, 1980–98*

	All firms			Direct writers			N.J.-only firms[a]		
Year	PIP	BIL and PDL	Physical damage	PIP	BIL and PDL	Physical damage	PIP	BIL and PDL	Physical damage
1980	84	96	104	25	26	30	1	1	1
1981	88	96	103	25	26	29	0	1	0
1982	83	92	99	22	24	28	0	2	0
1983	82	89	96	22	24	28	2	2	2
1984	77	86	89	21	23	28	2	3	2
1985	71	82	87	19	22	26	2	2	1
1986	68	75	77	20	23	26	2	1	1
1987	66	74	76	19	21	24	1	1	0
1988	65	71	79	18	19	24	1	0	1
1989	68	73	84	17	18	22	1	2	2
1990	70	71	81	17	18	21	6	4	4
1991	70	73	79	16	17	20	5	5	5
1992	71	74	81	17	17	21	4	4	4
1993	72	76	77	16	16	16	5	6	6
1994	69	76	74	15	16	16	6	8	7
1995	66	70	72	15	15	16	5	7	7
1996	64	70	71	15	15	15	5	4	6
1997	58	65	65	14	14	15	4	5	5
1998	58	65	64	14	14	15	4	5	5

Source: See table 3-4.

a. These are firms that have *positive* direct written premium in New Jersey only.

sive amounts of their private passenger business into their newly formed subsidiaries. The Insurance Department stated that between 1990 and 1993, 1.3 million of the state's 4.3 million drivers were moved to New Jersey–only, wholly owned subsidiaries. As of June 30, 1993, over three quarters of a million drivers were covered by just two of these: Prudential Property and Casualty Company of New Jersey (487,887) and State Farm Indemnity Co. (287,077).[113]

In May of 1998, the New Jersey Insurance Department fined General Accident Insurance Co. of America over a half-million dollars for shrinking its market share and turning away customers. A department spokes-

113. Joe Donohue, "Car Insurers Maneuver to Limit New Jersey Losses," *Newark Star-Ledger*, January 3, 1994. Since our data set has been aggregated to the group level, some of the large New Jersey writers would not be captured in table 3-11 as New Jersey–only writers since they would show up as offspring of parents that write business in other states.

person said, "We believe they were trying to withdraw from the state entirely." The department fined four other insurers for similar activity in the preceding year.[114]

Despite General Accident's attempt to protect its surplus, some insurers may have been more optimistic about the prospects for New Jersey. Progressive and GEICO were reportedly considering re-entering the market, and two insurers, albeit small ones, the Provident Washington Company and State National Insurance Company, filed applications in the summer of 1999 to write business in New Jersey.[115] Provident Washington has about 1,350 policies in force in the market.

Although the marginal effects of regulation on the distribution system and number of firms writing in the market are more appropriately determined by multivariate analysis, this review of the New Jersey experience presents a strong *prima facie* case that the law and regulatory environment have affected both. Many firms have departed, and more have tried. Without the state's exit barriers and their support by the state supreme court, even more firms would have abandoned ship. Firms could not recover the opportunity cost of capital because they were saddled with inadequate rates and with claims costs and a pool population that would ensure high loss ratios.

Availability and the Residual Market

From the passage of elective no-fault to the depopulation of the pool with the closing of the Market Transition Facility, New Jersey has relied extensively on the residual market mechanism. There have been markets in states—private passenger insurance in New Jersey and Massachusetts, pre-reform workers' compensation in Maine—where rates at times have been so inadequate that a large share of the state's risks have been unable to secure coverage in the voluntary market. New Jersey has had binding price constraints, and the market has been in disarray.

Table 3-12 shows the direct written premium for liability (bodily injury and property damage) and physical damage coverages in both the New Jersey and national residual markets. New Jersey has long been an "All Star" in the realm of rate inadequacy, with over 20 percent of the entire

114. Joseph N. DiStefano, "Philadelphia Insurer Fined for Refusing to Write New Jersey Policies," *Philadelphia Inquirer*, May 7, 1998.

115. Randy Diamond, "Reforms Tempt Some Major Auto Insurers. Firms Taking New Look at Covering New Jersey," *Bergen Record*, November 29, 1999.

Table 3-12. *New Jersey versus Countrywide Direct Written Premium, Residual Market, 1980–98*
Dollars (with last three digits omitted), unless otherwise indicated

| | New Jersey | | Countrywide | | |
Year	Personal property liability	Physical damage	Personal property liability	Physical damage	N.J. percent of total[a]
1980	387,115	151,012	1,865,050	666,532	21.3
1981	470,079	172,472	1,926,999	700,794	24.5
1982	569,541	208,426	2,017,081	763,778	28.0
1983	676,035	246,332	1,996,070	732,526	33.8
1984	651,033	229,048	2,043,160	719,941	31.9
1985	763,614	328,793	2,692,019	1,037,454	29.3
1986	801,181	418,518	3,372,660	1,402,602	25.5
1987	896,682	541,232	4,026,688	1,753,938	24.9
1988	956,171	583,141	4,670,321	1,953,762	23.2
1989	875,269	495,839	5,033,053	1,835,689	20.0
1990	867,043	477,508	4,997,172	1,576,901	20.4
1991	820,043	388,124	4,504,943	1,294,760	20.8
1992	469,178	169,782	4,096,391	857,461	12.9
1993	126,156	31,157	3,695,330	592,673	3.7
1994	143,566	36,762	3,877,800	580,191	4.0
1995	170,924	43,149	3,644,089	568,370	5.1
1996	172,722	43,224	3,323,769	518,506	5.6
1997	192,253	47,423	2,819,786	495,823	7.2
1998	164,694	42,406	2,257,483	453,794	7.6

Source: AIPSO (1985–99).

a. *New Jersey as a percent of the total residual market private passenger written premiums* = columns 2 + 3 divided by columns 4 + 5.

U.S. residual market for private passenger automobile insurance premium from 1980 to 1991. However, it reached legendary status with the adoption of the Joint Underwriting Association in 1983, when the state accounted for over one-third of the nation's residual market. The depopulation effects of the Market Transition Facility finally became visible in 1992 and peaked in 1993, when New Jersey's residual market share was 3.7 percent. This is in line with the state's share of the entire U.S. market, voluntary and residual, which was approximately 4.4 percent of countrywide private passenger business in 1993. It is troubling to note that New Jersey's share of the countrywide pool has increased monotonically since its low point in 1993.

Table 3-13. *New Jersey Residual Market Activity, 1985–97*
Units as indicated

Year	Total registrations	Written car-years Total insured[a]	Written car-years Residual market	Percent car-years in pool	Difference: registrations − insured years[b]
1985	4,366,000	3,939,653	1,638,404	41.6	426,347
1986	4,720,000	3,961,962	1,697,384	42.8	758,038
1987	4,907,269	4,022,711	1,771,106	44.0	884,558
1988	5,170,926	3,960,338	1,714,118	43.3	1,210,558
1989	5,100,936	4,009,720	1,489,210	37.1	1,091,216
1990	5,124,320	3,971,240	1,336,325	33.6	1,153,080
1991	5,001,507	3,941,379	1,059,887	26.9	1,060,128
1992	5,076,259	4,143,130	433,690	10.5	993,129
1993	5,123,861	4,439,034	97,317	2.2	684,827
1994	5,117,494	4,669,129	114,001	2.4	448,365
1995	5,194,831	4,536,829	137,812	3.0	658,002
1996	5,217,874	4,552,196	145,574	3.2	665,678
1997	5,161,045	4,626,543	129,271	2.8	534,502

Source: AIPSO (1985–1999).
a. Liability coverage.
b. Rough indicator of the number of uninsured motorists.

The JUA insured over 40 percent of written car-years in the state from the mid-1980s until the 1988 passage of the flex-rating provision, $250,000 PIP limit, and verbal threshold. Table 3-13 details the residual market activity from 1985 to 1997. Its share of written car-years dropped with the depopulation that accompanied the Market Transition Facility, and it reached its low of 2.2 percent of written car-years with the last policy expiration of the MTF in 1993.

The uninsured motorist problem has been severe in New Jersey. Affordability is an issue for many low-income drivers, and the basic policy described earlier is designed to help address it.[116] It is impossible to know exactly the size of the problem, and various proxies, including liability claims in cases involving uninsured motorists, have been used to get a sense of its magnitude. The Insurance Research Council estimates that 12 percent

116. For a literature review and brief discussion of the impact of price on the uninsured motorist population, see Schmit and Ma (2000).

of New Jersey drivers are uninsured.[117] The last column of table 3-13 shows the difference between registrations and written car-years in New Jersey. For the latest year available, there is a 10.4 percent differential between registered vehicles and exposure units, a value close to the IRC's finding. The gap between registrations and written car-years increased from 426,347 in 1985 to 1,210,558 in 1988. It remained around a million until 1993, when it decreased to 684,827—a drop of 31 percent in one year. Insurance prices were lower that year because the surcharging stopped, and the state had a take-all-comers rule in place. Many consumers saw prices drop 20 percent, and some uninsured drivers probably came in from the cold. Although the take-all-comers rule helped in this regard, it also put insurers in the position of having to insure cheats.

Fraud

Most evidence about fraud in New Jersey is anecdotal. Unfortunately, there is a great deal of it. The problem has been considered so serious that combating it was one of the four cornerstones of the Automobile Insurance Cost Reduction Act. The new Office of Insurance Fraud has been established in the Division of Criminal Justice. During its first full year of operation, it opened 344 new criminal investigations, prosecuted 87 cases with 134 defendants, got 78 convictions, and sent 20 percent of the convicted to jail.[118] Although the office is young, it has prosecuted "staged accidents (arrange for collisions)," "faked accidents (accidents which have never occurred)," "give-up schemes (arrange for someone to get rid of a car)," and using "runners (to solicit accident victims as patients)." These types of cases are not unique to New Jersey, and insurers have seen them all, but they are not the major source of fraudulent cost. That honor goes to the building up of costs associated with legitimate accidents. In 1994 the New Jersey insurance commissioner estimated that 10 percent of *all* insurance claims were fraudulent, and that the fraud rate was higher in automobile insurance.[119] The Insurance Research Council has estimated

117. Insurance Research Council (1999).
118. Office of Insurance Fraud Prosecutor (2000).
119. Herb Jaffe, "Insurance Chief Foresees Lower Rates for Drivers," *Newark Star-Ledger*, August 8, 1994.

that roughly 20 percent of paid losses are generated by the fraud rate and claims build-up.[120] This estimate, based on 1995 data, is identical to the one Governor Florio gave for the state for 1991.[121] Richard Derrig and his colleagues have estimated the extent of the build-up problem.

In a 1994 paper, Derrig, Weisberg, and Chen reported that in the state of Massachusetts, nearly half of 1989 bodily injury liability claims appeared to involve build-up.[122] The Automobile Insurers Bureau has an active research program to develop fraud detection measures for use in auto insurance. Their research team and colleagues have used linear models, fuzzy set theory, and neural network analysis to improve methods of claims fraud detection.[123] Such measures, coupled with strict enforcement and prosecution, are called for in the New Jersey market.

New Jersey borders two cities, New York and Philadelphia, that actually have auto insurance rates higher than some New Jersey territories.[124] Drivers in those cities can save money by fraudulently registering their cars in rural New Jersey areas. Between 1988 and the end of 1992, the Insurance Department received 30,000 rate evasion reports, and in 1990 the fraud squad found that approximately 40 percent of the 13,000 cases it investigated were claims submitted by rate evaders.[125] The Insurance Department conducted a Sunday morning raid in May 1991. They found 1,147 cars with New Jersey tags parked in Philadelphia and New York City; 944 were found to be fraudulent registrations.[126]

New Jersey has been a home to fraud and theft rings. Allstate and other insurers have been aggressive in pursuing and prosecuting suspected systems abusers. In 1997 Allstate filed suit against 1,200 people in North Jersey, the largest alleged fraud ring known in the country.[127] In August 2000

120. Insurance Research Council (1996).
121. Angela Stewart, "State Launches Crackdown on Car Rate Evaders," *Newark Star-Ledger*, January 3, 1992.
122. Derrig, Weisberg, and Chen (1994).
123. For linear models, see Weisberg and Derrig (1993). See Cummins and Derrig (1993) for an excellent review of earlier econometric work, including three papers by Cummins. For neural network analysis, see Brockett, Xia, and Derrig (1998).
124. For a discussion of high rates in cities and the related problem of uninsured drivers, see Smith and Wright (1992).
125. Stewart, "State Launches Crackdown on Car Rate Evaders."
126. Stewart, "State Launches Crackdown on Car Rate Evaders."
127. "Allstate Asks Court to Halt Litigation of Suspect's Claims," *Best's Review Property/Casualty*, vol. 98, no. 12 (1998), p. 106.

it filed against another alleged fraud ring of 241 people in Camden County in South Jersey.[128] Camden Fire Insurance Company filed suit in October 1996 against an 800-person alleged fraud ring in Passaic County.[129]

New Jersey has had virtually all of the fraudulent schemes seen elsewhere in the country, including fake auto inspection stickers and car theft rings.[130] Although auto theft is down, New Jersey has had 4 of the top 100 auto theft areas in the country. The National Insurance Crime Bureau reported that in 1994 one of every thirty-two cars was stolen in Jersey City, one in every fifty-six in Newark, and one of every ninety-three in Trenton. For the latter two cities, this was an improvement over the one in forty-eight and one in fifty-nine, respectively, in 1993.[131] With such statistics it is not surprising that theft and fraud have played a major role in New Jersey's high claims costs.

High Claims Costs

The effects of the law and its changes and of the cost factors that have been discussed can be seen in table 3-14, which compares indices of claim severity for New Jersey and the United States using the 2000 Insurance Research Council (IRC) study of auto injury claims.[132] Claim severity has grown faster than medical care inflation for bodily injury liability (BIL), property damage liability (PDL), and PIP in New Jersey, and it has grown faster in New Jersey than in the country. New Jersey started with a higher severity base for each claim type. BIL in New Jersey has grown from $7,592 in 1980 to about $19,600 in 1998 ($7,592 × 2.58 = $19,587); nationwide the amount is much lower, growing from a base of $4,955 in 1980 to around $9,600 in 1998. Thus BIL severity in New Jersey is over

128. Ruquet (2000).

129. Tim Smart, "Accidentally on Purpose," *Business Week*, June 30, 1997.

130. For example, see Robert Hanley, "Fake Auto Inspection Stickers Lead to Arrest of 2 Merchants," *New York Times*, February 11, 2000; see also Alan Feuer, "Police Break Up Car-Theft-Insurance Ring," *New York Times*, February 3, 2000. Passaic County has been referred to as the "car theft capital of the world" (Ruquet, 2000).

131. National Insurance Crime Bureau (1996).

132. Insurance Research Council (2000). The IRC is a division of the American Institute for Chartered Property Casualty Underwriters, one of the leading educational organizations in the property liability area. It trains, examines, and certifies insurance professionals. The IRC, a nonprofit research division of the institute, has done a series of research studies on the costs of private passenger insurance. I have used their latest cost study in table 3-14.

Table 3-14. *New Jersey and National Indices of Claim Severity versus Consumer Price Index (CPI), 1980–98*[a]

		Claim severity indices					
		New Jersey[b]			Countryside[c]		
Year	CPI-urban all items	BIL	PDL	PIP	BIL	PDL	PIP
1980	1.00	1.00	1.00	1.00	1.00	1.00	1.12
1981	1.10	1.08	1.12	1.17	1.12	1.12	1.12
1982	1.17	1.09	1.22	1.29	1.19	1.20	1.24
1983	1.21	1.18	1.32	1.41	1.26	1.28	1.37
1984	1.26	1.29	1.41	1.47	1.36	1.38	1.44
1985	1.31	1.41	1.49	1.84	1.44	1.50	1.50
1986	1.33	1.61	1.61	1.91	1.52	1.62	1.58
1987	1.38	1.78	1.79	2.09	1.61	1.76	1.67
1988	1.44	1.91	2.01	2.40	1.74	1.91	1.81
1989	1.50	2.05	2.34	4.12	1.83	2.04	1.95
1990	1.59	2.31	2.41	4.81	1.92	2.14	2.22
1991	1.65	2.36	2.45	5.75	2.04	2.17	2.28
1992	1.70	2.23	2.50	6.41	2.09	2.22	2.40
1993	1.75	2.28	2.59	6.01	2.14	2.32	2.49
1994	1.80	2.22	2.68	4.57	2.05	2.45	2.52
1995	1.85	2.33	2.90	5.03	2.00	2.63	2.57
1996	1.90	2.44	2.91	4.78	1.88	2.78	2.59
1997	1.95	2.50	3.03	5.07	1.91	2.87	2.74
1998	1.98	2.58	3.06	5.26	1.93	2.96	2.79

Source: Derived from Insurance Research Council (2000, table A-32 [N.J.] and table A-1 [countrywide]).

a. 1980 base year = 100.

b. 1980 New Jersey severity base (1980): BIL = $7,592; PDL = $748; PIP = $1,496.

c. 1980 countrywide severity base (1980): BIL = $4,955; PDL = $679; PIP = $1,434.

twice as great as that for the country as a whole. When New Jersey adopted the verbal threshold in 1988, PIP severity, as expected, increased. From 1984 to 1992, the years of the JUA-MTF regimes, the IRC data sample did not include claims frequency and severity for the New Jersey residual market. Hence, to the extent that pool severity was greater than voluntary market severity, the indices in table 3-14 are conservative for this period when the state operated without an assigned risk plan.

For its analysis of territorial frequency and severity, the IRC averages data over a three-year period, and for a broader exposure base, it uses data from both the ISO and the National Association of Independent Insurers.[133] Countrywide claim frequencies for 1998 were 1.17 per 100 insured cars for BIL, 4.09 for PDL, and 1.87 for PIP.[134] On a base of 12.4 million earned car-years in New Jersey, the IRC found frequency rates of 1.37 for BIL, 3.83 for PDL, and 2.73 for PIP. The ratio of BIL to PDL is a good indicator of both potential litigation and severity of claims costs. Nationwide the ratio of BIL to PDL claims was 28.7 percent. In New Jersey the ratio of BIL to PDL claims was 35.7, but it was *75 or more* in five of New Jersey's twenty-seven territories. In those territories 75 percent or more of PDL claims included BIL involvement.

Conclusion

New Jersey is an expensive place to do business: it is strictly regulated; labor and automobile repair costs are high; there may be upwards of a half-million uninsured motorists; it has higher than average frequency for BIL and PIP; and its BIL-to-PDL ratio is higher than the national average. State Senator Gerald Cardinale summarized his view of the rise in premiums in the state: "In short, the rise in insurance premiums in New Jersey has been partly caused by the unwillingness of many policyholders and others to accept the concept of a trade-off."[135] Some of these "others" have been state legislators. It is easier to install a benefit system that is rich and hide behind price suppression through regulation than to admit that we live in a world of constraints.

New Jersey is a state where it is incredibly difficult to get rate relief. The law has changed in the last two years, but rate regulation has not: twenty-nine of thirty-two rate filings have been rejected, and the three others received only partial approval.[136] Other requests for rate increases are pending (see table 3-2).

The state law is an exercise in social engineering, affecting firms' market shares, dictating whom a firm can take as a customer, and preventing

133. This information was provided by Elizabeth Sprinkel of the Insurance Research Council.

134. For these and the rest of the data in this paragraph, see Insurance Research Council (2000, table A-1 and appendix table B-31).

135. New Jersey State Senate (1997, p. 4).

136. Although the percentage of the business insured by the assigned risk plan is low, it is worth recalling that New Jersey has a take-all-comers rule, which mandates that insurers take risks. If insurers were free to reject risks when rates were grossly inadequate, the residual market share would probably increase rapidly.

market exit. As a result, New Jersey probably has fewer firms writing business and less competition than it would under different regulatory schemes. The law and its administration have subjected drivers and insurers to unnecessary costs and burdened them with needless administration. It has limited the choices that would enable families with different resource levels to make insurance selections that are in their own best interest.

There have been recent improvements. Reinstituting the assigned risk plan with market-driven incentives for cost containment, providing choice in PIP benefit levels, strengthening the fraud provisions of the law, and introducing tier rating are a few. But important reforms have still not come. It is time for New Jersey to join the deregulation bandwagon.

The market, left to its own devices, is a miraculous thing. It is more than capable of allocating capital and arriving at fair prices and returns. There is no need for a regulatory bureaucracy to impede competition, restrict choice, and suppress price. Prior approval rate regulation should be dismantled in New Jersey. It is not even clear that firms should be required to report prices before they use them; but if reporting were required, it should be for informational purposes only, that is, to use and file.

Willing parties are best suited for determining contract conditions. If the state feels a need to intervene, it should set minimum standards (for example, 15/30/5 BIL-PDL coverage), and then it should get out of the way and let the market work. If the state wants to foster choice, it should allow for a true no-fault choice (no tort, period), as well as the verbal threshold and the limitation on lawsuit options. If people want true no-fault and have the ability to pay for it, someone will market it, and people will buy it. If they do not want it, it will assume its place, alongside the beta video format, in the dustbin of market history.

The Insurance Department can be an information provider, as it is attempting to do now with its price comparisons that give consumers information on cost savings under different choices. All rates, plans, convention blanks, filing information, and insurance expense exhibits—paid for by consumers who purchase the insurance product—should be posted to the department's web page.

The industry has minimal antitrust exemption. It does not need it, and the free enterprise system can do quite well without it. The state, court rulings notwithstanding, should not be in the business of profit regulation. Excess profit laws are anticompetitive: they not only hurt the lucky, they hurt the efficient. They are barriers to entry, require needless reports, and waste taxpayer and policyholder money. Each line of insurance and each coverage sold by a company should meet the market test of competition. Someone who owns a home in suburban New Jersey and does not drive should not subsidize the driving excesses of immature eighteen-year-olds.

The state should eliminate barriers to exit. Although entry is relatively easy, firms will think three times about entering the market if they know they cannot get out. New Jersey needs an optimal number of "Metropolitans," and they should not be selected by regulators but rather by the pursuit of economic self-interest.

Crime pays. If we want to continue to fight fraud, we should lower the net benefits by increasing the costs of engaging in the crime and lowering the probability of success. New Jersey has made a leap forward by establishing the Office of the Insurance Fraud Prosecutor, but the penalties for both auto theft and fraud should be increased. Similarly, we need to know when someone is driving an uninsured vehicle. *If* we are going to require compulsory liability insurance, then we should get serious about creating a National Center for Insurance Coverage. Computer technology could provide notification within 24 hours of any policy lapse. When one does, tags should come off of a vehicle, and fraudulent tag use should bear a heavy fine or imprisonment.

It is not at all clear whether state coercion will achieve optimal levels of fraud and insolvency and numbers of uninsured motorists. It is clear that the provision of greater information and less regulation and bureaucracy will improve efficiency in the New Jersey market.

Illinois has had a free market for private passenger automobile insurance for over twenty years. The sky did not fall when Illinois adopted open competition, and private passenger automobile insurance has been depoliticized in that state. The political will to move to a free market probably does not currently exist in New Jersey. However, the legislature could make moves that would provide a transition to open competition. Any legislative changes—eliminating the take-all-comers rule, removing barriers to entry and exit, providing greater flexibility in pricing, repealing excess profit provisions—cannot be seen as temporary. If New Jersey wants to capture more of the benefits of competition, then insurers who want to leave the state, as well as those we would like to attract to our market, must be convinced that they will have every opportunity to compete for business and normal profits without the fear that they will be held captive by the state if they remain or enter the New Jersey private passenger market.

As this book goes to press, the new rating territories proposed by the commission have yet to be adopted, and the medical cost rules designed to reduce costs have not all been finalized. Some of the optimism that greeted the passage of the 1998 reforms and the 15 percent mandatory rate rollback is fading. The set and size of rate increase applications pending (table 3-2) and the rumblings in the state capital are reminders that the legislature is up for election in the fall. The governor's race will heat up this summer. And those who win will have New Jersey automobile insurance on their minds.

References

AIPSO. 1985–1999 (various issues). *AIPSO Facts: A Handbook for the Automobile Insurance Residual Market.* Johnston, R.I.

Bartlett, Dwight K., Robert W. Klein, and David T. Russell. 1999. "Attempts to Socialize Insurance Costs by Voluntary Insurance Markets. The Historical Record." *Journal of Insurance Regulation* 17: 478–511.

Beale, David T., Leonard Shambon, and Anne Hogan. 1970. *Automobile Insurance in New Jersey.* Princeton: Center for Analysis of Public Issues.

Bertie, Marjorie M. 1991. *Hit Me—I Need the Money.* San Francisco: ICS Press.

Brockett, Patrick L., Xiaobua Xia, and Richard A. Derrig. 1998. "Using Kohonen's Self-Organization Map to Uncover Automobile Bodily Injury Claims Fraud." *Journal of Risk and Insurance* 65: 245–74.

Browne, Mark J., and Brenda J. Wells. 1999. "Claims Adjudication in the Personal Automobile Insurance Residual Market." *Journal of Risk and Insurance* 66: 275–90.

Cummins, J. David. 1990. "Multiperiod Discounted Cash Flow Ratemaking Models in Property-Liability Insurance." *Journal of Risk and Insurance* 57: 79–109.

Cummins, J. David, and Richard A. Derrig. 1993. "Fuzzy Trends in Property-Liability Insurance Claims Costs." *Journal of Risk and Insurance* 60: 429–65.

Cummins, J. David, and Sharon Tennyson. 1992. "Controlling Automobile Insurance Costs." *Journal of Economic Perspectives* 6: 95–115.

Cummins, J. David, and Mary Weiss. 1991. "The Structure, Conduct and Regulation of the Property-Liability Insurance Industry." In *The Financial Condition and Regulation of Insurance Companies: Conference Series No. 35,* edited by Richard W. Kopcke and Richard E. Randall, 117–54. Federal Reserve Bank of Boston.

———. 1992. "Regulation and the Automobile Insurance Crisis." *Regulation: The Cato Review of Business and Government* 15: 48–59.

Cummins, J. David, and others. 1974. "Consumer Attitudes toward Auto and Homeowners Insurance." University of Pennsylvania, Wharton School.

Derrig, Richard A., H.I. Weisberg, and X. Chen. 1994. "Behavioral Factors and Lotteries under No-Fault with a Monetary Threshold: A Study of Massachusetts Automobile Claims." *Journal of Risk and Insurance* 61: 245–75.

Hansler, Herman. 1982. *An Assessment of the New Jersey No-Fault Automobile Insurance Reformation Act.* Trenton, N.J.: New Jersey Department of Banking and Insurance.

Harrington, Scott E., and Greg Niehaus. 1998. "Race, Redlining, and Automobile Prices." *Journal of Business* 71: 439–69.

Insurance Information Institute. 1989. *Auto Insurance Issues.* New York.

Insurance Research Council. 1996. *Fraud and Buildup in Auto Injury Claims: Pushing the Limits of the Auto Insurance System.* Malvern, Pa.

_____. 1999. *Uninsured Motorists.*

_____. 2000. *Trends in Auto Injury Claims: 2000 Edition.*

Jaffee, Dwight M., and Thomas Russell. 1998. "The Causes and Consequences of Rate Regulation in the Auto Insurance Industry." In *The Economics of Property Casualty Insurance,* edited by David F. Bradford, 81–112. University of Chicago Press.

Keeton, Robert E., and Jeffrey O'Connell. 1967. *The Need for Legal and Insurance Reform.* Homewood, Ill.: Dow-Jones-Irwin.

Lascher, Edward L., Jr. 1999. *The Politics of Automobile Insurance Reform.* Georgetown University Press.

Lascher, Edward L., Jr., and Michael R. Powers. 1997. "Expert Opinion and Automobile Insurance Reform. An Empirical Assessment." *Journal of Insurance Regulation* 16 (2): 197–222.

Ma, Yu-Luen, and Joan T. Schmit. 2000. "Factors Affecting the Relative Incidence of Uninsured Motorists Claims." *Journal of Risk and Insurance* 67: 281–94.

National Association of Insurance Commissioners. 2000. *State Average Expenditures and Premiums for Personal Automobile Insurance in 1998.* Kansas City, Mo.

National Insurance Crime Bureau. 1996. *Vehicle Theft Rate Study.* Palos Hills, Ill.

New Jersey Department of Banking and Insurance. 1998a. "Auto Insurers Tier Filing Status, Updated November 17, 1998" (http://states.naic.org/nj/tiergraf.htm [July 18, 2000]).

_____. 1998b. *Bulletin 98-03. Tier Rating Plans and Underwriting Rules.* Trenton, N.J.

_____. 1998c. *In the Matter of the Imposition of a Surcharge for Recoupment of the Property-Liability Insurance Order Guaranty Association Assessment Due November 2, 1998, and Imposed Pursuant to N.J.S.A. 17:30A-8a(3).* Order A98-152, December 1, 2000.

_____. 1998d. *UEZ Company Results.* Revised February 19, 1998.

_____. 1999a. "Basic Auto Policy Becomes Available." *New Jersey Insurance Reporter.* Winter.

_____. 1999b. *Bulletin 99-06. Voluntary Written Exposures and Primary Classification Data.*

_____. 1999c. "Hartford Group Must Return $3.2 Million To Consumers." *New Jersey Insurance Reporter.* Fall.

_____. 1999d. *In the Matter of Reduction in Rates to Be Made Pursuant to Section 67 of the Automobile Insurance Cost Reduction Act, P.L. 1988, c. 21.* Order A99-102, January 4, 1999.

_____. 1999e. *In the Matter of the Filing of Quarterly Tier Exposure Reports by All Insurers Writing Voluntary Private Passenger Automobile Insurance.* Order A99-135, May 3, 1999.

_____. 1999f. "Urban Enterprise Zone Making Auto Insurance More Accessible in Cities." *New Jersey Insurance Reporter.* Fall.

_____. 2000a. *Annual Report, 1998–1999.*

_____. 2000b. *Automobile Insurance Shopping Guide 2000.*

_____. 2000c. *Bulletin 00-13. Voluntary Written Exposure and Primary Classification Data.*

_____. 2000d. *Consumer Handbook on Tier Rating 2000.*

_____. 2000e. *1999 Private Passenger Auto Insurance Premium Comparison.*

New Jersey Department of Law and Public Safety. Office of Insurance Fraud Prosecutor. 2000. *Annual Report 1999.* Trenton, N.J.

New Jersey State Senate. Commerce Committee. 1997. *Public hearing, May 12, 1997.* Trenton, N.J.

Pauly, Mark, Howard Kunreuther, and Paul Kleindorfer. 1986. "Regulation and Quality Competition in the U.S. Insurance Industry." In *The Economics of Insurance Regulation,* edited by Jorg Finsinger and Mark V. Pauly, 65–107. St. Martin's Press.

Ruquet, Mark E. 2000. "Passaic Seen as 'Fraud Central.' " *National Underwriter,* Property/Casualty Edition 104 (37) pp. 9, 14, 16–17.

Schlesinger, Harris, and J-Matthias Graf von der Schulenburg. 1993. "Consumer Information and Decisions to Switch Insurers." *Journal of Risk and Insurance* 60: 591–615.

Smith, Eric, and Randall Wright. 1992. "Why Is Automobile Insurance in Philadelphia So Damn Expensive?" *American Economic Review* 82: 756–72.

Suponcic, Susan J., and Sharon Tennyson. 1998. "Rate Regulation and the Industrial Organization of Automobile Insurance." In *The Economics of Property-Casualty Insurance,* edited by David F. Bradford, 113–38. University of Chicago Press.

Tassini, John R. 2000. *In the Matter of GSA Insurance Company's Request for a Private Passenger Automobile Insurance Rate Increase, Initial Decision.* Office of Administrative Law, docket no. BKI 10882-98, agency docket 98-2514. January 6, 2000.

Tennyson, Sharon. 1993. "Regulatory Lag in Automobile Insurance." *Journal of Risk and Insurance* 60: 36–58.

_____. 1997. "The Impact of Rate Regulation on State Automobile Insurance Markets." *Journal of Insurance Regulation* 15: 502–23.

Weisberg, H.I., and R.A. Derrig. 1993. *Quantitative Methods for Detecting Fraudulent Automobile Bodily Injury Claims.* Boston: Automobile Insurers Bureau.

COMMENT ON CHAPTERS 2 AND 3
Richard A. Derrig

The well-documented case studies of Massachusetts by Sharon Tennyson, Mary Weiss, and Laureen Regan (TWR) and of New Jersey by John Worrall cover not only a combined fifty to sixty years of auto insurance regulation, but also many of the major issues that give rise to such regulation. My discussion highlights the similarities and differences in the issues identified by these studies and contrasts each state's regulatory responses. For example, regulatory actions in both states drove major national companies from the auto markets (see tables 2-9 and 2-10 in TWR and table 3-10 in Worrall), but the remaining companies are primarily agency companies in Massachusetts and direct writers in New Jersey. Subsidies abound in class and territorial rating in both states, through rate caps and other devices. Rate classifications are restricted in Massachusetts but not in New Jersey. Both studies point to the increased costs of regulation in terms of reduced incentives for cost control on the part of the insured population, and TWR provide estimates of those costs in Massachusetts. Fraud plays a prominent role in both studies. The discussion concludes with an examination of the prospects for change to less regulation, as in the South Carolina case study, paying particular attention to those players, other than regulators, whose interests shape the payment system and therefore the style of regulation needed.

Operating Characteristics: Massachusetts versus New Jersey

At the 1999 Auto Insurance Report National Conference, Vincent J. Dowling Jr., a senior analyst at Dowling and Partners, presented an analysis of the relatively profitable years for private passenger auto insurance since 1993 and the unprofitable future years predicted as price cutting began to enter the market. His formula for "managing through the auto rate cuts" was "better state selection." It should come as no surprise to readers of the TWR and Worrall case studies that the two states that were identified as "high regulatory environment/risk and low profitability prospects" were Massachusetts and New Jersey. This cynical view stemmed not from underwriting the underlying physical risks of car accidents and bodily injuries, but rather from the prospect of high costs combined with rate suppression by the regulators—a reality, based on the historical record.

The Massachusetts and New Jersey case studies reveal similar regulatory philosophies but quite dissimilar insurance market mechanisms to obtain those philosophical ends. For example, both states reacted to national company exits (as indicators of collapsing markets) by passing major reform laws, Massachusetts in 1988 and New Jersey in 1998. Both laws promised rate and premium reductions—13 percent for Massachusetts and 15 percent for New Jersey—and the potential for reduced costs—property costs for Massachusetts (see figure 2 below) and medical and fraud costs for New Jersey.[1] However, these changes were not expected to take place within the same market. Therefore, to give the reader a context for "reform" and prospects for the future, table 1 summarizes the features of both the Massachusetts and New Jersey markets, as identified by the case study authors.

Massachusetts and New Jersey are northeastern states with urban centers combined with scattered rural patches. For 1998 the private passenger auto insurance market in New Jersey had an exposure base of about 25 percent more insured cars than Massachusetts. New Jersey is the number one ranked state in average expenditures, and its market, at $5.2 billion, is almost 70 percent larger than that of Massachusetts. The recent rate cuts in Massachusetts have driven its average expenditure rank to tenth in the nation in 1998, and its rank will most likely drop lower in 2001 (see figure 2 below). Both case studies portray market histories that have reduced the number of participating firms and raised the concentration ratios, with four firms writing about 50 percent in both markets in 1998. Regulation of rates in the two states differs in details: in Massachusetts, competition must occur below rates set by the state, whereas in New Jersey, companies compete under strict prior approval and changing residual market mechanisms. These competitive models have led to the undesirable long-term market view expressed by Dowling and the emergence of a market dominated by domestic companies in Massachusetts (see TWR, table 2-9) and one that treats prior approval as a rate-suppressing delay mechanism in New Jersey (see Worrall, table 3-2).

Curiously, New Jersey has followed the national trend of increasing direct writer market share (70 percent in 1998) while Massachusetts has

1. The mandatory reductions required by both states' reform laws were based on the assumption that *all* potential cost reductions were realized. That realization never appeared in Massachusetts and has yet to appear in New Jersey.

Table 1. *Features of Private Passenger Auto Insurance Markets in Massachusetts and New Jersey, 1989 and 1998*
Units as indicated

Feature	Year	Massachusetts	New Jersey
Direct written premium	1998	3.1	5.2
(billions of dollars)	1989	2.5	3.9
Exposure (millions of car-years)	1998	3.7	4.6
	1989	3.3	4.0
Average expenditure rank	1998	816 (10)	1,138 (1)
(dollars; rank in parentheses)	1989	728 (5)	983 (1)
Direct loss ratio	1998	67.7	64.7
	1989	74.9	81.3
Underwriting profit (percent)	1998	−8.6	−4.0
	1989	−9.5	−19.1
Number of firms	1998	38	65
	1989	43	76
Residual market (percent)	1998	10.6	3.1
	1989	68.7	37.1
Direct writers (percent)	1998	21	70
	1989	23	62
Concentration: Herfindahl index	1998	932	865
	1989	632	759
Four-firm concentration	1998	49	53
	1989	39	49
Entries	1988–2000	10	8
Exits	1988–2000	30	14
Excess profits test		None	2.5 percent for 3 years

Source: Most entries are taken from the TWR (Massachusetts) and Worrall (New Jersey) studies. Some Massachusetts values are based on the author's estimates using data from his own sources; some New Jersey values are based on the author's estimates using data from Worrall (for example, New Jersey written premium for 1989: $3.9 billion = 4.0 × $983).

retained agency company dominance (79 percent in 1998). This disparity is most likely due to the state-set single-rate system in Massachusetts, with a separate state-set minimum for agents' commissions, which has encouraged competition at the wholesale level for agency books of business rather than competition for individual policyholders. The results for these two states in the 1990s vividly illustrate the climate produced by each version of strict regulation.

Results from the 1990s

Massachusetts and New Jersey are high-cost states for auto insurance, largely as a result of the tort systems chosen to deal with bodily injury claims. As the studies covered in some detail, Massachusetts continues to use no-fault, first-party injury coverage with a relatively low dollar threshold for filing a tort claim, while New Jersey has had a choice system since 1972, with 90 percent choosing the no-fault option (see Worrall, table 3-6). Both no-fault systems are legislative attempts to deal with the strong incentives provided by the tort system to file noneconomic damage claims for injuries that are minor, exaggerated, or nonexistent.[2] Those excess claims drive up the costs relative to the ideal compensation system. To demonstrate the extent of excess claiming, figure 1 shows a timeline of the ratios of bodily injury liability (BIL)—tort—claims to property damage liability (PDL) claims for four states: California, Massachusetts, Michigan, and New Jersey. Industry analysts interpret these data as injury claims per accident.

BIL-to-PDL ratios are shown for Michigan as a benchmark for true injury tort claims, at about one injury claim per fourteen accidents. Michigan is taken as a benchmark because it uses a strict verbal threshold to enter the tort system.[3] Worrall cites the high BIL-to-PDL ratios of about 1 to 3 in the 1960s as a cause for New Jersey's adoption of elective no-fault in 1972. If that was an alarming level, the nearly steady 1-to-4 level of the 1990s illustrates one continuing cause of New Jersey's high costs, at about three times the benchmark level of BIL claims per accident. Massachusetts exacerbated its 1-to-5 ratio of the 1980s with its "reform law" (effective in 1989), which, as TRW note, raised the dollar threshold for tort and the compulsory personal injury protection and BIL limits. Rather than reduce the number of tort claims, the 23 percent ratio in 1988 climbed to 35 percent in 1993, as the compulsory tort limits were doubled from 1989 levels.[4] Recent Massachusetts ratios have remained steady at about 1 to 3, probably reflecting a limiting effect from the Insurance Fraud Bureau activities. California ratios are shown to illustrate how bad things can get

---

2. Cummins and Tennyson (1992); Derrig, Weisberg, and Chen (1994); Abrahamse and Carroll (1999).

3. Abrahamse and Carroll (1999).

4. The change to $15/30 compulsory BIL limits was effective January 1, 1991, and $20/40 became effective January 1, 1993.

Figure 1. *Bodily Injury Claims per 100 Accidents, 1984–98*

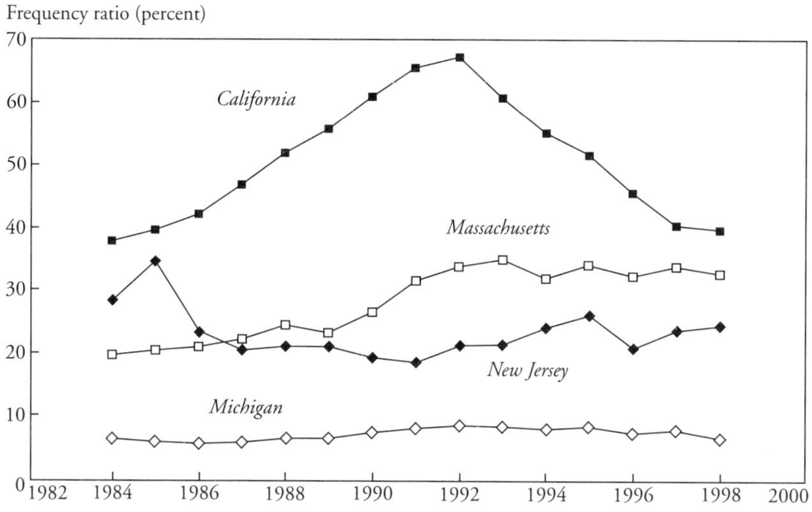

Frequency ratio (percent)

Source: Insurance Research Council (2000).

(a peak of two claims for every three accidents) when there is no realistic effort to control claim exaggeration and fraud through statutes and effective prosecution.

The Massachusetts auto vehicle damage reforms in 1989 were successful in reducing repair costs by virtue of lower labor rates and use of aftermarket parts and by reducing comprehensive costs for fire and theft.[5] The Massachusetts regulatory system reacted to the unintended deleterious effects of the "reform" law on bodily injury coverages by granting five consecutive double-digit rate increases over the period 1990–94, as the injury claim rate climbed.[6] Figure 2 shows the post-reform commissioner's rate changes from 1990 to 2001.

Figure 2 vividly demonstrates that overall rate changes were largely a reflection of the changes in bodily injury rates. The five bodily injury increases were followed by seven decreases (1995–2001), with overall rates decreasing about 25 percent from 1994. The dramatic injury coverage rate increases were taking hold at the same time that cost control measures,

5. Derrig (1997).
6. Weisberg and Derrig (1992); Weisberg and Marter (1992).

Figure 2. *Changes in Auto Insurance Rates, Massachusetts, 1989–2001*

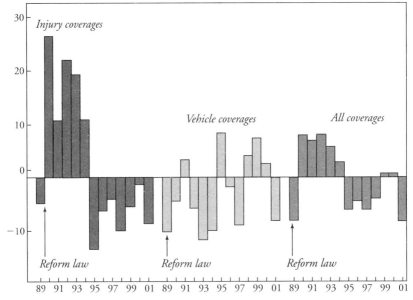

Annual percentage change

Source: Automobile Insurers Bureau of Massachusetts compilation of historical rate decisions.

including the actions of the Insurance Fraud Bureau, were being effective.[7] This combination of increased revenue and decreased costs led to four years of underwriting profits. Figure 3 compares underwriting results in Massachusetts and countrywide from 1990 to 1999. On average, the results were about the same, but the intermediate results reflect an interesting regulatory response. The realization of large profits from 1992 through 1995 gave way to large discounts and deviations from the commissioner's rate level from 1996 through 1999 (table 2), with reduced levels of discounts in 2000 and 2001.[8] This scramble for lower rates, especially for good drivers, produced a price war for market share that has led to two insolvencies, several mergers, and rate suppression designed to eliminate the competition (compare figures 3 and 4).[9] As a side note, the 1990–2000 Massachusetts

7. Derrig and Zicko (2000).
8. The average combined discount and deviation was 5.5 percent in 2000 and is estimated to be 3.5 percent in 2001.
9. The four-firm concentration was 51 percent in 2000.

Figure 3. *Direct Underwriting Profits for Private Passenger Automobile Insurance, Massachusetts versus Countrywide, 1990–99*

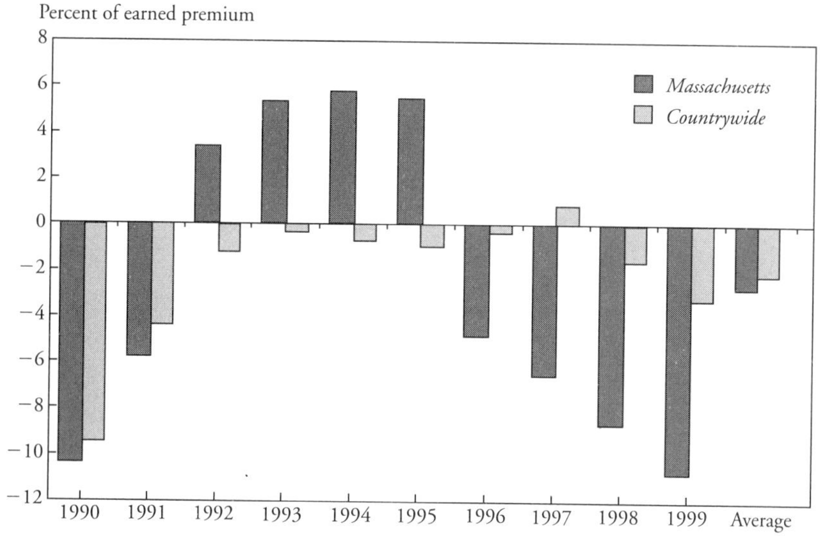

Percent of earned premium

Source: National Association of Insurance Commissioners (2000).

experience is one experimental validation of Worrall's hypothesis that excess profits laws are unnecessary: economic incentives will do the job just fine.

Figure 4 demonstrates what the underwriting results would have been had the commissioner's rate level been used without discounting. One consequence of the rate decreases of 1997–99 was that state rates were driven toward competitive levels, thereby reducing the companies' competitive discounting. This aversion to market prices rather than controlled prices is a hallmark of the Massachusetts and New Jersey style of regulation. For reference, table 2 and figure 5 show the comparable underwriting results including New Jersey.

The large negative New Jersey underwriting results appear to include both normal underwriting results plus the various charges and taxes to fund the defunct joint underwriting association and market transition facility deficits from the 1980s. Whatever the makeup of the payouts shown in the underwriting results, New Jersey was clearly due for the 1998 "reforms" that Worrall describes in great detail.

Figure 4. *Direct Underwriting Profits for Private Passenger Automobile Insurance, Massachusetts (Excluding Premium Effects of Competition) versus Countrywide, 1990–99*

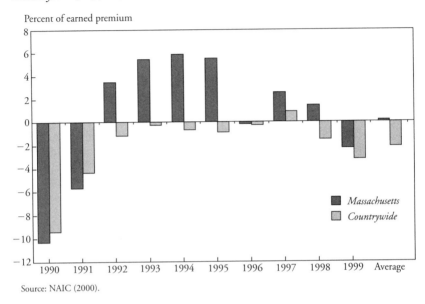

Source: NAIC (2000).

Figure 5. *Direct Underwriting Profits for Private Passenger Automobile Insurance, Massachusetts and New Jersey versus Countrywide, 1990–99*

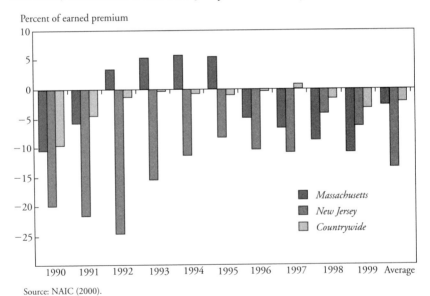

Source: NAIC (2000).

Table 2. *Underwriting Profitability*
Percent

| Year | Massachusetts | | | New Jersey underwriting profit | Countrywide underwriting profit |
	Underwriting profit on commissioner's rate level[a]	Average discount or deviation	Underwriting profit		
1990	−10.4	0.0	−10.4	−19.8	−9.5
1991	−5.7	0.0	−5.7	−21.5	−4.4
1992	3.4	0.0	3.4	−24.5	−1.2
1993	5.4	0.0	5.4	−15.3	−0.3
1994	5.8	0.0	5.8	−11.2	−0.7
1995	5.5	0.0	5.5	−8.2	−0.9
1996	−0.2	−4.4	−4.8	−10.2	−0.3
1997	2.6	−8.5	−6.5	−10.7	0.9
1998	1.4	−9.2	−8.6	−4.0	−1.5
1999	−2.3	−7.6	−10.7	−6.2	−3.2
Average	0.1	−3.0	−2.7	−13.2	−2.1

Source: NAIC (2000) and unpublished data from Automobile Insurers Bureau of Massachusetts.

a. The underwriting profit on the commissioner's rate level is derived from the NAIC reported Massachusetts Underwriting Profit data (p. 219) and the AIB compilation of average earned premium discounts or deviations according to this formula:

Massachusetts underwriting profit on commissioner's rate level = 1 − [(1 − NAIC Mass. underwriting profit) * (1 + discount/deviation)]

Prospects for Change

Given the discussion here and the extensive details of the operation of the Massachusetts and New Jersey markets for the last two decades in these case studies, what is the chance of a new, deregulated regime in either state? Illinois-style "no rate regulation" would seem out of the question. Possibly one paradigm for change could be the South Carolina model discussed in chapter 4 by Martin Grace, Robert Klein, and Richard Phillips.

Deregulation of the Massachusetts and New Jersey markets along the lines of the current South Carolina experiment would require overcoming formidable obstacles that have been in place for years:

—opposition from consumer groups that have captured the insurance departments;
—general reluctance to relinquish the rate suppression tool;

—embedded cross-subsidies and rating restrictions;

—unwillingness of the other players to change a familiar system;

—ineffectiveness of economic fairness and cost control incentive arguments in this political arena;

—willingness of some eternally optimistic companies to provide a market.

In both Massachusetts and New Jersey, auto insurance systems are highly visible local political issues. Worrall documents the importance of the 1998 reform proposals in the closely contested gubernatorial election, while TWR observe that the mechanism of one annual rate change for all in Massachusetts proved highly politicizing. Throw in high costs generated by the other players (see below), and the weight of the evidence favors little or no foreseeable change.

Insurance departments, especially in Massachusetts and New Jersey, react to high costs on behalf on the consumer through rate suppression, rather than staking out a position that lowers the costs.[10] The departments cede that problem to the players instead of representing the consumer, or even better, acting as the fair governmental arbiter on the issues. Rate suppression here means the willful underpricing of the insurance product, either directly—as in the state-set ceiling rate in Massachusetts—or indirectly—as in the prior approval delays and fantasy residual market mechanisms in New Jersey. The case studies demonstrate that unless rate suppression is used sparingly—an unlikely event given the two- to three-year delay in the accounting and reporting systems for rate making—the end result will be "crisis" followed by a "reform." New Jersey appears to be in the early stages of the post-reform era with an uncertain future, while Massachusetts is just entering the acute suppression stage.[11] The Massachusetts regulator first had to eliminate the competitive discounting before classic rate suppression could begin. That seems to have occurred with the 8.3 percent decrease in the commissioner's rates for 2001.

More important than elimination of the suppression tool by deregulation is dealing with the embedded rate subsidies. New Jersey has built-in rate caps for some high-cost youthful classes and territories. Senior citizens are also capped, but their driving habits (low mileage, high levels of experience) may make the caps nonbinding. Massachusetts has youth and urban

10. See Harrington (1992).

11. The 8.3 percent decrease in 2001 rates (figure 2) follows the large underwriting loss in 1999 (figure 3).

caps as well but also has additional subsidies arising from restricted rate classes, a subsidized residual market, and even an unintended subsidy from an embedded method that has been shown to be actuarially inappropriate. As both case studies point out, subsidies create higher overall costs by not allowing the true cost to be known (excessive injury claiming in urban areas, as an example) and addressed. In table 2-16 TWR estimate that regulation (read: subsidy-induced higher costs) accounts for about 12 percent of increased bodily injury liability costs and about half as much (7.5 percent) of property damage liability. Massachusetts adds additional costs, about 25 percent for bodily injury and 44 percent for property damage, according to the TWR regression.[12]

The severity of the subsidy obstacle can be illustrated by a recent decision by the commissioner in Massachusetts. As TWR document, Massachusetts in fact has a competitive rating statute for auto insurance that needs to be "suspended" each year by the finding that competition is not possible in the upcoming rate year. Such a finding has been made each year since 1979, including the most recent years, when insurers were competing for good drivers even to the extent of a price war for market share. The 2000 decision notes: "These discounts and deviations, individually and in combination, effectively make private passenger automobile insurance available to a large number of consumers at a range of prices. Thus current market conditions permit consumers to shop on the basis of price, as well as on the basis of considerations such as service."[13] Honk if that passage describes a competitive market. The decision goes on to say: "In 1977, when fully competitive rating was allowed, the cost of insurance for these two groups of drivers escalated dramatically. Public policy and past experience support a shift to competition only when mechanisms are in place to ensure that under a new system drivers in urban areas and those with less experience will not be, as they were in 1977, confronted with extraordinary rate increases." This issue of "rate shock" to the subsidized drivers is the official—and practical—obstacle to deregulation in Massachusetts, and to a lesser extent in New Jersey.

The case studies point to reform laws as solutions to market crises in New Jersey (several times) and Massachusetts (in 1989). A common feature of these reform efforts is the offer of substantial rate relief from some high "crisis" level of costs and rates. Since the potential solutions are the result of

---

12. Massachusetts has had the highest property damage frequencies in the nation for many years. Bad driving is a matter of pride in the Bay State.

13. Commissioner Linda Ruthardt (2000, pp. 2–3).

a political process, it is the stakeholders that matter for the shape of the reform outcome. Who are these stakeholders, or players? For auto insurance one can quickly identify at least eight: insurers, policyholders and claimants, agents, personal injury attorneys, medical providers (especially chiropractors and physical therapists), auto repair shops, governmental agencies, and consumer groups. If the outcome of reform must be lower premiums, one or more of these players must provide for the lower cost solution, either in reality (preferred by insurers) or in promises usually unfulfilled. The legislators crafting such a solution will react to the weight of political pressure from the players as to the trade-offs involved (lower benefits, lower income, less subsidy, and so forth), hopefully to the benefit of all concerned. The point here, however, is that in the absence of a crisis, of a (near) collapse of the market, the players establish an equilibrium of sorts, where the first mover has to overcome the high hurdle of economically based inertia. Thus the expected outcome in the absence of a crisis is no change, or more likely, a "study" of the market for further analysis by the players.

The systematic stickiness provided by the mostly hidden subsidies may provide the highest hurdle to deregulation. The case studies describe the particulars of these subsidies in Massachusetts and New Jersey. Both make reference to the lack of cost-reducing economic incentives. Actuarial fairness, where each risk class bears its own cost level, provides arguments for eliminating subsidies, both on behalf of policyholders, who pay the subsidies, and for insurers, who must compete using inaccurate pricing. In reality, however, these arguments carry little weight in the political process of reform, either because the subsidies are small (for the payer) or hidden from the policyholder or because insurers seem able to adapt as long as there is an adequate rate level overall.[14]

The last obstacle is the insurers themselves. The ultimate weapon for an insurer is withdrawal from a market. Both Massachusetts and New Jersey have made withdrawal from the state a costly exit (and entry) barrier. Table 1 shows that forty-four firms have exited the two states since 1988, so it does happen. But the studies also show that up to this point in time, the remaining insurers continue to make a market, presumably based on the notion that deep losses will eventually be replaced by profit well into the future. That optimistic premise was seemingly realized in the Massachusetts results for 1992 through 1995 (table 2). But as David Cummins aptly

14. As Worrall points out, the joint underwriting association and market transition facility subsidies are the exceptions, since they are the proximate causes of two of New Jersey's documented crises.

points out in chapter 1, balancing out the underwriting results does not mean that the lost investment opportunities balance out as well. Therefore profits can be adversely affected. This imbalance is the most likely source of the return on equity deficit for Massachusetts auto insurers, tabulated by TWR at about 3 to 4 percent without capital gain considerations and about 6.5 to 7.5 percent with capital gains (see TWR table 2-6). It appears from the TWR and Worrall studies that insurers exit (or do not enter) only when long-term profits are expected to be low or nonexistent, or when they become insolvent. The withdrawal weapon is unlikely to carry much weight until it actually occurs in large market share quantities.

References

Abrahamse, Allan F., and Stephen J. Carroll. 1999. "The Frequency of Excess Claims for Automobile Personal Injuries." In *Automobile Insurance: Road Safety, New Drivers, Risks, Insurance Fraud and Regulation,* edited by Georges Dionne and Claire Laberge-Nadeau, 131–49. Boston: Kluwer Academic.

Cummins, J. David, and Sharon Tennyson. 1992. "Controlling Automobile Insurance Costs." *Journal of Economic Perspectives* 6 (2): 95–115.

Derrig, Richard A. 1997. "Auto Property Damage Cost Containment—A Billion Dollar Decade of Progress in Massachusetts." Automobile Insurers Bureau of Massachusetts, Cost Containment and Fraudulent Claims Payment Filing, Docket R97-37, July. Boston: Massachusetts Division of Insurance.

Derrig, Richard A., Herbert I. Weisberg, and Xiu Chen. 1994. "Behavioral Factors and Lotteries under No-Fault with a Monetary Threshold: A Study of Massachusetts Automobile Claims." *Journal of Risk and Insurance* 61 (2): 245–75.

Derrig, Richard A., and Valerie A. Zicko. 2000. "Prosecution Outcomes 1991 through 1999." Insurance Fraud Bureau of Massachusetts. Automobile Insurers Bureau of Massachusetts, Cost Containment and Fraudulent Claims Payment Filing, Docket R2000-11, July. Boston: Massachusetts Division of Insurance.

Harrington, Scott. 1992. "Rate Suppression." *Journal of Risk and Insurance* 59: 185–202.

Insurance Research Council. 2000. *Trends in Auto Injury Claims.* Malvern, Pa.

National Association of Insurance Commissioners. 2000. *Profitability by Line by State in 1999.* Kansas City, Mo.

Ruthardt, Linda. 2000. *Opinion, Findings and Decision on the Operation of Competition among Motor Vehicle Insurers,* Docket R2000-07, June 29. Boston: Massachusetts Division of Insurance.

Weisberg, Herbert I., and Sarah S. Marter. 1992. "Medical Expenses and the Massachusetts Automobile Tort Reform Law: A First Review of 1989 Bodily Injury Claims." *Journal of Insurance Regulation* 10 (4): 462–514.

Weisberg, Herbert I., and Richard A. Derrig. 1992. "Massachusetts Automobile Bodily Injury Tort Reform." *Journal of Insurance Regulation* 10 (3): 384–440.

MARTIN F. GRACE
ROBERT W. KLEIN
RICHARD D. PHILLIPS

4 | *Auto Insurance Reform: Salvation in South Carolina*

Each state has a story to tell about its regulation of private passenger automobile insurance. While many common factors affect auto insurance, their particular mix varies among states, leading to different regulatory policies and market outcomes. Auto insurance is a highly salient issue among consumers and voters. Unfortunately, the collision of economic forces and politics has caused troublesome problems in some state auto insurance markets. At the same time, certain states have avoided or mitigated these problems with regulatory and market reforms. Hence there are valuable lessons to learn in examining the regulatory experience in specific jurisdictions.

South Carolina's story of auto insurance problems and subsequent reforms offers hope to other states. High speeds on its rural highways, frequent and severe accidents, and a litigious environment combined to escalate auto insurance costs. The government responded with intensive regulation in an attempt to stem rising premiums and address concerns about unfair treatment of certain drivers. In addition to tight limits on rates and underwriting, South Carolina established the Reinsurance Facility (hereafter referred to as "the Facility") for the residual market, which

The authors express their appreciation to the Brookings Institution, the American Enterprise Institute, Robert Litan, and J. David Cummins for their support and guidance of this research. Numerous other individuals and organizations also have provided invaluable assistance and comments on earlier drafts. The views expressed here are solely those of the authors.

imposed a large subsidy from low-risk and "bad-risk" drivers to medium-risk drivers.[1] Its design and other regulatory factors caused the Facility to balloon to 42 percent of the state's insured vehicles in 1992 and generate huge deficits borne disproportionately by drivers across the state.

Growing consumer and political dissatisfaction with this situation eventually prompted the South Carolina legislature to enact Senate Bill 254 (1997 S.C. Acts 154), which revamped the regulatory system. Related legislation in 1999 (Senate Bill 399) helped to implement the reform program. Restrictions on rates and underwriting have been eased and the Facility and its subsidy are being phased out.

With most of the reforms becoming effective in 1999, it is too soon to determine their ultimate outcome, but the early prognosis is positive.[2] The number of insurers writing auto insurance has doubled with implementation of the reforms. Many insurers also have lowered their overall rate levels for auto insurance, reflecting declining claim costs and the easing of restrictions on risk classification and pricing. Some insurers have raised their rates in order to cover high-risk drivers that were previously relegated to the Facility. Consequently, and most important, the Facility is depopulating rapidly.

This chapter begins with a review of the system for auto insurance regulation in South Carolina and its historical antecedents. We then examine the structure of the market over the last decade, before and after reform. This is followed by a historical analysis of market conduct and performance that looks at several outcome measures, including prices, profits, availability, and claim costs. Our analysis includes an initial review of cost drivers that reveals some interesting patterns that warrant further investigation. We conclude by distilling the principal insights from South Carolina's experience.[3]

Auto Insurance Regulation in South Carolina

Like most other states, South Carolina utilized a prior approval regulatory system for auto insurance after the enactment of the McCarran-

---

1. In South Carolina, the Department of Insurance defines "bad-risk" drivers as those with multiple driving violations.

2. We refer to these changes as the "1999 reforms," reflecting their effective date.

3. A more detailed analysis of the South Carolina experience is provided in Grace, Klein, and Phillips (2001).

Ferguson Act in 1945. The states' imposition of uniform "bureau rates" for the principal property-casualty lines in the postwar years is well documented.[4] The constraints on price competition gradually eroded over time as insurers gained increasing flexibility to deviate from uniform prices. Some states eventually removed prior approval requirements for auto insurance rates to allow market forces to operate more freely. Other states, including South Carolina, retained prior approval requirements and tightened price limits when costs escalated. In South Carolina, insurers were not required to adhere to mandatory bureau rates, but were required to individually file rates for prior approval.[5]

In 1975 legislation took effect in South Carolina that comprised a number of regulatory provisions that were popular in the more activist states.[6] These provisions included

—compulsory liability insurance;
—mandatory service requirements for auto insurers;
—establishment of the Reinsurance Facility;
—implementation of a mandatory, uniform merit rating plan; and
—a limited number of designated agents allowed to sell insurance directly through the Facility.[7]

However, these regulatory provisions proved to be problematic in the years ahead. Subsequent legislative and regulatory tinkering made some improvements but failed to fully solve the problems. This led to the comprehensive restructuring in 1999 (based on legislation enacted in 1997). Below we review the most important elements of South Carolina's regulatory system and how they were modified in comparison with other jurisdictions. Figure 4-1 provides a historical timeline of key developments in South Carolina auto insurance regulation.

---

4. Joskow (1973); Hanson, Dineen, and Johnson (1974).

5. Until the early 1990s, insurers could voluntarily adopt rates (by reference) filed by advisory organizations and approved by the insurance department. In the early 1990s, South Carolina, like other states, moved to a prospective loss cost system. (See subsequent discussion.)

6. The use of a reinsurance mechanism for the residual market went beyond what most states established.

7. These were agents authorized to place insureds directly with the Facility. They were not subject to enforcement of the field underwriting requirements generally required of "voluntary market agents," nor were they compelled to properly classify insureds and charge the appropriate rate.

Figure 4-1. *Timeline of Auto Insurance Reforms, South Carolina, 1975–2003*[a]

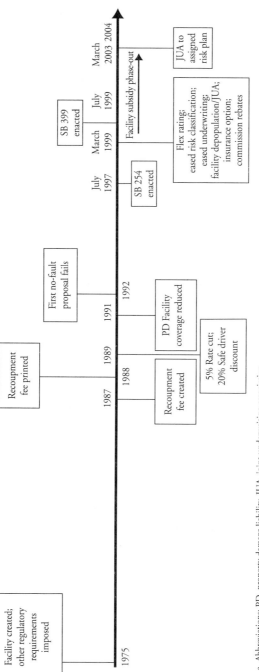

a. Abbreviations: PD, property damage liability. JUA, joint underwriting association.

Regulation of Price Levels

South Carolina required the prior approval of all private passenger auto insurance rates until 1999. At first glance the pre-1999 South Carolina system might appear similar to that of other prior approval states (see table 4-1). The South Carolina law contained the standard prohibitions against excessive, inadequate, and unfair rates. Insurers also were prohibited from employing socially unacceptable criteria in pricing and underwriting, such as race and religion. Insurers were required to file and receive regulatory approval of their auto insurance rates before they could be put into effect. Advisory organizations also played their typical role in submitting advisory loss costs for regulatory approval (full rates prior to 1991), which insurers could reference in their individual rate filings.[8]

There were some additional restrictions in South Carolina that were shared only with the most "activist" prior approval states (summarized in table 4-1 and discussed below). It also is necessary to look beyond statutes and regulations to the policies, procedures, and actions that enforced them. A number of observers have noted that regulatory stringency can vary greatly among states with similar systems.[9] In this respect, it appears that South Carolina enforced tighter price ceilings than the average prior approval state. This is reflected in the disposition of advisory loss cost filings. Table 4-2 shows that for bodily injury liability (BIL) coverage, regulators reduced advisory loss cost increases to a greater degree in South Carolina than in other states.

The apparent greater stringency of South Carolina regulation is also reflected in the Conning and Company rankings of states in terms of their insurance regulatory environments.[10] In periodic surveys conducted from 1984 to 1991, South Carolina's score declined from 3.2 to 2.4, and it ranked forty-fifth among fifty-one jurisdictions, indicating that insurers had a very negative view of its regulatory climate. In the 1994 survey, South Carolina's score improved to 4.5, and its rank rose to forty-first— better, but nothing to boast of.

On March 1, 1999, a "flex rating" system went into effect in South

8. The rating bureaus of the post-McCarran era were transformed into advisory organizations in the 1960s as most states moved away from mandatory bureau rate systems. Advisory organizations file advisory rates (prospective loss costs after 1992) and policy forms with regulators that are subject to prior approval in most states. Insurers may adopt approved advisory rates or loss costs by reference.

9. Klein (1986); Cummins, Phillips, and Tennyson (2000).

10. See Conning (1984, 1987, 1991, and 1994). Conning surveys in 1984, 1987, 1991, and 1994 use a relatively consistent approach in evaluating states' overall regulatory environment.

Table 4-1. *Key Auto Insurance Regulatory Provisions in South Carolina*

Provision	Pre-reform	Post-reform
Rates		
Filing and approval	Prior approval	Flex rating[a]
Risk classification	Restricted	Increased flexibility
Public rate hearings	Yes	No
Limits on underwriting	Highly restricted	Eased
Agent rebates	Disallowed	Allowed
Residual market		
Mechanism	Reinsurance Facility	JUA → assigned risk plan[b]
Subsidized	Yes	No
Compulsory insurance	Yes	No

a. See subsequent discussion.
b. JUA, joint underwriting association.

Carolina as one of its regulatory reforms. Under the new system, insurers do not need prior approval to implement rate changes (increases or decreases) that are less than or equal to 7 percent. Rate filings for more than a 7 percent change must still receive prior approval. Also, insurers are limited to one "flex" rate change (not requiring prior approval) during any twelve-month period. The insurance department also has approved larger rate changes, allowing insurers to differentiate their rate structures and risk portfolios.[11]

Restrictions on Rate Structures

Another issue with South Carolina's previous regulatory system was its constraints on risk classification and rating. While it is not uncommon for prior approval states to place some limits on insurers' rate differentials between risk classifications and geographic areas, South Carolina went further. Prior to Act 154, South Carolina statutes authorized the director of insurance to promulgate uniform classification systems, merit-rating plans, and rating territories and require insurers to grant safe driver discounts of no less than 20 percent. Rate differentials between territories also

11. In a competitive market, auto insurers tend to differentiate themselves in terms of the stringency of their underwriting standards and the characteristics of the drivers they insure. This specialization facilitates efficient, risk-based pricing of auto insurance and encourages drivers to lower their risk to qualify for lower rates.

Table 4-2. Advisory Loss Cost Filings for BIL, South Carolina versus Other States, 1991–99

	South Carolina percent change			Other states													
				Loss cost increases						Loss cost decreases							
				Indicated		Filed		Implemented		Indicated		Filed		Implemented		
Year	Indicated	Filed	Implemented	N[a]	Mean[b]	N	Mean	N	Mean	N	Mean	N	Mean	N	Mean	N	Mean
1991	33.9	33.9	23.0	39	13.7	30	12.2	30	11.9	6	-3.0	6	-3.0	6	-3.0		
1992	...	...	...	30	11.6	28	10.5	25	8.3	15	-7.7	15	-7.7	15	-7.7		
1993	...	...	...	16	14.3	15	9.9	13	8.1	27	-6.3	27	-6.3	27	-6.3		
1994	8.9	8.9	4.0	24	10.5	20	10.7	19	9.5	22	-6.1	22	-6.1	22	-6.1		
1995	2.4	2.4	1.1	33	9.2	30	7.4	30	7.4	12	-3.9	12	-3.9	12	-3.9		
1996	-10.7	-10.7	-10.7	22	7.4	21	6.4	20	6.4	22	-6.1	22	-6.1	24	-6.1		
1997	-14.9	-14.9	-14.9	4	8.5	3	2.7	3	2.7	42	-10.5	40	-10.4	39	-10.6		
1998	...	...	...	4	3.3	4	3.3	4	3.3	40	-10.3	38	-10.7	36	-10.7		
1999	-10.3	-10.3	-10.3	3	3.3	3	3.3	1	3.3	40	-9.2	38	-9.5	35	-9.3		

Source: Insurance Services Office (ISO), unpublished data.
a. Number of states in sample. Total of forty-seven states represented.
b. Percent.

Figure 4-2. *South Carolina Counties Ranked by Loss Ratio, BIL 1993–98*

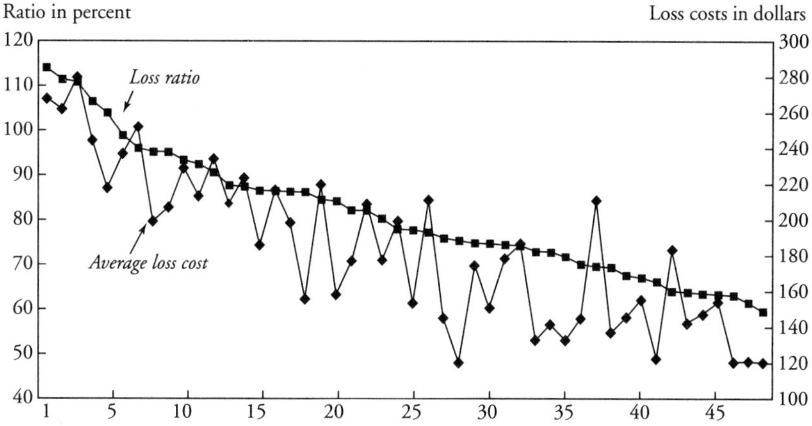

Source: South Carolina Department of Insurance, unpublished data.

were capped. Furthermore, merit rating was limited to a three-year experience period. An analysis by the National Association of Independent Insurers (NAII) indicated that in 1989 South Carolina was one of fourteen states with some form of explicit restriction on class or territorial rates for auto insurance.[12]

Rate compression occurs when regulators constrain price differentials between risk classifications or territories. To provide some preliminary evidence, consider figure 4-2, which reveals a direct relationship between average loss costs and loss ratios by county (BIL experience combined for 1993–98): premiums increase less than proportionately with average loss costs. This pattern is consistent with rate compression although not conclusive.[13]

The constraints on pricing and underwriting caused several problems. It limited insurers' flexibility in tailoring their pricing structures so that they might charge premiums corresponding to a driver's relative risk and expected loss. In practice this tended to prevent insurers from charging adequate rates to high-risk drivers. This contributed to the state's large residual market, despite a mandatory service—"take-all-comers"—

12. Diana Lee, NAII, in a letter to Helen Doerpinghaus, University of South Carolina, November 14, 1989.

13. As losses tend to fluctuate relative to premiums, one would expect loss ratios to be positively associated with loss costs.

requirement.[14] It also diminished incentives for high-risk insureds to improve their safety and hence would be expected to contribute to higher loss costs and exacerbate market and political pressures. "Forgiveness statutes," allowing drivers to expunge violations on their driving records in many counties, further compromised risk-based pricing. Finally, there was a perceived inequity in how the system's costs were allocated among different groups of drivers.

The easing of pricing constraints was one of the important reforms that became effective in 1999. Act 154 repealed the statutes for uniform classifications, merit rating, and rating territories, and the safe driver discount, although it also added a requirement that insurers provide an "appropriate" premium reduction for drivers age fifty-five and older who complete an approved driver training course.[15] Insurers are now allowed to file their own rating plans, and the Insurance Services Office (ISO) also is allowed to file its regular classification system. This should allow insurers to charge higher and more adequate rates for high-risk drivers and possibly lower rates for low-risk drivers. In turn, this should allow the market to function more freely and efficiently and improve incentives for safety.

Approach to Residual Market

South Carolina's residual market facility played a pivotal role in motivating regulatory changes. The Facility was somewhat unusual (in auto insurance) in that it utilized a reinsurance approach, a type of mechanism used by only two other states for auto insurance (New Hampshire and North Carolina). The policies of residual market insureds were serviced by voluntary market insurers who ceded all premiums and losses to the Facility and were compensated for servicing the policies. Insurers also were required to establish special statistical data reporting systems to track policies ceded to the Facility, further adding to their costs.

The problem with a reinsurance approach to residual markets is that servicing carriers bear the full cost of any loss control expenditures on Facility insureds, but they do not directly benefit from any resulting sav-

14. Insurers were required to accept insurance applications from any licensed driver, rather than exercising underwriting guidelines or discretion that might result in the rejection of applications from certain drivers who failed to meet an insurer's preferred underwriting standards. At the same time, an insurer could fully reinsure such drivers through the Facility.

15. Also, while insurers may file their own territorial plans, a rating territory may not be smaller than a county.

ings in claim costs. This diminishes servicing carriers' incentives to optimize loss control expenditures for Facility insureds, and they will be induced to under-invest in loss control measures. Also, designated agents who place insureds directly in the Facility are paid a fee to adjust the claims of these insureds. As this fee is a percentage of the claim amount, designated agents have little incentive to control claim costs—in fact, they have an incentive to inflate them. This can create a significant moral hazard problem and lead to higher loss costs, as demonstrated by several studies and explored later in this chapter.[16]

It also is apparent that the Facility rates, determined by regulators, were severely inadequate to cover its costs. There was a desire to maintain Facility rates that were "comparable" to voluntary market rates, but this became untenable because the Facility was subject to severe adverse selection. At least a couple of factors would have contributed to this. First, limits on Facility rates and relatively lax eligibility requirements led higher risk drivers to choose the Facility over the voluntary market when they had that option. Also, as explained above, certain agents were allowed to place insureds directly in the Facility, allowing drivers to enter by choice rather than through their rejection or cession by an insurer in the voluntary market.

Insurers also were induced to pass drivers to the Facility because of the limits on risk classification in the voluntary market.[17] The territorial and driver-class plan mandated by the state did not allow companies to price insureds according to their relative risk as indicated by their characteristics. This, coupled with suppression of overall rate levels, meant that insurers could identify insureds that would be expected to have greater claim costs than those contemplated in the regulated rate for a given class. Hence insurers were encouraged to cede these insureds to the Facility.

Because of these factors, the Facility grew rapidly and incurred large deficits that were assessed back against the voluntary market. Figure 4-3 plots the Facility market share from 1980 to 1998. The proportion of vehicles insured through the Facility increased from 20 percent in 1980 to 42 percent in 1992 and then decreased to 29 percent by 1998. The Facility's deficit and burden on the voluntary market moved in a similar pattern. Annual operating losses rose above $200 million in 1995 and then began

---

16. Harrington and Pritchett (1990) discuss this problem for the auto insurance market in South Carolina. Klein, Nordman, and Fritz (1993) and Danzon and Harrington (1998) also find evidence of this problem in workers' compensation insurance where reinsurance facilities are used for the residual market.

17. This is explained by Harrington and Pritchett (1990).

Figure 4-3. *Reinsurance Facility Market Share, 1980–98*

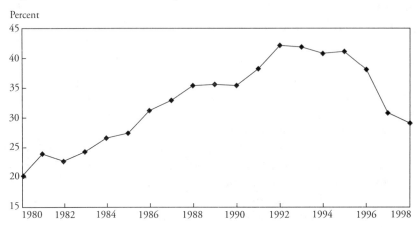

Percent

Sources: AIPSO (2001); South Carolina Department of Insurance, unpublished data.

to decline. The cumulative deficit incurred by the Facility through 1999 was $2.4 billion. These deficits were covered initially by assessments against voluntary market insurers and subsequently, starting in 1988, by recoupment fees (explained below) charged directly to insured drivers.

Suppression of both voluntary and Facility rates prompted some insurers to exit or retrench from the South Carolina auto insurance market in the 1980s. It also retarded the development of a viable voluntary nonstandard auto insurance market that could have covered high-risk drivers. These forces contributed to rapid growth in the Facility as the voluntary market shrank and the number of agents allowed to write coverage directly through the Facility increased.

In 1988 the system was changed to allow insurers to cover all Facility losses through a "recoupment fee," a direct surcharge to all policyholders.[18] The basic fee in 1988–89 for all coverages was $73 per vehicle: $40 for liability, $11 for personal injury protection, $18 for collision, and $4 for comprehensive coverages. Drivers who accumulated points for driving violations were required to pay specified multiples of the basic recoupment fee, which were increased in subsequent revisions of the fee schedule. For example, in 1998–99, a driver with no points paid a $44.32 recoupment fee, a driver with two points paid $830.20, and a driver with 5 points paid $2,075.50. A driver convicted of driving under the influence (DUI) paid $4,151.

18. Prior to the 1999 reforms, the recoupment fee was based on an insured's driving violations.

One important advantage of changing to the recoupment fee was that it made the subsidy to the Facility visible to drivers. Reinsured drivers also were required to pay this fee, which decreased the subsidy to Facility insureds. In essence, the direct burden of covering residual market deficits was moved from insurers to insureds. This ultimately helped catalyze the political support necessary for regulatory reforms. However, a given driver still did not know whether he was reinsured through the Facility. Also, Harrington and Pritchett argue that many drivers who paid the recoupment fee still received a subsidy. In essence, the basic structural problems that plagued the Facility were not fixed. Its size and deficits continued to grow, as did the recoupment fee paid by all insureds, particularly for those with driving violations.

Consequently, changing the residual market mechanism became a focal point of the reform legislation. Under the new law, the reinsurance Facility is being phased out over a three-year period that began March 1, 1999. Restrictions have been imposed on insurers' cessions to the Facility. Further, Facility rate levels for liability coverages will gradually be allowed to reach adequate levels, with annual rate increases limited to 10 percent. The recoupment fee has been capped and will be gradually phased out.

The Reinsurance Facility is being temporarily replaced by a joint underwriting association (JUA) and will ultimately be replaced by an assigned risk plan in 2003. A JUA was established as an intermediate step to ease the transition and avoid assigning a large number of drivers to insurers until the voluntary market had time to recover. Eligibility for the JUA has been tightened, and procedures have been implemented to channel as many drivers as possible into the voluntary market.

Market Structure Trends in South Carolina

South Carolina has a medium-size market for auto insurance, large enough to support numerous insurers and options to consumers. However, its pre-1999 regulatory climate depressed the number of companies supplying auto insurance.

Market Concentration

Table 4-3 tracks the number of insurance companies and groups in South Carolina over the period 1990–99. The number of insurer groups selling auto insurance dropped from 56 to 45 by 1998. In the Southeast

Table 4-3. *Market Concentration, South Carolina versus Southeast Region, 1990–99*

	South Carolina				Southeast region[a]			
Year	Unaffiliated companies[b]	Companies in groups[b]	Groups[c]	HHI[d]	Unaffiliated companies	Companies in groups	Groups	Average HHI
1990	2	78	56	1,195	15	184	99	1,082
1991	1	66	55	1,337	15	185	97	1,146
1992	2	54	45	1,454	13	183	96	1,129
1993	2	49	40	1,470	15	184	97	1,137
1994	2	48	41	1,476	13	182	96	1,129
1995	3	53	46	1,529	12	181	92	1,125
1996	4	51	45	1,538	11	184	93	1,136
1997	5	55	43	1,556	11	188	89	1,100
1998	4	61	45	1,540	8	194	87	1,085
1999	4	104	55	1,493	10	197	82	1,057

Source: National Association of Insurance Commissioners (NAIC), 1999 unpublished data.
a. Southeast region includes Alabama, Florida, Georgia, North Carolina, South Carolina, and Virginia.
b. Companies writing $100,000 or more in auto premiums each year.
c. Includes companies in groups plus unaffiliated singles.
d. Herfindahl-Hirschman index.

region (Alabama, Florida, Georgia, North Carolina, South Carolina, and Virginia), the average number of auto insurers declined marginally from 99 to 87.[19] While there were enough insurers in South Carolina to sustain workable competition, consumers had fewer choices. We should note that certain other southeastern states—Georgia and North Carolina—are also perceived to have relatively stringent auto insurance regulation.

The lower number of insurers contributed to higher market concentration in South Carolina, although it is probably not the sole cause. Table 4-3 also presents Herfindahl-Hirschman index (HHI) values for South Carolina's auto insurance market and compares them against regional averages over the last decade. In South Carolina, the HHI increased from 1,195 in 1990 to 1,540 in 1998.[20] In comparison, the regional average HHI remained relatively constant over this period and was 1,085 in 1998. Concentration in South Carolina did not reach a level that would generate concern about adequate competition, but it was an adverse trend exacerbated by regulation.

Fortunately, the trend toward fewer insurers and greater concentration reversed in 1999 with the implementation of regulatory and market reforms. The number of insurer groups (including unaffiliated single companies) selling auto insurance in South Carolina increased to 55 in 1999. The reforms also induced many groups to increase the number of their affiliated companies, expanding the options available to consumers. The number of insurance companies in the market doubled from 96 in 1998 to 192 in 1999, a remarkable turnaround in a short period of time.

Changes in the market shares of the leading insurer groups are also interesting. Table 4-4 indicates the premium volume and market shares of the top twenty insurers in 1999 and their positions in 1990 and 1995. The top three insurers—State Farm, Allstate, and Nationwide—have retained their rankings and increased their market share to a combined 60 percent over the decade. Several insurers, including Progressive, joined the top twenty during this period. Because insurers were able to cede unprofitable business to the Facility, larger insurers were able sustain operations in the state with retention of low-risk insureds and servicing fees from the Facility. Some smaller and nonstandard insurers may have encountered greater difficulty in sustaining operations in this environment.

19. Unless indicated otherwise, the term "insurer" refers to an insurer group consisting of multiple insurance companies as well as to single companies that do not belong to a group.

20. The Herfindahl-Hirschman index is equal to the sum of the squared market shares of all firms in the market. Higher values indicate greater concentration.

Table 4-4. *Change in Market Share, Top Twenty Auto Insurers in South Carolina, Selected Years, 1990–99*[a]
Units as indicated

Insurer	1999			1995			1990		
	DPW[b]	MS[c]	Rank	DPW	MS	Rank	DPW	MS	Rank
State Farm	492,538,487	30.8	1	402,598,169	32.3	1	268,251,658	28.1	1
Allstate Ins. Grp.	285,173,482	17.8	2	179,403,434	14.4	2	115,343,189	12.1	2
Nationwide	159,869,863	10.0	3	112,240,980	9.0	3	90,070,076	9.4	3
South Carolina Farm Bureau Mutual	94,950,158	5.9	4	83,890,758	6.7	5	n.a.	n.a.	n.a.
United Services Automobile Asn. Grp.	73,336,364	4.6	5	68,345,685	5.5	6	39,215,267	4.1	7
Royal & Sun Alliance USA	71,456,299	4.5	6	n.a.	n.a.	n.a.	n.a.	n.a.	n.a.
Berkshire Hathaway	68,418,185	4.3	7	30,716,887	2.5	8	n.a.	n.a.	n.a.
Seibels Bruce Grp.	61,107,485	3.8	8	65,415,861	5.3	7	55,540,966	5.8	5
American Modern Ins. Grp.	29,873,164	1.9	9	20,319,297	1.6	12	8,842,398	0.9	18
Citigroup	26,878,041	1.7	10	1,821,247	0.1	27	400,714	0.0	48
Auto-Owners Grp.	23,467,084	1.5	11	20,303,170	1.6	13	19,094,584	2.0	11
State Auto Mutual Grp.	22,454,133	1.4	12	21,412,530	1.7	11	17,175,907	1.8	12
CNA Ins. Grp.	22,200,612	1.4	13	24,221,611	1.9	10	n.a.	n.a.	n.a.
Great American Property & Casualty	17,731,300	1.1	14	14,078	0.0	53	1,683,134	0.2	34
Horace Mann Grp.	15,392,424	1.0	15	15,662,631	1.3	14	24,384,133	2.6	10
Companion LIC	14,193,491	0.9	16	29,849,502	2.4	9	3,075,806	0.3	29
Progressive Grp.	12,907,880	0.8	17	n.a.	n.a.	n.a.	n.a.	n.a.	n.a.
Hartford Fire & Casualty Grp.	11,023,875	0.7	18	2,359,701	0.2	26	3,405,900	0.4	27
Selective Ins.	9,266,012	0.6	19	9,401,878	0.8	15	9,288,069	1.0	17
Interfinancial	8,172,334	0.5	20	1,652,027	0.1	30	5,711,990	0.6	23

Source: See table 4-3.
n.a. Not available.
a. Top twenty as of 1999.
b. DPW, direct premiums written in dollars of given year.
c. MS, market share in percent.

Table 4-5. *Entries and Exits, South Carolina, 1990–99*[a]

	Entities at start of year		Entries		Exits		Net change	
Period	Number	Change[b]	Number	Change	Number	Change	Number	Change
1990	56	n.a.	4	n.a.	5	n.a.	−1	n.a.
1991	55	−2	5	25	15	200	−10	900
1992	45	−18	1	−80	6	−60	−5	−50
1993	40	−11	4	300	3	−50	1	−120
1994	41	3	9	125	4	33	5	400
1995	46	12	6	−33	7	75	−1	−120
1996	45	−2	3	−50	5	−29	−2	100
1997	43	−4	5	67	3	−40	2	−200
1998	45	5	19	280	9	200	10	400
1999	55	22	n.a.	n.a.	n.a.	n.a.	n.a.	n.a.

Source: See table 4-3.

n.a. Not available.

a. Calculated on a group and unaffiliated single basis. All entities counted with greater than $100,000 direct premiums written in private passenger auto lines of business.

b. In percent.

Entry and Exit

A reasonable flow of insurers in and out of a market facilitates competition and helps ensure an adequate supply of coverage. In a "normal" market that is "workably competitive," one would expect to see a small number of insurers both entering and exiting the market over time. Insurers that fail to respond to consumer needs efficiently and with reasonable profits would be expected to leave the market. New insurers entering the market can help respond to growing demand, promote innovation, lower prices, and pressure incumbent firms to improve. Even the threat of potential entry can foster market discipline. A high rate of exit can occur due to fierce competition, but it also can be caused by restrictive regulation and related market problems.

The experience in South Carolina appears to be influenced by restrictive regulation. Table 4-5 tracks market entries and exits in South Carolina over the last decade. Exits outpaced entries until 1997, when reform legislation moved forward and was enacted. One early indicator of the reform legislation's effects is the high number of entries into the South Carolina auto insurance market. As of August 2000, 105 new companies had entered the state's auto insurance market since March 1999. This is a clear indication that many more insurers believe the reforms will make it viable for them to write auto insurance in the state.

Prices and Profitability

Coincident with the March 1, 1999, effective date for the statutory changes, the Insurance Services Office filed new advisory loss costs and insurers filed new rating plans. ISO filed for an overall statewide 18.5 percent *decrease* in advisory loss costs, and it appears that at least some insurers also filed rate level decreases.[21] At first blush this might seem curious if insurers were subject to regulatory rate suppression and distortion prior to 1999. However, loss costs were declining in South Carolina as part of a national trend, although not as rapidly as in other jurisdictions.

Another indicator of general pricing activity are average premiums or expenditures on auto insurance in South Carolina compared with other states, as shown in table 4-6. In South Carolina, the average auto insurance premium increased from $616 in 1991 to $766 in 1998, a faster pace than in other Southeast states.[22] While this trend may seem to contradict the data on advisory loss cost and insurer rate filings, it is not inconsistent. Statistical data provided by the Department of Insurance reveals that the average premium for voluntary market insureds was $612 in 1993 and $621 in 1998, a 0.3 percent average annual growth rate. On the other hand, average premiums for Facility insureds increased from $649 to $981, an average annual growth rate of 9.1 percent.

Three historical measures of insurers' profitability can be used to judge rate adequacy. Loss ratios in South Carolina have remained higher than the national and regional averages but have declined in recent years to a more sustainable level, as shown in figure 4-4a. The state's loss ratio decreased from 90 percent in 1990 to 75 percent in 1998. Correspondingly, profits on insurance transactions, as a percentage of earned premiums, increased from −13 percent to −6 percent (figure 4-4b). The voluntary market loss ratio remained relatively stable over this period and was 64.6 percent in 1998. On the other hand, the Facility loss ratio increased from 97.3 percent in 1993 to 108 percent in 1996 and then fell to 70.9 percent in 1998.

---

21. The overall liability loss cost change was −12.5 percent and the overall physical damage loss cost change was −30.3 percent.

22. Based on data from the National Association of Insurance Commissioners (1999b).

Table 4-6. *Average Auto Insurance Premiums, South Carolina, Countrywide, and Other Southeast States, 1991–98*
Dollars, except as noted

Year	South Carolina Value	South Carolina Change[a]	Countrywide Value	Countrywide Change	Other Southeast states Ala.	Fla.	Ga.	N.C.	Va.	Average	Change
1991	615.89	...	685.56	...	560.41	727.60	677.73	522.39	603.11	618.25	...
1992	655.07	6.4	711.75	3.8	590.57	739.81	636.48	541.07	570.62	615.71	−0.4
1993	684.10	4.4	730.39	2.6	604.07	753.94	664.85	528.43	564.07	623.07	1.2
1994	680.80	−0.5	740.38	1.4	610.52	702.28	696.83	547.08	561.66	623.67	0.1
1995	675.93	−0.7	757.56	2.3	632.24	778.70	726.15	576.83	559.45	654.67	5.0
1996	698.30	3.3	780.11	3.0	661.62	823.65	761.75	594.79	608.87	690.14	5.4
1997	732.92	5.0	798.91	2.4	703.43	833.50	787.53	652.46	628.51	721.09	4.5
1998	766.23	4.5	797.23	−0.2	719.72	814.82	803.18	664.06	630.12	726.38	0.7
1991–98	...	24.4	...	16.3	...	...	...	...	...	...	17.5
Average	...	3.2	...	16.3	...	...	...	...	...	...	2.4

Source: NAIC (1999b).
a. Change expressed in percent.

Figure 4-4a. *Loss Ratios, 1990–99*

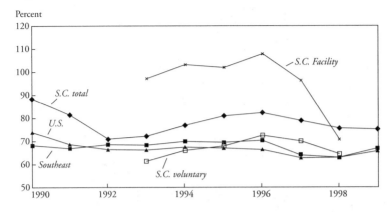

Figure 4-4b. *Profit on Insurance Transactions, 1990–99*

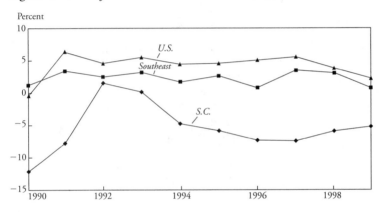

Figure 4-4c. *Rate of Return on Net Worth, 1990–99*

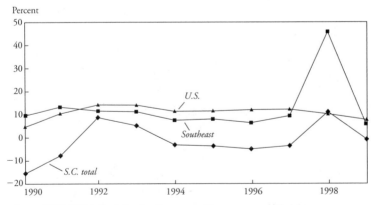

Source: NAIC (1999a); South Carolina Department of Insurance, unpublished data.

Finally, the estimated rate of return on net worth increased from −15 percent to 10 percent (figure 4-4c).

Availability

The availability of auto insurance is as important as its cost. With a residual market mechanism, the issue is not whether most drivers can obtain insurance but rather what options are available to them and their affordability. Some also might question whether residual market insureds receive the same quality of service as voluntary market insureds, although insurers may disagree that there is a difference. If rates are suppressed, insurers will be inclined to decrease their voluntary market writings, either forcing or encouraging drivers to secure coverage through the residual market. A large residual market creates problems for insurers and insureds. Operating deficits in residual market mechanisms and the subsidies necessary to cover them can burden the voluntary market and exacerbate the growth of the residual market. Drivers who choose to operate vehicles without liability insurance also are a concern if they lack sufficient financial resources to compensate people they harm.

Residual Market

The residual market problem is clearly evident in the South Carolina experience. Table 4-7 presents statistics on the volume of business in the Reinsurance Facility and its operating performance from 1993 to 1999. As shown earlier in figure 4-3, the Facility's share of insured vehicles continued to escalate from its inception and peaked at 42 percent in 1992. By 1995 the Facility insured more than 1 million private passenger vehicles. Its volume and market share then began to decline but still constituted almost 30 percent in 1998. The South Carolina Facility dwarfed the residual market mechanisms in most other jurisdictions, which rarely accounted for more than 1 to 2 percent of a state's insured vehicles. Massachusetts, New Jersey, and North Carolina are other states that have had large residual markets.

The Facility's operating results worsened with its growth. Its net operating loss (excluding revenues from recoupment fees) reached $200 million annually by 1995, approximately 40 percent of its earned premiums. By the end of 1999, the Facility had compiled a cumulative deficit of $2.4 billion.

Because of regulatory restrictions on risk-based pricing, it would be reasonable to surmise that certain driver groups would more likely be rein-

Table 4-7. *Operating Statistics for Reinsurance Facility, 1993–98*[a]
Thousands of dollars, except as noted

Year	Earned premiums	Losses incurred	Net UW results[b]	Net operating results		Residual MS[d]
				Amount	EP[c]	
1993	495,840	454,537	−143,236	−144,229	−29.1	41.8
1994	495,894	511,187	−194,354	−195,987	−39.5	40.6
1995	491,299	527,458	−197,694	−200,677	−40.8	41.0
1996	489,278	531,108	−200,006	−201,527	−41.2	37.9
1997	487,022	481,818	−152,842	−154,238	−31.7	30.7
1998	482,372	445,187	−115,959	−117,137	−24.3	29.3
1999	134,763	122,200	−30,878	−31,540	−23.4	n.a.

Source: AIPSO (2001).
n.a. Not available.
a. Results do not include offset of recoupment fees.
b. UW, underwriting.
c. EP, earned premiums, in percent.
d. MS, market share, in percent.

sured through the Facility than other groups. This is consistent with the geographic distribution of the Facility's share of insured vehicles. (See section on "Contributing Factors.") Interestingly, the Facility tends to account for a greater share of a county's vehicles in less densely populated areas. This appears contrary to the typical experience in many urbanized states.[23] If territorial base rates for lower-income, rural areas were compressed by regulators, it could have contributed to relatively more Facility placements from rural counties.

It appears that South Carolina's reform program is having its desired effect on shrinking the residual market. In 1998 the number of drivers added to the Facility averaged roughly 100,000 per month. In 1999 this figure dropped to 15,000–20,000.[24] Only sixty new policies had been written through the JUA as of September 1999. As of December 31, 1999, only 58,000 vehicles were insured in the Facility.

This rapid depopulation has been accompanied by significant improvement in the Facility's operating results. The operating deficit dropped to $21 million for fiscal year 1999 and will decline further with the movement toward adequate rates. Rate adequacy and depopulation reinforce each

23. See Klein (1996) and Harrington and Niehaus (1998).
24. R. Kevin Dietrich, "Insurance Reform Spurs Competition," *The State*, September 5, 1999; "Insurance Groups Double on Market since New Law," *Sun News*, August 1, 1999.

Table 4-8. *Ratio of Uninsured Motorist to BIL Claims, South Carolina, 1993–98*

Year	UM claims[a]	BIL claims	Ratio
1993	10,510	59,373	0.177
1994	12,106	65,937	0.184
1995	14,600	74,296	0.197
1996	16,575	76,996	0.215
1997	18,022	75,261	0.239
1998	16,271	64,644	0.252

Source: South Carolina Department of Insurance, unpublished data.
a. UM, uninsured motorist.

other and will ultimately confine the residual mechanism to the limited role it should play in a healthy marketplace.

Uninsured Motorists

Some additional indication of the availability (and implicitly the affordability) of auto insurance is provided by estimates of the number of uninsured motorists. A high number of drivers without insurance or other means to pay for damages they cause to others contributes to higher uninsured motorists premiums for those drivers who carry this coverage and externalizes costs to other parties. South Carolina has had a relatively high percentage of uninsured drivers despite its mandatory service and compulsory insurance requirements.[25] Even with these provisions, some drivers may attempt to avoid buying insurance because of its relatively high cost. Under the old system, some drivers facing high recoupment fees because of their driving records may have been especially inclined to forgo insurance.

It is difficult to produce precise estimates of the number of uninsured drivers, but the relationship of the number of uninsured motorists claims to the number of BIL claims provides some indication. Table 4-8 shows that the ratio of uninsured motorists claims to BIL claims in South Carolina has steadily increased from 0.177 in 1993 to 0.252 in 1998. Since Facility insureds generally experienced the greatest premium increases,

25. Consistent with this picture, a national study ranked South Carolina seventh among states in terms of the ratio of uninsured motorist claims to BIL claims (22 percent) for the period 1989–95 (Insurance Research Council, 1999c).

they may have been more likely to drop their insurance coverage, a phenomenon that would be consistent with studies of other auto insurance markets.[26]

Claim Costs and Factors

The cost of auto insurance claims and the factors that affect the frequency and severity of claims are important areas for investigation. First, rising costs tend to pressure the marketplace and can cause conflicts between insurers and regulators. Second, risk selection and the pricing of auto insurance influence drivers' incentives to prevent or mitigate losses.[27] Third, the tendency for people to file claims and lawsuits, the kind and severity of damages claimed, and the incidence of claim fraud affect costs and, in turn, can be affected by regulation. If regulation or other constraints distort insurance pricing, they can contribute to an escalating cycle of higher loss costs and regulatory conflicts. In this section we examine claim cost trends and conduct regression analyses of several factors contributing to claim costs.

Claim Trends

The cost of liability insurance is driven by the number and severity of accidents, the cost of injuries, the filing of claims, and the amount of litigation over accidents. South Carolina has a relatively high fatal accident rate of 2.6 per million vehicle miles driven, which ranks fifth among the states.[28] High speeds on its rural highways and poor road conditions are probably significant factors. Also, South Carolina's traffic laws appear to be more lenient than in other states.[29] Over time, fatal accident rates have declined countrywide and in South Carolina (to a lesser degree), partly due to safer vehicles and a crackdown on drunk drivers. At the same time, motorists are driving more miles, and severe accidents may remain a problem, even if they rarely involve fatalities.

Figures 4-5 through 4-11 plot trends in average loss costs, claim fre-

---

26. See Smith and Wright (1992).

27. For example, if drivers have reduced safety incentives, they may drive at higher speeds or be less likely to use safety belts. See Cummins and Tennyson (1992); Derrig and others (2000).

28. This information comes from the National Highway Safety Administration.

29. See Insurance Information Institute (2000).

Figure 4-5. *Average Loss Cost, 1983–99*

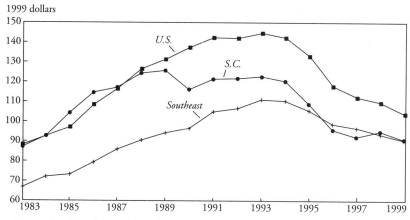

Source: National Association of Independent Insurers (NAII), Fast Track Monitoring System.

quency, and claim severity, by type of liability coverage for South Carolina, the region, and countrywide. All dollar amounts have been converted to "1999 dollars" to facilitate comparison. It appears that bodily injury liability (BIL) loss costs, driven by the frequency of BIL claims, constitute the most significant problem in South Carolina. Figure 4-5 indicates that the average BIL loss cost per exposure (earned car-year) in South Carolina steadily increased from under $90 in 1983 to $126 in 1989. The average loss cost declined in 1990, stabilized, and then began to decline further in 1994 back down to $90 in 1999. This trend has generally followed those in the Southeast and countrywide. Subsequent to 1987 the level of BIL loss costs in South Carolina has been lower than the countrywide average. However, the state's BIL loss costs exceeded the regional average until they began to converge in 1996.

Figures 4-6 and 4-7 decompose the frequency and severity elements of average BIL loss costs. The data indicate clearly that the frequency and not the severity of BIL claims is the cause of South Carolina's relatively high BIL costs. The frequency of BIL claims (claims per 100 exposures) in South Carolina has consistently exceeded the countrywide and regional averages. By contrast, the severity of BIL claims (dollars per claim) has remained considerably below the regional and national averages. The state's BIL frequency came closer to that of other states after 1994, when it dropped faster than regional and national trends. In South Carolina, BIL frequency peaked at 2.5 claims per 100 exposures in 1991 and fell to its

Figure 4-6. *BIL Frequency, 1983–99*[a]

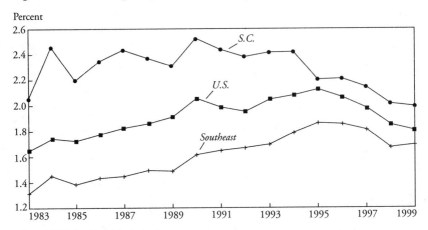

Percent

Source: NAII, Fast Track Monitoring System.
a. Frequency = claims per 100 exposures.

Figure 4-7. *BIL Severity, 1983–99*

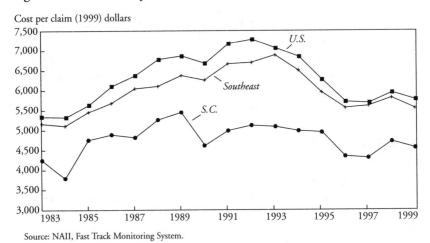

Cost per claim (1999) dollars

Source: NAII, Fast Track Monitoring System.

lowest level, 2.0, in 1999. By comparison, in 1999 the national average was 1.8, and the regional average was 1.7.

Declining BIL claim frequency may be due to improved safety features in vehicles, such as air bags and antilock brakes, which have benefited South Carolina as well as other states. Still, the state's frequency of BIL

Figure 4-8. *PDL Average Loss Cost: 1983–99*

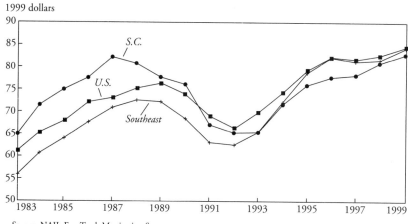

Source: NAII, Fast Track Monitoring System.

claims remains higher than other states, which could be influenced by the nature of its auto accidents—their tendency to involve bodily injuries and the severity of these injuries—as well as the tendency of accident victims to file claims and possibly lawsuits.

Examining property damage liability (PDL) claims experience provides further insights, as shown in figures 4-8 through 4-10. South Carolina's average PDL loss cost exceeded that of other states until 1992, when it fell into line with the regional and countrywide averages. The trend of South Carolina PDL loss costs has generally mirrored that of other states: costs increased till the late 1980s, fell, and then began to climb again in 1994–95. The average PDL loss cost reached its highest level in 1999 at around $83 in South Carolina, regionally, and nationwide. Hence escalating PDL costs do not appear to be specific to South Carolina; rather, they are a problem contributing to higher premiums across the country. One possible explanation for this phenomenon is that while vehicles have become safer, they also have become more expensive to repair after an accident.[30] Furthermore, the severity of PDL claims, not their frequency, has been the major cost driver (see figures 4-9 and 4-10).

It also is interesting to examine the ratio of BIL claims to PDL claims, shown in figure 4-11. A high BIL/PDL ratio could be caused by a high

30. For example, if air bags deploy even in a minor accident, they have to be replaced. Also, vehicles are being designed to absorb more of the force from a crash and transmit less of it to occupants.

Figure 4-9. *PDL Frequency, 1983–99*[a]

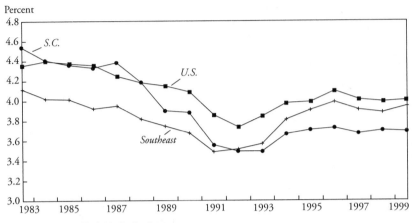

Source: NAII, Fast Track Monitoring System.
a. Frequency = claims per 100 exposures.

Figure 4-10. *PDL Severity, 1983–99*

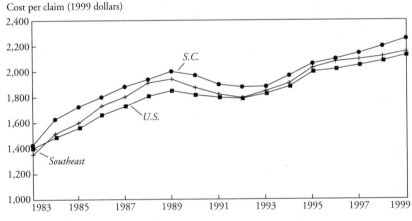

Source: NAII, Fast Track Monitoring System.

proportion of severe accidents causing bodily injuries, greater tendency to file claims for bodily injuries, or both. We see that this ratio is considerably higher in South Carolina than in other Southeast states and countrywide. It reached its peak near 70 percent in 1993 and has since declined to less than 55 percent in 1999. This is still 10 percentage points higher than the BIL/PDL claim ratio in other states.

Figure 4-11. *Ratio of BIL to PDL Claims, 1983–99*

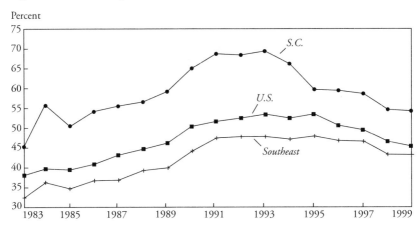

Source: NAII, Fast Track Monitoring System.

Possible Contributing Factors

A rigorous examination of auto insurance cost drivers is beyond the scope of this chapter, but it is useful to consider empirical evidence on some possible factors that warrant further investigation. In addition to traffic laws, driving conditions, driving behavior, and the accidents that result, the tendency to file and litigate claims could contribute to higher costs.

A review of auto insurance claims closed in 1997 revealed that 44 percent of bodily injury liability claims in South Carolina involved an attorney, ranking South Carolina eighteenth among the forty states with tort or add-on systems.[31] In this same survey, 80 percent of BIL claims dollars paid in South Carolina went to claimants represented by an attorney, ranking it thirteenth among the forty states. An associated survey of 180,000 households in 1998 indicated that 41 percent of South Carolina survey respondents filing auto insurance claims hired an attorney, ranking it eighteenth among forty-nine states and the District of Columbia (Hawaii was excluded). While these figures may not seem especially abnormal as they are only moderately above median levels, South Carolina's higher than average litigation incidence appears to be uncustomary among states with larger rural populations.

Then there is the issue of claim fraud, which is a significant problem

31. See Insurance Research Council (1999a and 1999b).

countrywide. A broad definition of claim fraud would include "padding" claims arising from real injuries as well as the filing of claims when there are no injuries or even an accident. The high ratio of BIL to PDL claims in South Carolina could be one indicator of what some experts have labeled "excessive claiming."[32] Hard data on claim fraud by state are not readily available, but anecdotes indicate that it is a concern in South Carolina. The state's attorney general recently instigated an insurance fraud project as one of his office's major initiatives.

While the literature suggests that higher auto insurance loss ratios and a greater tendency to file liability claims are more urban than rural phenomena, there is a curious alternative pattern among South Carolina's counties.[33] In table 4-9 the BIL loss ratios tend to be higher in the state's rural counties, a departure from the more common pattern in other states. Table 4-9 also reveals that the Facility market share and BIL/PDL claim ratio are higher in less densely populated areas, which also tend to have higher unemployment rates and lower household incomes. The positive association of loss ratios, residual market penetration, and BIL/PDL claim ratios with areas of low population density is contrary to expectation. Table 4-9 further indicates that rural counties had a greater percentage of collisions involving bodily injuries (based on state collision statistics) and alcohol, factors that also may contribute to the state's geographical pattern of claims.

Using econometric analysis, we examine four phenomena of interest: loss cost inflation; the residual market share; "excessive claiming" or fraud; and the demand for insurance. With pooled cross-sectional (county level) and time series data for the period 1993–98, we estimate several models that help to explain these phenomena. Our data set consists of statistical information on premiums and losses, by coverage (BIL and PDL), county, and voluntary and nonvoluntary markets. Our data also include several other demographic and economic variables available by county.[34] Table 4-10 lists all the variables used and their sources.

LOSS COST INFLATION   A key issue is how restrictive regulation serves to inflate loss costs. Suppression and compression of rates for all or certain

32. Insurance Research Council (1994); Abrahamse and Carroll (1999).

33. See Insurance Services Office and National Association of Independent Insurers (1988) for an analysis of auto insurance costs in large urban areas compared to nonurban areas.

34. Data on some economic and demographic variables were not available by year. In such instances, we used data for the year most closely corresponding to our sample period.

groups of drivers distort price signals and diminish incentives for safety and controlling losses. Thus our primary interest is to test the hypothesis that counties with large Facility market shares will have higher loss inflation rates. There are two reasons to suspect this relationship exists. First, suppression of rates for drivers in the Facility weakens their incentives to drive safely and may encourage more risky behavior. It is possible that drivers providing the subsidies, in the form of recoupment fees, will have increased incentives to minimize risky behavior. However, the combined effect of these two factors in a county is indeterminate. Second, although insurers no longer are financially liable for the losses of drivers ceded to the Facility, they do adjust their claims. As discussed earlier, this would be expected to reduce servicing carriers' incentives to control claim costs. Thus for both reasons we expect the growth rate in liability loss costs will be higher in counties with a greater percentage of the drivers in the Facility.

To test the hypothesis that loss growth rates for BIL and PDL claims will be a function of the size of the residual market in the county, we estimate the following regression equation:

$$\ln(G_{ijt}) = a + \theta R_{ijt} + \boldsymbol{\beta}' X_{ijt} + \varepsilon_{ijt},$$

where $\ln(G_{ijt})$ is the natural logarithm of the ratio of losses incurred per exposure unit in line of insurance i in county j for year t relative to the value of the same variable in year $t-1$; R_{ijt} is the percent of exposure units in line of insurance i in county j for year t insured by the Facility; X_{ijt} is a set of control variables expected to differentially influence liability growth rates across each county; a, θ, and the vector $\boldsymbol{\beta}'$ are estimated parameters; and ε_{ijt} is the error term. We estimate the loss growth equations separately for BIL and PDL and separately for voluntary and Facility vehicles.

There are five variables in our tests to control for other factors likely to influence the growth rate in losses. First is a variable equal to the level of losses incurred per exposure unit for a given coverage. This variable is lagged one year as we hypothesize that current growth rates will be a decreasing function of the prior year's average loss level.

The second control variable is the median household income in the county. The reason for including this variable depends on the coverage we are investigating. Household income was included in the PDL growth rate regressions because we expect that high-income households will tend to own more expensive vehicles, which would have a positive effect on the growth of PDL losses. For BIL, higher income individuals will have a higher

Table 4-9. *Bodily Injury Claim Costs and Economic Variables by County in Descending Order of Loss Ratio*
Percent, except as noted

County	BIL 1993–98		Facility MS 1998[b]	Bodily injury claim		BIL/PDL claims 1993–98	Median household income[a]	Unemployment rate	Population density[d]	Vehicle density[d]	Collisions involving	
	Loss cost[a]	Loss ratio		Frequency[c]	Severity[a]						Bodily injury	Alcohol
Clarendon	268.25	114.1	40.0	3.43	7,830	102.8	17,645	10.0	46.9	25.3	33.8	8.0
Allendale	262.51	111.5	43.4	3.97	6,604	107.5	15,013	8.6	28.7	12.7	53.4	5.8
Dillon	280.06	110.9	50.2	4.28	6,546	124.8	18,365	10.1	71.9	36.9	37.1	5.7
York	244.90	106.6	26.2	2.76	5,668	63.2	31,288	5.5	156.3	129.7	30.4	5.1
Lee	218.70	104.2	38.4	4.10	5,329	115.6	18,174	6.5	45.0	24.4	36.9	7.6
Marlboro Co.	237.73	99.0	38.1	3.51	6,764	105.6	17,825	12.5	69.3	35.3	47.9	6.1
Marion	252.39	96.2	52.7	3.71	6,803	111.5	19,226	12.4	24.6	13.5	32.5	5.9
Chester	199.95	95.4	34.0	3.67	5,441	87.9	23,054	13.5	55.4	33.8	36.6	4.0
Union	208.06	95.3	25.8	2.49	5,380	64.4	21,526	9.3	59.9	36.9	39.6	5.7
Hampton	229.69	93.6	40.6	3.17	7,242	104.0	18,615	8.6	32.5	17.1	23.7	5.7
Georgetown	213.92	92.6	33.9	3.28	6,523	86.7	23,981	8.6	56.8	32.2	41.6	4.4
Darlington	234.68	90.8	33.7	3.34	7,018	94.0	22,642	7.9	110.1	64.1	46.1	8.4
Colleton	209.93	88.0	43.1	3.68	5,710	108.8	20,617	8.1	32.5	18.3	37.8	5.3
Berkeley	223.97	87.7	36.5	3.43	6,536	80.3	29,106	4.7	117.1	69.7	35.2	4.9
Lancaster	186.55	86.8	32.2	3.22	5,795	79.7	25,320	8.7	99.3	64.7	33.2	6.0
Jasper	217.35	86.7	40.8	3.16	6,879	88.1	18,071	5.8	24.2	11.9	25.9	4.5
McCormick	199.00	86.5	29.3	3.21	6,191	97.4	18,068	11.0	61.2	29.5	47.4	7.5
Edgefield	156.73	86.5	25.1	2.50	6,274	69.8	23,021	6.0	36.6	22.7	40.7	5.4
Florence	220.28	84.8	33.8	3.55	6,206	85.5	24,264	5.9	143.1	82.9	35.6	4.6
Barnwell	159.12	84.4	26.2	2.69	5,906	84.9	23,501	14.2	37.0	22.2	44.3	5.5
Orangeburg	177.68	82.4	33.9	3.34	5,325	91.0	20,216	8.3	76.7	42.9	34.3	5.3
Dorchester	209.44	82.4	30.1	3.31	6,325	77.5	30,764	4.7	144.5	90.3	28.8	3.4
Fairfield	178.01	80.6	41.3	3.30	5,394	95.2	21,484	11.8	32.5	18.3	43.5	5.4
Pickens	199.91	78.2	22.5	2.19	5,517	54.8	26,336	5.3	189.1	127.6	29.4	7.0

County												
Calhoun	154.38	77.9	34.7	2.68	5,764	84.0	23,750	9.2	33.6	21.5	42.4	8.1
Horry	211.57	77.5	32.5	3.07	6,894	73.1	24,959	7.7	127.0	79.9	29.7	4.6
Anderson	146.19	76.1	19.8	2.40	6,102	62.4	25,748	6.6	202.2	141.3	33.1	4.2
Abbeville	121.33	75.6	24.9	2.16	5,621	65.3	23,170	8.3	47.0	31.6	38.8	6.6
Cherokee	151.83	75.0	26.5	2.54	5,979	66.2	24,655	6.9	113.2	71.2	37.1	6.1
Bamberg	179.03	74.6	35.9	3.41	5,244	95.9	17,496	10.6	43.0	20.9	39.3	4.0
Saluda	187.27	74.4	25.7	2.11	6,529	66.0	22,176	4.8	36.3	24.2	33.4	3.9
Laurens	133.81	73.1	26.2	2.56	5,222	69.9	24,905	6.6	81.5	51.9	37.7	4.8
Aiken	142.38	73.0	22.4	2.50	5,700	64.0	29,994	4.9	112.7	75.7	32.6	4.7
Williamsburg	133.83	71.9	51.6	3.56	6,883	106.7	18,409	8.9	40.9	20.1	41.9	7.9
Kershaw	145.78	70.1	29.5	2.34	6,235	69.5	28,282	8.6	60.1	40.2	36.1	5.8
Charleston	211.31	69.8	31.2	3.56	5,930	77.2	26,875	4.9	321.7	180.2	37.7	3.1
Spartanburg	138.07	69.4	25.1	2.80	5,244	66.4	26,941	5.5	279.7	185.6	32.1	5.4
Sumter	146.60	67.7	33.4	3.37	6,177	87.3	22,387	9.4	132.8	82.2	31.1	4.6
Greenwood	123.43	66.4	25.4	2.18	5,669	54.7	23,584	7.1	130.6	85.4	29.9	3.6
Beaufort	183.74	64.2	25.0	2.42	7,584	64.7	30,450	4.2	113.2	86.0	28.6	3.6
Greenville	143.11	64.0	26.2	2.62	5,459	59.1	29,088	4.9	404.3	274.9	24.3	3.7
Lexington	148.17	63.6	24.4	2.68	5,522	65.7	32,914	4.1	239.1	169.8	31.6	4.7
Chesterfield	154.77	63.5	36.5	2.66	5,820	85.3	21,069	5.9	48.3	29.7	39.1	9.0
Newberry	121.31	63.3	26.5	1.95	6,233	64.6	23,405	5.5	52.6	34.9	39.1	5.8
Oconee	121.76	61.7	19.6	2.09	5,816	61.2	25,723	7.7	92.0	65.7	34.0	5.8
Richland	121.06	59.8	29.8	3.54	5,296	72.5	28,848	4.6	377.4	220.7	29.1	3.3
Total	...	...	...	...	...	...	1,082,950	...	...	...	...	...
Weighted average	156.16	67.3	29.0	3.01	6,090	63.2	...	7.7	113.9	71.9	32.6	4.6
Mean	174.88	75.0	100.0	...	...	100.0	23,542	...	105.2	66.4	35.7	5.4

Sources: S.C. Department of Insurance, unpublished data; S.C. Department of Public Safety (2001); Bureau of the Census, *Statistical Abstract 2000*.

a. Dollars

b. MS, market share.

c. Frequency—number of claims incurred/100 car-years earned.

d. Per square mile.

Table 4-10. *Variables Used in Regression Analyses*

Variable	Data years	Source
Year	...	...
County name	...	...
County land area in square miles	...	CCDB
Total resident population	1993–96	CCDB
Percent of population		
Male	1993–96	CCDB
Age 15–19	1993–96	CCDB
Age 20–24	1993–96	CCDB
Age 65+	1993–96	CCDB
Below poverty level	1993	CCDB
Household language not English	1990	CCDB
Living in rural area	1990	CCDB
Number of vehicle thefts	1993–95	CCDB
Number of serious crimes	1993–95	CCDB
Number of households	1990	CCDB
Median household income	1990	CCDB
Civilian unemployment rate	1993–96	CCDB
Percent service establishments offering legal services	1992	CCDB
Number of registered vehicles: 1998	1998	SCDC
Number of registered vehicles: 1990	1990	SCDC
Number of registered vehicles: interpolated	1993–98	...
Percent bodily injury exposures in Facility	1993–98	SCDI
Percent property damage exposures in Facility	1993–98	SCDI
BIL claims per exposure unit	1993–98	SCDI
PDL claims per exposure unit	1993–98	SCDI
Ratio: BIL frequency to PDL frequency	1993–98	SCDI
Earned premium per exposure unit		
All coverages	1993–98	SCDI
All coverages, private market	1993–98	SCDI
All coverages, Facility	1993–98	SCDI
BIL losses		
Per exposure unit	1993–98	SCDI
Per exposure unit, private market	1993–98	SCDI
Per exposure unit, Facility	1993–98	SCDI
PDL losses		
Per exposure unit	1993–98	SCDI
Per exposure unit, private market	1993–98	SCDI
Per exposure unit, Facility	1993–98	SCDI

Source: Bureau of the Census, *County and City Data Book* (CCDB); South Carolina Department of Commerce (SCDC), unpublished data; South Carolina Department of Insurance (SCDI), unpublished data.

opportunity cost of visiting the doctor. Therefore we expect income to be negatively related to the growth of BIL losses.

The third control is a population density variable equal to the total population in the county divided by the number of square miles in the county. BIL losses are expected to grow faster in densely populated counties because the costs of goods and services have increased there at a greater rate.

The number of legal establishments divided by the number households in the county was included to control for the likelihood of attorney involvement in the claims process. As discussed above, previous research indicates that attorney involvement tends to increase the size of damage awards. We expect persons with greater access to legal counsel will be more likely to engage a lawyer for auto liability claims, which will tend to increase the cost of these claims. Also, a larger supply of lawyers might prompt some to more actively offer their services to persons involved in auto accidents. This effect should be greater for BIL than for PDL as there is greater opportunity to inflate BIL claims.[35]

Finally, we included year indicator variables to control for year-specific shocks or effects that could be important given the changing attitudes toward the automobile insurance system in South Carolina over this time period.

Liability growth rate models are estimated using weighted least squares since we anticipate larger and more populous counties to experience less random fluctuation in their auto insurance losses from year to year. The square root of the number of registered vehicles in a county is used as our weight for these regressions. To moderate the effects of extreme values, all equations were estimated using the natural logarithm of each explanatory variable and the dependent variable.

Table 4-11 presents the loss cost inflation regression results estimated separately for BIL and PDL coverages and voluntary and Facility markets for the years 1994–98. The primary variable of interest, the percent of the market insured by the Facility, is significantly and positively related to the growth rate for BIL losses in both the Facility and voluntary markets. This result is consistent with the hypothesis that suppressed residual market rates reduce safety incentives for Facility drivers in a county. This result also is consistent with insurers having reduced incentives to control the cost of claims involving Facility insureds.

Interestingly, the estimated relationship between the size of the Facility

---

35. Property damages should be fairly easy to verify, but alleged bodily injuries are more difficult to verify or challenge.

Table 4-11. *Loss Cost Inflation Regression, All South Carolina Counties, 1994–98*[a]

Independent variable	Dependent variable			
	Bodily injury liability		Property damage liability	
	Voluntary market	Facility market	Voluntary market	Facility market
Intercept	6.861***	11.081***	1.868*	1.560*
	(1.871)	(1.377)	(1.001)	(0.817)
BIL loss per exposure unit$_{t-1}$ voluntary market	−0.696*** (0.081)	...	...	...
BIL loss per exposure unit$_{t-1}$ Facility	...	−0.863*** (0.050)	...	...
PDL loss per exposure unit$_{t-1}$ voluntary market	...	...	−0.501*** (0.060)	...
PDL loss per exposure unit$_{t-1}$ Facility	...	...	...	−0.554*** (0.053)
Percent BIL exposure units in Facility	0.420*** (0.124)	0.468*** (0.093)	...	...
Percent PDL exposure units in Facility	...	...	0.080 (0.065)	0.075 (0.055)
Median household income	−0.288 (0.189)	−0.525*** (0.146)	0.041 (0.108)	0.101 (0.092)
Number legal establishments per household	0.107** (0.049)	0.112*** (0.038)	0.034 (0.029)	0.023 (0.025)
Population density	0.098** (0.045)	0.105*** (0.035)	0.047* (0.028)	0.084*** (0.023)
Year indicator = 1995	−0.080 (0.059)	−0.211*** (0.043)	−0.093*** (0.036)	−0.076** (0.031)
Year indicator = 1996	0.130** (0.056)	−0.112** (0.044)	−0.034 (0.036)	−0.046 (0.032)
Year indicator = 1997	0.063 (0.062)	−0.142*** (0.048)	−0.066 (0.040)	−0.048 (0.035)
Year indicator = 1998	−0.063 (0.066)	−0.496*** (0.051)	−0.066 (0.042)	−0.187*** (0.037)
Adjusted R^2 (percent)	62.7	78.5	33.5	54.2

Source: Authors' calculations based on data from sources listed in table 4-10.
*Significant at the 10 percent level.
**Significant at the 5 percent level.
***Significant at the 1 percent level.
a. The dependent variable in each model is the natural logarithm of the ratio of losses incurred per exposure unit in year t relative to year $t-1$. Except for the year indicator variables, the independent variables are all included in logarithmic form. The model was estimated using weighted least squares with the weight equal to the square root of the number of registered vehicles in the county. Standard errors are in parentheses.

market and the BIL inflation rate is similar in both the voluntary and Facility markets. This outcome could be consistent with the following interpretations. First, the reduced incentives for safety by Facility insureds might increase the number of accidents between themselves and voluntary market drivers, thus driving up the cost for drivers in both markets. This seems like a plausible explanation given the large number of Facility insureds in many counties over this time period (often greater than 40 percent of the market). Second, other structural problems in the county may be driving BIL growth rates higher, and the large size of the Facility market could be the outcome of those problems and not necessarily a causal factor. Based upon conversations with industry officials and after considering other research that has addressed the same question using other data, this second phenomenon seems less likely to be the driver of loss cost inflation and more likely to be the outcome of suppressed rates for certain classes of drivers.[36]

The Facility market share is not significantly related to the growth rate for PDL claims, which differs from the result for BIL. One possible explanation is that the subsidy to the Facility for PDL was not as great as the subsidy for BIL. The difference in subsidy levels could induce insureds to purchase higher BIL limits relative to PDL limits, which would contribute to higher BIL costs.[37] Another possibility is that PDL claims are easier to verify and more difficult to pad than BIL claims. Thus the reduced incentives insurers have to control loss costs may have a smaller impact on the PDL portion of a claim since property damages are less costly to verify.

The log of the number of lawyers per capita is positive and significant in the BIL regressions but not significant in the PDL growth rate regressions. Thus there is some evidence that a greater supply of legal services increases the growth rate of BIL claim costs.

The log of median household income variable is significant only in the BIL growth rate regression for the Facility market, providing only mixed support for the hypothesis that individuals with lower opportunity costs are more likely to engage in excessive claiming behavior. There is no support for the hypothesis that PDL growth rates were higher for counties with higher incomes. Finally, population density is significantly positive in all of the regressions, implying that liability loss costs rose more rapidly in urban areas.

The year indicator variables suggest there was a slight downward trend in loss growth rates consistent with nationwide trends for this time period.

36. See Danzon and Harrington (2000).

37. Butler (1994) finds a similar effect between increases in benefit levels and the growth rates for workers' compensation insurance costs.

The main difference across each model is that the year dummy variables indicate that BIL growth rates in the Facility market experienced a strong decrease in 1998 as the depopulation of the Facility began to accelerate.

FACILITY MARKET SHARE   Our research and that of others suggest that the residual market plays a role in increasing claim costs if its rates are inadequate.[38] Furthermore, as mentioned earlier, the reinsurance mechanism used by South Carolina decreased insurers' incentives to spend money to control loss costs in the claims adjustment process. The next set of regressions examines factors that may have contributed to a higher proportion of vehicles being reinsured through the Facility. Accordingly, we estimate an ordinary least squares regression where the dependent variable for the analysis is the log of the percent of BIL exposures in the Facility. The regression was estimated over the full set of observations by county for the years 1993–98.

The independent variables in our model measure several economic and demographic factors. One question motivating the specification of our model is whether there was a tendency for regulators to compress rates more for lower income areas of the state, which could contribute to a higher Facility market share in these areas. High costs of automobile insurance can induce some drivers to forgo the insurance market and drive as uninsured motorists. Research suggests that subsidizing low-income drivers might enhance efficiency to the extent that it induces them to purchase coverage, eliminating or significantly reducing the externality created by uninsured motorists.[39] We include two variables to test this "income redistribution" hypothesis: the percentage of county population with income below the poverty line and the percentage of county population living in a rural area. We expect positive signs on both estimated coefficients.

Three variables are included to control for high-risk drivers hypothesized to have a greater likelihood of being involved in an accident or in filing a claim: the percentage of the county population that is male, the percentage of the population aged fifteen to twenty-four, and the "serious" crime rate. The crime rate variable equals the number of serious crimes reported to police divided by the population of the county. We expect all three variables to have positive coefficients to the extent that insurers subject to price suppression are unable to charge adequate rates to cover the

38. See Danzon and Harrington (1998).
39. Smith and Wright (1992).

costs associated with underwriting drivers more likely to experience accidents or file claims because of these factors.

The percentage of the population older than sixty-five was also included for two reasons. First, although the number of accidents per miles driven by drivers after age sixty-five tends to increase, older drivers also drive less than younger ones. Thus we predict the number of accidents involving older drivers is likely to be lower, all else equal. Second, it is possible that insurers are less likely to cede older drivers to the Facility to the extent the driver has had a long relationship with the insurer. For both reasons we expect the sign on this variable to be less than zero.

As before, we include year indicator variables to control for year-specific effects. The Facility market share decreased over our sample period as incremental regulatory improvements were made and comprehensive reform legislation was enacted in 1997. Also, consistent with our earlier tests, the independent variables and the dependent variable were estimated in logarithmic form to minimize the potential for outliers to significantly impact the coefficient estimates.

Data from the estimated regression shown in table 4-12 lend support to our hypotheses. Both the log of the percentage of the population living below the poverty line and the log of the percentage of population living in rural areas were strongly positive. This is consistent with our expectation that regulators used the Facility to restrict rates more in rural, low-income areas in an effort to keep insurance affordable for their residents.[40] To the extent that this limited rates for drivers in these areas, they would be recipients of a subsidy. The subsidy would be expected to attract more drivers to the Facility (through designated agents), and the compression of voluntary market rates would prompt insurers to cede more drivers to the Facility.

The log of the percentage of males in the population is positive and statistically significant, consistent with the observation that males tend to be higher risk and the hypothesis that a greater percentage of male drivers would be ceded to the Facility. Interestingly, the log of the percentage of the population age fifteen to twenty-four was negative and significant. One possible explanation for this result, which is contrary to our hypothesis, may be that younger drivers are more likely to forgo any insurance coverage, including coverage in the Facility, to the extent they are "judg-

---

40. However, this does not conflict with the hypothesis that regulators may attempt to limit rates for low-income urban areas. Urban poverty may be a more significant problem in some states and rural poverty a bigger problem in others, such as South Carolina.

Table 4-12. *Size of the Facility Market Regression, All South Carolina Counties, 1993–98*[a]

Independent variable	Coefficient	Standard error	t statistic	p value
Intercept	0.2942	0.2831	1.0394	.2996
Percent population below poverty line	0.4106	0.0283	14.4917	.0000
Percent population in rural area	0.1738	0.0211	8.2255	.0000
Percent population age 15–24	−0.1168	0.0701	−1.6676	.0966
Percent population age 65+	−0.2898	0.0474	−6.1096	.0000
Number serious crimes per population	0.0788	0.0196	4.0300	.0001
Percent population male	1.1398	0.2824	4.0353	.0001
Average premium voluntary/ Facility market ratio	0.8876	0.1262	7.0349	.0000
Year indicator = 1994	−0.0014	0.0258	−0.0547	.9565
Year indicator = 1995	−0.0349	0.0265	−1.3149	.1897
Year indicator = 1996	−0.0386	0.0274	−1.4085	.1602
Year indicator = 1997	0.0049	0.0484	0.1019	.9189
Year indicator = 1998	0.0018	0.0595	0.0305	.9757
Adjusted R^2 (percent)	74.8			

Source: Authors' calculations based on data from sources listed in table 4-10.

a. Dependent variable is the natural logarithm of the ratio of bodily injury exposure units in the Facility divided by the total number of bodily injury exposures in both the voluntary and Facility markets. All independent variables were included in logarithmic form except the year indicators.

ment proof."[41] The percentage of the population age sixty-five or older was significantly negative, consistent with our expectations. The log of the number of serious crimes per capita is significantly positive, supporting the hypothesis that insureds in high-crime areas are likely to have higher loss costs, which induces insurers to cede these drivers to the Facility.

EXCESSIVE CLAIMING AND FRAUD   Next, we investigate why the ratio of BIL claims to PDL claims is relatively high in South Carolina. The average ratio of BIL frequency to PDL frequency over the time period 1983–99 was 59 percent in South Carolina compared to 47 percent for the Southeast region. Our model identifies factors that contributed to the relatively high number of BIL claims in the state. The dependent variable

41. See Shavell (1986).

is the commonly used measure of (the log of) the ratio of BIL to PDL claims. We hypothesize this ratio is affected by variations in the nature of the auto accidents that occur, as well as the tendency for people to file claims, legitimate or not.

A measure of vehicle density is used to control for the types of accidents that occur in a county. Vehicles traveling in densely populated areas are less likely to do so at speeds that would lead to more serious accidents. Since minor accidents are likely to cause only property damage, we expect the ratio of BIL frequency to PDL frequency to be negatively related to vehicle density.[42] Two proxies for vehicle density are tested separately: the number of registered vehicles per capita and the number of registered vehicles per household. Both variables are tested since it is not clear which is the better proxy for the actual density of vehicle miles driven per mile of roadway. The a priori expectation is that both variables will be negatively related to the ratio of BIL to PDL claims.

As discussed earlier, the Facility market share may be positively related to the ratio of BIL to PDL claims as it reduces insureds' incentives to avoid accidents or to avoid filing excessive claims due to restrictions on risk based pricing. In addition, insurers have diminished incentives to investigate questionable claims since they would not benefit from any resulting savings in claim costs. For both reasons we expect the Facility market share to be positively related to the ratio of BIL to PDL claims.

Two independent variables were included to control for the opportunity cost of filing a claim or, in the extreme, of participating in fraudulent claiming behavior: countywide unemployment rate and median household income. We expect a positive sign on the unemployment rate variable (lower opportunity cost of time) and a negative sign on the median household income variable (higher opportunity cost of time).

Finally, we include two variables designed to test the hypothesis that the costs of participating in organized schemes to file auto insurance claims will be lower for individuals who live in tight-knit communities: the percentage of households using a primary language other than English and the percentage of the population living in a rural area. Positive signs on both variables would be consistent with this hypothesis.

Table 4-13 displays the regression results. Of primary interest for this study is the coefficient on the Facility market share variable. The estimated sign is positive and significant in all four regressions, providing additional

42. See Cummins and Tennyson (1992).

Table 4-13. *Excessive Claiming Regression, All South Carolina Counties 1993–98*[a]

Independent variable	Model 1	Model 2	Model 3	Model 4
Intercept	1.8590*	5.5423***	5.0054***	9.0632***
	(0.974)	(1.218)	(1.402)	(1.734)
Unemployment rate	0.0932***	0.1115***	0.1322***	0.1574***
	(0.034)	(0.034)	(0.039)	(0.039)
Number registered vehicles	−0.5657***	...	−0.5017***	...
per capita	(0.127)		(0.123)	
Number registered vehicles	...	0.1193	...	0.1475
per household		(0.178)		(0.176)
Percent population in rural	0.0623**	−0.0163	5.3136***	6.3491***
area	(0.027)	(0.044)	(1.865)	(1.963)
Percent BIL exposure units in	0.5418***	0.5523***	0.4363***	0.4209***
Facility	(0.061)	(0.061)	(0.068)	(0.073)
Percent population with	0.0404	0.0907**	0.0524	0.0975***
primary language not English	(0.035)	(0.037)	(0.034)	(0.035)
Median household income	−0.1592*	−0.4884***	−0.4604***	−0.8329***
	(0.096)	(0.137)	(0.136)	(0.183)
Interaction term:				
(Rural pop.) ×	...	...	−0.5117***	−0.6200***
(Median household inc.)			(0.182)	(0.192)
Year indicator = 1994	0.1181***	0.0921**	0.1136***	0.0879**
	(0.035)	(0.036)	(0.033)	(0.035)
Year indicator = 1995	0.2556***	0.2028***	0.2512***	0.2003***
	(0.037)	(0.040)	(0.037)	(0.040)
Year indicator = 1996	0.2892***	0.2031***	0.2742***	0.1901***
	(0.038)	(0.043)	(0.037)	(0.042)
Year indicator = 1997	0.3847***	0.2663***	0.3505***	0.2318***
	(0.043)	(0.051)	(0.042)	(0.052)
Year indicator = 1998	0.3717***	0.2204***	0.3249***	0.1727***
	(0.050)	(0.062)	(0.049)	(0.064)
Adjusted R^2	0.7154	0.6991	0.7228	0.7108

Source: Authors' calculations based on data from sources listed in table 4-10.
*Significant at the 10 percent level.
**Significant at the 5 percent level.
***Significant at the 1 percent level.
a. Dependent variable is the natural logarithm of the ratio of BIL claims to PDL claims. All independent variables in logarithmic form except year indicators. Standard errors are shown in parentheses.

support for the hypothesis that the Facility reduced incentives for both insureds and insurers to control the filing of BIL claims. The coefficient is economically meaningful because a 10 percent increase in the size of the Facility would lead to a 4 to 5 percent increase in the number of BIL claims filed per PDL claim.

There also is strong support for the opportunity cost hypothesis as the unemployment rate is positive and significant in each regression and the income variable is negative and significant in each regression. There is only mixed support for our hypothesis concerning the costs of organizing excessive or fraudulent claiming behavior in a tight-knit community. The variable concerning percent of population with other than English as their primary language is positive in all four regressions but only significant in the models that use the number of vehicles per household as the vehicle density proxy (models 2 and 4). The percentage of the population living in rural areas is not statistically significant in models 1 and 2. However, this changes when we add a variable for the interaction of median household income and rural population in models 3 and 4. In this formulation the rural population variable becomes significantly positive and the interaction term is significantly negative. Thus it is possible that people living in rural areas are more likely to file claims, all else equal, but this tendency is mitigated as income rises.

Finally, the number of vehicles per capita is negative and significant, consistent with the hypothesis that accidents tend to be more frequent but less severe in areas with higher traffic density. The number of vehicles per household measure is insignificant in both regressions. The difference in results across vehicle density proxies suggests that these measures may be imperfect proxies and that other variables, like the percentage of miles driven in urban areas, might be a better measure of traffic density and more closely correlated with the average speed of automobiles involved in accidents.

DEMAND FOR INSURANCE   The final set of analyses is designed to estimate the relationships between the price of automobile insurance and demand for coverage in the voluntary market and the Facility. As suggested by previous studies, the size of the welfare loss due to the distortion of prices by regulation will depend upon how sensitive the demand for insurance is relative to changes in price.[43] Likewise, attempts to reduce the price of insu-

___

43. Blackmon and Zeckhauser (1991); Jaffee and Russell (1998).

rance can be welfare enhancing to the extent the price reductions encourage uninsured motorists to purchase insurance.[44] Thus it is important to account for consumers' sensitivity to price.

So that our work is comparable with prior research, we use insurance demand equations similar to those employed by Jaffee and Russell.[45] Specifically, the dependent variable in our analysis is the (log) number of insured exposure units per household in either the voluntary market or the Facility. The independent variables are median household income and population density (variables that should be related to the use of alternative transportation) and other variables designed to serve as proxies for the effective price of insurance in both the voluntary and involuntary markets. Price is calculated as the premium per exposure unit for all insurance coverages in either the voluntary or Facility market. All dollar amounts have been converted to real (1998) dollars using the Consumer Price Index.[46]

The results reported in table 4-14 are very similar to those reported by Jaffee and Russell using data from the California auto insurance market. The first two models use the ratio of prices between the voluntary and Facility markets and suggest both markets are sensitive to pricing differences between them. Specifically, the estimated coefficient on the insurance premium ratio in the voluntary market regression is −0.477, suggesting that a 1 percent increase in the ratio between voluntary and Facility market premiums will reduce the amount of insurance purchased in the voluntary market by 0.477 percent. Likewise, a 1 percent increase in the insurance price ratio will increase the amount of Facility market insurance by 1.8 percent. The same elasticity estimates reported by Jaffee and Russell were −0.72 in the voluntary market and 2.3 in the residual market, respectively.

One can draw further insights into the price elasticity of insurance by estimating demand where the prices for voluntary and Facility market insurance are included separately. In the voluntary market regression (fourth column), the own-price elasticity is −0.69 while the Facility market pre-

44. Smith and Wright (1992).

45. Jaffee and Russell (1998).

46. The specification used by Jaffee and Russell is slightly different than the one reported here. Specifically, Jaffee and Russell scale the dependent and income variables by population and not by the number of households. We use households because it seems reasonable to assume that the purchase of automobile insurance is a household decision. In addition, Jaffee and Russell's measure of congestion was the percentage of the population using public transportation. This variable is arguably a better proxy for access to alternative forms of transportation. Unfortunately, we were unable to obtain a similar measure in South Carolina. Finally, our effective premium variables contain all coverages and not just the mandatory BIL and PDL coverages.

mium elasticity is 0.30. Thus a 1 percent increase in the premiums in both markets would reduce by -0.39 percent the amount of private market insurance demanded as indicated by the difference between the two elasticities. Likewise, a 1 percent increase in the premiums in both markets would increase the amount of Facility market insurance by 0.40 percent.[47] A Wald test rejects the null hypothesis of equal elasticities for the two price variables at the 1 and 5 percent levels in the voluntary and Facility market insurance demand regressions, respectively. Thus the results shown in table 4-14 provide further evidence that the demands for insurance in both the voluntary and Facility markets were sensitive to price in the same market as well as the price in the cross-market. In addition, the net effect of price increases in both markets had a significant impact on the amount of insurance purchased in the Facility relative to the amount purchased in the voluntary market.

Conclusions

From the mid-1970s through 1998, South Carolina intensively regulated auto insurance. Rate levels and structures were restricted, insurers' underwriting discretion was limited, and large cross-subsidies were channeled through its residual market. Contrary to political expectations, but consistent with economic theory, these regulatory measures worsened market conditions. The distortion of economic incentives escalated costs and prices and caused the residual market to balloon. All drivers were surcharged to cover residual market deficits, and surcharges were especially severe for insureds with multiple points for driving violations. This led to growing public dissatisfaction with the existing system.

After several earlier attempts failed, the legislature was successful in enacting a comprehensive regulatory reform package that became effective in 1999. South Carolina's prior approval system was replaced by flex rating, and restrictions on risk-based pricing and underwriting were substantially eased. The Reinsurance Facility and its large subsidies are being phased out and replaced temporarily by a JUA and ultimately by an

---

47. Again, these estimates are very close to those shown by Jaffee and Russell (1998). Specifically, they report that the voluntary market insurance own-price elasticity was -0.84 and the cross-elasticity was 0.42. The own-price elasticity in the assigned risk market was -1.9 and the cross-elasticity was 2.5. Interestingly, Jaffee and Russell report the difference between the own-price elasticity and the cross-elasticity was not significant at the 5 percent level in either the voluntary or assigned risk markets.

Table 4-14. *Demand for Insurance Regression, All South Carolina Counties 1993–98*[a]

Independent variable	Voluntary market	Facility market	Voluntary market	Facility market
Intercept	−11.3301*** (0.758)	−1.4427 (1.246)	−8.2022*** (1.230)	−4.9621** (2.043)
Median household income	1.1624*** (0.081)	0.2031 (0.132)	1.0910*** (0.082)	0.2834** (0.137)
Population density	−0.1233*** (0.019)	−0.1655*** (0.031)	−0.1022*** (0.019)	−0.1892*** (0.032)
Ratio: voluntary/Facility market premium	−0.4771*** (0.174)	1.8010*** (0.286)	...	...
Voluntary market premium	...	...	−0.6931*** (0.184)	2.0441*** (0.305)
Facility market premium	...	...	0.3000* (0.180)	−1.6017*** (0.299)
Year indicator = 1994	0.0041 (0.037)	0.0510 (0.060)	0.0020 (0.036)	0.0534 (0.060)
Year indicator = 1995	0.0785** (0.037)	0.0740 (0.062)	0.0614* (0.037)	0.0933 (0.062)
Year indicator = 1996	0.1010*** (0.038)	0.1043 (0.063)	0.0734* (0.039)	0.1354** (0.064)
Year indicator = 1997	0.0986 (0.067)	0.3633*** (0.110)	0.1252* (0.066)	0.3334*** (0.110)
Year indicator = 1998	0.1198 (0.082)	0.4705*** (0.135)	0.1669** (0.082)	0.4174*** (0.137)
Adjusted R^2 (percent)	61.5	32.8	62.8	35.9

Source: Authors' calculations based on data from sources listed in table 4-10.
*Significant at the 10 percent level.
**Significant at the 5 percent level.
***Significant at the 1 percent level.
a. Regression performed using two-stage least squares. Dependent variable is the natural logarithm of the number of earned exposure units, for the particular market, relative to the number of households in the county. The average premium variables equal the total earned premium for all coverages, for the particular market, relative to the number of earned exposure units in the county. All variables, except the year indicators, are included in logarithmic form. Standard errors are shown in parentheses.

assigned risk plan required to charge adequate rates. This means that the hated recoupment fees have been substantially curtailed and will ultimately be eliminated for "clean" drivers. Compulsory liability insurance requirements also have been modified to allow some drivers to meet their obligations through means other than insurance.

With most of the reforms becoming effective in 1999, it is too soon to determine their ultimate outcome, but the early prognosis is positive. The number of insurers writing auto insurance has doubled with the implementation of the reforms. Many insurers have implemented more refined risk classification and pricing structures, as well as alternative policy options for consumers. It also appears that overall rate levels have continued to fall, possibly reflecting declining claim costs as well as the easing of restrictions on risk-based pricing. At the same time, many of the insureds that were previously subsidized are probably paying higher premiums. Most important, the Facility is depopulating rapidly.

References

Abrahamse, Allan F., and Stephen J. Carroll. 1999. "The Frequency of Excess Claims for Automobile Personal Injuries." In *Automobile Insurance: Road Safety, New Drivers, Risks, Insurance Fraud and Regulation,* edited by Georges Dionne and Claire Laberge-Nadeau, 131–49. Boston: Kluwer Academic.

Automobile Insurance Plans Service Office (AIPSO). 2001. *AIPSO Facts, 2000.* Johnston, R.I.

Blackmon, Glenn B., and Richard Zeckhauser. 1991. "Mispriced Equity: Regulated Rates for Auto Insurance in Massachusetts." *American Economic Review* 81 (2): 65–69.

Bureau of the Census. 2000. *Statistical Abstract of the United States 2000.* Washington.

Butler, Richard J. 1994. "Economic Determinants of Workers' Compensation Trends." *Journal of Risk and Insurance* 61 (3): 383–401.

Conning Insurance Research and Publications. 1984. *Shifting Regulatory Priorities for the Property-Casualty Studies Business.* Hartford, Conn.

_____. 1987. *Regulatory Survey of the Property-Casualty Studies Industry.*

_____. 1991. *Regulatory Survey of the Property-Casualty Studies Industry.*

_____. 1994. *1994 Property-Casualty Regulatory Survey: How Far Is the Camel's Nose Inside the Tent?*

Cummins, J. David, Richard D. Phillips, and Sharon Tennyson. 2000. "Regulation, Political Influence, and the Price of Automobile Insurance." Working paper, Georgia State University.

Cummins, J. David, and Sharon Tennyson. 1992. "Controlling Automobile Insurance Costs." *Journal of Economic Perspectives* 6 (2): 95–115.

Danzon, Patricia M., and Scott E. Harrington. 1998. *Rate Regulation of Workers' Compensation Insurance.* American Enterprise Institute.

_____. 2000. "Rate Regulation, Safety Incentives, and Loss Growth in Workers' Compensation Insurance." *Journal of Business* 73 (4): 569–96.

Derrig, Richard A., and others. 2000. "The Effect of Population Safety Belt Usage Rates on Motor Vehicle-Related Fatalities." Working paper. Boston: Massachusetts Automobile Insurance Rating Bureau.

Grace, Martin F., Robert W. Klein, and Richard D. Phillips. 2001. *Auto Insurance Reform: The South Carolina Story.* Georgia State University, Center for RMI Research.

Hanson, Jon S., Robert E. Dineen, and Michael B. Johnson. 1974. *Monitoring Competition: A Means of Regulating the Property-Liability Insurance Business.* Milwaukee: NAIC.

Harrington, Scott E., and Greg Niehaus. 1998. "Race, Redlining, and Automobile Insurance Prices." *Journal of Business* 71(3): 439–69.

Harrington, Scott E., and S. Travis Pritchett. 1990. "Automobile Insurance Reform in South Carolina." *Journal of Insurance Regulation* 8 (4): 422–45.

Insurance Information Institute. 2000. *The Fact Book 2000.* New York.

Insurance Research Council. 1994. *Auto Injuries: Claiming Behavior and Its Impact on Insurance Costs.* Malvern, Pa.

_____. 1999a. *Injuries in Auto Accidents: An Analysis of Auto Insurance Claims.*

_____. 1999b. *Paying for Auto Injuries: A Consumer Panel Survey of Auto Accident Victims.*

_____. 1999c. *Uninsured Motorists.*

Insurance Services Office and National Association of Independent Insurers. 1988. *Factors Affecting Urban Insurance Costs.* New York and Des Plaines, Ill.

Jaffee, Dwight M., and Thomas Russell. 1998. "The Causes and Consequences of Rate Regulation in the Auto Insurance Industry." In *The Economics of Property-Casualty Insurance*, edited by David F. Bradford, 81–112. University of Chicago Press.

Joskow, Paul L. 1973. "Cartels, Competition, and Regulation in the Property-Liability Insurance Industry." *Bell Journal of Economics* 4(2): 375–427.

Klein, Robert W. 1986. "Regulatory Stringency and Market Performance in Private Passenger Automobile Insurance." Ph.D. dissertation, Michigan State University.

_____. 1996. *Preliminary Analysis of Urban Auto Insurance Markets.* Kansas City, Mo.: National Association of Insurance Commissioners (NAIC).

Klein, Robert W., Eric C. Nordman, and Julienne L. Fritz. 1993. *Market Conditions in Workers' Compensation Insurance.* Kansas City, Mo.: NAIC.

National Association of Insurance Commissioners. 1999a. *Profitability by Line by State in 1998.* Kansas City, Mo.

_____. 1999b. *State Average Expenditures and Premiums for Personal Automobile Insurance in 1998.*

Shavell, Steven. 1986. "The Judgment Proof Problem." *International Review of Law and Economics* 6 (1): 45–58.

Smith, Eric, and Randall Wright. 1992. "Why Automobile Insurance in Philadelphia is so Damn Expensive." *American Economic Review* 82 (4): 756–72.

South Carolina Department of Public Safety. 2001. *South Carolina Traffic Collision Fact Book 1999.* Columbia, S.C.

DWIGHT M. JAFFEE
THOMAS RUSSELL

5 Regulation of Automobile Insurance in California

Because auto insurance is a critical consumer service, regulation in this market has a direct and important impact on consumer welfare.[1] In addition, because regulation in this industry occurs at the state level, auto insurance provides a particularly useful laboratory for evaluating the more general effects of regulation and deregulation. In this chapter we evaluate the regulation of California's automobile insurance market.

The study of the effects of regulation is frequently contentious; therefore we note immediately that our conclusions differ substantially from those of others in this volume. Those studies systematically conclude that regulation has created serious damage, deregulation has been highly successful, or both. In contrast, we conclude that although auto insurance has been highly regulated in California since 1988, the effects of this regulation have been benign, our study finding none of the traditional negative effects of regulation.

For providing data and useful comments, we extend special thanks to David Appel; Severin Borenstein; Patricia Born; Herman Brandau, Kenneth Cooley, and William Sirola; Jim Bugenhagen, Laura Dietrich, and Kathryn Tyrrell; Joyce Choy and Shawn Dadah; J. David Cummins; William G. Hamm; and Harvey Rosenfield. None of them, of course, is responsible for any errors on our part.

1. By way of background, we recommend two recent review studies of the auto insurance market, Cummins and Tennyson (1992) and Harrington (2000).

Our analysis is based on the passage of California referendum Proposition 103. This ballot initiative was passed on November 7, 1988, dramatically altering the regulatory environment of the property and casualty insurance industry in the state. Prior to that, California was ranked among the states with the least degree of auto insurance regulation. Passage of Proposition 103 transformed California to a state among those with the greatest degree of auto insurance regulation in the United States.

Although Proposition 103 has components directed at all lines of property-casualty insurance in California, by far its major impact has been on auto insurance. Proposition 103 thus represents a benchmark for state auto insurance regulation in much the same way that the state's earlier Proposition 13 (which limited local government expenditures to a fixed amount of property tax revenue) represents a benchmark for local funding of public expenditures.

The passage of Proposition 103 allows us to carry out an "event study" to contrast the performance of the state's auto insurance market in low and high regulatory regimes.[2] On the surface, Proposition 103 seems ideal for this purpose: more than a decade has passed since its passage, allowing us to observe both the transitory and continuing effects of the new regulatory environment. On closer inspection, however, unraveling the effects of this change is complicated by a number of confounding factors. First, at about the same time the regulatory regime changed, a major California Supreme Court decision, *Moradi-Shalal* v. *Fireman's Fund* (henceforth *Moradi-Shalal*), substantially limited the conditions under which insurance companies could be sued. Second, changes occurred in California's auto safety regulations over the post–Proposition 103 period, the most important being the strict enforcement of seat belt and driving-under-the-influence laws. Thus our analysis attempts to separate the influence of these factors from the effects of Proposition 103 itself.

This chapter examines the behavior of the industry following the passage of Proposition 103. We test three key predictions of economic theory regarding the expected effects of insurance market regulation: firms will exit from the industry, the state's assigned risk pool will expand, and firms in the regulated industry will earn a lower rate of profit. The results of our analysis lead us to conclude that none of the predicted negative effects of

2. Homeowners' insurance in California also faced a major recent crisis as a result of the Northridge earthquake in 1994, an event that leveled a large area near downtown Los Angeles, creating approximately $12 billion in insured losses. For the regulatory impacts of the Northridge quake on homeowners' and earthquake insurance in California, see Jaffee and Russell (2000).

auto insurance regulation occurred in California following the passage of Proposition 103. In this sense the California data and experience are sufficiently unique to suggest that even if most regulation is harmful, benign or good regulation is not an oxymoron.

Proposition 103: The New Regulatory Framework

Although Proposition 103 passed in November 1988, a series of judicial challenges requiring administrative orders delayed its full implementation for several years. However, by January 1995, the key features of the new regulatory environment were all in place.[3] What follows is a brief review of the provisions of the proposition as modified by subsequent judicial and administrative actions.[4]

Premium Rollback

Given the fact that property-casualty insurance was generally viewed as a competitive industry in which policyholder-owned firms held a significant market share, perhaps the most surprising provision of the proposition was its requirement for a premium rollback and freeze. Specifically, for a period of one year—November 1988 to November 1989—all automobile and other property-casualty insurance rates were frozen at 80 percent of their levels on November 8, 1987.[5]

This provision was immediately but unsuccessfully challenged in the courts, and after a number of legal findings and administrative law rulings, in August 1991 Insurance Commissioner John Garamendi issued emergency orders limiting the rebate requirement to those firms that earned in excess of a "fair profit," defined as a 10 percent rate of return. This rate of

3. The date January 1995 coincides with the election of a new pro-industry insurance commissioner, Charles Quackenbush. When Mr. Quackenbush left office in the fall 2000, he faced various accusations, including charges that he had misdirected insurance industry contributions to a nonprofit entity he may have controlled. None of these issues directly involved Proposition 103 or auto insurance.

4. This section draws on "Proposition 103—Main Provisions and Status," found on the web page for the Foundation for Taxpayer and Consumer Rights" (www.consumerwatchdog.org/insurance/fs/fs000324.php3 [July 2001]). See also Rosenfield (1998) for a law review article focused on Proposition 103. Harvey Rosenfield is president of the Foundation for Taxpayer and Consumer Rights, a major sponsor of Proposition 103.

5. Since rates had been rising, the 1987 benchmark would have required a de facto rate rollback of more than 20 percent.

return standard replaced the original proposition wording, which exempted firms only if a rebate "substantially threatened . . . [them] . . . with bankruptcy." The Garamendi orders were again challenged in court, but in August 1994 the California Supreme Court essentially upheld the Garamendi formula.[6] On November 22, 1994, the process of ordering rollbacks finally began.

To date over \$1.2 billion in rebates have been paid. Of the 600 companies affected by the proposition, all but a handful have now settled.[7] Of the state's ten largest insurers (by market share), nine gave rebates (that is, made payments with interest to their customers of 1988 and 1989). In 2000 the largest auto insurer, State Farm, was excluded under the Garamendi rate of return formula.

As a side effect of the proposition, by administrative order all insurance companies that challenged the rollback had their rates frozen. This in effect froze most property-casualty insurance premiums in California for the five-year period from late 1989 (most firms had updated their year-ahead premiums just before the November 1988 election) through 1994.

Prior Approval of Rates

Before 1988 rate changes in California were at the discretion of the insurer. Under Proposition 103 rate increases and decreases have to be justified to the insurance commissioner before they take effect. Subject to certain conditions, rate filings are deemed approved sixty days after public notice. Public hearings are discretionary for increases of less than 7 percent and 15 percent for personal and commercial auto insurance, respectively. The process includes an important role for "public interveners" who argue on behalf of consumers, with their fees paid by the insurance companies. A "fair return" or other rate of return limit is not applied in these prior approval decisions because the rate of return criterion was applied only in the initial Proposition 103 rollback of premiums. No regulations have been issued yet to govern the prior approval process, so applications are handled on an ad hoc basis. However, the newly installed commissioner

6. In *20th Century v. Garamendi* (8 Cal. 4th 216 [1994]), the California Supreme Court ruled that "not only is the rate making formula not inconsistent, it is not confiscatory, discriminatory or demonstrably irrelevant to legitimate policy."

7. Details may be found on the Department of Insurance web page (www.insurance.ca.gov [July 2001]).

in 2000, Harry Low, has announced that a set of proposed regulations will soon be released for comment.

Rate-Setting Formula

Prior to passage of the proposition, insurance companies based auto insurance rates on a number of factors, including the address of the insured. This led to perceived rating anomalies, including cases in which drivers living on opposite sides of a street sometimes faced premiums that differed by a factor of two. Proposition 103 replaced territorial-based or zip code rating with a formula based on three factors: the insured's driving record, number of miles driven, and number of years of driving experience. Other factors were allowed, but only if they could be shown to be statistically associated with risk.

This provision was also subject to legal challenge and eventually administrative interpretation. In September 1996 a set of regulations was issued to govern the setting of rates. The basic spirit of Proposition 103 was preserved though the regulations were far from easy to apply.[8] Most recently, on December 28, 2000, the right to use zip codes was reinstated by the decision of the California 1st District Court of Appeals. The judges held that where a driver lives (not how he drives) is the most important factor in gauging risk and that ignoring this factor makes rates arbitrary. This decision was appealed to the California Supreme Court, which refused to hear the case, so zip codes can now be used for rating auto insurance in California.

Good-Driver Discount

Proposition 103 required that good drivers be offered a discount at least 20 percent below the rate that otherwise would have been charged for coverage; it also required that all good drivers be offered policies. The criteria to be a "good driver" include at least three years of driving experience, no more than one violation point during the previous three years, and no fault in an accident involving death or damage greater than $500. While this may sound fairly innocuous, the "must take all good drivers"

---

8. The exact mechanics of the rating process can be obtained from the California Department of Insurance, "Auto Rating Factor Regulations" (www.insurance.ca.gov/LGL/Arf_regs.htm [July 2001]).

Figure 5-1.

1999 Automobile Insurance Survey

California Department of Insurance

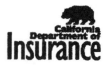

RESULTS

Based on the information you entered, the following profile and results most closely resemble your situation. Please contact a company representative for an actual quote. Please note: THIS IS NOT A PREMIUM QUOTE.

Standard Coverage Married Couple (no children driving), Husband & Wife have no violations or accidents, Berkeley

Company Name	Annual Premium	Company Name	Annual Premium
21st Century:	1,846	Hartford:	2,252
AAA:	2,464	Infinity:	6,996
Allstate:	2,248	Liberty Mutual:	3,395
California Capital:	2,686	Mercury:	2,672
Civil Service Employee:	2,100	Millers Ins:	3,813
Clarendon:	6,132	National General:	3,338
CNA Personal:	2,839	Nationwide:	2,324
Coast National:	2,494	Pacific Specialty:	N/A
Colonial Penn:	2,314	Progressive:	2,243
CSAA:	2,496	Safeco:	1,893
Explorer:	3,264	State Farm:	3,048
Farmers:	6,407	Sterling Casualty:	N/A
Financial Indemnity:	5,004	Superior Ins:	3,033
Fireman's Fund:	3,052	Travcal:	2,846
Galway:	4,039	USAA:	1,941
GEICO:	3,684	Viking of Wisconsin:	6,994
Generali US Branch:	4,032	Wawanesa:	1,663

Profile (32A)

requirement has a substantial thrust, since it limits the ability of the companies to circumvent the three-factor rating plan by refusing to provide insurance to certain consumers.

Other Provisions

Proposition 103 brought about other important changes in California's regulatory environment. First, it required that the insurance commissioner be elected for a term of four years; previously the commissioner had been appointed. The proposition also affected the legal status of insurance companies by removing their exemption from the state's antitrust laws. In addition, California's civil rights and consumer protection laws were extended to the industry, and banks were allowed to sell insurance (over 100 banks are now authorized to do so).

Presumably to prevent firms from leaving the state, insurers were forbidden to cancel policies except under certain specified conditions. The California Supreme Court later ruled that this did not prevent a company from exiting the State in toto.

Finally, Proposition 103 effected a further series of changes: brokers were allowed to discount commissions in order to rebate premiums, groups were permitted to negotiate a rate reduction, and the commissioner was required to provide a comparison shopping data base. With respect to the last, California's Department of Insurance has responded with an outstanding web page, which includes detailed information regarding insurance firms doing business in California, a complaint database, and a comparison shopping quote page that far exceeds in quality anything else available on the web.[9] Figure 5-1 shows a sample output for a quote request in Berkeley.

Taken together, the provisions of Proposition 103 amount to a major shift in the regulatory environment. The rest of our analysis explores the consequences that might be expected to flow from such an increase in regulation and then compares them with the changes that actually occurred.

Predicted Effects of Proposition 103

Because Proposition 103 made widespread changes to the regulatory environment in California, the behavior of insurance firms could be expected to change in a number of ways. Two major provisions were:

9. See www.insurance.ca.gov.

—the premium rollback and subsequent five-year rate freeze, and

—the change from an open rate-setting environment to one of prior approval.

In analyzing the effect of these two changes, we do not assume that the insurance industry "captured" the regulatory environment.[10] The intensity with which the industry opposed Proposition 103—$60 million was spent during the election—suggests that insurance companies saw little opportunity to use the new regulations to their advantage, at least in the short run. Furthermore, election of pro-consumer John Garamendi as insurance commissioner made early capture even less likely. For this reason we interpret these two provisions of Proposition 103 at face value.

Price Rollback and Freeze

Basic economic analysis suggests that the effect of a price rollback depends on the competitive structure of the industry. If firms are earning rents, a price rollback would redistribute these rents to consumers, the classic justification for price controls. A priori, however, there is no obvious reason why the industry should have been earning rents.

Six hundred firms were subject to the rebate requirement, with about half of them writing auto insurance. Moreover, Robert Klein, writing with respect to the industry in 1993 when any anticompetitive results of Proposition 103 should have become evident, concluded that "an analysis of the structure and performance of the personal auto and homeowners markets suggests that both of these markets are fairly competitive at the national and state level."[11] Klein's market share and Herfindahl-Hirschman (HHI) indexes for California are shown in table 5-1.

This conclusion is echoed by Scott Harrington, who states, "Economists generally agree that market structure and ease of entry are highly conducive to competition in auto, homeowners, workers' compensation, and most other property-liability insurance lines." He goes on to say that "most academic economists would agree that those levels of concentration would make noncompetitive pricing behavior a remote possibility."[12]

If we agree that the structure of the industry approximated that of textbook-perfect competition, firms would be making close to a normal rate of

10. For a discussion of this concept, see Stigler (1971), Posner (1974), and Peltzman (1976).
11. See Klein (1995, p. 17).
12. Harrington (2000, pp. 16–17).

Table 5-1. *Market Concentration Indexes for California Auto Insurance*

	CR_4[a]	CR_8	CR_{20}	HHI
Private passenger auto line	56.9	79.2	89.0	1,027
Homeowners line	59.8	72.6	87.3	1,197

Source: Klein (1995).

a. CR_x is the combined market share, based on written premiums of the top x insurer groups. HHI is the sum of the squared market shares of all insurer groups. The Department of Justice guidelines consider a market with an HHI of 1,000 or less to be unconcentrated.

return at pre–Proposition 103 prices. A price rollback would therefore be expected to lower price below long-run average cost and in this way cause exit from the industry. In the textbooks, where firms are identical, all firms would exit. This, of course, is too extreme. In any real world version of long-run equilibrium, some adjustment is always occurring, and some firms, being more efficient than others, will earn rents. These rents would cushion the effects of the price cut, and if they were large enough, they would allow these firms to stay in the industry. Moreover, there are many opportunities for cross-subsidization across lines and states, and this might allow firms to stay if they felt their long-term prospects were good. Finally, as Harrington has noted, state-specific investments would be lost by immediate exit, and this, together with other exit costs, could delay leaving.[13]

However, price cuts of more than 20 percent would be expected to cause at least the weaker brethren among insurers to leave the state, especially since the prospects for future rate increases, once the initial challenge to the rollback was rejected, must have seemed rather bleak. Therefore, the first prediction of standard economic analysis would be a decline in the number of firms writing property-casualty insurance in the state.

The predicted effect of the subsequent price freeze depends on the future path of market prices in the absence of the freeze. Often this counterfactual evidence is not available, but in this case market prices in the rest of the United States do provide one proxy for market prices in California. In fact, these U.S. prices were rising. Based on this proxy, price controls would be expected to lead to availability problems, although it is also important to analyze the comparative loss experience in California and the rest of the United States.

Within the auto insurance industry, availability problems are reflected, often dramatically, in an increase in the number of drivers forced to pur-

13. Harrington (2000, p.35).

chase insurance through the state's assigned risk pool. Therefore, the second prediction of standard economic theory would be expansion in the size of the state's assigned risk pool. The price freeze would also create forces that would be expected to lower the observed rates of return for insurance firms in California. This would be the third prediction of economic theory.[14]

Prior Approval

Compounding these negative effects of price controls, the move to prior approval as enforced by an elected pro-consumer commissioner would be expected to have similar effects. According to Harrington, prior approval with a regulatory lag can be expected to impose "direct costs of administration and costs of compliance; delays in adjusting rates to trends in losses and expenses; greater variation in availability over time; greater variation in insurer profits over time and increased uncertainty for insurers."[15] These costs must eventually be paid by consumers, but in the context of Proposition 103, rates were frozen, so there was no way for firms to pass them on.

To summarize, given the regulatory changes brought about by Proposition 103, economic theory provides three predictions:

—firms will leave the industry,
—availability problems will lead to an increase in the size of the assigned risk pool, and
—rates of return will fall.

We now examine what actually happened.

Firm Entry and Exit

Although the original 20 percent rollback provision was somewhat blunted, over $1.2 billion in rate reductions were eventually made under Proposition 103. As just noted, these price cuts were expected to drive mar-

14. Falling profit rates should be reflected in a decline in stock returns for publicly traded insurance firms with California property-casualty earnings exposure. Some event studies related to Proposition 103 found that this was the case. See Fields and others (1990); Fields, Ghosh, and Klein (1998); Shelor and Cross (1990); Szewczyk and Varma (1990). However, more recent studies failed to find evidence of a declining rate of return. See Grace, Rose, and Karafiath (1995); Brockett, Chen, and Garven (1999).

15. Harrington (2000, p. 32).

Table 5-2. *Firms and Groups Selling Auto Insurance in California, 1984–99*[a]

	Firms				Groups[b]			
Year	Entering	Exiting	Existing year end	Exiting market share[c]	Entering	Exiting	Existing year end	Exiting market share
1984	n.a.	n.a.	296	n.a.	n.a.	n.a.	113	n.a.
1985	34	33	297	4.61	17	18	112	3.953
1986	19	37	279	0.94	13	19	106	0.63
1987	22	29	272	0.90	10	15	101	0.16
1988	21	28	265	1.80	9	17	93	0.44
1989	13	31	247	3.53	7	6	94	1.93
1990	15	12	250	0.27	5	1	98	0.13
1991	16	**44**	222	**2.93**	**14**	**21**	91	0.26
1992	**22**	**32**	212	0.67	**11**	9	93	0.004
1993	**24**	**28**	208	**1.35**	10	**14**	89	0.64
1994	**29**	23	214	0.71	10	7	92	0.50
1995	20	25	209	0.54	5	5	92	0.001
1996	14	15	208	0.26	4	5	91	0.003
1997	20	19	209	0.16	6	5	92	0.15
1998	**31**	3	237	0.07	**15**	1	106	0.000
1999	0	9	228	1.05	8	4	110	0.42
Avg.	20	25	241	1.32	10	10	98	0.62

Source: National Association of Insurance Commissioners (NAIC) data from California Department of Insurance (www.insurance.ca.gov/docs/FS-MarketShare.htm [October 2001]).
n.a. Not available
a. Bold indicates years after 1988 with above average number of exiting or entering firms or groups.
b. A group is one or more firms under common ownership. Each firm is in precisely one group.
c. In percent.

ginal firms out of the market and in this way reduce the size of the industry. Yet in looking at the number of firms and size of the industry after passage of the proposition, there seems to be little evidence that this was in fact the case.

Table 5-2 shows data from 1984 to 1999 for the number of insurance firms and insurance groups with positive insurance premiums in California. The number of insurance firms declines from 265 in 1988 to 208 in 1993. There are a number of reasons, however, why this result is not an indication of firms fleeing California in response to Proposition 103:

—Most of the departing firms were members of insurance *groups*. However, the groups themselves remained active in the California market. For example, from 1988 to 1993, there was a net loss of only four groups from the California market. Furthermore, certain provisions of Proposition 103 provided a motivation for groups to consolidate the number of member firms.[16]

—From 1988 to 1993, a sizeable number of groups also *entered* the California market, and indeed for 1991 and 1992 the number of entrants was above average. Large numbers of new entrants would seem unlikely if Proposition 103 were seen as a harsh regulatory regime being imposed on a competitive industry.

—The market share of the exiting groups was quite small. For example, from 1989 to 1993, the accumulated market share of the exiting groups was only 2.96 percent, and this does not consider the offset from the new entrants over the same period.

—There were economy-wide trends during the late 1980s and early 1990s that caused a number of large insurance groups to leave the auto insurance market in a number of states, not just California. Thus some of the exits should not be attributed to Proposition 103.[17]

—The market shares of the top firms were very stable, as shown in table 5-3.

Overall, we conclude that the pattern of exit and entry in the California auto insurance market following Proposition 103 was well within the normal entry and exit pattern of a competitive industry. The hypothesis that a price rollback and freeze would reduce the number of firms and size of the industry seems to be rejected by the data, all of which point to the perhaps unexpected conclusion that despite Proposition 103, after 1988 it was "business as usual."[18]

16. The motivating provisions were the requirements that "good drivers" receive a discount of at least 20 percent relative to what that firm would have otherwise charged them and that all firms must offer insurance to all good drivers (a take-all-comers requirement for good drivers). Furthermore, since as much as 80 percent of the state's drivers met the good-driver standard, even the high-risk subsidiary of an insurance group was likely to have many good drivers among its customers. After Proposition 103 these drivers could insist that they be transferred to the low-risk subsidiary of the same group so as to benefit from that firm's lower premiums. Groups that attempted to avoid the take-all-good-drivers requirement soon faced lawsuits from the Department of Insurance. In the end the only alternative was to consolidate high- and low-risk subsidiaries so that higher premiums for the previously low-risk customers could offset some of the reduction in premiums for the previously high-risk customers.

17. For example, Travelers withdrew from the California auto insurance market, but it also withdrew from eight other states at the same time. Also, while Aetna was threatening to leave California's auto insurance market, it was actually leaving other states, such as Arizona.

18. A similar conclusion can be found in Viscusi and Born (1999).

Table 5-3. *Written Premium and Market Share by Year, 1987–95*[a]
Units as indicated

Company name	Premium and market share[b]								
	1987	1988	1989	1990	1991	1992	1993	1994	1995
State Farm Auto	915(15.7)	1141(15.9)	1258(16.30)	1319(16.7)	1398(18.1)[c]	1381(18.8)	1355(18.4)	1329(18.3)	1349(17.8)
California State Auto Assn.	588(10.1)	735(10.2)	818(10.6)	877(11.1)	806(10.5)	765(10.4)	762(10.4)	763(10.5)	776(10.3)
Farmers	579(9.9)	661(9.2)	749(9.7)	825(10.4)	834(10.8)	756(10.3)	740(10.1)	879(12.1)	931(12.3)
Allstate	575(9.9)	676(9.4)	841(10.9)	824(10.4)	789(10.2)	683(9.3)	625(8.6)	500(6.9)	461(6.1)
Auto Club of Southern California	544(9.3)	526(7.3)	558(7.2)	589(7.4)	562(7.3)	547(7.4)	544(7.5)	553(7.6)	598(7.9)
Twentieth Century	304(5.2)	365(5.1)	332(5.3)	440(5.6)	475(6.1)	509(6.9)	544(7.4)	542(7.5)	641(8.5)
Mercury Casualty	163(2.8)	206(2.9)	202(2.6)	208(2.6)	178(2.3)[d]	130(1.8)	124(1.7)	108(1.5)	105(1.4)
United Services Auto	157(2.7)	167(2.3)	171(2.2)	172(2.2)	186(2.4)	184(2.5)	177(2.4)	170(2.3)	164(2.2)
State Farm Fire and Casualty	80(1.4)	164(2.3)	178(2.3)	175(2.2)	…[e]	…	…	…	…
GEICO	79(1.4)	77(1.1)	94(1.2)	79(1.0)	62(.8)	60(.8)	37(.5)	54(.7)	55(.7)

Source: California Department of Insurance.

a. Market share shown in parentheses.

b. Premium in millions of dollars; market share in percent.

c. From this year forward State Farm Fire and Casualty was merged with State Farm Mutual.

d. From this year forward Mercury Casualty was split into Mercury Casualty and Mercury Insurance.

Assigned Risk Pool

Because auto insurance is generally required to drive a car, all states have created some form of assigned risk pool, residual market, or joint underwriting agency to provide auto insurance to consumers who have been rejected by the voluntary market. When regulations force automobile insurance premiums below their cost, economic theory predicts that insurance firms will refuse to sell such insurance to customers. These customers will then be forced to become uninsured or enter the residual market. The link between rate suppression and assigned risk pools is made very clear by Harrington: "In short, the best way to ensure availability and therefore a small residual market is to deregulate rates."[19]

Before 1988 California had a large and active assigned risk pool (ARP), and the above analysis would predict that the pool should have expanded after the passage of Proposition 103. The evidence, however, points in the opposite direction. In figure 5-2 the dashed line shows the percentage of all insured cars in California that are in the ARP: the line starts at 5.7 percent in 1988, peaks at 8.4 percent in 1989, and then declines steadily, reaching its low point of 0.3 percent at the most recently available observation in 1998. In short, starting with over 1 million cars at the time Proposition 103 was passed, the pool now has shrunk to approximately 50,000 cars.

We are not suggesting that Proposition 103 created this result; two other factors explain most of this decline. First, there was a nationwide downtrend in the size of ARPs: between 1989 and 1998, the national percentage of all insured cars in ARPs fell from 6.9 percent to 2.3 percent (while California's percentage fell from 8.4 percent to 0.3 percent). Second, in 1991 California raised the average annual premium for its ARP by about 85 percent (from $724 to $1,340). In figure 5-2 this is shown as a steep increase in the ratio of ARP to voluntary market premium. Prior to that rate increase, a substantial number of California's drivers were finding that premiums in the ARP were actually lower than in the voluntary market, so they "volunteered" to join the residual market. After the premium increase, this was no longer true, and the percentage of drivers in the ARP declined sharply, to under 1 percent of all insured cars by 1993.

However, even if the decline in the ARP cannot be claimed as a ben-

19. Harrington (2000, p. 20).

Figure 5-2. *California's Assigned Risk Pool (ARP), 1988–98*

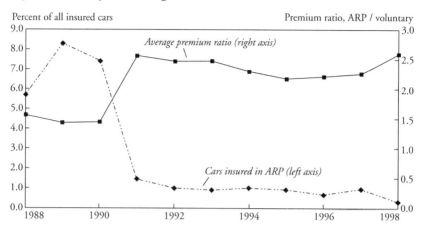

Source: Automobile Insurance Plan Service Office, *AIPSO Facts: A Handbook for the Automobile Insurance Residual Market*, 1993 and 1999 editions.

efit of Proposition 103, there is no evidence of the opposite. In particular, Proposition 103 was already in effect when the premiums in the ARP were almost doubled to reach parity with the voluntary market—not evidence of a clumsy and premium-constraining regulatory mechanism.[20]

On October 10, 1999, California governor Gray Davis signed bills creating the pilot Low Cost Automobile Insurance Program, which is administered by the state's ARP. The program is designed to provide auto insurance to low-income drivers, possibly with the additional benefit that it would reduce the number of uninsured drivers in the state.[21] As of the end of October 2000, only 434 low-income policies had been issued, although tens of thousands of policies were initially expected. In addition, many of these drivers have only switched from higher-cost policies in the standard market. This represents further evidence that California's voluntary insurance market appears to be meeting the needs of most drivers.

20. Moreover, in an October 2000 interview, Director Richard Manning of California's ARP indicated that almost all the drivers now remaining in the ARP would be considered "uninsurable" by almost any standard due to their records for driving under the influence, multiple accidents, and the like. Thus there is no evidence that otherwise insurable risks are being placed in the ARP due to suppressed premiums in the voluntary market.

21. California ranks among the states in the country with the highest proportion of uninsured drivers. Jaffee and Russell (1998) discuss the welfare benefits that can occur when insurance premiums are suppressed in order to reduce the number of uninsured drivers.

Figure 5-3. *Average Insurance Expenditure per Insured Car, California versus the Rest of the United States (USX), 1982–98* [a]

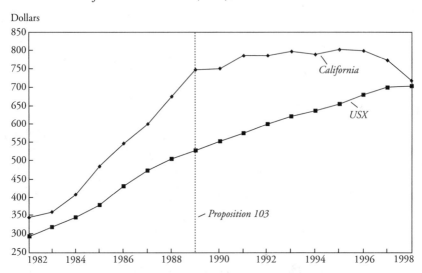

Source: National Association of Insurance Commissioners (NAIC), *State Average Expenditures*, various years; A. M. Best, "Average Auto Premiums by State," *Best's Review*, March 1990, pp. 14, 99–101.

a. The average expenditure is derived by computing total expenditures on all forms of auto insurance (liability, comprehensive, and collision) and then dividing by the total number of insured cars.

Premiums and Profit Rates

The third prediction of economic theory is a decline in the rate of profits during the period in which the price freeze was binding. An immediate question, of course, is whether or not the price freeze in California was binding in this period. To answer this question, we look at the growth in average auto insurance premiums in California relative to those for the rest of the United States (denoted as USX). Figure 5-3 shows summary data for the average insurance expenditure per insured car. For the period *prior* to Proposition 103 (1982–89), the annual growth of California's average premium was 11.70 percent, compared to the average growth in USX of 8.76 percent, indicating a *relative premium growth* for California of 2.94 percent. For the decade immediately *after* passage of Proposition 103 (1989–98), California's relative premium growth is −3.69 percent, meaning that California auto premiums rose significantly less than in the rest of the country.

Figures 5-4 to 5-6 show comparable graphs for each of the components

Figure 5-4. *Average Liability Premium per Insured Car, California versus USX, 1987–98*[a]

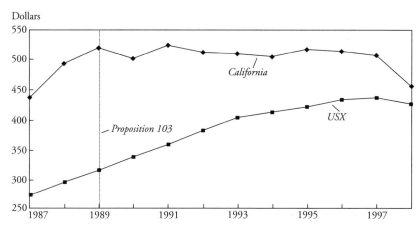

Source: NAIC, *State Average Expenditures.*
a. Without Proposition 103 (1987–89), California's relative growth was 1.86 percent. With Proposition 103 (1989–98), California's relative growth was –4.77 percent.

Figure 5-5. *Average Collision Premium per Insured Car, California versus USX, 1987–98*[a]

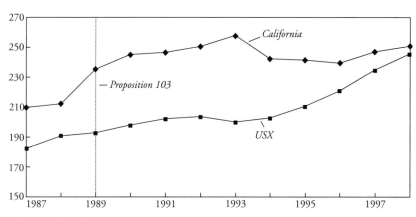

Source: See figure 5-4.
a. Without Proposition 103 (1987–89), California's relative growth was 3.08 percent. With Proposition 103 (1989–98), California's relative growth was –2.00 percent.

Figure 5-6. *Average Comprehensive Premium Insured Car, California versus USX, 1987–98*[a]

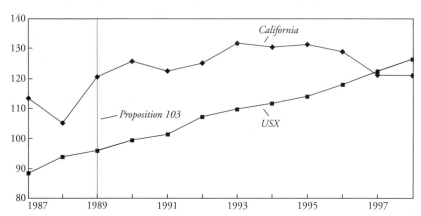

Source: See Figure 5-4.
a. Without Proposition 103 (1987–89), California's relative growth was –0.99 percent. With Proposition 103 (1989–98), California's relative growth was –3.08 percent.

of personal auto insurance: liability, collision, and comprehensive. Each of these graphs starts in 1987, since that is the earliest year for which premium data by component are available. In each case, prior to Proposition 103, the California premium is substantially higher than the equivalent premium for USX. After passage of Proposition 103, the California premium shows significant negative growth relative to the USX premium. Indeed, by 1998 the difference between the California and USX premiums is negligible.

The clear implication of figures 5-3 to 5-6 is that subsequent to the passage of Proposition 103, the auto insurance costs for California consumers fell sharply relative to average costs nationwide. Of course, this coincidence in timing does not necessarily imply a causative link, an issue we examine in the following section. A quantitative measure of this consumer gain can be derived by comparing the actual premiums that occurred in California with an estimate of what California premiums would have been had they followed the same pattern as the national average. These computations are presented in table 5-4.

More precisely, table 5-4 is based on the assumption that, starting with the actual 1989 California premium for any component, the hypothetical premium in each succeeding year is determined by applying the actual annual premium growth rate for USX for that component.[22] In each suc-

---

22. A similar methodology was employed by the National Insurance Consumer Organization (1992), with periodic updates in reports circulated by the Foundation for Taxpayers and Consumer Rights.

Table 5-4. *Hypothetical Auto Premium Savings, 1990–98*
Units as indicated

Component	Premium[a]		Insured cars[b]	Prop. 103 savings[c]
	Actual	No Prop. 103[d]		
Liability				
1990	501.34	554.15	13.22	698
1991	522.95	587.32	13.64	878
1992	510.71	624.75	13.54	1,544
1993	508.05	659.06	13.45	2,031
1994	502.76	673.36	13.87	2,366
1995	514.53	686.57	13.89	2,390
1996	511.14	705.37	14.32	2,781
1997	504.00	709.87	16.45	3,387
1998	452.23	692.15	17.83	4,278
Total liability savings				20,353
Collision				
1990	245.19	241.43	8.48	−32
1991	246.35	246.69	9.54	3
1992	250.32	248.03	9.73	−22
1993	257.50	243.72	9.77	−135
1994	241.68	246.85	10.49	54
1995	240.93	256.25	10.54	161
1996	238.91	268.87	11.00	330
1997	246.33	285.45	11.87	464
1998	249.97	298.41	12.61	611
Total collision savings				1,434
Comprehensive				
1990	125.80	125.01	9.75	−8
1991	122.58	127.42	10.18	49
1992	125.15	135.00	10.39	102
1993	131.76	138.10	10.43	66
1994	130.41	140.48	11.07	111
1995	131.30	143.45	11.20	136
1996	128.91	148.32	11.59	225
1997	121.04	153.89	12.45	409
1998	120.90	158.84	13.10	497
Total comprehensive savings				1,587
Total savings				23,374

Source: NAIC, *State Average Expenditures and Premiums for Personal Automobile Insurance,* 1990, 1996, and 2000 editions.

a. In dollars.

b. In millions.

c. In millions of dollars. Proposition 103 savings = (No Prop. premium − actual premium) × number of insured cars.

d. For 1990 the No Prop. 103 premium equals the growth rate of the corresponding USX component premium times the actual California premium in 1989. For subsequent years the No Prop. 103 premium equals the growth rate of the corresponding USX premium times the computed No Prop. premium of the preceding year (as in a dynamic simulation).

cessive year, the USX growth rate is applied to the computed California premium for the preceding year, in the manner of a dynamic simulation. The initial year of the computation is 1990.[23] The computations are for the three main auto insurance components—liability, collision, and comprehensive.

As shown in the bottom line of table 5-4, total savings for the full nine-year period are over $23 billion. The annual saving in 1998 alone is $5.4 billion, which represents over 42 percent of the actual total auto insurance premiums in California in that year ($12.8 billion). The liability component constitutes by far the major part of the accumulated savings (over $20 billion) because basically all insured cars have liability insurance and because premium savings per insured car for this component were significantly higher both proportionately and in absolute size. Coincidentally or not, the consumer activist groups that promoted Proposition 103 focused on liability insurance costs, since this coverage is required by law.

But where did the transfer of $23 billion come from? For a competitive industry, this transfer, acting as if it were a tax, should lower the rate of return, at least relative to a baseline such as the rate of return in the overall U.S. auto insurance industry. Figures 5-7 and 5-8 show the return on net worth for the liability and physical damage components of auto insurance. Figure 5-7 shows impressive *increases* in the profit rate for liability coverage since 1990 for both California and USX, with an equally impressive *relative increase* for the California industry. As for physical damage coverage, figure 5-8 indicates a major downturn in profit rates since 1990 for both California and USX, but still no significant *relative* decline for California.[24] These data thus fail to confirm the third prediction of standard theory, namely a declining relative rate of return, especially for the important liability component of auto insurance.[25]

---

23. This was the first year that Proposition 103 was likely to have strongly influenced premiums. By the time the proposition passed in November 1988, many companies had already set their premium schedules for 1989, and most firms initially refused to lower their premiums in 1989 as called for in the proposition.

24. Consistent with our finding for California, Bajitelsmit and Bouzouita (1998) find no effect of regulation on profit rates for the U.S. auto insurance industry.

25. As mentioned in an earlier footnote, several event studies indicated that, at the time that Proposition 103 passed and at other key dates, stock market values fell for auto insurance firms with significant business in California, presumably on the expectation of falling profit rates. The results presented here indicate that, in fact, profit rates did not fall.

Figure 5-7. *Return on Net Worth for Liability Component, 1985–1998*[a]

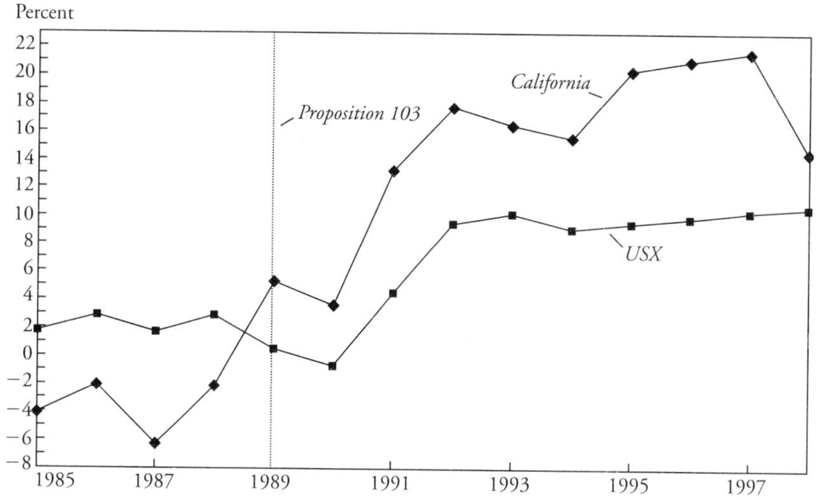

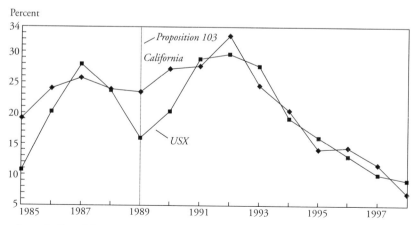

Percent

Source: NAIC, *Annual Statement*, various years.

a. Before Proposition 103 (1985–89), California's relative return on net worth was –3.84 percent. After Proposition 103 (1990–98), California's relative return on net worth was 7.96 percent.

Figure 5-8. *Return on Net Worth for Physical Damage Component, 1985–98*[a]

Percent

Source: See Figure 5-8.

a. Before Proposition 103 (1985–89), California's relative return on net worth was 3.52 percent. After Proposition 103 (1990–98), California's relative return on net worth was 0.66 percent.

Alternative Forces Determining Insurance Premiums in California

The discussion in the previous section demonstrated that following passage of Proposition 103, California auto insurance premiums declined sharply, both absolutely and relative to the levels in the rest of the country. We now investigate a variety of factors that may have caused this phenomenon. The framework for our approach is illustrated by figure 5-9. The variable to be explained is *earned premiums*, shown at the far right of the figure. One step back (to the left) are the *proximate determinants* of earned premiums—incurred losses, underwriting expenses, and underwriting profits. A further step back (in the two leftmost columns) are the *fundamental factors*—those forces that have created the observed trends in the proximate determinants. These determinants and factors are each discussed in turn.

Proximate Determinants of Auto Insurance Premiums

An identity links incurred losses, underwriting expenses, and underwriting profits with auto insurance premiums: It can be applied on a per insured car basis:

$$premiums = losses + expenses + profits,$$

where *premiums* are premiums per car, *losses* are the incurred losses per car, *expenses* are the underwriting expenses per car, and *profits* are the underwriting profits per car, computed as the residual.

Table 5-5 shows the results of applying this equation as a first difference from 1990 to 1998.[26]

The top half of table 5-5 shows the liability component of auto insurance. The relative result (California—USX) shows that California consumers benefited from lower liability premiums while simultaneously the California auto insurance industry achieved higher profits. Lower premiums and higher underwriting profits coincided because the two determinants of insurance costs—incurred losses and underwriting expenses—

---

26. Data for earned premiums are from NAIC, *State Average Expenditure and Premiums for Personal Automobile Insurance*. Incurred losses and underwriting expenses are from NAIC's *Annual Statement* data, which are formatted as ratios to earned premiums. In Table 5-4, we separated physical damage into its comprehensive and collision components. We are unable to do this in Table 5-5 because NAIC's *Annual Statement* data do not provide this disaggregation.

Figure 5-9. *Fundamental Factors, Proximate Determinants and Earned Premiums*

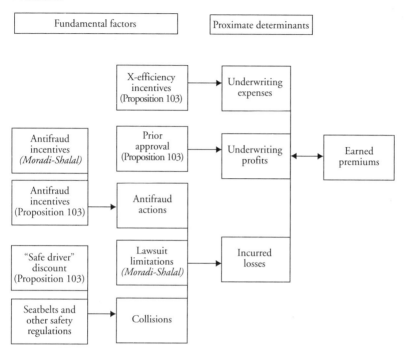

were both falling. The bottom half of table 5-5 shows the physical damage component of auto insurance. Here, too, California consumers benefited from lower insurance premiums, although the relative profits from physical damage underwriting fell slightly. Relative incurred losses and underwriting expenses for physical damage did not decrease to the same extent as they did for the liability component of insurance costs.

In table 5-5 the decline in incurred losses is quantitatively the most important cost determinant for the declining relative insurance premiums. We next consider what fundamental forces may have created this substantial decline in incurred losses.

Collisions and Incurred Losses

A change in the number of collisions is the most obvious factor that may explain the change in incurred losses. The top half of table 5-6, taken from

Table 5-5. *Auto Insurance Premiums and Proximate Determinants, 1990 and 1998*
Dollars unless otherwise indicated

				Change		
	Per insured car		Per insured car		Percent	
Determinants	1990	1998	1990–98	Calif. − USX[a]	1990–98	Calif. − USX
Liability component						
Earned premium						
California	501	452	−49	−133	−9.8	−34.7
USX	339	423	84	...	24.9	...
Incurred losses						
California	381	239	−142	−133	−37.3	−34.1
USX	280	271	−9	...	−3.2	...
Underwriting expenses						
California	189	183	−5	−48	−2.8	−36.6
USX	127	170	43	...	33.8	...
Underwriting profits						
California	−68	30	98	48	nc	nc
USX	−69	−18	50	...	nc	...
Physical damage						
Earned premium						
California	288	306	18	−55	6.3	−18.8
USX	291	364	73	...	25.1	...
Incurred losses						
California	165	197	32	−17	19.4	−7.4
USX	183	232	49	...	26.8	...
Underwriting expenses						
California	92	112	20	−16	22.1	−17.4
USX	92	129	36	...	39.5	...
Underwriting profits						
California	31	−3	−34	−22	nc	nc
USX	16	3	−12	...	nc	...

Source: Authors' calculations based on NAIC, *State Average Expenditures* and *Annual Statement*.
n.c. Not computed because some of the underlying profit values are negative, making the percentage change meaningless.
a. USX, rest of the United States.

table 5-5, shows the percent changes in incurred losses for California and USX over the period 1990–98. The bottom half of table 5-6 provides data on the number of collisions for California and USX during the same period for three categories of collisions. The first category is collisions with fatalities. Between 1990 and 1998, the number of such collisions per insured car decreased 51.1 percent in California and 14.9 percent for USX—an additional decline in California of 36.2 percent. For collisions with injuries only, the additional decline in California was 25.6 percent, and for collisions with property damage only, the additional decline was 17.2 percent.

Overall, these results demonstrate a significant improvement in California's relative driving safety. The data are consistent with a simple model in which relative percentage improvements in driving safety, as measured by reductions in vehicle collisions, are a fundamental force creating comparable reductions in the relative percentage of incurred insurance losses. The data also suggest that this improvement was particularly pronounced for the most severe type of accidents, with the highest and second highest reductions for those with fatalities and injuries, respectively. For the combined category of collisions with either fatalities or injuries, the relative percentage change was −25.8 percent.

Collisions with fatalities or injuries generally create liability claims. It is thus interesting that the percent decline for incurred liability insurance losses (−34.1 percent) actually exceeds the percent decline in fatality or injury collisions (−25.8 percent). This suggests that while driving safety may have been a major influence in lowering incurred losses, other factors may also have played a role, as our discussion below confirms.

In addition to liability claims, collisions generally create physical damage; thus the value for total collisions shown at the bottom of table 5-6 is relevant for comparison with incurred losses for physical damage insurance. Here, in contrast to the liability component, the percent change in relative incurred losses (−7.4 percent) is substantially less than the relative percentage decline in total collisions (−21.2 percent). However, approximately one-third of physical damage losses relate to comprehensive coverage (such as car theft), which is independent of driving safety. Thus we would only expect about two-thirds of the percent decline in collisions to be reflected in physical damage insurance premiums. Although this helps reconcile the relative decline in physical damage premiums with the greater relative decrease in total collisions, other factors also must have played a role—for example, a rising relative cost of repairs for those collisions that did occur.

Table 5-6. *Incurred Losses and Vehicle Collisions, 1990 and 1998*
Units as indicated

	Dollars per insured car		Percent change	
	1990	1998	1990–98	Calif. − USX
Incurred losses				
Liability component				
California	381	239	−37.3	−34.1
USX	280	271	−3.2	...
Physical damage				
California	165	197	19.4	−7.4
USX	183	232	26.8	...
	Number per 1000 insured cars		Percent change	
Type of collision				
With fatalities				
California	0.353	0.172	−51.1	−36.2
USX	0.287	0.245	−14.9	...
With injuries				
California	17.895	10.602	−40.8	−25.6
USX	15.606	13.242	−15.1	...
With fatalities or injuries (subtotal)				
California	18.248	10.775	−41.0	−25.8
USX	15.894	13.487	−15.1	...
With only property damage				
California	23.516	16.297	−30.7	−17.2
USX	33.093	28.632	−13.5	...
Total collisions				
California	41.764	27.072	−35.2	−21.2
USX	48.987	42.119	−14.0	...

Source: National Highway Traffic Safety Administration (1998); California Highway Patrol, *Annual Report of Vehicle Traffic Collisions,* 1998; and table 5-5.

The next step is to consider what fundamental factors might have led to the observed improvements in California's driving safety. Two factors seem important. The first factor is the increasing rate of seatbelt use and other improvements for safe driving (such as better road construction and tougher enforcement of driving-under-the influence [DUI] laws). This factor is independent of Proposition 103. The second factor is the premium structure created by Proposition 103, in particular, the mandated "safe driver" discount, which provides a potentially important financial incentive for safe driving.

SEAT BELTS AND CALIFORNIA'S SAFE DRIVING EXPERIENCE   Over the same time period for which we are evaluating Proposition 103, California was creating and enforcing the most stringent seat belt laws in the United States. Here are some facts about the state's seat belt laws:[27]

> —California's first seat belt use law went into effect on January 1, 1986. Only eight other states had implemented laws earlier (all during 1985).
> —California was the first, and remains one of only fifteen states, with *primary* ("standard") enforcement, meaning that car occupants can be ticketed just for not using seatbelts.
> —California is one of fifteen states that require *all occupants* in the car to wear seatbelts.
> —California is one of ten states with *no exempt classes* of vehicles.

As of 1998, 88.6 percent of California drivers wore seatbelts, compared to a national average of 68.7 percent—a 20 percentage point differential. California had the highest ratio in the country, a position it had maintained since the data were first collected.[28]

A "back of the envelope" computation provides a rough estimate of what percentage of California's low relative collision rate can be attributed to its high relative rate of seat belt use. The established rate of seat belt effectiveness in reducing fatalities and injuries in the United States is about 50 percent.[29] As noted just above, California's seat belt usage rate

---

27. See National Highway Traffic Safety Administration (1998) and other materials available on their web page (www.nhtsa.dot.gov/people [July 2001]).

28. National Highway Traffic Safety Administration (1999b).

29. An excellent source of effectiveness statistics is the National Highway Traffic Safety Administration (1999a). For example, the "official" effectiveness rate for fatalities is 45 percent (p. 12); for moderate injuries, 53 percent (p. 15); and for serious injuries or worse, 67 percent. (p. 17).

is approximately 20 percentage points higher than the national average (88.6 percent versus 68.7 percent). Therefore, about 10 percentage points of reduced injury and fatality rates can be attributed to California's intensive use of seat belts. As shown in table 5-6, in 1998 the number of collisions with fatalities or injuries in California was below the USX average by about 20 percentage points (= 1 − [10.8/13.5]). Thus about 50 percent (10 percentage points out of 20) of California's reduced rate of collisions with fatalities or injuries can be attributed to its greater use of seat belts.

Two other factors may explain the remaining 50 percent of California's reduced rate of collisions. First, California has been a leading state in reducing driving under the influence of alcohol. Second, the state made significant improvements in the safety of its roadways during the 1990s.[30] These factors, however, are not easily evaluated with a "back of the envelope" computation. Instead, a pooled, cross-state, time series regression analysis is the proper method for evaluating the impact of all aspects of improved driving safety (including greater seat belt use) on incurred insurance losses. Such a study, of course, would have to control for all other systematic influences on incurred losses (including regulatory regime, number of miles driven per car, and so on). Although cross-sectional auto insurance studies do exist, they are not in a form that can answer our specific questions.[31] We hope to carry out such a study in the near future.

PREMIUM STRUCTURE AND PROPOSITION 103   As noted earlier, Proposition 103 requires that auto insurance be provided to all drivers who meet its "good driver" criteria and that the premium charged such good drivers be at least 20 percent less than what the insurance firm would have otherwise charged them. Thus, as a result of this premium incentive, Proposition 103 might well have the effect of creating safer drivers. It is noteworthy that previous studies do find that drivers are sensitive to insurance premiums when deciding whether to own a car, or if they own a car,

---

30. We do not consider air bags because cars in all states share the same air bag features, and thus the effects of air bags should be reflected in the national data that we are using as our baseline. In fact, to the extent that California's benign climate creates an older stock of autos, the air bag effect might actually work in reverse.

31. For cross-sectional auto insurance studies, see Cummins and Weiss (1991, 1992), Grabowski, Viscusi, and Evans (1989), and Harrington (2001).

whether to insure it.[32] There is even direct empirical evidence that financial incentives encourage safer driving.[33] More complete conclusions regarding the effects of Proposition 103 incentives on safe driving, however, would require a new pooled, cross-state, time series regression analysis, as just described.

Of course, incentives for safer driving created by regulatory actions are not necessarily welfare enhancing. The problem is that while consumers will respond to the good-driver premium incentives by driving more safely, the benefit in reduced insurance claims may not be worth the perceived costs of safer driving. On the other hand, there may also be social externalities to safer driving—for example, fewer innocent, third-party injuries and fatalities. Thus, from a technical perspective, it is an open issue whether the safe driver components of Proposition 103 are welfare enhancing. Nevertheless, it seems fair to conclude that any increases in driver safety possibly induced by Proposition 103 are likely to be judged by the public as unequivocally beneficial.

Reducing Auto Insurance Fraud and Dissipative Expenses

We now consider a second set of factors, different from driving safety, that may explain the absolute and relative declines in California's incurred insurance losses during the post-Proposition 103 period. Harvey Rosenfield, for example, argues that Proposition 103 effected a significant decrease in fraudulent claim payments and in dissipative expenses.[34] His key assumption is that, prior to Proposition 103, auto insurance premiums were based on a "cost pass-through" system, in which the costs of fraud and dissipative expenses were simply passed through to insurance premiums. Then, when Proposition 103 placed a ceiling on premium levels, the firms had to control fraud and their expenses in order to maintain their profits levels.

Rosenfield reinforces his case by comparing the observed profit rates of

---

32. Blackmon and Zeckhauser (1991); Jaffee and Russell (1998). Further evidence is available in California, as well as in some other states, since drivers that receive a moving violation may have the option to take eight hours of driver education in order to remove the violation from the driving record that is made available to insurance companies. Through direct observation the authors can confirm that many individuals with apparently high hourly opportunity costs attend these classes, suggesting that they expect to avoid a significant increase in their auto insurance costs as a result.

33. Cummins and Weiss (1999); Dionne, Gourieroux, and Vanasse (1999).

34. Rosenfield (1998, p. 121).

the insurance industry in California to the rest of the country. As shown in figures 5-7 and 5-8, no significant decline occurs in the relative rate of return earned by California's auto insurance industry, and, in fact, a significant absolute and relative increase in the rate of return occurs in the liability component of the industry. These results are particularly consistent with significant savings from antifraud activity if fraud occurs primarily with liability claims. This is plausible because it is much easier for an insurance firm to verify a physical damage claim than one for pain and suffering.

In making this argument, it is essential to explain why insurance firms did not find it in it their best interest to control fraud and expenses even before the passage of Proposition 103. A possible mechanism for this effect is based on the consumer ill will that an insurance firm may elicit when it falsely accuses a customer of fraud. This, in turn, may create a "bad equilibrium" in which all firms in the industry ignore insurance fraud to avoid the reputation for falsely accusing their customers. In this situation it is possible that a major regulatory change such as Proposition 103 may push the system toward an alternative "good" equilibrium, in which all firms in the industry fight fraud and reduce dissipative expenses.

Data on the amount of auto insurance fraud would, of course, provide a quantitative estimate of the effectiveness of antifraud activities, but we are unaware of any direct measurements. Available empirical studies provide evidence concerning fraudulent claims by looking at indirect or proxy measures of fraud.[35] For example, the ratio of the number of bodily injury liability (BIL) claims to the number of property damage liability (PDL) claims is sometimes proposed as a fraud index.[36] The idea is that fraud most commonly arises with BIL claims, whereas PDL claims provide a baseline for the number of real accidents.

Figure 5-10 shows this ratio for California and USX. The BIL/PDL claim ratio for USX rises slowly during the 1980s and early 1990s, then stabilizes in the late 1990s. The California BIL/PDL claim ratio, in contrast, rises steeply until about 1991; then it declines equally sharply, reaching about the same value in 1999 as it had in 1983.

It is tempting to associate the decline in California's BIL/PDL claim ratio after 1991 with the passage of Proposition 103, but there are two confounding factors that make the proper interpretation of figure 5-10 difficult. First, California's rising rate of seat belt use during the 1990s

35. Abrahamse and Carroll (1999); Caron and Dionne (1999); Crocker and Tennyson (1999); Cummins and Tennyson (1996); Weisberg and Derrig (1991).
36. Cummins and Tennyson (1996).

Figure 5-10. *Ratio, Bodily Injury to Physical Damage Claims per 100 Insured Cars, 1983–99*

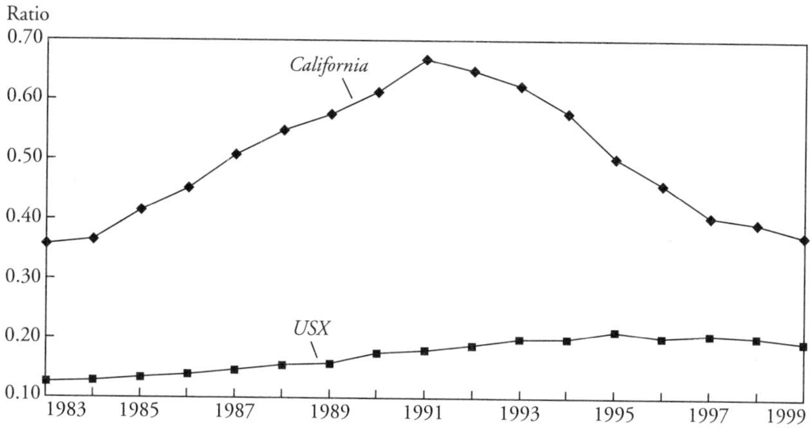

Ratio

Source: National Association of Independent Insurers, Fast Track data.

would also create a declining pattern for the BIL/PDL claim ratio, since seat belts sharply reduce bodily injuries but do not reduce property damage. Second, in figure 5-10 both the rising pattern in the 1980s and the falling pattern in the 1990s are fully consistent with a California Supreme court decision (*Moradi-Shalal*), which had its effect just about 1990 and which eliminated a whole class of bodily injury lawsuits against insurance companies. (See subsequent discussion.) Thus the BIL/PDL claim ratio would provide useful information on antifraud activity only if it were used as the dependent variable in a cross-section regression analysis, in the form suggested earlier, with proper controls for the other factors that may have influenced the ratio.

At this time there is only anecdotal evidence, but it strongly suggests that antifraud activities in California have significantly reduced the amount of auto insurance fraud in the last ten years. For example, the largest category of press releases on the web page of California's Department of Insurance refers to cases of auto insurance fraud that have been apprehended. Given the possibility that auto insurance fraud has significantly declined, it is certainly plausible that Proposition 103 may have provided the impetus.

In addition to its possible effect in controlling fraud, Proposition 103 may also have contributed to an across-the-board cost-cutting exercise within the insurance industry. With firms facing a de facto freeze on premiums, control of costs became essential for preservation of profits. As table 5-5 shows, underwriting expenses declined sharply in relative terms between 1990 and 1998.

The view that firms do not always operate at minimum cost was first suggested by Harvey Leibenstein[37] (1966). More recent work has found evidence consistent with the "x-efficiency" view that firms grow fat (with respect to costs) when they grow wealthy.[38] In this view, firms cut costs when they are in economic distress, and to the extent that a freeze in premiums created economic distress, we would expect firms to try hard to control both underwriting expenses and fraud.

Third-Party Lawsuits and Related Legal Issues

Another important factor may explain the absolute and relative declines in California's incurred auto insurance losses since 1988. In the *Moradi-Shalal* v. *Fireman's Fund* case of 1988, the California Supreme Court reversed its earlier 1979 decision in *Royal Globe Insurance Company* v. *Superior Court* and denied third parties the right to sue insurance companies for bad faith damages.[39] Furthermore, the *Moradi-Shalal* ruling continues in force today, although challenges from the consumer activist community also continue. For example, two referendum proposals restoring the right to sue another person's insurer were offered in the March 2000 election (Propositions 30 and 31), but both failed, each receiving only about 25 percent of the votes. Unfortunately for researchers, the timing of *Moradi-Shalal* coincides almost exactly with the passage of Proposition 103, confounding the role each played in the decline of incurred losses for auto insurance in California.

In a recent paper, the Foundation for Taxpayer and Consumer Rights has actively argued that the *Moradi-Shalal* case has sharply reduced liability claims paid by auto insurance companies in California.[40] The ratio of bodily injury liability to property damage liability claims in California (figure 5-10) shows the thrust of the evidence, namely that bodily injury

---

37. Leibenstein (1966).

38. Severin Borenstein, and Joseph Farrell, "Do Investors Forecast Fat Firms? Evidence from the Gold Mining Industry," draft, July 12, 1999.

39. 46 Cal.3d 287 (1988) and 23 Cal.3d 880 (1979), respectively. The injured third party always has the right to sue the primary party that created the injury. Given that the insurance firm has much deeper pockets, the right to sue the insurance firm directly is much more valuable.

40. Foundation for Taxpayer and Consumer Rights, "The Low-Balling of the California Auto Insurance Claim" (www.consumerwatchdog.org/insurance/rp/rp000156.pdf [July 2001]).

claims have fallen sharply since about 1991. Data on the frequency and the average size of claims as well as the number of auto insurance lawsuits all show a very similar pattern. This trend is certainly consistent with the view that while the *Royal Globe* case in 1979 opened the floodgates to more and larger bodily injury claims, the *Moradi-Shalal* case in 1988 closed them. The problem, however, is that the same evidence is broadly consistent with a reduction in bodily injury claims due to either safer driving or fewer fraudulent claims.

It is also a matter of major debate in California whether the *Moradi-Shalal* decision represents good public policy. The Foundation for Taxpayer and Consumer Rights argues that the decision allows the insurance industry to "low ball" or reject claims unfairly, which would conform with the downward trend shown in figure 5-10 and other similar evidence. The insurance industry, in contrast, argues that the decision has acted as a strong deterrent against fraudulent claims, consistent with the same evidence.

Our interest in the current context, however, is focused on whether or not the *Moradi-Shalal* decision represents another major factor, alongside safer driving and fewer fraudulent claims, that can explain the sharp relative decline in California's incurred insurance losses, and thereby the decline in California's auto premiums. William Hamm performed a pooled, cross-state, time series regression analysis on behalf of the insurance industry to provide evidence against Propositions 30 and 31.[41] Using average liability premium as the dependent variable, this study found that reductions in average premiums up to14.5 percent could be attributed to *Moradi-Shalal.* On the basis of this evidence, our preliminary conclusion is that the *Moradi-Shalal* decision does represent an important third factor.[42]

Profit Margins

Up to this point, this discussion has focused on a set of factors, such as improved driving safety and constraints on third-party lawsuits, that reduced the costs faced by auto insurance firms. We now consider the extent to which the cost reductions were actually passed through to consumers in the form of lower premiums.

41. Hamm (2000).

42. We hope to obtain further information about this issue from our own cross-state regression analysis, planned for the near future, which will also focus on incurred losses and accidents as dependent variables.

To the extent that the prior approval provisions of Proposition 103 slowed down the pass-through of reduced costs, profit margins in the industry would rise. Since underwriting profits are one of the proximate determinants of premiums (see figure 5-9), an increase in profit margins would cause premiums to fall by less than they would have if the industry had remained unregulated. This possibility that regulation causes margins to increase during a period of falling costs has been noted by a number of authors.[43] This margin-increasing mechanism is based on the time lag between rate filing and rate approval, a lag that holds up prices during a period of falling costs.[44] However, it could also be the product of firms' reluctance to reduce premiums by the full amount when costs are falling, because if their costs rise in the future, they might have difficulty obtaining regulatory approval for an increase in premiums.[45]

The evidence supporting the regulatory lag hypothesis is mixed. Studies by Scott Harrington and Gregory Niehaus and by Sharon Tennyson found evidence that current inverse loss ratios for automobile insurance have a larger dependence on lagged values in states with prior approval. However, an analysis by Barbara Stewart found that prior approval regulations had little or no effect on loss ratios in commercial lines.[46]

The evidence for California is presented in figure 5-11, using dollar profit margins (earned premiums − [incurred losses + underwriting expenses] per insured car).[47] Consistent with the regulatory lag hypothesis, dollar profit margins rose more in California than in the rest of the country throughout the period after prior approval.[48] By 1998 the relative profit margin in California was higher than in the rest of the nation by approximately $50.

43. See, for example, Harrington (1984), Cummins and Outreville (1987), Tennyson (1993), and Fung and others (1998). An excellent review may be found in Harrington and Niehaus (2000).

44. This possibility is relevant only to the liability component of California auto insurance since underwriting costs for the physical damage component were steadily rising during the 1990s.

45. This cost averaging requires a noncompetitive industry in the short run. Given the costs of entry and exit, it is certainly possible that firms would not have incentive to take advantage of the short-term rents.

46. Harrington and Niehaus (2000, p. 681); Tennyson (1993); Stewart (1984).

47. Profit margins are also commonly computed as (price − average cost)/price, that is, as a percentage profit margin. The percentage profit margin must be used when computing an aggregate profit margin for a multiproduct firm, since dollar profit margins are not comparable across different products. We believe that the dollar profit margin is appropriate for our current case with average auto insurance premiums. However, we have performed comparable computations based on the percentage profit margin and obtain very similar results.

48. Since our intent is to compare the profit margins of California and the rest of the United States, we have not included investment income because it would not be a differentiating factor.

Figure 5-11. *Dollar Profit Margins, Liability Component, 1990–98*[a]

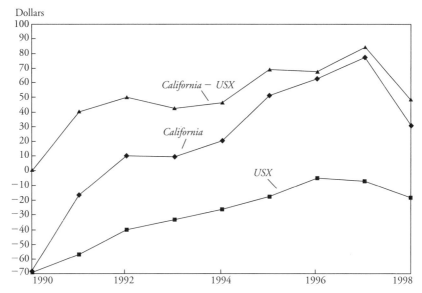

Source: Authors' calculations based on data from NAIC, *State Average Expenditures* and *Annual Statement*.
a. Dollar profit margins = earned premiums – (incurred losses + underwriting expenses) per insured car.

Taken at face value, figure 5-11 is consistent with the hypothesis that Proposition 103 created a positive regulatory component in California auto insurance premiums, raising the premiums approximately $50 per insured car—more than 10 percent of the average premium paid in 1998. However, the regulatory lag hypothesis is not the only explanation for these data. As Emilio Venezian noted, the behavior of profit margins in the U.S. insurance industry also supports an extrapolative forecasting model in which recent past losses are used as a basis for forecasting future losses.[49] Venezian's model uses an estimation period of three years and an extrapolation period of two years, and shows that this generates a second-order autoregressive process for margins with a period of about six years.[50] When industry forecasts of losses are extrapolative, a state such as California, with a drop in costs relative to the average, will see its profit margins rise.

49. Venezian (1985).
50. To be sure, this forecasting methodology fails to satisfy the canons of full information rational expectations forecasting. It may be worth pointing out, however, that naive extrapolative forecasting models seem to describe forecasting behavior even of professional forecasters of corporate earnings. See Darrough and Russell (2002).

How much of the increase in profit margins is due to regulatory lag and how much is due to industry forecasting methods is still an open question. With enough years of data, a regulatory change such as Proposition 103 provides the perfect experiment to measure this. Under the regulatory lag hypothesis, the passage of Proposition 103 would be expected to change the value of the coefficients in the second-order autoregression scheme, which is known to characterize the time series behavior of the profit margin. In the absence of such data, and given the very limited understanding of why insurance margins behave cyclically in the first place, we see no scientific basis at this time for quantifying the effects of Proposition 103 on margins.

Lower Quality Auto Insurance

There is still another way that the predictions of economic theory regarding regulation might be reconciled with the apparently successful changes that actually occurred in California's auto insurance market: a reduction in the quality of insurance. Declining premium levels and rising industry profit rates can occur under increased regulation if the quality of the underlying insurance product is falling at the same time. Unfortunately, we are unaware of any dependable direct measure of insurance quality. However, what data are available do *not* confirm any significant decline in auto insurance quality over the last decade.

First, on the anecdotal level, little or no public attention appears to be directed to the issue of declining insurance quality. For example, the web page of the Foundation for Taxpayer and Consumer Rights—the major consumer activist group opposing the auto insurance industry—allocates a great deal of space to the level of auto insurance premiums and to legal limitations such as *Moradi-Shalal*, but it makes no reference at all to insurance quality.

Second, although data on industry expenses in California, as shown in table 5-5, do indicate declining absolute expenses (for the liability component) or at least declining relative amounts (for the physical damage component), the magnitudes are small compared to the declines in direct losses incurred. Furthermore, there are no grounds for attributing the declining expenses to lower insurance quality rather than, as suggested in the previous section, to a reduction in dissipative expenses.

Third, on the special web page maintained by California's Department of Insurance (DOI) for auto insurance complaints, the counts are remarkably low. Specifically, the DOI publishes a "justified complaint ratio," derived from the number of annual complaints that the DOI has judged to be justified divided by the number of exposures (policies). For the fifty largest auto insurance companies in 1998, the aggregate complaint ratio was 0.000053, which is to say 0.0053 percent or 5.3 complaints per 100,000 exposures.[51] This appears to be a very low complaint ratio, certainly consonant with the general lack of public attention to this issue.

Overall, we do not feel that a declining level of auto insurance in California is a significant factor in understanding the sharply declining auto premiums and incurred losses (both absolute and relative) in California over the last ten years.

Summary: Factors Determining Insurance Premiums

We have investigated an extensive list of factors that may be responsible for the significant decline in both absolute and relative auto insurance premiums in California during the 1990s. We focused on the sharp decline in incurred losses in auto liability insurance as the major proximate determinant of the declining premiums, and then considered what factors may have created the sharp decline in incurred losses.

Two key factors independent of Proposition 103 have been identified: greater driving safety (with a focus on increased seat belt use) and elimination of third party lawsuits against insurance companies for bad faith (the *Moradi-Shalal* case). We estimate that, roughly, 50 percent of the relative decline in collisions with injuries or fatalities is due to greater seat belt use, and up to 14.5 percent of the relative decline in auto insurance premiums is attributable to *Moradi-Shalal.* At this time, we are unable to quantify the impact of other forms of increased driving safety, such as reductions in DUI and more safely designed roadways. Our analysis also identified two key factors directly linked to Proposition 103 that could account for some of the decline in incurred liability insurance losses. The first factor is the good-driver discount required by Proposition 103, which provides a strong financial incentive for safer driving. The second factor is the proposition's constraint on premium levels, which created an incentive for insurance firms to enforce more aggressive antifraud programs and otherwise reduce dissipative expenses in order to maintain their profit rates.

Finally, our analysis identified one factor, an increase in profit mar-

---

51. This has been computed by adding up the total number of complaints for the fifty companies and dividing by the total exposure of these companies. The DOI shows only the fifty largest companies in a single table, although the complaint ratio can be called up for any specific firm writing auto insurance in California. See "2000 Consumer Complaint Study" (www.insurance.ca.gov/docs/FS-ComplaintStudy.htm [July 2001]).

gins, that would tend to raise, not lower, auto premiums in California. This factor may be linked to the prior approval provisions of Proposition 103, but there is currently no quantitative assessment of this effect.

Conclusion

There is a widespread presumption among economists that, good intentions aside, regulation of a competitive industry frequently distorts market incentives and thus ends up doing more harm than good. In the context of insurance markets, the harm to consumers is thought to arise from a number of factors. For example, by holding prices down, prior approval regulation is thought to cause firms to exit the market, reducing availability and forcing consumers into incentive-challenged assigned risk pools. Prior approval is also thought to increase costs in other ways that ultimately lead to increases, not decreases, in premiums.

Contrary to the standard expectation, our analysis shows that none of the commonly predicted negative effects of regulation seem to have arisen from the 1988 passage of Proposition 103 in California. Indeed, taking post–Proposition 103 industry performance at face value (in comparison with the average U.S. performance), the effects of the regulatory regime introduced by this proposition seem to have been remarkably benign.

The problem, however, is that industry performance after a regulatory shift cannot be taken at face value. Regulatory shifts take place within a general economic environment, and changes in this environment can easily have just as much impact on industry performance. For example, the partial deregulation of the electricity industry in California in 1996 was followed by a period of unexpectedly large input price increases. Within this new environment, the failure to deregulate the retail price of electricity undid the benefits of the partial deregulation. Had input prices fallen, as most industry experts expected, the deregulation experiment might well be judged very positively today.

As we have shown, the regulation of auto insurance in California took place against a background of sharply falling loss costs, an input environment exactly the opposite of that for energy. In this case, the regulation of premiums by prior approval becomes quite consistent with declines in premiums and increases in profits, and the ceteris paribus predictions of economic theory no longer hold.

Here then is the fundamental scientific challenge: how to separate the effects of the regulatory shift from those of the simultaneous change in the economic environment? Our analysis isolated two major contemporaneous changes in the insurance industry in California. At approximately the same time the industry was adapting to Proposition 103, there were major improvements in California's driver safety record, which resulted from strict enforcement of seat belt and DUI laws and possibly other factors. Meanwhile, the legal environment changed significantly when the *Moradi-Shalal* decision ended the right of third parties to sue insurance companies for bad faith settlements. Both of these environmental changes had the effect of reducing loss costs: the safety improvements decreased the frequency and severity of accidents, and the *Moradi-Shalal* decision facilitated the control of fraud.

As discussed earlier, it would require a careful cross-state analysis of the determinants of premiums and losses to disentangle the effects of all these factors. In this chapter we have conducted only a partial analysis of the relative effects of the regulation and the environment, and based on this we find:

—no evidence of the "traditional" adverse consequences to be expected from Proposition 103, such as firm exit, an expanding assigned risk pool, or declining industry profit rates;

—Proposition 103 may have had a positive effect by encouraging safer driving (through the incentive of the required safe driver discount for insurance premiums) or by causing firms to control fraud and dissipative expenses (improving x-efficiency) by limiting their ability to pass such costs on to their customers;

—Proposition 103 may have had a detrimental effect on auto insurance premiums by increasing profit margins.

Taken together, these findings suggest that drivers in California have little to regret from the passage of Proposition 103 and the regulatory regime it introduced.

References

Abrahamse, Allan, and Stephen Carroll. 1999. "The Frequency of Excess Claims for Automobile Personal Injuries." In *Automobile Insurance: Road Safety, New Drivers, Risks, Insurance Fraud, and Regulation*, edited by Georges Dionne and Claire Laberge-Nadeau, 131–49. Boston: Kluwer Academic.

Bajitelsmit, Vickie L., and Raja Bouzouita. 1998. "Market Structure and Performance in Private Passenger Automobile Insurance." *Journal of Risk and Insurance* 65 (3): 503–14.

Blackmon, B. Glenn, and Richard Zeckhauser. 1991. "Mispriced Equity: Regulated Rates for Auto Insurance in Massachusetts." *American Economic Review* 81 (2): 65–69.

Brockett, Patrick L., Hwei-Mei Chen, and James R. Garven. 1999. "A New Stochastically Flexible Event Methodology with Application to Proposition 103." *Insurance: Mathematics and Economics* 25 (2): 197–217.

Caron, Louis, and Georges Dionne. 1999. "Insurance Fraud Estimation: More Evidence from the Quebec Automobile Insurance Industry." In *Automobile Insurance: Road Safety, New Drivers, Risks, Insurance Fraud, and Regulation*, edited by Georges Dionne and Claire Laberge-Nadeau, 175–82. Boston: Kluwer Academic.

Crocker, Keith, and Sharon Tennyson. 1999. "Costly State Falsification or Verification: Theory and Evidence from Bodily Injury Liability Claims." In *Automobile Insurance: Road Safety, New Drivers, Risks, Insurance Fraud, and Regulation*, edited by Georges Dionne and Claire Laberge-Nadeau, 120–30. Boston: Kluwer Academic.

Cummins, J. David, and Francois Outreville. 1987. "An International Analysis of Underwriting Cycles in Property-Liability Insurance." *Journal of Risk and Insurance* 54(2): 246–62.

Cummins, J. David, and Sharon Tennyson. 1992. "Controlling Automobile Insurance Costs." *Journal of Economics Perspectives* 6 (2): 95–113.

———. 1996. "Moral Hazard in Insurance Claiming: Evidence from Automobile Insurance." *Journal of Risk and Insurance* 12 (1): 29–50.

Cummins, J. David, and Mary A. Weiss. 1991. "The Effect of No Fault on Automobile Insurance Loss Costs." *Geneva Papers on Risk and Insurance* 16 (1): 20–38.

———. 1992. "Incentive Effect of No Fault on Automobile Insurance: Evidence from Insurance Claim Data." In *Contributions to Insurance Economics*, edited by Georges Dionne, 445–70. Norwell, Mass.: Kluwer Academic.

———. 1999. "The Incentive Effects of No Fault Automobile Insurance." In *Automobile Insurance: Road Safety, New Drivers, Risks, Insurance Fraud, and Regulation*, edited by Georges Dionne and Claire Laberge-Nadeau, 283–308. Boston: Kluwer Academic.

Darrough, Masako, and Thomas Russell. 2002. "A Positive Model of Earnings Forecasts." *Journal of Business* (forthcoming).

Dionne, Georges, Christian Gourieroux, and Charles Vanasse. 1999. "Evidence of Adverse Selection in Automobile Insurance Markets." In *Automobile Insurance: Road Safety, New Drivers, Risks, Insurance Fraud, and Regulation*, edited by Georges Dionne and Claire Laberge-Nadeau, 13–46. Boston: Kluwer Academic.

Fields, Joseph, Chinmoy Ghosh, and Linda S. Klein. 1998. "From Competition to Regulation: The Six-Year Battle to Regulate California's Insurance Markets." *Risk Management and Insurance Review* 1 (2): 54–71.

Fields, Joseph, and others. 1990. "Wealth Effects of Regulatory Reform: The Reaction to California's Proposition 103." *Journal of Financial Economics* 29 (Nov./Dec.): 233–50.

Fung, Hung-Gay, and others. 1998. "Underwriting Cycles in Property and Liability Insurance: An Empirical Analysis of Industry and By-Line Data." *Journal of Risk and Insurance* 65 (4): 539–61.

Grabowski, Henry, W. Kip Viscusi, and William Evans. 1989. "Price and Availability Tradeoffs of Automobile Insurance Regulation." *Journal of Risk and Insurance* 56 (2): 275–99.

Grace, Elizabeth V., Lawrence C. Rose, and Imre Karafiath. 1995. "Using Stock Return Data to Measure the Wealth Effects of Regulation: Additional Evidence from California's Proposition 103." *Journal of Risk and Insurance* 62 (2): 271–85.

Hamm, William. 2000. *The Economic Effect of Propositions 30 and 31.* Emeryville, Calif.: Law and Economics Consulting Group (January 13).

Harrington, Scott E. 1984. "The Impact of Rate Regulation on Prices and Underwriting Results in the Property-Liability Insurance Industry: A Survey." *Journal of Risk and Insurance* 51 (4): 577–623.

_____. 2000. *Insurance Deregulation and the Public Interest.* AEI-Brookings Joint Center for Regulatory Studies.

_____. 2001. "The Effects of Prior Approval Rate Regulation of Auto Insurance." Paper presented at the conference on Insurance Rate Regulation: A View from the States, AEI-Brookings Joint Center for Regulatory Studies, January 18, 2001.

Harrington, Scott E., and G. Niehaus. 2000. "Volatility and Underwriting Cycles." In *Handbook of Insurance,* edited by Georges Dionne, 657–86. Boston: Kluwer Academic.

Jaffee, Dwight, and Thomas Russell. 1998. "The Causes And Consequences of Rate Regulation in the Auto Insurance Industry." In *The Economics of Property-Casualty Insurance,* edited by David Bradford, 81–112. University of Chicago Press.

_____. 2000. "Behavioral Catastrophe Insurance: The Case of the California Earthquake Authority." Paper prepared for NBER Insurance Conference, Cambridge Mass., February.

Klein Robert. 1995. "Market Structure and Performance in Personal Auto and Homeowner's Insurance." *NAIC Research Quarterly* 1 (1): 13–29.

Leibenstein, Harvey. 1966. "Allocative Efficiency versus X-efficiency." *American Economic Review* 56 (June): 392–415.

National Highway Traffic Safety Administration. 1998. "Standard Enforcement Saves Lives: The Case for Strong Seat Belt Laws. Section IV: Successful Examples." (www.nhtsa.dot. gov/people/injury/airbags/seatbelt/ [July 2001]).

_____. 1999a. *Fourth Report to Congress: Effectiveness of Occupant Protection Systems and Their Use.* Department of Transportation. May 1999.

_____. 1999b. "1998 State Shoulder Belt Use Survey Results." Research Note. (www.nhtsa.dot.gov/people/ncsa/1998userates.html [July 2001]).

National Insurance Consumer Organization. 1992. *A Consumer Triumph: Proposition 103 Revisited.* Alexandria, Va.

Peltzman, Sam. 1976. "Toward a More General Theory of Regulation." *Journal of Law and Economics* 19 (August): 211–40.

Posner, Richard A. 1974. "Theories of Economic Regulation." *Bell Journal of Economics* 5 (2): 335–58.

Rosenfield, Harvey. 1998. "Auto Insurance: Crisis and Reform." *University of Memphis Law Review* 29 (Fall): 69–135.

Shelor, Roger M., and Mark L. Cross. 1990. "Insurance Firm Market Response to California Proposition 103 and the Effects of Firm Size." *Journal of Risk and Insurance* 57 (4): 682–90.

Stewart, Barbara D. 1984. "Profit Cycles in Property-Liability Insurance." In *Issues in Insurance,* edited by John D. Long and Everett D. Randall, 273–334. Malvern, Pa.: American Institute for Property and Liability Underwriting.

Stigler, George. 1971. "The Theory of Economic Regulation." *Bell Journal of Economics* 2 (1): 3–21.

Szewczyk, Samuel, and Raj Varma. 1990. "The Effect of Proposition 103 on Insurers: Evidence from the Capital Market." *Journal of Risk and Insurance* 57(1): 671–81.

Tennyson, Sharon L. 1993. "Regulatory Lag in Automobile Insurance." *Journal of Risk and Insurance* 60 (1): 36–58.

Venezian, Emilio. 1985. "Ratemaking Methods and Profit Cycles in Property and Liability Insurance." *Journal of Risk and Insurance* 52: 477–500.

Viscusi, W. Kip, and Patricia Born. 1999. "The Performance of the 1980s California Insurance and Liability Reforms." *Risk Management and Insurance Review* 2 (2): 14–33.

Weisberg, Herbert, and Richard Derrig. 1991. "Fraud and Automobile Insurance: A Report on the Baseline Study of Bodily Injury Claims in Massachusetts." *Journal of Insurance Regulation* 9 (4): 497–541.

COMMENT ON CHAPTER 5

David Appel

Dwight Jaffee and Thomas Russell (JR) have written an interesting and provocative paper. It is provocative in the sense that it provides a striking contrast to the fairly persistent finding that stringent price regulation in competitively structured markets tends to produce inefficiencies and market failures. It is also surprising in that it finds that a regulatory policy fashioned in the voting booth—by only the slimmest of margins—ultimately confers massive benefits on both consumers and insurers. According to the results reported by JR, Proposition 103 appears to have increased insurer profits, lowered accident rates, and also provided consumers $23 billion in savings over the past decade.

In contrast to these unabashed benefits, many economists would predict that such a regulatory policy would likely impose significant cross-subsidies and lead to large welfare losses. This traditional view is difficult to reconcile with the one proposed by JR. In this brief comment I provide some data and observations that may help to do so.

Prices and Costs of Auto Insurance

I will focus primarily on the finding that consumers have saved $23 billion due to the passage of Proposition 103, since this is perhaps the most dramatic result reported by JR. To reach this conclusion, JR assume that absent Proposition 103, the annual rate of change in auto insurance premiums in California would have equaled the rate of change in the United States excluding California (USX).[1] Since auto premiums in USX increased by approximately 33 percent between 1989 and 1998, while in California they were relatively stable (decreasing by approximately 10 percent in the last year), the savings have been substantial. This is shown graphically in figure 1.

Figure 1 shows annual premiums for auto liability insurance in both

1. In this final version of the paper, JR are somewhat more circumspect about the causes of the apparent savings than they were in the original draft. However, while they allow for the possibility that cost decreases in California explain much of the "savings," they continue to report the computations suggesting that Proposition 103 was indeed a binding constraint on insurance rate increases in California during the past decade.

Figure 1. *Average Written Liability Premium per Insured Car-Year,*
1989–98

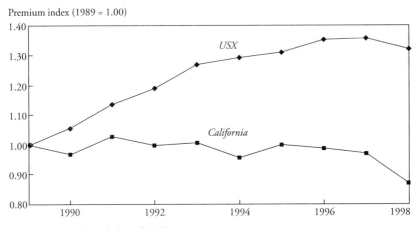

Premium index (1989 = 1.00)

Source: Insurance Research Council (2000).

California and USX, expressed as an index (1989 = 1.00). (I restrict my
analysis to liability insurance, since that coverage represents nearly 90
percent of the estimated $23 billion of savings.) As can be seen, premi-
ums in USX have indeed increased regularly over the past decade, while
in California they have been fairly level, with a small decline in the most
recent year. To compute annual dollar savings, JR take the product of
the difference between the indexes (expressed in dollar terms) and the
number of insured vehicles per year. As noted, this is equivalent to the
assumption that but for Proposition 103, auto insurance premiums in
California would have increased at the same rate as in the rest of the
nation.

My initial response is that this finding is inconsistent with the views
of industry observers in California, who argue that absent Proposition
103, rates in California would have declined more quickly than they actually did.[2] The logic behind this argument is that since insurers believed
that rate rollbacks were imminent, territorial rating was about to be abolished, and rate increases might be difficult or impossible to achieve under
the new prior approval regulatory regime, they failed to take rate decreases

2. I have been personally involved in a substantial amount of the litigation surrounding Proposition 103 and have also represented insurers in regulatory proceedings in California since the enactment of the law. My comments are, of course, conditioned on this experience.

when cost conditions indicated these were appropriate. In my view there is substantial evidence to support this hypothesis.

Standard actuarial and economic principles indicate that insurance rates should be cost based, that is, premiums should be set to cover the costs that policyholders impose on insurers, with an appropriate margin to compensate insurers for the risk they bear. Furthermore, when markets are either competitively structured or reasonably contestable (for example, minimal entry barriers and adequate potential competition), prices tend to be cost based, as theory would predict. As many of the chapters in this volume indicate, there is little evidence that insurance markets would fail to achieve these competitive outcomes absent rate suppression or the threat of confiscation by regulators.

In contrast to these fundamental pricing principles, I argue that auto insurance markets in California failed to reflect completely declining cost conditions in the state during the post–Proposition 103 period. If this hypothesis is correct, consumers in California will have suffered a welfare loss due to the imposition of strict prior approval regulation. Figures 2 through 4 show loss costs and premiums for California and USX during the post–Proposition 103 period.

Figure 2 is analogous to figure 1, showing indexes of liability loss costs per insured vehicle in both California and USX for the period 1989 through 1998 (1989 = 1.00). Notice that for USX, liability loss costs per vehicle increased at a roughly constant rate over the decade, with the 1998 value nearly 30 percent higher than the 1989 value. This cost increase is consistent with the cumulative rate increase of approximately 33 percent over the same period shown in figure 1. However, in California the situation is somewhat different: although costs increased in the first year, they then leveled off and began a rather steady decline, resulting in a cumulative 20 percent decrease in costs over the decade. This decline was not, however, matched by commensurate premium decreases during the 1990s: as shown in figure 1, California rates remained relatively constant through the decade, except for a 10 percent decline in 1998.

Figures 3 and 4 highlight these contrasts. In figure 3, USX cost and premium levels are shown together, and as expected they follow very similar patterns: rates increase over time as costs increase. Note the difference in figure 4, however, which displays patterns in California. Costs increase initially, but beginning in 1991 they start a sustained decline that is not accompanied by comparable rate decreases.

It might be argued that even absent changes in the regulatory environ-

Figure 2. *Average Liability Loss Cost per Insured Car-Year, 1989–98*

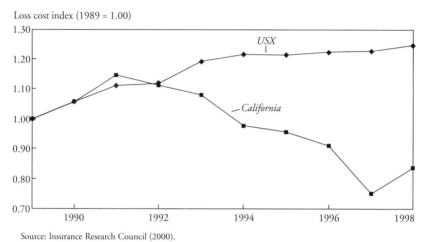

Loss cost index (1989 = 1.00)

Source: Insurance Research Council (2000).

Figure 3. *Loss and Premium per Insured Car-Year, United States except California, 1989–98*

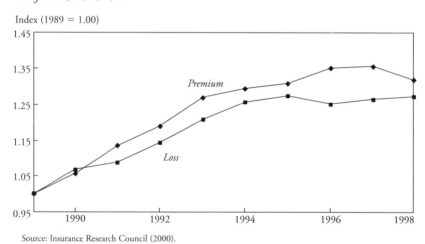

Index (1989 = 1.00)

Source: Insurance Research Council (2000).

ment, the observed cost decreases through most of the 1990s would not have produced rate decreases in California. For example, if rates of return in the period before 1993 had been inadequate, the patterns noted above might be consistent with a normal return over the entire decade—substandard returns in the first half of the period offset by supranormal returns in

Figure 4. *Loss and Premium per Insured Car-Year, California, 1989–98*

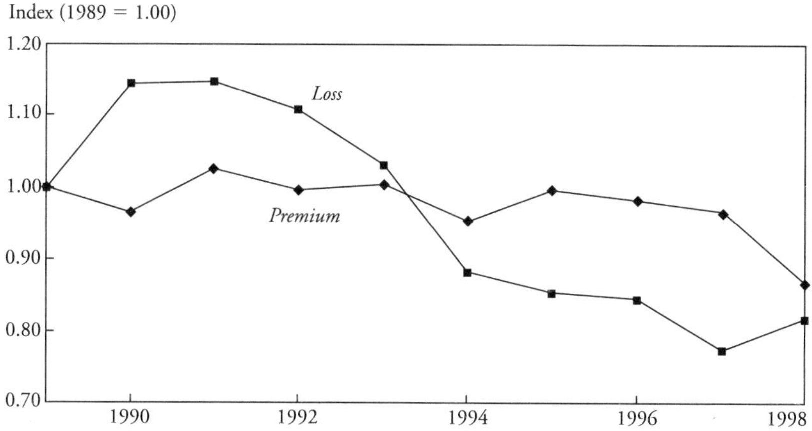

Index (1989 = 1.00)

Source: Insurance Research Council (2000).

the latter half. Under such circumstances the relative stability of rates in California might be understandable.

The facts, however, do not support such an interpretation. As JR show in their paper, profit margins in California exceeded those in USX at the beginning of the Proposition 103 period and then increased relative to the rest of the country throughout the decade.[3] I believe this is prima facie evidence that the regulatory environment induced insurers to defer rate reductions in response to declining costs; in effect, insurers retained the increased profits as a hedge against future regulatory risk.

Such behavior on the part of insurers can be seen as a rational response to the increased uncertainty associated with the Proposition 103 regulatory regime.[4] As evidence of this uncertainty, note JR's comment that "no regulations have been issued yet to govern the prior approval process, so applications are handled on an ad hoc basis." This is despite the fact that the insurance department began to hold hearings about rating factors as early as 1990. In addition, for more than a decade after the passage of

3. JR are more circumspect about attributing the increase in profit margins to lags induced by Proposition 103.

4. The hypothesis that Proposition 103 increased uncertainty for California insurers is consistent with the results of event studies such as those of Fields, Ghosh, Kidwell, and Klein (1990) and others cited in footnote 14 of JR.

Proposition 103, insurers were faced with the prospect that territorial rate making would be prohibited, severely limiting their ability to achieve adequate rates.[5] Under such circumstances the failure to reduce rates in response to declining costs is perhaps understandable.

Determinants of Auto Insurance Cost Reductions

What caused the improvement in California's loss costs in the first place? JR hypothesize that some of the effect may be due to the passage of Proposition 103, particularly the good-driver discount and take-all-comers provisions; however, they acknowledge that testing such a hypothesis would be confounded by the coincidence of several other developments with the passage of the initiative.[6] While they hesitate to quantify the impact of these two factors precisely, JR suggest that in combination they might be responsible for approximately two-thirds of the decline in costs.[7]

I would note several points with respect to the good-driver discount. First, JR claim that the incentive effects of a discount for safe driving could have substantially reduced accident rates and injury costs in the state. The good-driver discount stipulates that anyone classified as a good driver must receive a discount of 20 percent and may not be denied coverage by any insurer. Since the definition of a good driver was sufficiently liberal to include more than 90 percent of the drivers in the state, most drivers' rates in fact declined only negligibly.[8] That is, in order to comply with the law, insurers tended to raise their basic rates by about 20 percent so that the discount merely brought good-driver rates back to initial levels.

5. As noted by JR, one provision of Proposition 103 specified the order in which variables were to enter the rate-making process and restricted the ability to rate on a territorial basis. This provision, which was widely viewed as an attempt to impose cross-subsidies from rural to urban areas, was strongly opposed by insurers. On January 4, 2001, the California Appellate Court upheld a ruling permitting territorial rating, stating that "unrefuted evidence establishes that territory is a more important determinant of the risk of loss than any other single factor." This ruling appears to put to rest nearly thirteen years of appeals on this matter. See Ron Panko, "Calif. Appellate Court Upholds Territory as Insurance Rating Factor," *BestWire* (A.M. Best wire service), January 4, 2001.

6. These include a 1988 California Supreme Court decision, *Moradi-Shalal* v. *Firemans Fund,* that limited the right to sue insurance companies for bad faith, as well as increased enforcement of the state's seat belt law. For evidence on the impacts of seat belt laws, see Derrig and others (2002).

7. Specifically, JR suggest that 50 percent of the reduction in the rate of auto accidents in California can be attributed to increased seat belt use, and they claim that cost reductions of perhaps 14.5 percent are attributable to the *Moradi-Shalal* case.

8. Hunstead (1995). Hunstead indicates that 92 percent of all drivers qualified for the good-driver discount.

Of course, incentive effects depend only on the existence of a rate differential, not on whether an individual's rate actually declines. However, California is hardly the only state in which significant penalties for a bad driving record (or discounts for a good record) exist. In most states insurance companies apply tiered rating plans, which provide discounts for "preferred risks"—that is, drivers with favorable records. Such discounts can vary widely but typically range from about 10 to 25 percent of premium, or amounts similar to the discounts in California.[9] It would also be instructive to look at the experience of other jurisdictions that have experimented with penalties for bad driving records, since in some cases surcharges far in excess of 20 percent will have been imposed for various driving infractions.[10] One wonders whether such punitive rules had a salutary impact on accident costs in those states.

In any event, as JR acknowledge, testing the efficacy of good-driver discounts requires estimating a model of insured accident costs using a pooled cross-sectional time-series data set, with appropriate independent variables to control for many of the factors that affect accidents and claims. This would include, of course, a variable that adequately measures the safe driving discounts that are available either through state mandates (as in California) or through market mechanisms (as in virtually all other states). In addition, if the model intends to explain auto insurance rates, it should properly focus on *insured* accident costs, not just accident rates, since auto insurance premiums are not always highly correlated with auto accident rates.

One may wonder why insurance premiums are not necessarily highly correlated with accident (or fatality) rates, and in general the answer lies in differential claim behavior on the part of insured drivers. It is well known that in some states insurance costs are driven by aggressive claim filing and a willingness to build up claim costs so as to exceed certain thresholds, thus permitting recovery of noneconomic damages associated with auto injuries. California in the late 1980s and early 1990s was, in fact, such a jurisdiction. Evidence is found in the relationship between bodily injury and property damage liability claims.

Typically, an auto accident involving two vehicles results in a property damage liability (PDL) claim; therefore PDL claims are a reasonable proxy for accident frequency across insured drivers. However, not all accidents

9. This assessment is based on my review of preferred, standard, and nonstandard auto rate filings.

10. For example, New Jersey experimented with the DIP (Driver Improvement Program) in the 1990s.

Figure 5. *Frequency of Bodily Injury Liability to Property Damage Liability Claims, 1985–98*

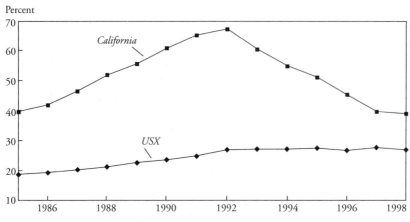

Percent

Source: Insurance Research Council (2000).

give rise to bodily injury liability (BIL) claims; only in the case of personal injury should such claims be filed. Thus, all other things being equal, the ratio of BIL to PDL claims is an indicator of the aggressiveness of claiming behavior on the part of drivers. In addition, this ratio is widely used as an indicator of the potential for fraud in the insurance system.[11]

If one reviews the history of this ratio in California and in the United States excluding California during the relevant time frame, a potential explanation for the cost reductions in California emerges. Figure 5 shows BIL claims expressed as a percentage of PDL claims. As is evident from the graph, that ratio was increasing steadily in California throughout the 1980s and into the early 1990s. It peaked in 1992, at a level approximately two and a half times the USX average, and then began a fairly dramatic, steady decline that continued for the remainder of the decade. By contrast, in USX the BIL-to-PDL ratio continued to increase throughout the decade. To the extent that elevated levels of this ratio fairly proxy fraud and claiming behavior, one would expect costs to have declined in California, relative to the rest of the nation, from 1992 on.

For evidence on cost changes, review figure 2. This graph shows that liability costs per insured vehicle in California did in fact peak in 1991 and declined steadily thereafter, a finding that is entirely consistent with the

11. Cummins and Tennyson (1992).

BIL-to-PDL ratios shown above. Equally consistent is the experience in USX, where the BIL-to-PDL ratio increases, and loss costs per insured vehicle also increase continuously through the decade.

JR hypothesize that the declining costs in California are in some way related to Proposition 103, since the price caps imposed under the law would have induced insurers to control costs and more fully address fraud. However, given that the cost decline began at least three years after the passage of Proposition 103, one might question whether the price controls associated with the initiative actually engendered the observed savings. Also, while this was a period of intense focus on insurance fraud in California, JR provide no evidence that it was in response to the rate rollback and freeze. If anything, the data would seem to support a finding that the increase in antifraud activity was a response to the continuing escalation in fraud, as evidenced by the increasing BIL-to-PDL ratio.[12]

Other Issues

The principal focus of my comments has been on putative savings to consumers. However, I would note that this chapter raises a number of other issues that are related directly to Proposition 103 and to rate regulation more generally.

Residual Market

JR note that contrary to the predictions of economic theory, the residual market in California did not grow in response to the rate caps imposed by Proposition 103. This is not at all surprising in light of the fact that residual market rates were increased by approximately 85 percent after the passage of the initiative, a point noted by JR.[13] That fact, combined with the take-all-comers and good-driver discount provisions of Proposition 103, suggests that the residual market would shrink significantly.

12. During the same time period in California, there was a significant amount of attention directed to workers' compensation fraud, which was viewed as an equally important problem. This increased attention to insurance fraud in general would likely have affected the attitude toward auto fraud as well.

13. JR claim that the 85 percent rate increase in the residual market shows that under Proposition 103 there is "not evidence of a clumsy and premium-constraining regulatory mechanism." I would note that assigned risk rates in California were specifically excluded from Proposition 103 and that rate approval standards for ARP rates were different from those under the proposition (in particular, the ARP rates must be actuarially sound, a provision that does not appear in the language of Proposition 103).

Rate Cross-Subsidies

As noted earlier, one of the most important provisions of Proposition 103 was that it required insurers to use a specific, hierarchical order of rating variables in the determination of the individual insured's premium. I would argue that those provisions (which required safety record, miles driven, and years of experience to dominate any other rating variables) were intended to remove territory from the rate determination process. Since expected costs for urban drivers clearly exceed those for rural drivers, such rules would ultimately impose significant cross-subsidies from rural to urban consumers. In considering the social welfare implications of a regulatory scheme such as Proposition 103, it is critical to attempt to measure (or at least to identify) the extent of the welfare losses associated with such rules.[14]

California Workers' Compensation

It is interesting to note that while California was transitioning from being the least regulated to one of the most regulated auto insurance systems in the country, its workers' compensation system was moving in exactly the opposite direction—from the most to the least regulated state. It would be instructive for JR to look at the workers' compensation experience for a test of the benefits of deregulation. For example, in the year preceding the deregulation of the workers' compensation market in California, employers paid roughly $4.33 per $100 of payroll to insure their workplace injury exposure, while two years after deregulation that cost had fallen by more than 45 percent, to $2.34 per $100 of payroll.[15]

Conclusions

As I said at the outset, Jaffee and Russell have written a most provocative paper, challenging the conventional wisdom that increased regulatory control in an otherwise competitive market leads to unfavorable economic outcomes. I believe they have much more work to do, however, to prove their point. Most important, they have to consider the cost side of the

14. It is fair to say that the procedures ultimately adopted by the insurance department did permit territory to enter into the rate determination process.
15. Workers' Compensation Insurance Rating Bureau (2000).

insurance equation and control for as many determinants of costs as possible before concluding that regulation has produced benefits for consumers. To their credit, JR recognize this and indicate several times that they are proceeding along that path, to estimate a cross-sectional time-series model of insurance prices and costs. I look forward to the results of their study.

References

Cummins, J. David, and Sharon Tennyson. 1992. "Controlling Automobile Insurance Costs." *Journal of Economic Perspectives* 6: 95–115.
Derrig, Richard A., and others. 2002. "The Effect of Safety Belt Usage Rates on Motor Vehicle Related Fatalities." *Accident Analysis and Prevention* 34 (forthcoming).
Hunstead, Lyn. 1995. "Measuring and Modifying the Effects of Auto Rating Factors." *Journal of Insurance Regulation* 14 (2): 159–87.
Insurance Research Council. 2000. *Trends in Auto Injury Claims: 2000 Edition.* Malvern, Pa.
Workers' Compensation Insurance Rating Bureau. 2000. *California Workers' Compensation Accident Year Experience.* San Francisco.

STEPHEN P. D'ARCY

6 | *Insurance Price Deregulation: The Illinois Experience*

One of the primary advantages of state regulation of insurance is the opportunity it presents for experimentation with different forms of regulation. Most of these experiments are planned, during which a state adopts a specific form of regulation in order to accomplish certain specified goals. Others are more serendipitous, where the exact form of regulation was not specifically intended. This is the case in Illinois, where there is currently no specific rating law applicable to auto insurance. How this situation arose, how the current system operates, and the effectiveness of allowing competition to determine auto insurance rates are covered in this chapter. However, a brief review of the history of insurance regulation is first necessary to provide an understanding of the circumstances that led to the Illinois experience.

History of Insurance Regulation

Insurance regulation arose in this country long before the federal government became actively involved in regulatory activities and even before

The author wishes to thank Robert Litan and David Cummins for their support and guidance on this project. Other individuals who have provided assistance with this project include Rep. Shirley Bowler, Martin Grace, Anne Gron, Scott Harrington, Robert Heisel, Roger Kenney, Rodger Lawson, Phil O'Connor, Judy Pool, Gary Ransom, Dick Rogers, and Sharon Tennyson.

the United States was formed. An early example of regulation was the charter granted in 1752 by the Commonwealth of Pennsylvania to Ben Franklin's Philadelphia Contributorship for the Insurance of Houses from Loss by Fire. This charter provided specific requirements that the company had to meet and served as a form of regulation by legislation.[1] The lag between payment of a premium and receipt of services, combined with the contingent nature of the services, created a situation in which regulation was felt necessary to assure the consumer that the promised benefits would, in fact, be paid. In most cases the regulation simply required the insurer to publish financial information to allow policyholders to ascertain the company's financial condition. In addition to being a benefit to consumers, regulation also helped insurers. By providing some assurance that the insurers were able to stand behind their promise to pay benefits, insurance became a more valuable, and salable, product.

In colonial days the formation of stock companies was restricted to limit competition with Crown corporations. For this reason the early charters were issued only to mutual insurers. This restriction ended upon independence. In 1794 Pennsylvania issued a charter to the first stock insurance company, the Insurance Company of North America, which was another example of regulation by legislation. More general statutory reporting requirements that applied to insurance companies, as well as other financial institutions, were enacted in Massachusetts in 1807 and New York in 1827. These regulations, though, were aimed at promulgating information, not regulating rates.[2]

Insurance regulation provided the opportunity to tax the industry, both to cover the cost of regulation as well as to support other governmental functions. The first tax on insurance in the United States was levied by Massachusetts in 1785, in the form of a stamp tax.[3] The first premium tax, which is the common current form of taxation, was enacted by New York in 1824.[4] In addition to raising revenue, taxation was used to protect local insurance companies. Massachusetts again instigated this activity in 1827 with a 10 percent premium tax on insurers not domiciled in the state. Eight states, including New York, responded with similar legislation.[5] The New York premium tax rates were 10 percent on insurers not domiciled

1. Day (1970).
2. Day (1970).
3. Kimball (1960).
4. Patterson (1927).
5. Mehr and Cammack (1980, p. 234).

in the state but zero for domestic insurers.[6] Illinois enacted a law in 1844 that taxed the total premiums of out-of-state insurers.[7] By 1996 premium taxes paid by insurance companies in all states totaled $9.1 billion, a figure well in excess of the cost of regulation.[8]

The dominant form of property-liability insurance prior to the early twentieth century was fire insurance. One notable feature about this risk during this period was the propensity for fires to become catastrophes, with devastating losses occurring in New York (1835), Chicago (1871), Boston (1872), and San Francisco (1906). Due to the regional nature of many early insurers, in part fostered by protectionist regulations, the catastrophic losses led to significant insolvencies among insurers, and fire insurance was generally unprofitable over the period of 1791 to 1850.[9] The New York fire of 1835 demonstrated the problem of New York's protectionist tax laws, as twenty-three of the twenty-six fire insurers operating in the city went bankrupt.[10] After the Chicago and Boston fires of the 1870s, approximately 75 percent of the country's fire insurers went bankrupt.[11] As a result of this experience, the primary regulatory concern at the time became preventing rates that were inadequate, for an insurer that charged too low a premium in a given area would be able to dominate market share locally, exposing it to the risk of insolvency in the event of a major fire.

The fire insurance industry began to deal with the problem of inadequate rates in the early 1800s by establishing local associations to control price competition.[12] The objective of these organizations was to establish rates within a region that would provide for an adequate return, protect insurers from ruinous competition, and reduce the risk of insurer insolvencies. However, these early organizations were voluntary and had no ability to prevent insurers from undercutting their rates and instigating a price war. Eventually the compact system developed, in which companies agreed to adhere to the rates the association developed, and companies that did not join the compact were prevented from cooperating with member insurers. These nonmember companies would not be able to share infor-

---

6. Lilly (1976).
7. Grace and Skipper (1990).
8. Insurance Information Institute (1998, p. 38).
9. Kimball and Boyce (1958).
10. Lilly (1976).
11. Grace and Barth (1993, p. 8).
12. Day (1970).

mation with member companies, obtain or provide reinsurance with member companies, or, in some cases, be represented by agents that also represented members of the compact. Unfortunately for the industry, the early compacts were not especially successful. By 1866 the National Board of Fire Underwriters was established with similar goals, operating on the countrywide level.

The Chicago and Boston fires of the 1870s and the resulting wave of bankruptcies led to significant changes for the fire insurance industry. First, the National Board of Fire Underwriters began to focus on fire prevention and data collection.[13] More important, the regional associations were able to enforce the compact agreements more effectively. By 1880 the compact system was considered to be working effectively.[14] This assessment, though, may have been as much the result of an absence of catastrophic fires as it was due to the operation of the compact. However, this success in restricting competition resulted in the passage of anticompact legislation in many states in the 1880s and 1890s.[15] The San Francisco fire of 1906, sparked by an earthquake, again caused significant bankruptcies among insurers and led to another rethinking of regulatory policy.

The most influential analysis of insurance regulation during this era was the report of a joint committee of the New York Senate and Assembly chaired by Senator Merritt. Although most of the recommendations dealt with policy forms, agents, and fire prevention, the salient aspect of the Merritt committee report on insurance rates criticized competition in rates and strongly supported rating bureaus, but indicated that they should be subject to state regulation.[16] The National Convention of Insurance Commissioners (NCIC) came out with similar findings in 1914, even proposing that membership in rating bureaus be mandatory.[17] This focus on insurance solvency and support for the anticompetitive behavior of rating bureaus then set the stage for the next development in insurance regulation. Kansas had already enacted the first rating law that allowed joint rate-making under regulatory supervision, adopting this approach in 1909.[18] By 1944 eighteen states regulated fire insurance rates.[19]

13. Day (1970, p. 8).
14. Wandel (1935).
15. Day (1970).
16. Mehr and Cammack (1980, p. 236).
17. Day (1970, p. 20).
18. Day (1970).
19. Mertz (1965).

The findings of the Merritt committee and the NCIC illustrate one of the common problems of regulation: it often focuses on the environment that previously existed and develops solutions to deal with the past problems, not recognizing that the situation has actually changed. Both studies supported joint ratemaking due to the risk of catastrophic fires. However, the San Francisco fire of 1906 was the last of the great city-destroying fires in the United States. The lessons of that fire, and social and technological developments, led to a significant reduction in the risk of catastrophic fire. In fact, despite population growth and inflation, the $350 million loss from the San Francisco fire was not surpassed even in nominal terms until the 1989 Texas fire at the Polyolefin plant that caused $750 million in losses. In inflation-adjusted terms, the San Francisco fire loss was almost four times as large as the largest (in nominal dollars) fire loss in history, the Oakland firestorm of 1991 that caused $1.5 billion in losses.[20]

Another development that dramatically affected the insurance environment of the early twentieth century was the introduction of the "reasonably priced, reliable, and efficient" Model T by Henry Ford in 1908, only two years after the San Francisco fire and a few years prior to the Merritt committee and NCIC reports.[21] The automobile not only revolutionized the transportation system in this country, it also caused a major shift in the property-liability insurance industry as well, as automobile insurance soon replaced fire insurance as the largest line of business. The primary risk of automobile insurance was liability, not damage to the property itself. Also, automobiles were not subject to the fire peril or other catastrophic exposures to the same extent that buildings and their contents were. The regulatory role envisioned by the Merritt committee and the NCIC did not, and perhaps could not, encompass such a dramatic shift in the industry.

State regulation of insurance developed in this country even though the Constitution reserved for the federal government the power "to regulate commerce . . . among the several states." In the early 1800s, as an attempt to escape state regulatory restrictions, some insurers tried to get the U.S. government to assert regulatory control over the industry, likely based on the opinion that federal regulation would be less intrusive than state regulation. This attempt was not successful. The first major legal challenge to state regulation occurred when Samuel Paul, an agent for a New York

20. Insurance Information Institute (1998, p. 71).
21. Henry Ford Museum and Greenfield Village, "The Life of Henry Ford" (www.hfmgv.org/exhibits/hf [January 2002]).

insurer, wrote a fire policy for a Virginia insured. The Commonwealth of Virginia claimed that Paul had to obtain a license in Virginia. Paul refused and continued to write fire insurance until he was arrested, convicted, and fined.[22] He then used the commerce clause as a basis to contest this treatment. In 1869 the Supreme Court ruled against Paul by finding that insurance was not commerce within the meaning of the interstate commerce clause. First, insurance was not considered commerce since it was intangible and not a good or a service. Second, since insurance policies do not take effect until delivered to the policyholder, they were held to be local contracts, even if written by an insurer from a different state.[23] This contorted ruling allowed states to continue regulating the business of insurance.

This strained interpretation of commerce held for seventy-five years. During this time several significant federal antitrust laws were enacted: the Sherman Act of 1890 that provided for regulation of monopolies and prohibited restraint of trade or commerce, the Clayton Act of 1914 that dealt with anticompetitive mergers, the Federal Trade Commission Act of 1914 that addressed the issue of fair trade, and the Robinson-Patman Act of 1936 that prohibited ratemaking in concert and provided specific guidelines for pricing differentials within a single company.

The extensive antitrust activity, strongly supported by both economic theory and practical experience, prohibited the formation of monopolies, the operation of cartels, and joint pricing activity in most areas of the economy.[24] Only in situations where monopolies were clearly in the public interest due to significant economies of scale (as in the case of electric utilities) would monopolies be tolerated, although still subject to extensive regulation. Joint activities were allowed (such as tire companies working together to develop standardization in tire sizes), but joint pricing was clearly prohibited under the federal antitrust statutes.

The insurance industry was fortuitously exempt from the early antitrust legislation thanks to *Paul* v. *Virginia*. However, the nature of the insurance business is such that joint pricing activities can actually serve the public interest by fostering new entry, which serves to promote competition, and by reducing the risk of mispricing, which restrains premium levels. The unique feature of insurance that generates this anomaly is that the cost of the insurance product is not known until well after it is sold, when

22. Mehr and Cammack (1980, p. 679).
23. Mehr and Cammack (1980, p. 680).
24. Morgan (1976).

the losses that the policy covers have occurred and been settled. For almost all other goods and services that consumers purchase, the price is set after they have been produced, making the pricing question relatively straight-forward.[25] Insurance, however, is pricing the future. The more historical information that a company has on which to base the forecast of future losses, the more accurate the price can be. A company that has no historical information would simply not be able to price a new line of business realis-tically, which would prevent any risk-averse entity from writing a new line of business. A small insurer, if allowed to use only its own loss experience, would be at a severe competitive disadvantage because random error would lead to prices that diverge significantly from the correct values, and compe-tition would lead to their obtaining few overpriced risks but many under-priced risks, increasing insolvency risk for the company. Allowing or mandating insurers to share past loss experience benefits all insurers by ena-bling them to generate more reliable prices. Consumers also benefit from accurate insurance pricing, as insolvency risk is reduced and insurers, with less uncertainty, are able to reduce the risk load that would be needed.

The genesis of the case that overturned *Paul* v. *Virginia* began in 1922, when the state of Missouri tried to reduce the rates of the regional rating bureau. The industry responded by filing numerous lawsuits to prevent this action. The result was a negotiated plan finalized in the late 1930s that included payments to state officials. The Missouri attorney general chal-lenged this settlement and asked the U.S. Department of Justice to get involved since many of the members of the Southeastern Underwriters Association (SEUA) were domiciled in states other than Missouri.[26] The SEUA was a fire-rating bureau that required members to adhere to the promulgated rates, prohibited members from providing reinsurance for nonmembers, prevented agents of member companies from representing nonmembers, and placed other restrictions on competition. Although sub-ject to state regulation, by making payments to state regulators as part of the negotiated settlement, the bureau effectively eliminated restrictive reg-ulation. The SEUA was charged with violating the federal antitrust laws regarding restraint of trade and anticompetitive behavior. The SEUA's

---

25. It could be argued that contractors bidding on projects face similar uncertainty. However, in most cases their hourly labor and construction material costs are known and could be fixed prior to pricing the project. The only uncertainty is the number of hours of labor involved. This uncertainty is unique to the specific project, and no social benefit would be gained by having contractors work together to set the project price.

26. Grace and Barth (1993).

defense rested on the finding in *Paul* v. *Virginia* that insurance was not commerce and therefore insurers were not subject to federal antitrust laws.

In 1944 the Supreme Court held that insurance was indeed commerce and that policies written by insurers not domiciled in the state in which the policyholder resided were interstate commerce, subject to federal jurisdiction.[27] This ruling immediately subjected the insurance industry to the full force of the antitrust laws and abolished the authority of all state insurance departments for any regulatory activity involving insurers not domiciled within the state. Given the drastic impact of this ruling, the courts delayed the application of the ruling to give legislators, both state and federal, an opportunity to deal with this new statutory environment.

As a result of considerable pressure exerted by states (facing the loss of both regulatory authority and significant tax revenue) and insurers, Congress passed Public Law 15, better known as the McCarran-Ferguson Act, less than eighteen months after the SEUA decision. The law stated that the continued regulation of the insurance industry by the states was in the public interest and affirmed the right of the states to continue regulating and taxing insurance companies. The law suspended the application of the existing federal antitrust laws to insurance until 1948 and then allowed state regulation to supercede federal antitrust laws (except for cases of boycott, coercion, or intimidation—actions alleged under the SEUA case). Furthermore, the McCarran-Ferguson Act specified that no federal law should be considered applicable to insurance unless specifically stated within the legislation. Commentary that accompanied the law expressed that the intent of the legislation was to promote competition within the industry.

This situation created divisions within the insurance industry. Bureau companies needed state regulation in order to be exempt from federal antitrust laws that prohibited joint pricing activities. Large independent insurers set rates by themselves and thus were not subject to federal antitrust laws; therefore they did not require any state regulatory system to allow them to continue to operate. Also, the degree of regulation needed to supercede the federal antitrust laws was not clear. Some argued that rates had to be subject to specific approval, while others held that competitive rating would be sufficient.

In 1944 only seven states had been regulating auto insurance rates.[28] More states, but still not all, regulated fire and workers' compensation rates.

27. Mehr and Cammack (1980, p. 681).
28. Mertz (1965, p. 9).

The McCarran-Ferguson Act inspired all states to adopt rate regulation over the next few years. The National Association of Insurance Commissioners proposed model legislation for rate regulation that allowed for three different approaches to rate regulation: mandatory bureau rates, prior approval, and open competition.[29]

The combined effect of the SEUA decision and the McCarran-Ferguson Act spurred all states to adopt some form of rate regulation by 1951.[30] In most cases the regulation took the form of prior approval laws because of legitimate concern that competitive rating laws might not satisfy the act's legal requirement that states regulate rates. However, several states, including California, did adopt open competition rating laws that were later held sufficient to replace the federal antitrust laws.[31]

The evident success of the open competition laws led to several analyses of rate regulation during the 1960s. One significant study on insurance rate regulation in this era was conducted by the New York Insurance Department in 1969. This report supported competition as a means of ensuring appropriate rates and proposed that New York adopt an open competition rating law.[32] New York did, in fact, adopt an open competition form of rate regulation effective in 1970.

The environment in which the industry operated had changed significantly. The risk of catastrophic fire losses had declined due to strengthened building codes and effective fire departments, the number of independent insurance companies that did not belong to rating bureaus had grown, and automobile insurance, which did not have the same catastrophic loss potential, had become increasingly important to property-liability insurers. With the risk of catastrophic losses having been reduced significantly, competition could work effectively to maintain reasonable rates within the industry.

Rate Regulation in Illinois

Like many other states, Illinois enacted a prior approval rating law for automobile insurance in 1947. This format was adopted, in part, due to

29. Grace and Barth (1993).

30. Mertz (1965).

31. *California League of Independent Insurance Producers* v. *Aetna Casualty and Surety Co.*, 175 F. Supp. 857 (N.D. Calif. 1959).

32. New York Insurance Department (1969).

concern that competitive rating would not suffice to exempt insurers from federal antitrust laws. In 1969, in line with the general movement in progressive states toward competitive rating systems, the state legislature enacted an open competition law that became effective January 1, 1970, replacing the prior approval law. This legislation included a sunset clause that caused the open competition rate regulatory law to expire in August 1971. The intent apparently was either to renew the rate regulatory law or to revise this legislation after a brief experiment. However, a stalemate in the state legislature prevented either proposal from being enacted, so the rate regulatory law in Illinois expired and was not replaced. Thus Illinois became the only state in the country without a rate regulatory law.

The lack of a rating law caused some concern that the federal antitrust laws could be applied to joint ratemaking in Illinois. In response, the rating agencies, including Insurance Services Office (ISO), stopped promulgating rate manuals in Illinois.[33] Instead, ISO distributed loss costs, essentially the pure premiums without any loading for expenses. It was left to the member companies to add a provision for expenses and reprint the manuals with these independently determined premium levels.[34]

The relative success of the competitive system has dissuaded the state legislature from enacting any rate regulatory law, so Illinois continues to operate in a completely open competition environment for most lines of business, including private passenger auto insurance. In effect, the argument over rate regulation has focused on whether to enact a competitive rating law or to continue to operate without any rating law. Illinois is the state of domicile of the two largest personal lines writers, State Farm and Allstate. Since these insurers set rates independently, they do not require state rate regulation in order to be exempt from federal antitrust laws. Their presence has provided support for the competitive rating environment.[35] Rates for the involuntary automobile insurance market in Illinois are regulated. Also, regulations mandate that whatever rates companies do charge for auto insurance must be filed with the insurance department no later than ten days after their first use. Additionally, legislation restricts insurers from charging different rates within the city of Chicago. Thus

33. Over the next twenty years, ISO shifted to providing loss costs in all states to encourage more independent ratemaking.

34. At least one company, confused by the different format, used the loss costs as premiums. Not surprisingly, the loss ratios were quite high and the company soon caught its error.

35. Personal communication with Phil O'Connor, former director of the Illinois Department of Insurance, January 18, 2001.

whatever rates apply to any one portion of the city are the rates that apply throughout the city for that insurer. There are no restrictions on rates in Chicago relative to other areas within the state.

Even though insurance rates in the voluntary market are not regulated, the Illinois Insurance Department does not take a laissez-faire approach to insurance regulation. The department regulates insurance solvency and market conduct and analyzes the insurance market to make sure that competition is serving to provide coverage. In fact, since the department is not required to regulate rates, it can focus its efforts on other aspects of insurance regulation that are more widely regarded as being useful and necessary.

Illinois is the only state in the country without a rate regulatory law. All other states have either restrictive rate regulations, requiring companies to obtain specific approval before adopting new rates, or have provisions in their rating laws that allow the insurance department to disapprove rates that have been filed. Insurers in these states must provide varying levels of supporting documentation for rates. The information requirements and regulatory review process in each state are costly, both to the insurance department and to insurers. The Illinois experience can shed light on whether rate regulation is necessary or beneficial. If not, then other states can achieve the benefits of the Illinois system by repealing their rate regulatory laws.

Prior Research on Automobile Insurance Rate Regulation

Many studies have addressed the effect of rate regulation from a variety of viewpoints. The Department of Justice, in a study on the effect of state regulation, commented that the experience in three open competition states (California since 1947, Illinois since 1969, and New York since 1970) clearly illustrated the benefits of competitive rating laws.[36] Early studies found that rate regulation tended to raise auto insurance rates, but these were based on experience through the 1970s.[37] However, more recent studies have determined that since the 1980s, rate regulation has had the effect of lowering auto insurance rates.[38] Other studies have found no significant effect of the type of rate regulatory law, although the con-

36. U.S. Department of Justice (1977, pages 31–34).
37. Joskow (1973); Ippolito (1979).
38. Harrington (1984a, 1987); Grabowski, Viscusi, and Evans (1989).

centration level is an important variable.[39] Rate regulation has also been found to lower the number of insurers writing in a state and reduce the market share of direct writers, assumed to be the lower cost writers.[40] Rate regulation tended to make it harder for residents to find insurance and increased the residual market size within the state.[41]

One problem with studies on the effect of rate regulation is the determination of what, in fact, constitutes rate regulation. Most prior studies have determined the type of rate regulation based on the rating law in effect in a given state. State-made rates, mandatory bureau rates, and prior approval rating laws are generally considered to be strict regulation. File-and-use rating laws are also sometimes included as strict regulation but other times are categorized as competitive rating. Use-and-file and no-filing states (and sometimes file-and-use states) are considered to use competitive rating.[42] However, in practice there are considerable differences in the application of a rating law, with some prior approval states routinely approving all filings and some file-and-use states that frequently disapprove rate filings, forcing companies to refile new rates until the insurance department finally accepts them.

An alternative measure of rate regulation is based on perceived regulatory restrictiveness, derived from a survey of insurers operating within a state.[43] Conning Company, an insurance management service and investment broker, has periodically performed such studies and promulgated the results to clients. Initially, these studies were based on the 30 largest states (based on premium volume), but starting in 1984 they were expanded to all states and then in 1991 to all states and the District of Columbia.[44] One advantage to using the Conning studies is that regulation is measured, not based on a dummy variable value of 0 or 1, but on a scale with a much wider range (from 1 to 51, based on recent studies). The disadvantages of the Conning studies are their reliance on subjective opinion, which may reflect historical rather than current practices, the infrequency of the analyses, and the limited number of states originally included in each survey.

Although the two regulatory variables are correlated ($R = 0.589$),

39. Bajtelsmit and Bouzouita (1998); Gron (1995).
40. Harrington (1984b); Suponcic and Tennyson (1998); Tennyson (1991, 1993, and 1997).
41. Cummins and Weiss (1992).
42. Harrington (1984b); Tennyson (1991).
43. D'Arcy (1982, 1985); Grabowski, Viscusi and Evans (1989).
44. Conning Company (1980 and 1994).

there are some notable differences in state results. For example, the Conning Company survey ranks Michigan as forty-seventh, forty-fifth, and forty-fifth in the 1984, 1991, and 1994 surveys, respectively, regarding relative freedom to manage personal lines business. However, Michigan has had a competitive rating law for automobile insurance over this entire time period. Alternatively, Alaska ranked seventh in 1991 and North Dakota ranked fourth in 1994, but both had prior approval rating laws in force for auto insurance for over twenty years. In effect, measuring regulation is an inexact process regardless of the approach taken. However, Illinois was ranked second (to California) in 1984 and first in both 1991 and 1994 by the Conning survey, confirming the freedom insurers have in Illinois in regard to automobile insurance rates.

One clear fact about automobile insurance regulation is that Illinois represents a unique regulatory environment since it is the only state operating completely without a rate regulatory law. Given the size of the state, the diversity of residential and driving conditions, and the length of time this arrangement has been in place, any benefits of or problems related to this unregulated environment would be clearly evident. Thus Illinois represents an excellent case study of the effect of not regulating automobile insurance.

Studies of the Illinois Experience

Given its unique position, Illinois has been the subject of a number of studies on the effect of competitive rating. A set of interviews conducted with small insurers operating in the state in the 1970s found general support for insurance regulation and indicated that these insurers believed that markets were competitive.[45] Two rate studies conducted in the 1970s found that automobile insurance rates in Illinois tended to be lower than in similar geographical areas in other states.[46] Another study indicated that loss ratios in Illinois for automobile insurance declined over the first five years that competitive rating was in effect.[47] A study by Cummins and Weiss reported that 150 insurers were writing auto insurance in Illinois in 1990, more than in any other state, compared to an average number of 97 insurers per state.[48]

45. Long and Mehr (1981).
46. Illinois Department of Insurance (1977, 1979).
47. Witt (1977).
48. Cummins and Weiss (1992).

Figure 6-1. *Illinois Market Concentration, Private Passenger Automobile Insurance, 1992–98*

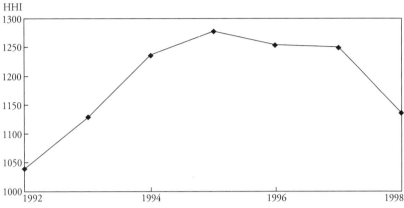

Source: Illinois Department of Insurance (2000).

Under legislation adopted in 1986, during a period when it was hard to obtain coverage for some commercial liability risks, the director of insurance is required to report to the general assembly annually on issues related to cost containment and insurance availability. These studies provide extensive information about the state of the automobile insurance market, among other lines. Included in the 2000 report are data about the Herfindahl-Hirschman index (HHI) (see figure 6-1), the number of insurers that had filed private passenger rates in 1998 (221), the number reporting written premium in the city of Chicago (192), and the size of the automobile residual market in Illinois compared with national figures (see figure 6-2).[49] All these indications support the finding that the current regulatory system is working in Illinois.

Economics of Insurance Regulation

The pervasive nature of insurance regulation has engendered almost as many viewpoints about the need for and nature of insurance rate regulation as there are different forms of regulation. These arguments can be used to form a variety of testable hypotheses about the effect of insurance rate regulation.

49. Illinois Department of Insurance (2000).

Figure 6-2. *Automobiles in Residual Market, Illinois versus United States, 1994–98*

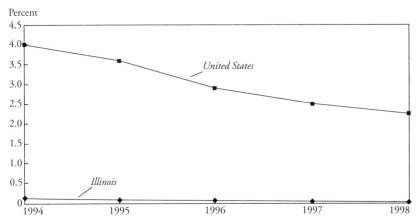

Source: Illinois Department of Insurance (2000).

Proponents of rate regulation argue that rate regulation is necessary to protect the public from adverse effects that an unregulated environment would produce. Exactly what those effects would be are not clear. However, regulatory laws consistently state that insurance rates must not be excessive, inadequate, or unfairly discriminatory, hence implying that unregulated rates could tend in any of these directions. Taking them one at a time allows the formation of three distinct hypotheses of regulatory protection.

Joskow proposes that in the absence of regulation, insurers could form cartels that would lead to excessive rates.[50] If rate regulation protects policyholders in this manner, then rates in unregulated states, and in Illinois especially, will tend to be excessive. Unfortunately, it is not possible to determine if rates are excessive, or inadequate, on an absolute scale for an individual line of business. Determining the appropriate profit margin for an insurer as a whole, or even of the industry in aggregate, remains an unsolved problem despite extensive analysis of insurance financial results. A proper analysis requires access to a considerable level of financial detail that is not publicly available and often not even readily available within the firm.

50. Joskow (1973).

This issue has been studied extensively by the National Association of Insurance Commissioners and many others.[51] One problem is determining the appropriate components of investment income to include in the profit measure.[52] Another problem deals with the appropriate risk adjustment for insurance cash flows. The complications are compounded when trying to measure the appropriate profit level for an individual line of business by state, since neither investment income nor capital is specifically allocated by line by state. Thus determining whether rates are excessive in unregulated markets on an absolute scale cannot be accomplished. However, it is possible to compare the relative profit level by state by examining the one measurable component of profits that varies from state to state: the loss ratio.

If rate regulation does protect policyholders from excessive rates, then the loss ratio in states with restrictive rating laws would be higher than the loss ratio in states with competitive rating laws. On the other hand, the loss ratio in Illinois, without any rate regulation, would be lower than in states with competitive rating laws. If regulated rates are adequate, then insurers would be willing to write business at regulated rates. Thus the size of the residual market should be no higher in regulated states than in other states, including Illinois. Individuals might decide not to insure for a variety of reasons, including the inability to afford insurance coverage and the driver's perception of the cost of coverage compared to the risk of a loss. Since rates in regulated states would be adequate while rates in competitive rating states would be excessive, there should be fewer uninsured vehicles in states with regulation than in competitive states. However, there should be no difference in insolvency assessments by type of regulation.

The early calls for insurance rate regulation were to protect the industry, and the public, from inadequate rates and the resulting insolvencies when catastrophic losses occurred. This view is encompassed by the requirement that rates not be inadequate. If rate regulation protects policyholders from inadequate rates, then the loss ratio in states with restrictive rating laws would be lower than the loss ratio in states with competitive rate regulation, and the loss ratio in Illinois would be higher than that in competitive rating states. Also, since unregulated rates would be inadequate, insurers would not be willing to write all risks. Thus the residual market

51. NAIC (1970 and 1984). For additional studies on the appropriate profit margin for property-liability insurers, see Cummins (1990, 1991); D'Arcy and Doherty (1988); D'Arcy and Garven (1990); D'Arcy and Dyer (1997); D'Arcy and Gorvett (1998); Feldblum (1996); Van Slyke (1999).

52. D'Arcy (1990).

share would be lower in regulated states and higher in Illinois. If unregulated insurers charged inadequate rates, then the number of drivers that elected not to insure would decline. Thus the proportion of drivers without insurance would be higher in regulated states and lower in Illinois. Additionally, if unregulated insurers tend to charge inadequate rates, then more insurers will become insolvent in competitive rating states and even more in Illinois, so the number and size of insolvencies will be larger. Thus the insolvency assessments will be lower in states that regulate insurance and higher in Illinois.

Another objective of rate regulation is to ensure that rates are not unfairly discriminatory. Fair discrimination, which is allowed, has been held to apply if the rate differentials simply reflect differences in expected losses. Unfair discrimination would be if the rates for some policyholders did not represent the cost of providing coverage. If insurers as a whole are unfairly discriminating against particular risk classes, then unregulated insurers would be more profitable. Individuals that are unfairly discriminated against in unregulated states would be more likely to use the residual market and less likely to purchase insurance. Thus in regulated states the loss ratio would be higher and in Illinois the loss ratio would be lower than in competitive rating states. The size of the residual market would be lower in regulated states and higher in Illinois. Also, fewer drivers would be uninsured in regulated states, and more in Illinois. Regulation would not affect insolvency assessments.

The hypotheses developed above all rest on the premise that rate regulation fulfills a useful purpose. An opposing position is that rate regulation is detrimental to the insurance market. This position is based on the economic theory that competition will drive prices to the appropriate level. If the price of insurance is above a firm's marginal cost, then the firm will lower its price to increase market share. Competition will continue to drive prices down to the marginal cost level of the most efficient firm. Firms would be unwilling to write business below marginal cost since that would generate losses. Because this effect works in the absence of regulation, any regulation would only serve to disrupt the market. Several theories have been developed based on this premise.

One theory is that rate regulation suppresses rates below the appropriate level.[53] Based on this theory, the loss ratio in regulated states would be higher than in competitive rating states. The loss ratio in Illinois should

53. Harrington (1992).

be equivalent to that in competitive rating states. If regulation suppresses rates, then insurers would be less willing to write risks in regulated states, so the residual market share would be higher in regulated states. There should be no difference in residual market size in Illinois compared to other competitive rating states. Since regulation keeps rates below the fair cost, this theory predicts that fewer drivers will be uninsured in regulated states. There should be no difference between Illinois and competitive rating states. Finally, since regulation keeps rates below the appropriate rate level, more insolvencies will occur in states with rate regulation. Illinois should be similar to competitive rating states.

An alternative theory of rate regulation, termed capture theory, presumes that the regulated industry will gain control of the regulatory process and utilize it to increase profit levels.[54] Based on this theory, loss ratios would be lower in regulated states than in competitive rating states. The loss ratio in Illinois should be equivalent to that in competitive rating states. Since rates in regulated states would be higher than necessary, the size of the residual market would be lower in regulated states. More drivers would be uninsured in regulated states due to the excessive rates insurers would charge. Since rates in regulated states would be excessive, the rate of insolvency would be lower in those states. In all instances, Illinois should not be different from competitive rating states.

Peltzman expands on capture theory by allowing for differing levels of interest group pressure, depending on the economic conditions.[55] At times the regulated industry will prevail, specifically during recessions or other difficult economic times; but at other times consumer groups will prevail, specifically during economic expansions or other favorable economic conditions. Thus regulation will serve to increase profit levels when financial results are poor and to reduce profit levels when financial results are more favorable, having the effect of reducing the variability of results.[56]

Based on this theory, termed maximization of political support, the effect of regulation will fluctuate with market conditions. The countrywide loss ratio for automobile insurance tended to increase during the period

---

54. Stigler (1971).

55. Peltzman (1976).

56. D'Arcy (1982) finds support for Peltzman's theory by examining profitability by line of business. Regulation reduced profitability for auto insurance, a line for which consumers would bring the greatest pressure to bear on regulators. Conversely, regulation increased profitability for homeowners' insurance, a line in which consumers would play a less forceful role and in which the industry could offset the losses in auto insurance.

Figure 6-3. *Countrywide Automobile Insurance Loss Ratios, 1980–98*[a]

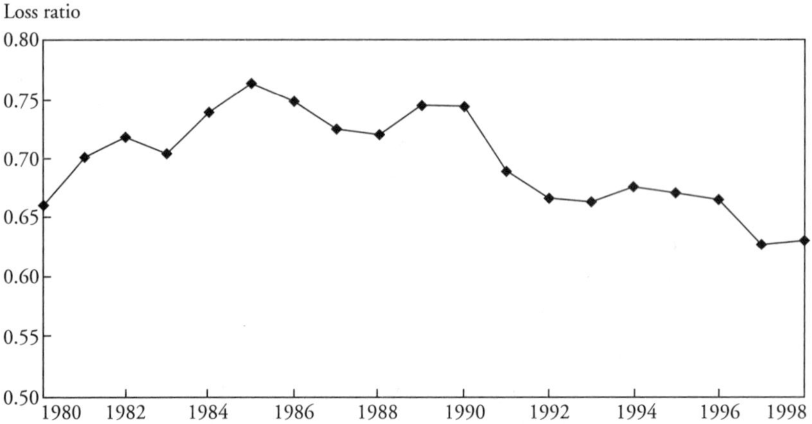

Loss ratio

Source: A. M. Best and NAIC.
a. Loss = incurred losses/earned premium.

1980–90 and then declined from 1991 to 1998 (figure 6-3). Increasing loss ratios indicate strong competition by insurers, which would suggest that they would not be the dominant pressure on regulators. When loss ratios are declining, insurers are raising rates faster than loss costs, which reflects their greater influence on the regulatory process. Based on this theory, the coefficients of the regulatory variables should differ over the sample periods, with loss ratios in regulated states being higher than in competitive states for the first period and lower than in competitive states in the latter period. In Illinois, without any regulation, the loss ratios should be the same as in competitive states. Over the entire period, results would be less variable in regulated states. This theory would also suggest that the size of the residual market would also vary with the cycle. The residual market would be larger in regulated states in the first period (when consumers dominate the regulatory process) and lower in the second period (when the industry would dominate the process). The number of uninsured drivers would be lower in regulated states during the first period (when rates are suppressed by consumer influence) and higher in the second period. Insurer insolvencies would also follow a cycle, but due to the lag between insolvency problems developing and insolvency assessments being made, this cannot be ascertained from this sample.

A final theory of regulation, termed market disruption, is proposed here. Under this theory rate regulation is unnecessary for auto insurance, since competition will serve to price this product in line with expected costs. Rate regulation will not necessarily lead to inadequate rates in the long run, since insurers can respond to inadequate rates by refusing to write unprofitable business, reducing the level of service provided to lower costs, and even withdrawing from the market if necessary. However, rate regulation will disrupt the rating process. Loss ratios will be more variable in regulated markets and less variable in Illinois. Insurers will have fewer rate changes in regulated states and the rate changes will be, on average, larger. In Illinois the rate changes will be more frequent and smaller. Since insurers will refuse to write unprofitable business in the voluntary market, the residual market will be larger in regulated states and lower in Illinois. Finally, since regulation distorts the normal market functions, insolvencies will be more frequent and more costly in regulated states and less frequent and less costly in Illinois.

Table 6-1 summarizes the predicted results based on the different economic theories of regulation. These theories predict a variety of results. The remainder of this chapter will take advantage of the different forms of regulation applied in the insurance markets to determine which, if any, of these theories can be supported by empirical evidence.

Analysis of the Illinois Experience

Illinois is the only state in the nation that does not formally regulate insurance rates for the voluntary automobile insurance market. The Department of Insurance does obtain all rate manuals and monitors the insurance market by examining the level of competition and premium levels. It also regulates residual market rates, market conduct, and insurance solvency. However, rates are not subject to approval and cannot be disapproved, leaving insurers free to charge whatever rates market conditions dictate. This unique position sets Illinois apart from all other states by providing a completely competitive market for insurance. Illinois is not simply similar to other states that have competitive rating laws; by not having a rate regulatory law, Illinois represents a significantly different regulatory environment. Analysis of the Illinois experience can provide insight into whether rate regulation is necessary or even useful. Thus, in the analysis of the experience, a dummy variable representing Illinois is used to determine if there are any measurable effects under this system.

Another dummy variable is used to represent states that regulate insu-

Table 6-1. *Predicted Results Based on Economic Theories*

| | Loss ratio | | | | Rate change activity | | | | Residual market | | Uninsured vehicles | | Insolvency Assessments | |
| | Level[a] | | Variability | | Number of changes | | Size of changes | | | | | | | |
Theory	REG[a]	Illinois	REG	Illinois	REG	Illinois	REG	Illinois	REG	Illinois	REG	Illinois	REG	Illinois
Regulation protects against:														
Excessive rates	+	−	…	…	…	…	…	…	0	0	−	0	0	0
Inadequate rates	−	+	…	…	…	…	…	…	−	+	+	−	−	+
Unfairly discriminatory rates	+	−	…	…	…	…	…	…	−	+	−	+	0	0
Alternative theories														
Rate supression	+	0	…	…	…	…	…	…	+	0	−	0	+	0
Capture theory	−	0	−	…	…	…	…	…	−	0	+	0	−	0
Maximization of political support	±	0	−	0	…	…	…	…	±	0	±	0	…	…
Market disruption	0	0	+	−	−	+	+	−	+	−	…	…	+	−

a. REG, regulated states.

rance rates. This variable follows the definition used by Harrington, which classifies as regulated an environment with state-made rates, any form of prior approval law, or a file-and-use law with prior approval required for deviations from rates filed by rating bureaus (see chapter 7). If rates are regulated, the state value is 1. Otherwise, the value is 0, which would apply to states that have file-and-use rating laws, use-and-file laws, filing-only laws, no filing laws, flex rating with a large flex rating band, or no rating law at all, as is the case for Illinois. When results over time are analyzed, the average of the dummy variables for each year over the appropriate time period is used.

A second classification of regulation uses the Conning Company rankings of states based on freedom to manage personal lines business. This variable ranges from 1 to 51. Since this variable is only available for 1984, 1991, and 1994, it is used only to analyze results over a period of time. In each case the average value for the appropriate years is used.

The first analysis of the Illinois experience is a comparison of loss ratios by state. In prior studies of regulation, the loss ratio (or its inverse) has been used as a proxy for the price of insurance. The loss ratio is determined by dividing incurred losses (sometimes including loss adjustment expenses) by the earned premium. The incurred losses available for this study are calendar year values, meaning that they represent paid losses and changes in loss reserves during a particular year (or calendar quarter) for all claims outstanding, not just those that occurred in the current time period. Thus reserve changes on claims from prior years can affect the values.[57]

The source of information for this comparison is annual data for 1980 to 1998 from page 14 of insurance companies' annual statements.[58] Table 6-2 shows the results of three regressions: for the entire time period, the period 1980–90 (when loss ratios were generally rising), and 1991–98 (when loss ratios were generally falling). In each case the coefficients of regulation and of Illinois are insignificantly different from zero. Thus none of the theories that predict a significant effect of regulation on the level of the loss ratio are supported.

The maximization of political support theory predicts that the volatility of the loss ratio will be lower in states where rates are regulated and higher in Illinois. The market disruption theory predicts that the volatility of the loss ratio will be higher in states where rates are regulated and lower in Illinois. The standard deviation of the loss ratio by state over the

57. Weiss (1985).
58. Database generated by David Cummins from data provided by A.M. Best Company and NAIC.

Table 6-2. *Loss Ratio, Linear Regressions, 1980–98*[a]

Independent variable	1980–98		1980–90		1991–98	
	Coefficient	t statistic	Coefficient	t statistic	Coefficient	t statistic
Regulation	−0.0460	1.115	0.0079	1.485	−0.0003	−0.048
Illinois	−0.0133	−0.916	−0.0188	−0.994	−0.0063	−0.282
R^2	0.264	...	0.244	...	0.102	...
N	950	...	550	...	400	...

Source: Author's calculations based on data from A.M. Best and NAIC.

a. The dependent variable is the ratio of direct losses incurred divided by direct premiums earned by state for private passenger automobile insurance. Regulation is a dummy variable set equal to 1 for states with prior approval regulatory laws and equal to zero otherwise. Illinois is a dummy variable set equal to 1 for Illinois and equal to zero otherwise.

period 1980–98 was calculated and used as the dependent variable in several regressions, with the results shown on table 6-3. The regulation variable is the average of the yearly dummy variables for restrictive regulation over the period 1980–98. Thus a state that had a prior approval law for the entire period would have a value of 1, whereas a state that had a competitive rating law for the entire period would have a value of 0. An alternative measure of regulation used in this study was the average Conning state ranking over the years 1984, 1991, and 1994. This value could range from 1 (if a state had been ranked as providing the most freedom to manage personal lines business) to 51 (if a state had been ranked as the most restrictive each year).[59] A dummy variable representing Illinois was also included in some of the models.

In model 1 regulation was the only explanatory variable, and restrictive regulation was shown to significantly (at the 10 percent level) increase the variability, as predicted by the market disruption theory. In model 2 the dummy variable for Illinois was the only explanatory variable, and the results were not significant. When both regulation and Illinois were included as explanatory variables, each had the expected sign based on the market disruption theory, but neither was significant. When the Conning ranking was used to represent regulatory restrictiveness, the results were significant (at the 1 percent level) in the direction predicted by the market disruption theory. These results show that variability was higher for states that regulated restrictively and thus provide support for the market disruption theory.

59. In fact, Illinois had the lowest value at 1.33 and New Jersey had the highest value at 50.33.

Table 6-3. *Standard Deviation of Loss Ratio, Linear Regressions*[a]

Independent variable	Model 1		Model 2		Model 3		Model 4	
	Coefficient	t statistic	Coefficient	t statistic	Coefficient	t statistic	Coefficient	t statistic
Regulation	0.011	1.733*	...	...	0.01	1.617	...	...
Illinois	...	...	−0.014	−0.678	−0.007	−0.371	...	...
CC ranking	...	...	...	...	...	...	0.001	3.192**
R^2	0.059	...	0.009	...	0.062	...	0.175	...
N	50	...	50	...	50	...	50	...

Source: Table 6-2.
*Significant at the 10 percent level.
**Significant at the 1 percent level.

a. The dependent variable is the standard deviation of the loss ratio for private passenger automobile insurance (direct losses incurred divided by the direct premiums earned) by state over the period 1980–98. Regulation is a dummy variable set equal to 1 for states with prior approval regulatory laws and equal to zero otherwise. Illinois is a dummy variable set to equal 1 for Illinois and zero otherwise. CC ranking is the Conning and Company average ranking of each state based on freedom to manage personal lines business.

Table 6-4. *Private Passenger Automobile Rate Level Change, 1990–99*

| | Company 1 | | Company 2 | |
| | Number of | | Number of | |
State	changes	Average[a]	changes	Average
Competitive rating				
Colorado	11	3.53	9	3.54
Illinois	9	3.28	14	3.73
Kentucky	8	4.38	13	4.18
Michigan	10	3.43	9	2.49
Minnesota	11	3.19	13	2.73
Missouri	10	3.24	15	2.33
Ohio	12	1.9	11	2.45
Oregon	8	3.94	12	2.74
Virginia	11	1.99	14	3.51
Wisconsin	9	2.77	14	2.64
Average	9.90	3.17	12.40	3.03
Prior approval				
California	6	3.92	3	8.76
Connecticut[b]	5	7.9	11	2.79
Florida	11	4.99	13	3.69
Georgia	5	2.72	3	8.29
New Jersey	12	4.1	13	6.2
North Carolina	10	2.98	12	3.82
Pennsylvania	11	3.7	14	4.34
South Carolina	4	4.75	2	2.59
Texas	15	3.72	12	4.77
Average	8.78	4.31	9.22	5.03
t statistic	0.825	−2.019*	1.771	−2.560*
Average overall	9.37	3.71	10.89	3.98

Source: Author's calculations.
* Significant at the 5 percent level.
a. Average absolute value of rate changes.
b. Connecticut was a prior approval state from 1994 to 1999. Between 1990 and 1993, the state had a competitive rating law.

Several insurers provided confidential rate change information for the period from 1990 through 1999. Table 6-4 shows the number of rate changes two insurers made in selected states and the average absolute value of those rate changes, along with the results of t tests comparing sample means based on one-tailed tests. The number of rate changes is lower in prior approval states, but the difference is not significantly different from zero, for both companies. On the other hand, the average (absolute value) size of rate changes in prior approval states is significantly higher (at the 5 percent level) for both companies. Table 6-5 reports the results of additional regressions that test the effect of regulation on the number of rate changes and the average size of those changes for the pooled sample. The market disruption theory suggests that regulation will reduce the number of rate changes and increase the size of those changes. In Illinois, changes should be more frequent and smaller. Although the coefficients for Illinois are not significant, regulation does reduce the number of rate changes (significant at the 10 percent level) and increase the size of rate changes (significant at the 1 percent level). The Conning Company ranking also shows a significant effect (at the 5 percent level) for the size of rate changes, again providing support for the market disruption theory.

The next question addressed is whether any of the problems with automobile insurance are exacerbated in Illinois compared with other states or by restrictive rate regulation. First, is insurance coverage readily available to the public in the voluntary market? One measure of insurance availability is the size of the residual market—policyholders unable to obtain coverage in the voluntary market and instead purchase coverage through the state's residual market mechanism.[60]

Based on data provided by the Automobile Insurance Plans Service Office, the ratio of the number of written car-years insured in the residual market to the number of written car-years in the voluntary market was calculated for 1981 through 1998. Table 6-6 shows the results of a regression of residual market size as a function of the type of regulation, a dummy variable representing Illinois, and the proportion of the population residing in urban areas, both for the entire time period and for the periods 1981–90 and 1991–98. Restrictive regulation significantly increased the size of the residual market for all the time periods analyzed, providing support for the rate suppression and market disruption theories. The urban population proportion increased the size of the residual market for the

60. States have a variety of methods for handling the residual market. The most common is through an assigned risk plan, with those unable to obtain coverage in the voluntary market being assigned to insurers based on each insurer's voluntary market share. The insurer must then write the assigned risk for a set period, normally three years. Other states have a joint underwriting association (in which specified carriers write all residual market policies, but the losses are shared among all insurers), reinsurance facilities (in which insurers must write all applicants for insurance but can choose to reinsure selected drivers with the reinsurance plan, with losses from that plan spread among all insurers in the state), or state plans that provide coverage for those uninsurable in the voluntary market.

Table 6-5. *Effect of Regulation on Number and Average Size of Rate Changes, Linear Regressions*[a]

Independent variable	Model 1		Model 2		Model 3		Model 4	
	Coefficient	t statistic	Coefficient	t statistic	Coefficient	t statistic	Coefficient	t statistic
Regulation	−2.024	−1.715*	1.557	3.127***	...	...	...	...
Illinois	0.482	0.188	0.383	0.355	...	...	...	...
CC Ranking	...	...	...	...	−0.062	−1.677	0.039	2.367**
R^2	0.086	...	0.220	...	0.072	...	0.135	...
N	38	...	38	...	38	...	38	...

Source: Author's calculations based on data from table 6-4.

*Significant at the 10 percent level.
**Significant at the 5 percent level.
***Significant at the 1 percent level.

a. The dependent variable in models 1 and 3 is the number of rate changes made in each state during the period 1990–99 by two insurers that agreed to provide this information. The dependent variable in models 2 and 4 is the average absolute size of the rate changes by state made during this period by these insurers. Regulation is a dummy variable set equal to 1 for states with prior approval regulatory laws and equal to zero otherwise. Illinois is a dummy variable set equal to 1 for Illinois and equal to zero otherwise. CC ranking is the Conning Company average ranking of each state based on freedom to manage personal lines business.

Table 6-6. *Residual Market Size, Linear Regressions, 1981–98*[a]

Independent variable	1981–98		1981–90		1991–98	
	Coefficient	t statistic	Coefficient	t statistic	Coefficient	t statistic
Regulation	0.091	7.118**	0.137	6.544**	0.051	4.798**
Illinois	−0.027	−0.610	−0.054	−0.718	0.005	0.143
Urbanization	0.123	2.823**	0.296	4.124**	−0.060	−1.700*
R^2	0.062	...	0.101	...	0.061	...
N	900	...	500	...	400	...

Source: Author's calculations based on Automobile Insurance Plans Service Office, *AIPSO Facts*, various years.

*Significant at the 10 percent level.

**Significant at the 1 percent level.

a. The dependent variable is the ratio of the number of written car-years of private passenger, non-fleet vehicles covered for liability insurance that are insured in the residual market divided by those that are insured in the voluntary market. Regulation is a dummy variable set equal to 1 for states with prior approval regulatory laws and equal to zero otherwise. Illinois is a dummy variable set equal to 1 for Illinois and equal to zero otherwise. Urbanization is the percent of a state's population residing in urban areas based on Bureau of the Census classification.

entire period and for 1981 through 1990. Surprisingly, the coefficient of urbanization was actually significantly negative from 1991 through 1998. This result was due to the success that two highly urban states, Massachusetts and New Jersey, had in reducing the size of their residual markets in the 1990s at the same time that a relatively rural state, South Carolina, experienced a rapid growth in its residual market size.[61] The coefficients for Illinois were not significantly different from states with competitive rating laws in any of the time periods.

The other measurable characteristic that provides information on the effectiveness of a state's regulatory system is the percentage of drivers that do not purchase insurance coverage. The actual number of uninsured drivers is nearly impossible to measure. Some studies have compared the number of insured passenger vehicles with the number of registered vehicles by state in an attempt to measure the uninsured population. One problem with this method is due to differences in the classification of many vehicles, specifically the classification of many light trucks and minivans as commercial vehicles in state registration figures but as private passenger vehicles by insurers. This discrepancy requires adjusting the data to attempt to correct

61. In 1985, for example, the ratio of the residual market to the voluntary market in Massachusetts was 0.9781, in New Jersey was 0.7119, and in South Carolina was 0.3785. By 1993 the value had declined for Massachusetts to 0.1130 and for New Jersey to 0.0217, but in South Carolina the value had increased to 0.7118, the highest in the country.

for this problem or exercising caution in interpreting the results for individual states. The Insurance Research Council has determined an alternative method of estimating the uninsured driving population: comparing the uninsured motor vehicle claim frequency with bodily injury claim frequency.[62] This method is considered superior to a straight comparison of claims made under the uninsured motorist coverage by state since it adjusts for the general accident frequency rate across states.

The average ratios of uninsured motorist claim frequency to bodily injury claim frequency from 1980 through 1986 and 1989 through 1994 (1987 and 1988 are not available) are shown in table 6-7 for Illinois, the comparable states included in the rate change study cited above, all competitive rating states, and all prior approval states. Whereas there is little overall difference between the values for competitive rating states and prior approval states, either in the uninsured motorist claim ratios or the urban population, there are notable differences among the states. The effect of urban population on the uninsured motorist claim frequency ratio is evident. Given that the Illinois population is more urban than average, the slightly lower value for uninsured motorist claim frequency ratio is a favorable indication.

The results of a regression of type of regulation and percent of population residing in urban areas (where the incentive to avoid insuring would be the greatest due to higher insurance rates and higher poverty rates) against the uninsured motorist population are shown in table 6-8 for the entire time period data are available and for the two subperiods.[63] The urban population percentage has a very significant influence on the size of the uninsured population in each period. Neither the type of regulation nor the Illinois variable had a significant effect for the entire time period. However, the effect of regulation differed for the subperiods. As predicted by the maximization of political support theory, regulation reduced the size of the uninsured motorist population when loss ratios were rising (although not quite significantly) and increased it when loss ratios were declining (significant at the 5 percent level).

62. Insurance Research Council (1999); All-Industry Research Advisory Council (1989).

63. Prior studies on factors influencing uninsured motorist claims have yielded conflicting results about the effect of other variables. Ma and Schmit (2000) found that a significant effect was exerted by the percent of a state's population living in poverty (a variable highly correlated with urbanization); whether a state had a financial responsibility, compulsory insurance, or no-fault law; and the percent of the population residing in metropolitan areas. The Insurance Research Council (1999) found that insurance laws had only a limited impact. Neither study considered the type of rate regulatory law in effect.

Table 6-7. *Ratio of Uninsured Motorist to Bodily Injury Claims, 1980–86 and 1989–94*[a]

States	Ratio	Urban population (1990)[b]
Illinois	0.131	84.6
Always CR		
Colorado	0.303	82.4
Minnesota	0.149	69.9
Missouri	0.130	68.7
Ohio	0.133	74.1
Oregon	0.127	70.5
Virginia	0.151	69.4
Wisconsin	0.100	65.7
Average	0.156	71.5
PA to CR		
Connecticut	0.100	79.1
Kentucky	0.106	51.8
Michigan	0.141	70.5
Average	0.116	67.1
CR to PA		
California	0.235	92.6
Florida	0.241	84.8
Georgia	0.182	63.2
Average	0.219	80.2
Always PA		
New Jersey	0.100	89.4
North Carolina	0.044	50.4
Pennsylvania	0.144	68.9
South Carolina	0.166	54.6
Texas	0.164	80.3
Average	0.124	68.7
Average of all CR states	0.134	68.1
Average of all PA states	0.136	68.2

Source: Author's calculations based on data from the Insurance Research Council (1999) and All-Industry Research Advisory Council (1989).

a. Categories for comparable states: always CR, under competive rating for the entire 1980–94 period; PA to CR, started under prior approval and later shifted to competitive rating; CR to PA, started under competitive rating and then switched to prior approval; always PA, under prior approval for the entire period.

b. Percent of the state's population residing in urban areas based on Bureau of the Census classification.

Table 6-8. *Uninsured Motorist Population, Linear Regressions, 1980–94, Selected Years*[a]

Independent variable	1980–86, 1989–94		1980–86, 1989–90		1991–94	
	Coefficient	t statistic	Coefficient	t statistic	Coefficient	t statistic
Regulation	0.002	0.407	−0.008	−1.431	0.023	2.429*
Illinois	−0.025	−1.410	−0.019	−0.909	−0.037	−1.118
Urbanization	0.134	7.857**	0.123	6.126**	0.144	4.540**
R^2	0.087	…	0.086	…	0.131	…
N	650	…	450	…	200	…

Source: Insurance Research Council (1999) and All-Industry Research Advisory Council (1989).
*Significant at the 5 percent level.
**Significant at the 1 percent level.
a. Regulation is a dummy variable set equal to 1 for states with prior approval regulatory laws and equal to zero otherwise. Illinois is a dummy variable set equal to 1 for Illinois and equal to zero otherwise. Urbanization is the percent of a state's population residing in urban areas based on the Bureau of the Census classification.

Another indicator of the effectiveness of insurance regulation is the impact it has on insurer insolvency, in many regards the most important aspect of insurance regulation. Each state has a guaranty fund system that assesses all insurers in a state to compensate policyholders for the financial consequences of an insurer insolvency. All states except New York use a system in which assessments are made after an insolvency occurs; New York has a prefunded insolvency program. The total insolvency assessments for property-casualty insurers by state for the period 1992–98 were provided by the Alliance of American Insurers.[64] This is the best available information on the cost of insolvencies by state, but it is not ideal. First, the assessments cover all lines of business, not just private passenger automobile insurance. Second, assessments can be generated in one state due to the insolvency of an insurer domiciled in another state, for which the other state would have primary regulatory responsibility. Finally, there is a significant time lag between the effect of an adverse regulatory environment and the insolvency assessments. Thus the type of regulation in effect over an extended period of time needs to be considered when measuring this impact.

In the regression developed to examine the effect of regulation on insolvency costs, the dependent variable is the total insolvency assessments

64. Alliance of American Insurers, *Guaranty Funds: Assessments*, reports for years 1992–98, Downers Grove, Ill.

Table 6-9. *Ratio of Insolvency Assessments (1992–98) to 1992 Direct Written Premium, Linear Regressions*[a]

Independent variable	Model 1		Model 2	
	Coefficient	t *statistic*	*Coefficient*	t *statistic*
Regulation	0.009	1.548	...	...
Illinois	0.002	0.134	...	...
CC ranking	...	...	0.0004	2.135*
R^2	0.050	...	0.088	...
N	49	...	49	...

Source: Author's calculations based on data from the Alliance of American Insurers, *Guaranty Funds*, 1992–98, Downers Grove, Ill.

*Significant at the 5 percent level.

a. The dependent variable is the ratio of total property-casualty insurance guaranty fund insolvency assessments for all lines for the period 1992–98 divided by the 1992 direct written premium for all lines. Regulation is a dummy variable set equal to 1 for states with prior approval regulatory laws and equal to zero otherwise. Illinois is a dummy variable set equal to 1 for Illinois and equal to zero otherwise. CC ranking is the Conning Company average ranking of each state based on freedom to manage personal lines business.

by state over the period 1992–98 divided by the direct written premium for 1992 to adjust for the size of the insurance market during this period. The independent variables are the average type of regulation (as used earlier) in effect over the period 1980–98 (to reflect the lag effect), a dummy variable representing Illinois, and the average regulatory ranking from the Conning reports from 1984–94. The results are reported in table 6-9. The average type of regulation had a positive but not quite significant effect (*t* statistic 1.55). Illinois was also not significant. However, the Conning ranking was positive and significant at the 5 percent level. Thus, based on the Conning Company measure of regulatory restrictiveness, regulation increases the risk of insolvency. This finding supports the rate suppression and market disruption theories, and it refutes capture theory and the three theories based on regulatory protection.

The results of all the empirical tests are summarized in table 6-10, which also repeats the predicted results from table 6-1 for ease of comparison. In general, the results clearly refute the three theories based on regulatory protection. Thus, based on this analysis, regulation is not necessary to protect against excessive, inadequate, or unfairly discriminatory rates. The predictions of capture theory were also contradicted; the insurance industry has not captured the regulatory process to increase premiums and

Table 6-10. Predicted and Actual Results Based on Economic Theories

| | Loss ratio | | | | Rate change activity | | | | Residual market | | Uninsured vehicles | | Insolvency assessments | |
| | Level | | Variability | | Number of changes | | Size of changes | | | | | | | |
Theory	REG[a]	Illinois	REG	Illinois	REG	Illinois	REG	Illinois	REG	Illinois	REG	Illinois	REG	Illinois
Regulation protects against:														
Excessive rates	+	-	...	...	...	...	...	...	0	0	-	0	0	0
Inadequate rates	-	+	...	...	...	...	...	...	-	+	+	-	-	+
Unfairly discriminatory rates	+	-	...	...	...	...	...	...	-	+	-	+	0	0
Alternative theories														
Rate suppression	+	0	...	...	...	...	...	...	+	0	-	0	+	0
Capture theory	-	0	...	...	...	...	...	...	-	0	+	0	-	0
Maximization of political support	±	0	-	0	...	...	...	...	±	0	±	0	...	...
Market disruption	0	0	+	-	-	+	+	-	+	-	...	...	+	-
Results of empirical tests														
Regulation based on:														
Type of law	0	0	+	0	-	0	+	0	+	0	0/+	0	0	0
CC ranking[b]	...	...	+	...	0	...	...	...	...	...	...	...	+	...

a. REG, regulated states.
b. CC ranking is the Conning Company average ranking of each state based on freedom to manage personal lines business.

profits. The primary prediction of the rate suppression theory, that the loss ratio would be higher under regulation, is not supported, but the corollary predictions that regulation would increase the size of the residual market and insolvency assessments are supported. The prediction made by maximization of political support theory that regulation would reduce variability is contradicted, and the results provide no support for the divergent effects of regulation on the loss ratio or the size of the residual market. However, the variation in effect of regulation on the size of the uninsured market does support this theory. The only theory that is supported in almost every case is the market disruption theory. As it predicts, regulation increases volatility, reduces the number and increases the size of rate changes, and increases the size of the residual market and insolvency costs. Insurance regulation serves to disrupt the market, producing only negative effects.

On the other hand, the Illinois experience is not significantly different from other competitive rate regulation systems in any of the analyses. Even though private passenger automobile insurance is not subject to rate regulation in Illinois, the system appears to work just as effectively as in other states with competitive types of rating laws. By not actively regulating insurance rates, the insurance department saves resources and can direct efforts to more productive areas, including solvency and market conduct regulation. In addition, insurers are not burdened by a time-consuming regulatory process, with uncertain results and delays in applying needed rate levels, which saves money and thus further reduces the cost of insurance. The evidence seems to suggest that restrictive regulation induces market failure. In contrast, not regulating auto insurance rates at all seems to work just as effectively as competitive rating laws. The general conclusion that can be drawn from this analysis is that the lack of a rate regulatory law in Illinois has not had any unusual effect on profitability, rate level changes, size of residual market, number of uninsured drivers, or insolvency assessments.

Conclusion

The Illinois experience suggests that rate regulation for automobile insurance is unnecessary. Illinois has functioned without a rating law since 1971. Auto insurance is widely available from a large number of competitors. Rate changes are frequent, modest, and appear to follow claim experience. Loss ratios and the size of the uninsured and residual market, as well as insolvency assessments, are in line with that in states that have competitive rating laws. Thirty years of experience suggest that the automobile insurance market functions effectively without any rate regulation.

References

All-Industry Research Advisory Council. 1989. *Uninsured Motorists.* Oak Brook, Ill.

Bajtelsmit, Vickie L., and Raja Bouzouita. 1998. "Market Structure and Performance in Private Passenger Automobile Insurance." *Journal of Risk and Insurance* 65 (3): 503–14.

Conning Company. 1980. *Regulatory Review of the Property and Casualty Industry.* Hartford, Conn.

_____. 1994. *1994 Property-Casualty Regulatory Survey.*

Cummins, J. David. 1990. "Multi-Period Discounted Cash Flow Models in Property-Liability Insurance." *Journal of Risk and Insurance* 57 (1): 79–109.

_____. 1991. "Statistical and Financial Models of Insurance Pricing and the Insurance Firm." *Journal of Risk and Insurance* 58 (2): 261–303.

Cummins, J. David, and Mary A. Weiss. 1992. "Regulation and the Automobile Insurance Crisis." *Regulation* 15 (2): 48–59.

D'Arcy, Stephen P. 1982. "An Economic Theory of Regulation." Ph.D. dissertation, University of Illinois at Urbana-Champaign.

_____. 1985. "Perceived Restrictiveness of Property-Liability Insurance Rate Regulation." *Journal of Insurance Regulation* 3 (3): 307–14.

_____. 1990. "Investment Issues in Property Liability Insurance." In *Foundations of Casualty Actuarial Science,* chap. 8. New York: Casualty Actuarial Society.

D'Arcy, Stephen P., and Neil A. Doherty. 1988. *The Financial Theory of Pricing Property-Liability Insurance Contracts.* Homewood, Ill.: Richard D. Irwin.

D'Arcy, Stephen P., and Michael A. Dyer. 1997. "Ratemaking: A Financial Economics Approach." *Proceedings of the Casualty Actuarial Society* 84: 301–90.

D'Arcy, Stephen P., and James R. Garven. 1990. "Property-Liability Insurance Pricing Models: An Empirical Evaluation." *Journal of Risk and Insurance* 57 (3): 391–430.

D'Arcy, Stephen P., and Richard W. Gorvett. 1998. "A Comparison of Property/Casualty Insurance Financial Pricing Models." *Proceedings of the Casualty Actuarial Society* 85: 1–88.

Day, John G. 1970. *Economic Regulation of Insurance in the United States.* Automobile Insurance and Compensation Study, Department of Transportation.

Feldblum, Sholom. 1996. "Personal Automobile Premiums: An Asset Share Pricing Approach for Property/Casualty Insurance." *Proceedings of the Casualty Actuarial Society* 83: 190–296.

Grabowski, Henry, W. Kip Viscusi, and William N. Evans. 1989. "Price and Availability Tradeoffs on Automobile Insurance Regulation." *Journal of Risk and Insurance* 56 (2): 275–99.

Grace, Martin F., and Michael M. Barth. 1993. *The Regulation and Structure of Nonlife Insurance in the United States.* Financial Sector Development Department, World Bank.

Grace, Martin F., and Harold D. Skipper, Jr. 1990. "The Illinois Discriminatory Premium Tax: Time for Repeal?" *Southern Illinois Law Review* 14 (Spring): 345–99.

Gron, Anne. 1995. "Regulation and Insurer Competition: Did Insurers Use Rate Regulation to Reduce Competition?" *Journal of Risk and Uncertainty* 11 (September): 87–111.

Harrington, Scott E. 1984a. "The Impact of Rate Regulation on Automobile Insurance Loss Ratios: Some New Empirical Evidence." *Journal of Insurance Regulation* 3 (December): 182–202.

_____. 1984b. "The Impact of Rate Regulation on Prices and Underwriting Results in the Property-Liability Insurance Industry: A Survey." *Journal of Risk and Insurance* 51 (4): 577–623.

_____. 1987. "A Note on the Impact of Auto Insurance Rate Regulation." *Review of Economics and Statistics* 69 (February): 166–70.

_____. 1992. "Rate Suppression." *Journal of Risk and Insurance* 59 (2): 185–202.

Illinois Department of Insurance. 1977 and 1979. *Illinois Automobile Rate Study.* Springfield.

_____. 2000. *Annual Report to the Illinois General Assembly on Insurance Cost Containment.*

Insurance Information Institute. 1998. *The Fact Book 1998 Property-Casualty Insurance Facts.* New York.

Insurance Research Council. 1999. *Uninsured Motorists.* Malvern, Pa.

Ippolito, Richard A. 1979. "The Effects of Price Regulation in the Automobile Insurance Industry." *Journal of Law and Economics* 22 (April): 55–89.

Joskow, Paul. 1973. "Cartels, Competition and Regulation in the Property-Liability Insurance Industry." *Bell Journal of Economics* 4 (2): 375–427.

Kimball, Spencer. 1960. *Insurance and Public Policy.* University of Wisconsin Press.

Kimball, Spencer, and Ronald Boyce. 1958. "The Adequacy of State Insurance Rate Regulation: The McCarran-Ferguson Act in Historical Perspective. *Michigan Law Review* 56: 545–48.

Lilly, Claude. 1976. "History of Insurance Regulation in the United States." *CPCU Annals* 29: 99–115.

Long, John D., and Robert I. Mehr. 1981. *The Illinois System of Insurance Pricing—Practices and Attitudes of Selected Insurers.* Bloomington, Ind.: Insurance Research Associates.

Ma, Yu-Luen, and Joan T. Schmit. 2000. "Factors Affecting the Relative Incidence of Uninsured Motorists Claims." *Journal of Risk and Insurance* 67 (2): 281–94.

Mehr, Robert I., and Emerson Cammack. 1980. *Principles of Insurance.* 8th ed. Homewood, Ill.: Richard D. Irwin.

Mertz, Arthur C. 1965. *The First Twenty Years: A Case-Law Commentary on Insurance Regulation Under the Commerce Clause.* Kansas City, Mo.: National Association of Independent Insurers.

Morgan, Thomas D. 1976. *Economic Regulation of Business: Cases and Materials.* West Publishing Company.

National Association of Insurance Commissioners. 1970. "Measurement of Profitability and Treatment of Investment Income in Property and Liability Insurance." *Proceedings of the National Association of Insurance Commissioners* 2A: 719–951.

_____. 1984. "Report of the Investment Income Task Force." *Proceedings of the National Association of Insurance Commissioners* 2: 719–807.

New York Insurance Department. 1969. *The Public Interest Now in Property and Liability Insurance Regulation.*

Patterson, Edwin W. 1927. *The Insurance Commissioner in the United States.* Harvard University Press.

Peltzman, Sam. 1976. "Toward a More General Theory of Regulation." *Journal of Law and Economics* 19 (2): 211–40.

Stigler, George J. 1971. "The Theory of Economic Regulation." *Bell Journal of Economics* 2 (1): 3–21.

Suponcic, Susan J., and Sharon Tennyson. 1998. "Rate Regulation and the Industrial Organization of Automobile Insurance." In *The Economics of Property-Casualty Insurance,* edited by David F. Bradford, 113–38. University of Chicago Press.

Tennyson, Sharon L. 1991. "The Effect of Rate Regulation on Underwriting Cycles." *CPCU Journal* 44: 33–44.

———. 1993. "Regulatory Lag in Automobile Insurance." *Journal of Risk and Insurance* 60 (1): 36–58.

———. 1997. "The Impact of Rate Regulation on State Automobile Insurance Markets." *Journal of Insurance Regulation* 15 (4): 502–23.

U.S. Department of Justice. 1977. *The Pricing and Marketing of Insurance.* A report to the Task Group on Antitrust Immunities.

Van Slyke, Oakley E., ed. 1999. *Actuarial Considerations Regarding Risk and Return in Property-Casualty Insurance Pricing.* New York: Casualty Actuarial Society.

Wandel, William H. 1935. *The Control of Competition in Fire Insurance.* Lancaster, Pa.: Art Printing.

Weiss, Mary. 1985. "A Multivariate Analysis of Loss Reserving Estimates in Property-Liability Insurers." *Journal of Risk and Insurance.* 52 (2): 199–221.

Witt, Robert C. 1977. *The Automobile Insurance Rate Regulatory System in Illinois: A Comparative Study.* Illinois Insurance Laws Study Commission.

SCOTT E. HARRINGTON

7 Effects of Prior Approval Rate Regulation of Auto Insurance

State regulation of insurance rates varies across states, time, and lines of business. A large literature provides statistical evidence of rate regulation's effects on average rate levels in relation to claim costs, most commonly for private passenger automobile insurance, the largest and arguably most politically sensitive line of property-liability insurance.[1] A smaller body of work provides statistical evidence of rate regulation's effects on insurance coverage availability, volatility of underwriting results, prevalence of alternative distribution methods, and levels of nonclaim production costs. The customary approach classifies states by type of rating law—prior approval or competitive rating—and then compares the mean values of relevant performance measures between the groups, conditioning on one or more control variables.

Available evidence suggests three stylized facts concerning prior approval rate regulation. First, the average effect it has on rates in relation to claim costs, if any, varies over time.[2] Second, the effects of prior

I thank the American Insurance Association (especially Amy Bruins) for providing information on state rating laws and David Cummins for providing A. M. Best aggregate state data for the period 1980–98. David Cummins, Georges Dionne, Robert Litan, and Ted Moore provided helpful comments on an earlier version of this chapter.

1. For surveys of early work, see Harrington (1984, 2000) and Cummins, Phillips, and Tennyson (2001).

2. Saba (1978); Ippolito (1979); Harrington (1987); Grabowski, Viscusi, and Evans (1989); Morrow (1992).

approval rate regulation on rates vary among states with such laws.[3] Third, it is associated with larger residual market shares.[4] In addition, there is some (but not uniform) evidence that prior approval regulation increases the volatility of underwriting results.[5] Finally, it may also influence nonclaim production expenses and reduce the market shares of direct writers.[6]

This study estimates the conditional mean effect of prior approval rate regulation on the level of automobile insurance loss ratios, level of automobile insurance residual market shares, and volatility of loss ratios and growth rates in the average expenditure on automobile insurance (an indirect measure of rate volatility).[7] It does not consider the interesting and important question of whether rate regulation distorts consumer and insurer incentives for loss control and therefore increases claim costs and average rate levels for any given price-cost margin.

In this study annual, cross-state data for the fifty states during 1972 to 1998 are employed to analyze loss ratios and volatility of expenditure growth rates. Residual market shares are analyzed for the period from 1974 to 1997. Borrowing from a large literature that estimates cross-sectional models of expected returns in securities markets, I allow the mean effects of prior approval rate regulation and the control variables in my regression equations to vary each year and test whether the time-series average of each coefficient is significantly different from zero for the overall sample period and for three nonoverlapping subperiods.[8]

The analysis begins with an outline of the possible effects of prior approval regulation on prices, loss ratios, availability, and volatility. Subsequent sections describe the methodology and data used and then present the results of estimating the conditional mean effect of prior approval regulation on loss ratios, residual market shares, and the volatilities of loss ratios and expenditure growth rates.

---

3. Harrington (1986, 1987); Grabowski, Viscusi, and Evans (1989); Cummins, Phillips, and Tennyson (2001).

4. Ippolito (1979); Grabowski, Viscusi, and Evans (1989); Bouzouita and Bajtelsmit (1997).

5. MacAvoy (1977); U.S. General Accounting Office (1979); Witt and Miller (1981); Outreville (1990); Tennyson (1991); Barth and Feldhaus (1999).

6. Joskow (1973); Braeutigam and Pauly (1986); Pauly, Kleindorfer, and Kunreuther (1986); Gron (1995); Tennyson (1997); Suponcic and Tennyson (1998).

7. The loss ratio is an inverse measure of average price (see subsequent discussion).

8. For an example of estimates using cross-sectional models of expected returns in securities markets, see Fama and French (1992).

Conceptual Framework

A substantial body of research has stressed three main hypotheses concerning the effects of prior approval regulation.[9] According to the *capture* (or producer protection) hypothesis, regulators are captured by the insurance industry, with the result that prior approval raises average rates and thus reduces average loss ratios (ratios of losses to premiums). Given the competitive structure of the industry, supracompetitive rates would be expected to produce nonprice (service) competition that would increase product quality and prevent excess profits.

In contrast, the *rate suppression* (or consumer pressure) hypothesis posits that consumer pressure for low rates causes regulators to suppress rates periodically or even persistently. The predicted results include higher loss ratios, lower availability of coverage in the voluntary market, lower product quality, reduced entry, and increased exit. Although chronic rate suppression would probably be unsustainable without both strong consumer pressure for low prices and consumer myopia concerning its adverse effects on quality and availability, temporary rate suppression during periods of rapid claim cost growth is prima facie more plausible.

However, persistent rate suppression may be feasible for some groups of consumers if rate increases for other groups allow insurers to earn normal profits without significantly reducing average product quality.[10] Although average loss ratios would be largely unaffected by the resulting cross-subsidies, residual market shares would be larger because insurers would not provide coverage voluntarily to groups whose regulated rates are suppressed compared to competitive levels.

Thus chronic, temporary, or selective rate suppression would produce higher residual market shares in states with prior approval regulation. *Regulatory lag* could produce lower rate increases during hard markets or periods of rapid cost growth (temporary rate suppression) and larger rate increases or slower rate reductions in soft markets or periods of stable or declining claim costs.[11] If so, residual market shares

9. Ippolito (1979); Harrington (1984); Grabowski, Viscusi, and Evans (1989); Cummins, Phillips, and Tennyson (2001). See also the introduction to this volume by David Cummins and my monograph (Harrington, 2000).

10. Harrington and Doerpinghaus (1993).

11. Insurance markets historically have had alternating soft and hard market periods, especially for commercial lines of business. Soft markets are characterized by abundant availability of coverage and

would increase during the former periods and decline during the latter periods.

Regulatory lag would tend to increase the volatility of loss ratios over time.[12] Regulatory lag in states with prior approval could conceivably smooth rate changes in relation to changes in expected claim costs, which in turn could reduce the volatility of average expenditures by consumers over time. For example, if prior approval regulation tends to be counter-cyclical (that is, rates are depressed during hard markets and inflated during soft markets compared with competitive rating), loss ratio volatility would be higher than in competitive rating states, but regulatory lag could reduce volatility of rates and, therefore, of expenditures.

An alternative hypothesis is that regulatory lag and political pressure might lead to fewer but larger rate changes in prior approval states than in competitive rating states.[13] A strong and persistent surge in claim costs, for example, might initially be accompanied by rate suppression, followed by large rate increases to keep pace with expected costs and to halt declining availability and quality of coverage and deter insurer exit.[14] Similarly, prior approval regulation might initially delay rate decreases in the face of declining costs, with larger decreases ultimately filed and approved. These effects would tend to cause greater volatility in loss ratios, rate changes, and expenditure growth in prior approval states than in competitive rating states.

Methodology and Data

This section first describes the methodology and data used to analyze levels of loss ratios. I then describe my analysis of residual market shares and the volatility of loss ratios and expenditure growth rates.

Loss Ratio Analysis

To provide evidence of prior approval regulation's average effect on rates for private passenger automobile insurance (liability-related coverages

---

relatively stable or declining prices. Hard markets are characterized by limited availability of coverage and pronounced price increases.

12. See, for example, Witt and Miller (1981) and Tennyson (1991).

13. MacAvoy (1977); Tennyson (1991, 1993).

14. Regarding persistent increases in claim costs and rate suppression, see Kramer (1991). For a discussion of the consequences of rate suppression, see Harrington (1992).

and physical damage coverage combined), I analyze the adjusted loss ratio, which is defined as the sum of direct incurred losses and policy dividends divided by direct earned premiums.[15] The loss ratio is commonly used as an inverse measure of price. (A number of studies employ the inverse of the loss ratio, which is sometimes called the unit price.) One minus the loss ratio represents the (undiscounted) gross margin for insurer loss adjustment expenses, nonclaim expenses, and profits. Other things being equal, higher (lower) average loss ratios in states with prior approval regulation than in states with competitive rating laws would imply that prior approval regulation lowers (raises) average rates for any given level of expected claim costs.[16]

The basic approach used here involves estimating several versions of the following equation for each year during the 1972–98 period:

$$(7\text{-}1) \qquad Loss\ Ratio_{jt} = \alpha_t + \beta_t\, Prior\ Approval_{jt} + \gamma_t\,'\mathbf{X}_{jt} + \varepsilon_{jt}\,,$$

where for state j in year t, $Loss\ Ratio$ is the loss ratio, $Prior\ Approval$ is an indicator variable equal to one if the state has a prior approval law and zero if it has a competitive rating law (see below), $\mathbf{X}$ is a vector of control variables that could influence loss ratios apart from any effects of rate regulation, and ε is a statistical disturbance that reflects unexplained influences on the loss ratio. The parameters α_t, β_t, and η_t are allowed to vary over time. The key parameter, β_t, measures the average effect of prior approval regulation on loss ratios in year t, controlling for the influence of $\mathbf{X}$.[17]

For each year several versions of equation 7-1 are estimated using least squares, and then each coefficient is averaged over the 1972–98 period and the 1972–80, 1981–89, and 1990–98 subperiods. Given probable heteroskedasticity and autocorrelation in the yearly parameter estimates, I test whether the mean values are significantly different from zero using the ratio of the mean coefficient to its heteroskedasticity and autocorrelation consistent standard error.[18] These test statistics are referred to as t-ratios.

The time-varying parameter approach has several advantages. First,

15. Loss ratios were winsorized at the 0.5 and 99.5 percentiles of the sample distribution for 1972 to 1998 to reduce the effects of possible outliers.

16. Profitability measures that incorporate loss adjustment and nonclaim expenses are not analyzed here. Some expenses are reported by state, but only for recent years. Loss ratios are highly correlated with profitability measures that reflect such expenses, other expenses that are allocated among states, and allocations of investment income.

17. In more technical terms, the estimate of β_t is an estimate of the difference between the conditional mean loss ratio in prior approval and competitive rating states, conditioning on $\mathbf{X}_{jt}$.

18. Newey and West (1987).

annual estimates (and subperiod means) of the effects of prior approval regulation are informative in their own right. When compared with results from previous studies, they provide additional insight into temporal variation in regulation's effects. Second, intuition, financial models of insurance prices, and prior work on regulatory lag and the politics of rate regulation all suggest that the coefficients will vary (stochastically) over time due to changes in interest rates, technology (and thus production expenses), political pressure, and so on. As a result, statistical tests that assume that the parameters are constant over time will tend to reject the null hypothesis too frequently. A third and related advantage is that statistical tests based on the annual estimates are robust to cross-state correlation in the regression model disturbances, including any correlation due to regional factors.[19]

PRIOR APPROVAL   Table 7-1 provides definitions and data sources for the main variables used in the analysis. A state is classified as having a prior approval law in year t if it had either state-made rates, a strict prior approval law, a prior approval law with an express "deemer" provision (that is, rates are deemed approved if no action has been taken by regulators a specified number of days after the rates were filed), a modified prior approval law requiring prior approval for changes in the relation between premiums and expenses, or a file-and-use law that required prior approval of deviations from rates filed by a rate advisory organization. A state is classified as having a competitive rating law if it permitted file-and-use, use-and-file, filing only, file-and-use or use-and-file in a "competitive" market, or had flex rating with a large flex band.[20] Tables 7A-1 and 7A-2 in appendix 7A summarize the broad classification used and the types of laws in effect by state during the sample period.

19. Fama and French (2000) emphasize this third advantage in a different context. Allowing the parameters to vary over time precludes fixed effects estimation. Allowing for fixed state effects would require constraining variation of one or more of the parameters over time. Fixed (and random) effects estimation generally only allows for a specific form of cross-sectional correlation (for example, that which might arise from fixed or random time effects). Given that three-fifths of the states kept the same regulatory regime during 1972 to 1998, estimating the model with panel data and the conventional fixed effects estimator also would ignore information about regulation's effects in those states. After the conference presentation of this paper, I nonetheless estimated equation 7-1 with both fixed and random effects methods (allowing for year and state effects) for the 1972–98 period and the 1972–79, 1980–89, and 1990–98 subperiods. The results had the same implications as those reported in table 7-3.

20. Flex rating systems allow insurers to file and use rate changes without prior approval if the absolute rate change is within a specified range (the flex band).

Table 7-1. *Variable Definitions and Data Sources*

Variable	Description	Period	Source[a]
Loss Ratio	Loss ratio (adjusted for dividends)	1972–98	1972–92: A.M. Best Co. 1993–98: NAIC
Prior Approval	1 if prior approval rating law; 0 otherwise	1972–98	AIA (1992–99), U.S. GAO (1979), ISO (1990), Kansas Insurance Dept. (2000), state codes
Liability percent	Auto liability (including personal injury protection) direct (written) premiums/ total auto direct premiums	1972–98	1972–92: A.M. Best Co. 1993–98: NAIC
PIP percent	Personal injury protection (PIP) direct premiums/total auto direct premiums	1972–98	1972–92: A.M. Best Co. 1993–98: NAIC
Direct Writer percent	Direct writer share of auto direct premiums	1972–98	1972–92: A.M. Best Co. 1993–98: NAIC
Loss Cost	Average loss per liability written car-year in state divided by the mean average loss across states in year t	1972–98	Incurred losses 1972–92: A.M. Best Co. 1993–98: NAIC Written car-years AIPSO, *AIPSO Facts*
Residual Market percent	Residual market share of auto liability insurance written car-years	1974–97	AIPSO
Expenditure Growth	Percent growth in average auto insurance premium expenditure per liability written car-year/100	1973–98	Premiums 1972–92: A.M. Best Co. 1993–98: NAIC Written car-years AIPSO
Car-years$^{1/2}$	Square root of auto liability written car-years	1972–98	AIPSO
σ^2(Loss Ratio)	Unexplained volatility in Loss Ratio (squared, de-meaned residual from basic Loss Ratio equation)	1972–98	See Loss Ratio
σ^2(Expenditure)	Unexplained volatility in Expenditure Growth (squared, de-meaned residual from Expenditure Growth equation)	1973–98	See Expenditure Growth

a. A.M. Best, unpublished data; NAIC, National Association of Insurance Commissioners, unpublished data; AIA, American Insurance Association; GAO, General Accounting Office; ISO, Insurance Services Office; AIPSO, Automobile Insurance Plans Service Office.

Figure 7-1. *Number of States with Prior Approval Rate Regulation for
Private Passenger Automobile Insurance, 1972–98*

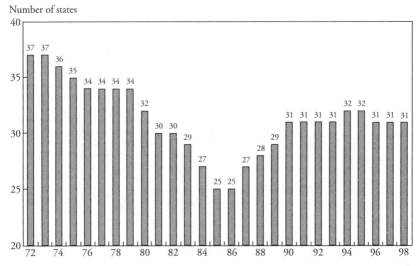

Source: American Insurance Association (1992–99); U.S. General Accounting Office (1979); Insurance Services
Office (1990); Kansas Insurance Department (2000); state codes.

Figure 7-1 plots the number of states with prior approval regulation
during the 1972–98 period. Beginning in the early 1970s, that number
declined from three quarters to half of the states by the mid-1980s. It subsequently increased to about three-fifths of the states in conjunction with
the surge in automobile insurance claim costs in the late 1980s.

Some specifications of equation 7-1 include indicator (dummy) variables for three states—Massachusetts, New Jersey, and South Carolina—
known for rigid rate regulation during much or all of the 1972–98
period.[21] The inclusion of dummy variables for those states provides
insight into the extent to which estimates of regulation's effects are influenced by a few heavily regulated states. The coefficient on the prior
approval variable then provides an estimate of prior approval regulation's
average effect in the remaining states with such laws.

CONTROL VARIABLES   The control variables were chosen to balance the
advantages of parsimony with the risk of omitted variables. Four main var-

21. State indicator variables for one or more states have been used to proxy for regulatory stringency
in a number of earlier studies.

iables are included that could be associated with differences in expected loss ratios among states in the absence of rate regulation:[22]

—Liability percent: the proportion of private passenger automobile premiums in the state that is represented by liability-related coverages (liability, medical, personal injury protection, and uninsured-underinsured motorists);

—PIP percent: the proportion of private passenger automobile premiums represented by personal injury protection (PIP) coverage;

—Direct Writer percent: the share of premiums written by direct writers (that is, insurers with exclusive agents, company employee systems, or direct sales);

—Loss Cost: the state's average loss per insured vehicle (incurred losses divided by liability written car-years) divided by the mean average loss for all states in the given year.

The coefficient on Liability percent provides an estimate of the effect on the loss ratio of substituting liability-related premiums for physical damage (and theft) premiums. Longer claims tails for liability-related coverages will tend to increase the expected loss ratio because insurers can earn more investment income on premiums before paying claims, thus reducing the premium that must be charged to fund expected claim costs. Higher claim settlement expenses for liability coverage will tend to reduce the expected loss ratio.

Given the inclusion of Liability percent, the coefficient on PIP percent provides an estimate of the effect on the loss ratio of substituting personal injury protection premiums associated with automobile no-fault or "add-on" laws for other liability-related premiums. Shorter claims tails for personal injury protection coverage compared to other liability-related coverages will tend to reduce the expected loss ratio because insurers will earn less investment income. Lower claim settlement expenses for personal injury protection coverage than for other liability coverages will tend to increase the expected loss ratio.[23] The coefficient on PIP percent (or on the other control variables) also will reflect any correlation during year t

22. In contrast to previous studies (such as Bajtelsmit and Bouzouita, 1998), a measure of market concentration as a control variable is not included. As explained in my 1984 paper, the high correlation between direct writer share and concentration might make it difficult to distinguish the effects of each variable.

23. Advocates of no-fault often stress that no-fault states should have higher loss ratios and thus deliver a higher percent of benefits per dollar of premiums than in traditional tort liability states.

between unexpected growth in incurred losses and PIP percent (or the other controls). The magnitude of the coefficients obtained for PIP percent and anecdotal evidence suggest unexpectedly large loss ratios in some states with no-fault laws.[24]

The coefficient on Direct Writer percent is expected to be positive given materially lower expenses for direct writers than for insurers that use independent agents and brokers.[25] The coefficient should diminish over time to the extent that such differences have diminished.

Loss Cost is included to allow for a possible nonproportional relationship between average premiums and average expected claim costs across states. It sometimes is argued, for example, that states with higher average losses will have higher loss ratios because some nonclaim production expenses may increase less than proportionately with expected claim costs. Dividing by the mean ratio of incurred losses to written car-years across states in a given year makes the coefficients on Loss Cost comparable over time. Given possibly material variation of average losses around the expected value that will be directly related to Loss Ratio, Loss Cost in the prior year is used as an instrument for Loss Cost in year t (except for 1972, where Loss Cost in 1973 is used). This procedure is designed to produce a consistent estimator.[26]

INTERACTION VARIABLES   If factors that influence differences in regulation's effects among prior approval states are correlated with the control variables, the coefficients on Prior Approval and the controls will reflect those influences. If, for example, any effect of prior approval regulation on loss ratios is greater in states with higher underlying costs of coverage, the coefficient on Loss Cost in equation 7-1 would tend to be biased upward, which in turn would tend to produce a downward bias in the coefficient on Prior Approval.

To check the robustness of the results, a model is estimated that includes interaction variables between Prior Approval and each of the con-

24. Harrington (1987); Witt and Urrutia (1983).
25. Berger, Cummins, and Weiss (1997).
26. See Harrington (1987) for further discussion. For convenience equation 7-1 was estimated with least squares (without adjusting the standard errors) rather than true instrumental variables. For years 1973–98 the predicted (fitted) value from a regression of Loss Cost$_{jt}$ on Loss Cost$_{jt-1}$ was used as an instrument for Loss Cost$_{jt}$. Because incurred loss data was not available for 1971, the fitted value from a regression of Loss Cost$_{j,1972}$ on Loss Cost$_{j,1973}$ was used for 1972. Data on written car-years for 1972 and 1973 was also not available; therefore values for those years were backfitted based on the two-year geometric growth rate using the first available data.

trols.[27] I interact Prior Approval and the difference between each control variable and its mean in year t in prior approval states. Defining the interaction variables using "de-meaned" controls has two advantages. First, the coefficient on Prior Approval provides an estimate of regulation's impact on the loss ratio for a state with average values of the control variables in prior approval states. Second, deducting the mean reduces the correlation between Prior Approval and the interaction variables (although the interaction variables themselves may still be highly correlated).[28]

Residual Market Share Analysis

Residual Market percent is analyzed to provide evidence of the average effect of prior approval rate regulation on coverage availability. Two versions of the following equation are estimated for each year during the 1974–97 period:[29]

$$(7\text{-}2) \quad Residual\ Market\ \%_{jt} = a_t + \beta_t\ Prior\ Approval_{jt} + \gamma_t{}'\ \mathbf{BIG}_{jt} + \varepsilon_{jt},$$

where for state j and year t, *Residual Market* is liability written car-years in the residual market divided by total (voluntary plus residual) liability writ-

---

27. Cummins, Phillips, and Tennyson (2002).

28. As a further robustness check, I considered the possibility that the presence of prior approval regulation could be correlated with the statistical disturbance, ε_{jt}, thus making the least squares estimator inconsistent. Following Cummins, Phillips, and Tennyson (2001), I estimated a selection model based on the two-step estimator of Heckman (1978). As an alternative, the model was also estimated using two-stage least squares, where the predicted probability that a state has prior approval regulation (from a probit model) was used as an instrument for Prior Approval. [Greene (1998) provides a concise explanation of the selection and instrumental variables approaches for models of "treatment" effects.] A variety of probit equations were estimated, including Liability percent, PIP percent, Direct Writer percent, Loss Cost, Loss Cost squared, and Car-Years[1/2] as regressors. Neither the selection model nor the two-stage least squares approach to allowing for possible sample selectivity or endogeneity of prior approval rate regulation produced reliable estimates. The yearly coefficients for Prior Approval were highly variable with implausible magnitudes (both negative and positive). The culprit appeared to be ill-conditioning (multicollinearity) of the regressors when the selection variable (the inverse Mills ratio) was included in equation 7-1 or when the predicted probability of having prior approval regulation was used as an instrument for Prior Approval. The unreliability of the results might in part reflect the relatively small sample size in the yearly cross-state regressions. Given these findings, it remains uncertain whether possible correlation between prior approval regulation and one or more omitted factors that could substantively affect loss ratios *in markets without prior approval regulation* could materially bias the least squares coefficient on Prior Approval in equation 7-1. While my attempts to provide empirical insight into this question in the context of the time-varying parameter approach were unsuccessful, I can think of no strong intuitive reason for material bias.

29. Results with the same implications were obtained using a log odds specification to allow for the fact that Residual Market percent is bounded by zero and is close to zero in many states.

ten car-years and **BIG** is a vector of dummy variables for five states (Massachusetts, New Hampshire, New Jersey, North Carolina, and South Carolina) with reinsurance facilities or related residual market mechanisms and large residual market shares during much of the 1974–97 period.[30] Without the state dummies, the coefficient on Prior Approval equals the difference in the mean value of Residual Market percent between states with prior approval and states with competitive rating. When the state dummies are included, the coefficient on Prior Approval equals the difference in the mean value of Residual Market percent between the remaining states with prior approval and states with competitive rating.

The coefficients on Prior Approval and the state dummies will reflect the effects of prior approval regulation on overall rate levels and any regulatory restrictions in prior approval states on rate classification and underwriting. I do not attempt to distinguish those influences apart from including the dummy variables for the five states that often have substantially restricted differences in rates across consumers compared to competitive pricing. Letting the parameters vary over time allows for changes in residual market share in prior approval and competitive rating states associated with temporal influences, such as the insurance underwriting cycle. The absence of other control variables in equation 7-2 reflects the assumption—based on both theory and evidence—that residual markets generally will be negligible when states allow insurers a large degree of freedom in pricing and rate classification.[31]

Loss Ratio Volatility

Unexplained (unpredictable) volatility in loss ratios is analyzed to provide evidence of the average effect of prior approval regulation on the vol-

---

30. The same notation is used for the parameters and disturbances in equations 7-1 and 7-2 and for the parameters in equation 7-3 (see below) to avoid notational clutter.

31. It is well known, for example, that some states with competitive rating environments (such as Illinois and Ohio) have negligible residual markets even though they have large urban centers with sizable low-income populations. The estimated effects of control variables included in prior studies of residual market shares may reflect correlation between the controls and the scope and intensity of price regulation, as opposed to their effects in markets that are substantially free from price regulation (Ippolito, 1979; Bouzouita and Bajtelsmit, 1997). The implications of those studies concerning the effects of rate regulation are nonetheless consistent with those reported here. Moreover, I obtained results with similar implications when Residual Market percent was regressed on Prior Approval, dummies for states with large residual market shares, and growth (current or lagged) in Loss Cost.

atility of insurers' underwriting results. The following equation is estimated for each year during the 1972–98 period:

(7-3) $\sigma^2(Loss\ Ratio)_{jt} \equiv (e_{jt} - e_{j.})^2 = a_t + \beta_t Prior\ Approval_{jt}$
$$+ \lambda_t'W_{jt} + v_{jt},$$

where for state j and year t, e_{jt} is the least squares residual from equation
7-1, $e_{j.}$ is the mean of e_{jt} for state j during the 1972–98 period, W is a vector of control variables, and v is a statistical disturbance. The loss ratio volatility measure, $\sigma^2(Loss\ Ratio)$, abstracts from (a) temporal variation in
average loss ratios in both prior approval and competitive rating states
caused by cyclical or other influences, (b) the (time-varying) effects of the
control variables on loss ratios, and (c) the mean unexplained component
of the loss ratio for state j, that is, the component that is unrelated to (a)
and (b). Regarding (c), if a state has either a positive or negative mean
residual over time from equation 7-1, that effect is removed from the volatility measure so as not to confound unexplained volatility with unob-
served effects of rate regulation or omitted variables.[32]

Four control variables are included in equation 7-3: Liability percent,
PIP percent, Loss Cost, and Car-Years$^{1/2}$ (in hundreds). Car-Years$^{1/2}$ is
included to allow for lower volatility as the number of insured exposures
increases.[33] A significantly positive (negative) mean coefficient on Prior
Approval for the overall sample period or any subperiod would provide
evidence of significantly larger (smaller) volatility in prior approval states
than in competitive rating states.

Volatility in Expenditure Growth Rates

An equation similar to equation 7-3 is used to test whether volatility in
the unexplained growth rate in the average auto insurance expenditure per
written car-year differs between prior approval and competitive rating
states. First equation 7-1 is estimated using Expenditure Growth in year t as
the dependent variable instead of Loss Ratio. Then the squared de-meaned

32. I also estimated models that defined volatility as the square of $y_{jt} - y_{j.}$, where y_{jt} equals the residual from equation 7-1 in year t plus the estimated coefficient for Prior Approval in year t. That volatility measure will reflect the influence of changes in the average effect of prior approval regulation
over time. The results had the same implications as those reported (see "Empirical Results").

33. Note that Car-Years$^{1/2}$ is not included to adjust for heteroskedasticity in the disturbance of the
loss ratio volatility equation; it is included because volatility should be related to the volume of written car-years.

residuals from the first step—denoted σ^2(Expenditure)—are regressed on Prior Approval, Liability percent, PIP percent, and Loss Cost.[34]

The analysis of volatility in expenditure growth rates provides an indirect test of whether volatility in rate changes differs between states with prior approval and competitive rating. As long as the short-run demand for automobile insurance coverage (per car-year) is relatively inelastic with respect to rates, expenditure growth rates should be positively related to rate changes. As discussed earlier, if prior approval produces less frequent but larger rate changes, it could increase the volatility of rate changes and of expenditure growth rates. Demand elasticity with respect to rate changes will reduce the correlation between rate changes and expenditure changes, thus reducing the power of the indirect test for differences in rate volatility between regulatory regimes using σ^2(Expenditure).

Empirical Results

This section first presents the results for the analysis of the level of loss ratios. I then describe the results of the residual market share and volatility analyses.

Rate Regulation and Loss Ratios

Table 7-2 presents descriptive statistics for the variables used in the analysis for all states and stratified by type of rating law. The mean loss ratios for prior approval and competitive rating states during the 1972–98 period are identical to the third decimal place (0.689 vs. 0.688, respectively).[35]

Figure 7-2 plots yearly mean loss ratios for the two broad regulatory regimes. The sample period included two severe hard market periods, 1975–76 and 1985–86. The latter hard market was much more severe for commercial liability insurance, and it followed a prolonged soft market for such coverages in the late 1970s and early 1980s. The overall property-

---

34. I winsorize Expenditure Growth at the 0.5 and 99.5 percentiles of the sample distribution. Similar results were obtained including Car-Years$^{1/2}$. I also estimated models that defined expenditure volatility as the square of $z_{jt} - z_{j.}$, where z_{jt} equals the residual in year t from estimating equation 7-1 with Expenditure Growth as the dependent variable in year t plus the estimated coefficient for Prior Approval in year t. The results had the same implications as those reported.

35. Consistent with the regression results reported later, a difference-in-means test for the mean Loss Ratio in prior approval and competitive rating states was not significant, whereas the means for Residual Market percent and volatility variables are significantly higher for prior approval states than for competitive rating states (at the 0.05 level or lower for each variable).

liability market was soft in most states through much of the 1990s. Although the patterns depicted in figure 7-2 are not sharp, they provide casual evidence that rate regulation tended to raise rates (in relation to claim costs) in soft markets and lower rates in hard markets. The mean loss ratios are virtually identical from 1972 to 1975, higher in prior approval states from 1976 to 1981, lower in prior approval states during the early 1980s, higher in prior approval states from 1986 to 1992, and approximately equal to those for competitive rating states from 1993 to 1998.

Least Squares Estimates

Table 7-3 reports mean coefficients for Prior Approval from estimating equation 7-1. Results are shown for equations with and without control variables and for the control variables plus interactions between Prior Approval and the de-meaned control variables. Results for the 1972–98 period and the 1972–80, 1981–89, and 1990–98 subperiods are presented, as are results for each equation with and without the dummies for Massachusetts, New Jersey, and South Carolina.[36]

The implications of the results reported in table 7-3 are broadly similar across specifications. For the overall 1972–98 period, the largest mean coefficient for the Prior Approval variable is 0.01 (1 percent), and it is weakly significant (t-ratio = 1.83). The largest mean coefficient for any subperiod is 0.02 during the 1972–80 period, with a t-ratio above two. Apart from the 1970s and from the model with controls and without state dummies for the 1990s, no t-ratio exceeds two. Thus the overall results indicate a positive but economically negligible and weakly significant relationship between prior approval regulation and loss ratios.

Table 7-4 shows mean coefficients for the control variables from estimating equation 7-1 without the Massachusetts, New Jersey, and South Carolina dummy variables. There is some evidence of lower loss ratios in states with a greater proportion of premiums represented by liability-related coverages, which could indicate that the higher loss adjustment expenses for such coverage outweigh the influence of the longer claims tail. There is evidence of a strong, positive relationship between loss ratios and PIP percent. Although consistent with the argument that no-fault laws deliver a higher proportion of premiums to consumers in the form of claim

---

36. The coefficients on the New Jersey and South Carolina dummy variables were generally large, positive, and highly significant but were generally insignificant for Massachusetts.

Table 7-2. Descriptive Statistics[a]

Sample and variables	Mean	SD	Skewness	Kurtosis	Minimum	Maximum	N
All states							
Loss Ratio	0.689	0.073	0.26	3.12	0.495	0.908	1350
Prior Approval	0.605	0.489	−0.43	1.18	0.000	1.000	1350
Liability percent	0.586	0.066	−0.08	2.61	0.377	0.776	1350
PIP percent	0.047	0.068	1.40	4.49	0.000	0.369	1350
Direct Writer percent	0.601	0.124	−0.76	3.22	0.210	0.837	1350
Loss Cost[b]	271	141	0.65	2.71	57	783	1350
Residual Market percent	0.042	0.090	3.40	16.46	0.000	0.732	1200
Expenditure Growth	0.057	0.060	0.59	4.228	−0.109	0.267	1300
σ^2(Loss Ratio) $\times$ 100	0.199	0.363	4.70	37.77	0.000	4.554	1350
σ^2(Expenditure) $\times$ 100	0.143	0.284	4.92	38.27	0.000	3.302	1300
Prior Approval							
Loss Ratio	0.689	0.076	0.19	3.13	0.495	0.908	817
Liability percent	0.589	0.071	−0.09	2.41	0.401	0.776	817
PIP percent	0.045	0.063	1.20	3.37	0.000	0.249	817
Direct Writer percent	0.583	0.134	−0.68	2.95	0.210	0.837	817
Loss Cost	278	153	0.61	2.45	57	783	817

Residual Market percent	0.064	0.110	2.54	10.10	0.000	0.732	715
Expenditure Growth	0.055	0.062	0.51	3.95	−0.109	0.267	781
σ^2(Loss Ratio) × 100	0.241	0.419	4.38	32.07	0.000	4.554	817
σ^2(Expenditure)×100	0.169	0.320	4.61	33.77	0.000	3.302	781
Competitive Rating							
Loss Ratio	0.688	0.066	0.39	2.88	0.524	0.908	533
Liability percent	0.582	0.058	−0.19	2.86	0.377	0.733	533
PIP percent	0.050	0.075	1.51	4.98	−0.002	0.369	533
Direct Writer percent	0.629	0.101	−0.51	2.40	0.369	0.810	533
Loss Cost	260	118	0.55	2.73	67	606	533
Residual Market percent	0.010	0.022	3.08	13.78	0.000	0.151	485
Expenditure Growth	0.060	0.055	0.78	4.66	−0.109	0.267	519
σ^2(Loss Ratio) × 100	0.134	0.240	3.78	20.62	0.000	1.814	533
σ^2(Expenditure) × 100	0.105	0.214	5.03	36.26	0.000	2.174	519

Source: Author's calculations.

a. See table 7-1 for detailed definition of the variables. SD is standard deviation. N is the number of observations.

b. The Loss Cost variable in this table is simply the average loss per car-year; it is not divided by the cross-state mean in year t. Values are in dollars for mean, standard deviation, minimum, and maximum.

Figure 7-2. *Mean Auto Insurance Loss Ratios by Type of Rating Law,*
1972–98

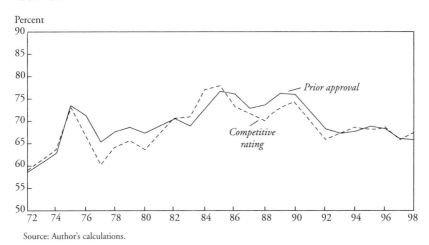

Source: Author's calculations.

payments than traditional tort systems, the large magnitude of the estimates suggests unexpectedly large loss ratios in the 1970s with a declining
impact over time. The mean coefficients for Direct Writer percent are positive and significant as expected, except for the 1981–89 subperiod, where
the mean is near zero. The mean coefficient for Loss Cost is positive and
significant for the overall period and each subperiod, but it is considerably
smaller in the 1990s than in earlier years.

Table 7-5 shows yearly coefficients for Prior Approval and *t*-ratios
using White standard errors.[37] Results are shown for equations estimated
with and without controls and with and without the three state dummy
variables. Figure 7-3 plots the yearly coefficients for Prior Approval for the
model with controls but no state dummies and the 95 percent confidence
interval (the estimate plus or minus two standard errors) for those estimates, again using White standard errors. The results confirm the basic
pattern illustrated in figure 7-2 and those shown in table 7-3. The 95 per-

37. White standard errors (White, 1980) are used since the statistical disturbance will likely be heter-
oskedastic, in part due to variation in the impact of prior approval regulation across states (compare with
Harrington, 1987). White standard errors have relatively poor finite sample properties. Long and Ervin
(2000) show that White standard errors are biased toward rejecting the null hypothesis in small samples,
but they find that a variant known as HC3 (see MacKinnon and White, 1985) has good properties even
for sample sizes as small as twenty-five. I replicated the tests using HC3 standard errors, and the resulting *t*-ratios generally were slightly lower than those presented here. I report results using White standard
errors because the HC3 standard errors assumed implausibly large values for a handful of the yearly
parameter estimates, presumably due to a ballooning effect for observations with high leverage.

Table 7-3. *Mean Coefficients and t-ratios for Prior Approval in Loss Ratio Equations, Selected Periods, 1972–98*[a]

Control variables and period	Without Mass., N.J., and S.C. dummies		With Mass., N.J., and S.C. dummies	
	Mean	t-ratio	Mean	t-ratio
None				
1972–98	0.010	1.83	0.005	0.97
1972–80	0.020	2.03	0.015	1.66
1981–89	0.007	0.59	0.001	0.10
1990–98	0.005	1.03	−0.001	−0.11
Liability percent, PIP percent, Direct Writer percent, Loss Cost				
1972–98	0.008	1.48	0.003	0.78
1972–80	0.019	1.92	0.014	1.73
1981–89	−0.002	−0.18	−0.005	−0.70
1990–98	0.006	2.03	0.000	0.16
Equation 7-1 controls plus Prior Approval– control interactions				
1972–98	0.008	1.68	0.004	0.90
1972–80	0.020	2.31	0.017	2.30
1981–89	−0.001	−0.07	−0.003	−0.53
1990–98	0.006	1.71	−0.001	−0.31

Source: Author's calculations.

a. Mean is the mean coefficient for Prior Approval for the period shown. The *t*-ratio is the mean divided by the Newey-West standard error. See table 7-1 for detailed definitions of the variables.

Table 7-4. *Mean Coefficients and t-ratios for Control Variables in Loss Ratio Equation, without Dummies for Massachusetts, New Jersey, and South Carolina, Selected Periods, 1972–98*[a]

Period	Liability percent		PIP percent		Direct Writer percent		Loss Cost	
	Mean	t-ratio	Mean	t-ratio	Mean	t-ratio	Mean	t-ratio
1972–98	−0.082	−2.02	0.198	4.57	0.035	2.24	0.062	4.70
1972–80	−0.041	−1.49	0.340	6.73	0.038	2.93	0.073	3.71
1981–89	−0.028	−0.94	0.173	3.79	−0.007	−0.29	0.089	5.41
1990–98	−0.176	−1.91	0.082	2.74	0.075	4.01	0.025	2.73

Source: Author's calculations.

a. Mean is the mean coefficient for Prior Approval for the period shown. The *t*-ratio is the mean divided by the Newey-West standard error. See table 7-1 for variable definitions.

Table 7-5. *Coefficients and* t-*values by Year for Prior Approval in Loss Ratio Equations, 1972–98*[a]

| Year | Without control variables | | | | With control variables | | | |
| | Without Mass., N.J., and S.C. dummies | | With Mass., N.J., and S.C. dummies | | Without Mass., N.J., and S.C. dummies | | With Mass., N.J., and S.C. dummies | |
	Coeff.	t-ratio	Coeff.	t-ratio	Mean	t-ratio	Coeff.	t-ratio
1972	−0.004	−0.42	−0.003	−0.32	0.002	0.20	0.002	0.18
1973	−0.001	−0.09	−0.004	−0.32	−0.006	−0.64	−0.007	−0.74
1974	−0.008	−0.62	−0.013	−1.01	−0.016	−1.64	−0.015	−1.49
1975	0.004	0.24	−0.003	−0.16	0.014	0.97	0.008	0.53
1976	0.037	2.26	0.034	2.19	0.041	3.03	0.027	2.35
1977	0.049	3.48	0.046	3.33	0.050	3.44	0.037	2.88
1978	0.035	2.04	0.029	1.69	0.037	2.46	0.031	2.04
1979	0.030	1.81	0.022	1.36	0.028	1.90	0.024	1.65
1980	0.036	2.30	0.030	1.93	0.021	1.43	0.024	1.57
1981	0.020	1.13	0.012	0.66	0.003	0.20	0.001	0.05
1982	−0.001	−0.06	−0.005	−0.30	−0.006	−0.48	−0.005	−0.40
1983	−0.021	−1.70	−0.022	−1.72	−0.025	−2.68	−0.022	−2.45
1984	−0.040	−2.77	−0.040	−2.64	−0.033	−2.21	−0.033	−2.18
1985	−0.012	−0.90	−0.014	−1.01	−0.014	−1.07	−0.012	−0.89
1986	0.027	1.61	0.018	1.02	0.016	0.94	0.010	0.55
1987	0.013	0.75	0.004	0.22	−0.004	−0.23	−0.012	−0.75
1988	0.037	2.50	0.030	1.97	0.029	2.27	0.022	1.82
1989	0.035	1.92	0.026	1.45	0.021	1.33	0.011	0.73
1990	0.016	0.84	0.007	0.40	−0.001	−0.04	−0.007	−0.43
1991	0.019	0.96	0.011	0.58	0.016	0.75	0.006	0.27
1992	0.025	1.69	0.023	1.48	0.024	1.36	0.021	1.14
1993	0.005	0.31	0.002	0.11	0.002	0.19	−0.003	−0.25
1994	−0.009	−0.81	−0.015	−1.47	−0.007	−0.54	−0.010	−0.91
1995	0.006	0.49	0.004	0.30	0.010	0.67	0.007	0.47
1996	−0.004	−0.24	−0.011	−0.71	0.010	0.57	0.004	0.21
1997	0.002	0.17	−0.007	−0.51	0.011	0.65	0.005	0.31
1998	−0.013	−0.82	−0.019	−1.19	−0.012	−0.77	−0.018	−1.12
Average	0.010	0.60	0.005	0.27	0.008	0.45	0.003	0.19

Source: Author's calculations.

a. The *t*-ratio is the coefficient (coeff.) divided by its White standard error.

Figure 7-3. *Yearly Coefficients for Prior Approval for the Loss Ratio Model with Controls, 1972–98*[a]

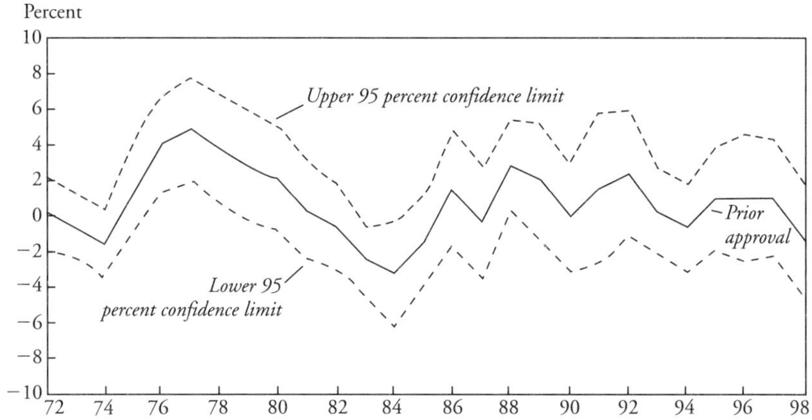

Source: Author's calculations.
a. Also shows ninety-five percent confidence band for prior approval coefficient using White standard errors. Control variables are included; Massachusetts, New Jersey, and South Carolina dummies excluded.

cent confidence interval encompasses zero in twenty-one of twenty-seven years. In the remaining six years, the estimate is positive in four years (1975–78, which included the 1975–76 hard market) and negative in two years (1983–84, which included the end of the early 1980s soft market).

Rate Regulation and Residual Market Share

The mean Residual Market percent during 1974 to 1997 was 6.4 percent in states with prior approval laws and only 1.0 percent in competitive rating states (see table 7-2; the difference is statistically significant at the 0.01 level). The standard deviation of Residual Market percent for prior approval states is five times as large as that for competitive rating states. Figure 7-4 plots the mean value of Residual Market percent over time for prior approval states; prior approval states excluding Massachusetts, New Hampshire, New Jersey, North Carolina, and South Carolina; and competitive rating states. The large increase in the mean for prior approval states up to 1990 clearly is attributable to those five states. Nonetheless, the mean for the other prior approval states consistently exceeds that for competitive rating states until 1996.

Table 7-6 presents mean coefficients from estimating equation 7-2

Figure 7-4. *Mean Residual Market Share of Written Car-Years by Type of Rating Law, 1974–97*[a]

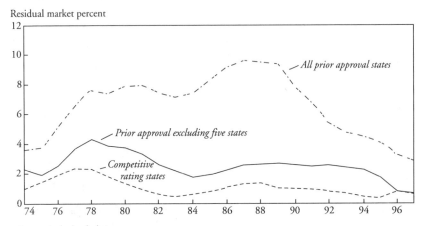

Residual market percent

Source: Author's calculations.
a. The five states excluded from the prior approval group are Massachusetts, New Hampshire, New Jersey, North Carolina, and South Carolina.

with and without the five state dummies for the overall sample period and three subperiods. Consistent with prior work, the results confirm an economically and statistically significant positive association between prior approval regulation and Residual Market share, even when the five states with alternative Residual Market mechanisms and large Residual Markets throughout much of the period are excluded from the comparison. (The mean coefficients for these five states were positive and highly significant for the overall period and most of the subperiods.)

For the remaining states, it would be difficult to distinguish to what extent the positive association between prior approval regulation and Residual Market share reflects regulation of overall rate changes, as opposed to any greater tendency for prior approval states to restrict rate classification or impose Residual Market rate caps or both. This issue is somewhat moot from a policy perspective, given the likelihood that deregulation of rate changes would be accompanied by less regulatory interference in rate differentials across consumers.

Loss Ratio Volatility

The mean of σ^2(Loss Ratio) during 1972 to 1998 for prior approval states is about 85 percent larger than the mean for competitive rating states

Table 7-6. *Mean Coefficients and* t-*ratios for Prior Approval in Residual Market Percent Equation, Selected Periods, 1974–97*[a]

Period	Without Mass., N.H., N.J., N.C., and S.C. dummies		With Mass., N.H., N.J., N.C., and S.C. dummies	
	Mean	*t-ratio*	*Mean*	*t-ratio*
1974–97	0.055	8.40	0.014	8.07
1974–81	0.046	5.40	0.016	4.57
1982–89	0.076	20.59	0.014	11.88
1990–97	0.042	6.13	0.012	3.80

Source: Author's calculations.

a. Mean is the mean coefficient for Prior Approval for the period shown. The *t*-ratio is the mean divided by the Newey-West standard error.

(0.0024 versus 0.0013; see table 7-2). A *t* test (not shown) using the ratio of the mean difference over time to its Newey-West standard error indicates that the difference is highly significant. Table 7-7 presents the mean coefficients for Prior Approval from estimating equation 7-3. The mean coefficient for Prior Approval is positive and highly significant for the overall period and the three subperiods for each specification. The *t*-ratios range from 3.14 to 10.09. These results provide strong evidence that the unexplained loss ratio volatility measure is higher on average in prior approval states than in competitive rating states. There also is evidence that loss ratio volatility is positively related to PIP percent and Loss Cost and, consistent with lower volatility in states with more exposures, negatively related to Car-Years$^{1/2}$.

Expenditure Growth Volatility

The mean of σ^2(Expenditure) during 1972 to 1998 for prior approval states is about 60 percent larger than the mean for competitive rating states (0.0017 versus 0.0011; see table 7-2). Table 7-8 presents the mean coefficients for Prior Approval from estimating equation 7-3. The mean coefficient for Prior Approval is positive and significant during the 1972–98, 1981–89, and 1990–98 periods. It is positive but not significant during the 1972–80 subperiod. These results provide substantial evidence that unexplained volatility in expenditure growth rates is higher on average in prior approval states than in competitive rating states. The evidence is consistent with greater volatility in rate changes in prior approval states, espe-

Table 7-7. *Mean Coefficients and t-ratios for Loss Ratio Volatility Equations, Selected Periods, 1972–98*[a]

Period	Prior Approval		Car-Years$^{1/2}$		Liability percent		PIP percent		Loss Cost	
	Mean	*t-ratio*	*Mean*	*t-ratio*	*Mean*	*t-ratio*	*Mean*	*t-ratio*	*Mean*	*t-ratio*
With car-years$^{1/2}$										
1972–98	0.104	10.09	−0.006	−3.10	...	...	...	...	...	...
1972–80	0.094	4.96	−0.006	−1.25	...	...	...	...	...	...
1981–89	0.104	5.27	−0.007	−2.36	...	...	...	...	...	...
1990–98	0.114	7.38	−0.005	−3.45	...	...	...	...	...	...
With car-years$^{1/2}$ and other controls										
1972–98	0.088	5.75	−0.010	−4.14	−0.003	−0.01	0.451	3.19	0.218	2.25
1972–80	0.060	5.27	−0.011	−1.91	−0.069	−0.26	0.210	0.70	0.423	2.34
1981–89	0.074	3.14	−0.012	−4.55	0.150	1.22	0.461	2.01	0.277	4.02
1990–98	0.129	6.02	−0.006	−4.64	−0.090	−0.13	0.682	3.12	−0.039	−0.39

Source: Author's calculations.

a. Mean is the mean coefficient for the period shown. See table 7-1 for variable definitions. Coefficients for Prior Approval, Liability percent, PIP percent, and Loss Cost are multiplied by 100. Coefficients for Car-Years$^{1/2}$ are multiplied by 1,000.

Table 7-8. *Mean Coefficients and* t-*ratios for Expenditure Volatility Equations, Selected Periods, 1972–98*[a]

Period	Prior Approval		Liability percent		PIP percent		Loss Cost	
	Mean	t-ratio	Mean	t-ratio	Mean	t-ratio	Mean	t-ratio
Without controls								
1972–98	0.061	3.40	...	...	...	...	...	...
1972–80	0.034	0.98	...	...	...	...	...	...
1981–89	0.047	3.78	...	...	...	...	...	...
1990–98	0.099	3.55	...	...	...	...	...	...
With controls								
1972–98	0.060	3.11	0.001	0.01	0.325	2.71	0.037	0.95
1972–80	0.032	1.10	−0.073	−0.29	0.361	1.83	0.074	1.52
1981–89	0.036	4.34	−0.032	−0.13	0.339	1.47	0.095	1.36
1990–98	0.109	3.08	0.100	0.48	0.279	1.75	−0.053	−0.95

Source: Author's calculations.

a. Mean is the mean coefficient for the period shown. See table 7-1 for variable definitions. Coefficients for Prior Approval, Liability percent, PIP percent, and Loss Cost are multiplied by 100.

cially since demand elasticity with respect to rate changes will reduce the strength of the relationship between expenditure growth rates and rate changes. There also is some evidence that expenditure growth volatility is positively and significantly related to PIP percent, although the *t*-ratio is less than two in each subperiod.

Conclusions

This study uses a time-varying parameter approach to provide evidence of the effects of prior approval regulation during the 1970s, 1980s, and 1990s on the level of loss ratios and residual market shares over time and on the volatilities of loss ratios and expenditure growth rates. The main results, which confirm and extend those of several previous studies, suggest that on average, prior approval regulation had little or no effect on the relationship between rate levels and claim costs over time, but it did reduce coverage availability and increased volatility for both insurers and consumers.

The estimated average effect of prior approval regulation on loss ratios during 1972 to 1998 is positive but small in magnitude and at best weakly significant, and it is largely due to experience in the 1970s. Thus there is little or no evidence that prior approval on average has a material effect on average rates for any given level of claim costs. This finding is consistent with an inability of rate regulation to reduce average rates materially and persistently in competitively structured markets without significantly reducing product quality or ultimately causing widespread exit by insurers.

However, prior approval regulation is reliably associated with lower availability of coverage. It is positively and significantly related to residual market shares, even when states with reinsurance facilities or related residual market mechanisms and the largest residual market shares are excluded from the comparison. Prior approval regulation also is reliably associated with greater volatility in loss ratios and expenditure growth rates after controlling for the influence of a number of other variables that could affect volatility.

References

American Insurance Association. 1992–98. *State Rating Law Survey.* Washington, D.C.
_____. 1999. *State Rate and Form Law Guide.*
Bajtelsmit, Vickie, and Raja Bouzouita. 1998. "Market Structure and Performance in Private Passenger Automobile Insurance." *Journal of Risk and Insurance* 65: 503–14.
Barth, Michael, and William Feldhaus. 1999. "Does Rate Regulation Alter Underwriting Risk?" *Journal of Insurance Issues* 22: 26–50.
Berger, Allen, J. David Cummins, and Mary Weiss. 1997. "The Coexistence of Multiple Distribution Systems for Financial Services: The Case of Property-Liability Insurance." *Journal of Business* 70: 515–46.
Bouzouita, Raja, and Vickie Bajtelsmit. 1997. "The Impact of Rate Regulation on the Residual Market for Automobile Insurance." *Journal of Insurance Regulation* 16: 61–72.
Braeutigam, Richard, and Mark V. Pauly. 1986. "Cost Function Estimation and Quality Bias: The Regulated Automobile Insurance Industry." *Rand Journal of Economics* 17: 606–17.
Cummins, J. David, Richard Phillips, and Sharon Tennyson. 2001. "Regulation, Political Influence, and the Price of Automobile Insurance." *Journal of Insurance Regulation* 20: 9–50.
Fama, Eugene, and Kenneth French. 1992. "The Cross-Section of Expected Returns." *Journal of Finance* 47: 427–65.
_____. 2000. "Forecasting Profitability and Earnings." *Journal of Business* 73: 177–75.
Grabowski, Henry, W. Kip Viscusi, and William N. Evans. 1989. "Price and Availability Tradeoffs of Automobile Insurance Regulation." *Journal of Risk and Insurance* 56: 275–99.
Greene, William. 1998. *LIMDEP User's Manual, Version 7.* New York : Econometric Software.

Gron, Anne. 1995. "Regulation and Insurer Competition: Did Insurers Use Rate Regulation to Reduce Competition?" *Journal of Risk and Uncertainty* 11: 87–111.

Harrington, Scott E. 1984. "The Impact of Rate Regulation on Prices and Underwriting Results in the Property-Liability Insurance Industry: A Survey." *Journal of Risk and Insurance* 51: 577–23.

———. 1986. "Regulation and Subsidies in Automobile Insurance." Unpublished manuscript, May.

———. 1987. "A Note on the Impact of Auto Insurance Rate Regulation." *Review of Economics and Statistics* 69: 166–70.

———. 1992. "Presidential Address: Rate Suppression." *Journal of Risk and Insurance* 59: 185–202.

———. 2000. *Insurance Deregulation and the Public Interest.* AEI-Brookings Joint Center for Regulatory Studies.

Harrington, Scott E., and Helen Doerpinghaus. 1993. "The Economics and Politics of Automobile Insurance Rate Classification." *Journal of Risk and Insurance* 60: 59–84.

Heckman, James. 1978. "Dummy Endogenous Variables in a Simultaneous Equations System." *Econometrica* 46: 931–59.

Insurance Services Office. 1990. *Personal Auto Insurance: Costs and Profits in Perspective.* New York.

Ippolito, Richard. 1979. "The Effects of Price Regulation in the Automobile Insurance Industry." *Journal of Law and Economics* 22: 55–89.

Joskow, Paul. 1973. "Cartels, Competition, and Regulation in the Property-Liability Insurance Industry." *Bell Journal of Economics and Management Science* 4: 375–427.

Kansas Insurance Department. 2000. *Report to the Kansas Legislature 2000 Session on Rate and Form Filings Laws in Other States.* Kansas City. March 1, 2000.

Kramer, Orin S. 1991. *Rate Suppression and Its Consequences.* New York: I.I.I. Press.

Long, J. Scott, and Laurie H. Ervin. 2000. "Using Heteroscedasticity Consistent Standard Errors in the Linear Regression Model." *American Statistician* 54: 217–24.

MacAvoy, Paul, ed. 1977. *Federal-State Regulation of the Pricing and Marketing of Insurance.* American Enterprise Institute.

MacKinnon, James G., and Halbert White. 1985. "Some Heteroskedasticity Consistent Covariance Matrix Estimators with Improved Finite Sample Properties." *Journal of Econometrics* 29: 305–25.

Newey, Whitney K., and Kenneth D. West. 1987. "A Simple, Positive Semi-Definite, Heteroskedasticity and Autocorrelation Consistent Covariance Matrix." *Econometrica* 55: 703–08.

Outreville, Jean Francois. 1990. "Underwriting Cycles and Rate Regulation in Automobile Insurance Markets." *Journal of Insurance Regulation* 8: 274–86.

Pauly, Mark V., Paul Kleindorfer, and Howard Kunreuther. 1986. "Regulation and Quality Competition in the U.S. Insurance Industry." In *The Economics of Insurance Regulation,* edited by Jorg Finsinger and Mark Pauly, 65–107. Macmillan.

Saba, R. 1978. "An Alternative Theory of the Regulation of Automobile Insurance." *Southern Economic Journal* 44: 469–76.

Suponcic, Susan, and Sharon Tennyson. 1998. "Rate Regulation and the Industrial Organization of Automobile Insurance." In *The Economics of Property-Casualty Insurance,* edited by David Bradford, 113–38. University of Chicago Press.

Tennyson, Sharon. 1991. "The Effect of Rate Regulation on Underwriting Cycles." *CPCU Journal* 44 (1): 33–45.

———. 1993. "Regulatory Lag in Automobile Insurance." *Journal of Risk and Insurance* 60: 36–58.

———. 1997. "The Impact of Rate Regulation on State Automobile Insurance Markets." *Journal of Insurance Regulation* 15: 503–23.

U.S. General Accounting Office. 1979. *Issues and Needed Improvements in State Regulation of the Insurance Business.*

White, Halbert. 1980. "A Heteroskedasticity-Consistent Covariance Matrix Estimator and a Direct Test for Heteroskedasticity." *Econometrica* 48: 817–38.

Witt, Robert W., and Harry Miller. 1981. "Price Competition, Regulation, and Systematic Underwriting Risk in Automobile Insurance Markets. *CPCU Journal* 34: 174–89.

Witt, Robert W., and Jorge Urrutia. 1983. "A Comparative Economic Analysis of Tort Liability and No-Fault Compensation Systems in Automobile Insurance." *Journal of Risk and Insurance* 50: 631–39.

Appendix 7A.

Table 7A-1. *Classification of States as Prior Approval (PA) or Competitive Rating (CR), 1972–98*

State	Rating law	State	Rating law
Alabama	PA	Missouri	CR
Alaska	PA	Montana	CR
Arizona	PA, 1972–80; CR, 1981–98	Nebraska	PA
		Nevada	CR, 1972–89; PA, 1990–98
Arkansas	PA, 1972–79, 1987–98; CR, 1980–86	New Hampshire	PA
California	CR, 1972–88; PA, 1989–98	New Jersey	PA
		New Mexico	PA, 1972–75, 1988–98; CR, 1976–87
Colorado	CR		
Connecticut	PA, 1972–83, 1994–99; CR, 1984–93	New York	CR, 1972, 1996–98; PA, 1973–95
Delaware	PA	North Carolina	PA
Florida	PA, 1972–74, 1987–98; CR, 1975–86	North Dakota	PA
		Ohio	CR
Georgia	CR, 1972–87; PA, 1988–98	Oklahoma	PA
		Oregon	CR
Hawaii	PA	Pennsylvania	PA
Idaho	CR	Rhode Island	PA
Illinois	CR	South Carolina	PA
Indiana	CR	South Dakota	PA, 1972–79; CR, 1980–98
Iowa	PA, 1972–87; CR, 1988–98	Tennessee	PA
Kansas	PA	Texas	PA
Kentucky	PA, 1972–82; CR, 1983–98	Utah	PA, 1972; CR, 1973–98
Louisiana	PA	Vermont	PA, 1972–84; CR, 1985–98
Maine	PA		
Maryland	PA, 1972–84, 1990–98; CR, 1985–89	Virginia	PA, 1972–73; CR, 1974–98
Massachusetts	PA	Washington	PA
Michigan	PA, 1972–80; CR, 1981–98	West Virginia	PA
		Wisconsin	CR
Minnesota	CR	Wyoming	PA, 1972–83; CR, 1984–98
Mississippi	PA		

Sources: American Insurance Association (1992–98, 1990), U.S. General Accounting Office (GAO; 1979), Insurance Services Office (ISO; 1990), Kansas Insurance Department (2000), state codes.

Table 7A-2. *Types of Rating Laws by State, 1972–98*[a]

State	Rating law	State	Rating law
Alabama	3: 1972–98	Montana	6: 1972–98
Alaska	3: 1972–98	Nebraska	3: 1972–98
Arizona	3: 1972–80; 5: 1981–98	Nevada	4: 1972–89; 2: 1990–98
Arkansas	3: 1972–79, 1987–98;	New Hampshire	2: 1972–98
	4: 1980–86	New Jersey	2: 1972–98
California	6: 1972–88; 3: 89–98	New Mexico	3: 1972–75, 1988–98;
Colorado	5: 1972–83; 4: 1984–98		4: 1976–87
Connecticut	3: 1972–83, 1994–99;	New York	4: 1972; 2: 1973–95;
	9: 1984–93		7: 1996–98
Delaware	2: 1972–98	North Carolina	2: 1972–76; 3: 1977–98
Florida	3: 1972–74, 1987–98;	North Dakota	3: 1972–98
	4: 1975–86	Ohio	4: 1972–98
Georgia	4: 1972–87; 3: 1988–98	Oklahoma	3: 1972–98
Hawaii	3: 1972–98	Oregon	4: 1972–98
Idaho	5: 1972–98	Pennsylvania	3: 72–98
Illinois	5: 72–98	Rhode Island	3: 1972–98
Indiana	4: 1972–98	South	3: 1972–98
Iowa	3: 1972–87; 8: 1988–98	Carolina	
Kansas	3: 1972–98	South Dakota	3: 1972–79; 8: 1980–98
Kentucky	3: 1972–82; 8: 1983–98	Tennessee	3: 1972–98
Louisiana	3: 1972–98	Texas	2: 1972–98
Maine	3: 1972–98	Utah	3: 1972; 5: 1973–98
Maryland	3: 1972–84, 1990–98;	Vermont	3: 1972–84; 8: 1985–98
	4: 1985–89	Virginia	3: 1972–73; 4:
Massachusetts	1: 1972–98		1974–89; 8: 1990–98
Michigan	3: 1972–80; 8: 1981–98	Washington	3: 1972–98
Minnesota	4: 1972–98	West Virginia	3: 1972–98
Mississippi	3: 1972–98	Wisconsin	5: 1972–98
Missouri	5: 1972–98	Wyoming	3: 1972–83; 8: 1984–98

Sources: American Insurance Association (1992–98, 1999), GAO (1979), ISO (1990), Kansas Insurance Department (2000), state codes.

a. Type of regulation indicated by the following numbers: 1, state-made rates; 2, prior approval without a deemer provision; 3, prior approval with a deemer provision (rates deemed approved if no regulatory action within a specified period; includes states that required prior approval of deviations from bureau rates and Alabama's modified prior approval law, which requires prior approval of changes in expense and profit loadings); 4, file-and-use (file on or before effective date); 5, use-and-file (file within specified period after effective date); 6, filing only (no time period specified); 7, flex rating (prior approval of changes outside of permissible range); 8, file-and-use or use-and-file in a competitive market.

COMMENT ON CHAPTER 7
Georges Dionne

In chapter 7 Scott Harrington analyzes the effects of insurance rate regulation on the automobile insurance market. He offers an econometric estimate of the effects of prior approval rate regulation on three variables: the level of automobile insurance loss ratio; the volatility of two variables—loss ratios and growth rates in average spending on automobile insurance—that are used as proxies for the volatility of insurance rates; and the level of residual market share for automobile insurance. The insurance loss ratio is a proxy for the inverse insurance price. Rate volatility is a concern for risk-averse participants in the market, and lower residual market share is an indirect measurement of the availability of insurance. The analysis uses cross-state data from all fifty states over the period 1972–98.

My comments are divided into two parts. I first discuss the author's methodology and argue that he has not emphasized the most appropriate estimation method to reach his study's objectives. I then discuss alternative ways of measuring welfare effects and the possibility of assessing the effects of rate regulation without reference to the strategic behavior of the different states.

The main findings of the study can be summarized as follows:

—Prior approval rate regulation is found to have a slightly positive effect on loss ratios over time, but the estimated effect is negligible and at best only weakly significant during the 1972–98 period. The significant findings also reflect the market experience of the 1970s. This positive effect is indeed quite weak.

—Prior approval rate regulation is associated with more highly volatile loss ratios and expenditure growth rates. This finding can be interpreted as a welfare loss to both risk-averse insurers and risk-averse consumers.

—Prior approval regulation is persistently and reliably associated with larger residual market shares, which can also represent a welfare loss.

I thank David Cummins, Robert Gagné, and Mathieu Maurice for their comments on an earlier version of this comment, and Sybil Denis and Claire Boisvert for their collaboration in the preparation of the final version.

These results can be interpreted as a net welfare loss, since the prior approval has little or no effect on insurance rates but increases both volatility and residual market shares.

Methodology

My discussion focuses on loss ratios, although its general thrust applies to all three estimations. To obtain his first finding, the author constructed a data set containing information on all fifty states in the United States for twenty-seven periods: a total of 1,350 observations. This type of data set is a complete panel, in the sense that there are no entries into (nor exits from) the sample: in other words, all fifty states are present over the twenty-seven periods. The sample is thus free from potential bias due to entries or exits. This sort of bias is often present in models that infer technological parameters from incomplete panel data. An example is the case where efficient firms enter and no efficient ones exit.[1] When a firm is absent for a number of periods, all the information relevant to this firm is missing for these periods. The major problem is to know whether the absence is explained by randomness (incomplete surveys) or by numerous factors that may affect the technological parameters (mergers, bankruptcies, and so forth). Usually a test for selectivity bias must be applied.

Panel data sets cannot be properly treated without an appropriate methodology. In his chapter Harrington uses a method that allows the parameters to vary over time (the Fama-French method). While he notes that the main results are robust to using fixed effects estimation, he almost exclusively emphasizes the time-varying parameter results. He claims that the panel method with state fixed effects is less appropriate because it does not take into account the regulation effects in states where regulation did not change. This is not necessarily true. Panel data can be used to control for both fixed or state effects and regulation effects.

There are currently two schools of thought about the effects of regulation. The first believes that regulation is necessary to reduce the effects of imperfect competition between insurers, particularly in states where only a few insurance firms operate. This school also believes that the existence of regulation in some states will affect the behavior of insurers in unregulated

1. See Baltagi (1995); Dionne, Gagné, and Vanasse (1998).

states, as there is always a probability that regulation will be extended to all states if the differences between insurance rates become too large. The second school believes that regulation has no effect: the variations observed are explained by differences in the markets before regulation and after deregulation. Insurance rates are said to be lower in unregulated markets because the insurers in these markets are more efficient, for example, and life is said to be easier for inefficient insurers in regulated markets.

If one thinks that the second interpretation is correct, a significant dummy variable might act as a proxy for insurer efficiency and not necessarily for any regulation effect. Cross-sectional analysis (or an average of cross-sectional analyses) cannot discriminate between the two stories. Panel data analysis, however, can distinguish between the two hypotheses by analyzing the loss ratios of states moving from a regulated to an unregulated status (and vice versa).

Another advantage of panel data analysis is that it lessens the problems associated with omitted variables.[2] What seem to be regulation effects may be obtained because some other real effects (potentially correlated with other explanatory variables) are not observable. Using information on many periods in a dynamic way can introduce control over unobservable variables. When omitted variables are correlated with the included variables, cross-sectional analysis will not provide adequate means of obtaining consistent coefficients for the effect of regulation. This is particularly true when coefficients vary over time, as can be seen in Harrington's table 7-5. Nor is it clear to me that one can take the average of coefficients when some are significantly different from zero and many others are not.

With panel data it is often assumed that the true model is one with constant parameters but variable intercepts over time and cross-sectional units. Harrington's method allows the intercept and the slopes to vary over time but does not allow for intercepts that vary across states. The variable intercepts approach in conventional panel data estimation methods can account for the unobservable features that distinguish states within any given period or over time. Consider the following simple example:

$$L_{it} = \alpha + \beta x_{it} + \mu_{it},$$

where L_{it} is the loss ratio in state i for period t, x_{it} is a dummy variable for regulation in state i for period t, and μ_{it} is a random term.

2. Hsiao (1986).

This random term is not necessarily independent from x_{it} and can be written as

$$\mu_{it} = \delta S_i + \lambda M_t + v_{it},$$

where S_i is an unobservable variable in state i, M_t is an unobservable market variable in period t, and v_{it} is a random term. Here μ_{it} is correlated with one unobservable state variable, S_i, and with a market variable, M_t, that varies over time. This correlation may affect the conclusions about the estimated parameter $\hat{\beta}$. Panel data methods are capable of obtaining a consistent estimate of β even if M_t and S_i are not observable. This correlation will introduce a variable intercept model (α_{it}) that will yield an appropriate $\hat{\beta}$ by eliminating the omitted-variable bias.

There are two standard methods of estimating models with panel data: the fixed effects model, where both the time and the state effect are controlled, and the random effects model. Because both the number of periods and the number of states being considered here are quite low, the fixed effects model can be applied by simply using twenty-seven dummies for the years (dates) and fifty dummies for the states and checking whether the coefficients and the t-student values are appropriate. Seventy-seven dummies with 1,350 observations is a manageable proposition. When the number of observations is very high—say, 30,000 individuals over ten years—one cannot use dummies for the individuals. In that case, one can turn to the random effects model, where the distribution of the random term must be analyzed.

Of course, matters are much more complicated when the endogenous aspects of regulation also enter into the equation. But here regulation is treated as only exogenous.

Macroeffects

On the aggregate level, it is interesting to observe (from Harrington's figures 7-1 and 7-2) that there is a strong relationship between variations in the number of rate-regulating states and variations in the mean loss ratios for both types of states (competitive rating and prior approval). This observation suggests a number of interesting areas for further research. Is there any causal connection between the two distributions at the macrolevel? In other words, is there any relationship between average loss ratios for auto

Table 1. *Deaths in Motor Vehicle Accidents per 100,000 Persons, 1994 and 1997*

Geographical area	1994	1997
United States	16.3	15.8
California	14.3	10.5
Illinois	15.0	11.7
Massachusetts	8.0	7.2
New Jersey	9.8	9.3[a]
South Carolina	22.6	23.8
Canada	10.9	9.6
Quebec	11.3	10.4
France	13.8	14.1

Sources: *Statistical Abstract of the United States, 1998;* Statistics Canada (1998); and data from the Organisation Nationale Interministérielle de la Sécurité Routière, France, 1998.
a. 1998.

insurance and the number of states that regulate? Or are these relationships to be explained only by the liability insurance crisis?

Can one test to see whether average rates (in both regulated and unregulated states) started to rise when the number of states with regulation started to decrease, and vice versa? Who are the leaders, the states that regulate or those that do not? Do regulators follow the market in the other states, or are insurers in unregulated states influenced by the behavior of regulators in states that do regulate?

Finding answers to such questions might help in predicting what effect complete deregulation in all fifty states might have on the auto insurance market. More generally, are there any strategic differences between states that regulate and those that do not? Furthermore, are market structures the same in regulated and unregulated states? Is the market less competitive in the regulated states (fewer insurers, more market power)?

Finally, I would like to point out a possible link between regulation and automobile accident fatality rates. Table 1 reproduces the number of deaths per 100,000 individuals in the states, provinces, and countries analyzed in this conference. Although many factors could cause differences in automobile accident fatality rates across regions, it is nonetheless interesting to observe that the number of deaths per 100,000 individuals is much lower in regulated states than in unregulated states. Rates in Canada and France are also lower than in the United States, where many states are not regulated. A recent article in *Insurance Day* reports that bodily injury claims are increasing in the United Kingdom.[3] According to some specialists, the driving force behind this finding is the pricing by insurers.[4]

As I show in chapter 9 of this book, deregulation should not be brought in too rapidly, and appropriate substitutes must be introduced to replace certain beneficial properties of regulation. In particular, I consider the commitment value of regulation.

Conclusion

I very much enjoyed reading Harrington's chapter. It reports interesting results that will likely influence the way the regulation of automobile insurance rates will be discussed in the United States over the coming years. However, the findings reported are not necessarily independent of the methodology used. I would therefore suggest that different methodologies be applied to the data set before any political decisions are based on this information.

References

Baltagi, B. H. 1995. *Econometric Analysis of Panel Data.* Chichester, U.K.: Wiley.

Danzon, P., and S. Harrington. 2001. "Workers' Compensation Rate Regulation: How Price Controls Increase Costs." *Journal of Law and Economics* (forthcoming).

Dionne, G., R. Gagné, and C. Vanasse. 1998. "Inferring Technological Parameters for Incomplete Panel Data." *Journal of Econometrics* 87 (December): 303–27.

Harrington, S., and P. Danzon. 2000. "Rate Regulation, Safety Incentives, and Loss Growth in Workers' Compensation Insurance." *Journal of Business* 73 (4): 569–95.

Hsiao, C. 1986. *Analysis of Panel Data.* Cambridge University Press.

Statistics Canada. 1998. "Mortality—Summary List of Causes, 1998." Ottawa.

---

3. N. Munns, "Bodily Injury Claims on Increase," *Insurance Day*, March 20, 2001, p. 8.

4. See Danzon and Harrington (2001) and Harrington and Danzon (2000) for similar analyses of workers' compensation insurance.

RICHARD J. BUTLER

8 | *Form Regulation in Commercial Insurance*

Since many states have deregulated insurance pricing, the main source of regulatory constraint for commercial insurers is approval of changes in contract language, or form regulation. This has become an important issue in the rapidly evolving market for risks traditionally handled through the insurance industry. Insurers face increasing competition from alternative risk transfer (ART) mechanisms, including self-insurance, captive insurance companies, finite risk reinsurance, and securitized products developed by investment banks and global reinsurers. While many states require that changes in contract language be approved by state regulators before new contract language or provisions can be employed, there are essentially no significant pricing or form restrictions on contracting in the ART market. This places insurers at a competitive disadvantage in markets where insurance needs to be customized to meet the changing needs of the consumer. Particularly in the commercial market, where agreements are reached between large well-informed firms and insurers, any significant delay in language approval "taxes" insurance transactions: such restrictions make insurance contracts

Support from the AEI-Brookings Joint Center for Regulatory Studies is greatly appreciated. Comments on this draft by Val Lambson, James Cardon, Mark Showalter, Robert Hartwig, Andy Whitman, David Appel, and David Cummins are also appreciated. The research assistance of Steven Butler is gratefully acknowledged, as are the useful references provided by Deb Scott and David Unnewehr and the help with the Dun and Bradstreet data by Hui Liao.

less attractive than ART contracts, place insurers at a competitive disadvantage relative to their unregulated competitors, and reduce the welfare of commercial customers.

A model illustrating the implicit tax effect of delayed innovation is developed in this chapter. That such taxes have shifted risk pooling from the commercial insurance to the ART market is suggested by data shown in table 8-1: during the last 20 years, the ART market share has grown steadily from one-fifth to one-third of the market, for a growth rate of about 2.5 percent a year in market share (this may understate the growth and level of the ART market to the extent that it doesn't include securitization).

While the ART market traditionally existed to avoid overinsurance, expand capacity, and diversify the spectrum of insurance risks, there are other reasons for the recent surge in ART market share.[1] Another plausible explanation of ART growth is that many of these financial mechanisms avoid the approval-delay tax. The largest ART mechanism, for example, is self-insurance, either through the direct retention of the risk or through wholly owned captive insurance.[2] Since no formal insurance contract is involved in risk retention, there are no forms to be reviewed for approval and thus the approval-delay tax is avoided entirely. Captive insurers are insurance entities created by noninsurance companies for the sole purpose of providing insurance to the company owning them. Formal contracts are involved when insuring with a wholly owned captive: the contract defines the application of the retention, the claims administration within the retention, and excess coverage over the retention. But this is not generally regulated. There has been a sharp increase in the number of rent-a-captive insurers, which should open up the alternative insurance market further for small and medium-size insureds; but these only avoid the delayed-approval tax when they are wholly owned by the insured.[3]

Another alternative for medium and small businesses is to join together in a risk retention group, combined to insure one another as a group, as permitted under the Product Liability Risk Retention Act of 1981. These risk retention groups (RRGs) must be chartered in one state but can operate in other states without licenses or the need to meet the

1. Swiss Re (1999).

2. In their excellent discussion of the ART market, Swiss Re excludes self-insurance as part of the ART market; however, they note that insurance captives are the most important mechanism in the ART market (1999, p 6). See also Conning (1999); Hartwig (2000).

3. Conning (1999).

Table 8-1. *Growth of the Alternative Risk Transfer Market, Selected Years, 1979–1997*

Units as indicated

Year	Traditional market		Alternative markets	
	Billions of dollars	Percent	Billions of dollars	Percent
1979	45.6	78.9	12.2	21.1
1983	51.0	73.9	18.0	26.1
1987	104.9	71.7	41.5	28.3
1990	109.8	69.4	48.4	30.6
1991	114.8	69.3	50.9	30.7
1995	132.5	67.7	66.1	33.3
1997	134.8	66.0	69.4	34.0

Source: Conning (1999).

state admission requirements that other insurers must meet. While RRGs must report details on their coverages, rates, and forms, the forms do not necessarily have to be approved by the state regulators. The number of such groups grew from forty-six in 1987 to about sixty-nine in 1997.[4]

Multiline-multiyear products are alternative risk transfer products that cover several lines of insurance over a number of years in order to "smooth" the costs (relative to any single one policy) of insurance. However, since these policies are offered through insurers, they are subject to the same delays (form regulation) that traditional policies are. Hence, to the extent that the movement to the alternative risk transfer market is a move to avoid form regulation costs, these products should not grow as fast as the rest of the ART market.

Whether or not other forms of alternative insurance—finite risk reinsurance or securitized products—are subject to form regulation depends largely on whether they are provided through insurance contracts or through other financial intermediaries such as investment banks. If they are provided through banks, then form regulation is generally avoided. Also, in states with insurance form regulation, nonadmitted insurers have been able to supply insurance coverage through surplus lines of insurance with less form regulation than admitted insurers. This helps to explain the growth in surplus lines of insurance coincident with the growth in the ART market.

4. Conning (1999).

Finite risk solutions spread risks for a firm over time through a multiyear contract. The regulatory implications of such policies are still not entirely clear; however, the chances of being regulated are reduced when noninsurance entities are involved rather than insurance companies. Securitized products include things like catastrophe bonds, insurance derivatives, and contingent capital.[5]

The Financial Services Modernization Act (Gramm-Leach-Bliley Act) of 1999 allows investment banks and insurers (and reinsurers) to affiliate within a holding company structure. Given this situation, commercial insurance contracts written through the insurance subsidiary will always entail additional, regulatory costs that are not present in securitization contracts written by the investment bank subsidiary and covering the same insurance need. From this perspective the implicit tax involved in form regulation lowers the value of the insurance subsidiary relative to the investment banking subsidiary, placing the former at a competitive disadvantage.

A simple model of insurance innovation is constructed in the next section to indicate the potential loss in consumer welfare when form regulation slows the speed at which insurance contracts can be innovated. Then empirical evidence on the size of the delays is presented, using information from a U.S. commercial insurer for 1999 form filings. Delays are substantial and shown to be strongly correlated with the extent of form regulation.

Subsequent analysis focuses on the differences between a form-deregulated state, Minnesota, and a relatively form-regulated state, New York. Again, the results indicate that form regulation substantially increases the time before contracts can be offered. Since it has a substantial negative impact on the welfare of businesses seeking new insurance products for their organizations, the question remains whether form regulation generates benefits to commercial buyers of insurance sufficient to offset the welfare costs. Therefore, additional empirical evidence on the potential benefits of form regulation is also provided and analyzed.

Welfare Costs of Delayed Innovation

A simple model of insurance innovation illustrates the problem with form regulation. Assume there is demand for a new insurance product, known to all commercial insurers. "New" insurance is broadly defined to

5. Hartwig (2000).

include not only coverage for new risks and changes in law and legal rulings that affect old risks, but new also includes changes in the way the insurance contract is structured to meet new institutional demands as well. These "institutionally related" changes would address many "recent" trends: the movement from monoline to package policies, the change from occurrence to claims-made contracts, the use of "absolute" pollution exclusions, and concern over concurrent cause coverage in earthquake insurance contracts.[6]

The market is assumed to be competitive in the sense that there are too many potential insurers to collude. Insurers set their prices to maximize profits for this new product once they are ready to enter the market. But they are overly optimistic in the sense that if they choose to enter, they assume that they will remain the lowest-cost producer throughout the period. That is, insurers are myopic agents playing a Bertrand game.[7]

Though the new insurance product is homogeneous from the consumer's perspective, it is not yet a "standard commodity" product like homeowners' or auto insurance policies. While the insurance innovation is homogeneous in its essential provisions no matter who offers the new policy, the insurers providing the new policy are not homogeneous: they differ in the time they need to get this product to market and in the cost of providing the policy once it comes to the market. The only fixed costs are the time costs of preparing the contract, and each firm's marginal costs are constant with respect to the level of their output. But one firm's marginal costs will differ in general from another's. All firms that enter this market will offer policies that are perfect (or near perfect) substitutes for each other.

Indeed, the differences in preparation time and premium costs between firms arise from differences in expertise in the new product area and differences in legal, underwriting, and marketing processes across insurers. Because the product is new, no one knows the bivariate distribution of preparation times and marginal costs across insurers: firms have no information about other insurers' potential preparation times or costs (that is, no one knows the means, variances, or correlation between preparation time and premium costs). The only publicly held knowledge, shared by all insurers and all insurance buyers, is the market demand for the current innovation and prior market transactions, including the current market price.

Market demand is specified over some fixed, long, time period (a year

6. Concurrent cause coverage exists when a policy will cover damage that arises from two causes, one that is covered by insurance and one that is not.

7. Bertrand games are those in which firms compete by setting a price (Mas-Colell, Whinston, and Green, 1995).

in our simulations below, but it could just as well be ten years). Because the contract period is "long," commercial insureds are assumed to insist on a "meet the lowest credible offer" clause in their contracts. This commercial contract clause provides the following option to the insured commercial risk: if another insurer enters a market with a lower price for the same product, the current insurer must meet the new price or withdraw so that the insured can obtain the lower price. Differences across firms in marginal costs, as well as the meet-the-lowest-credible-offer clause, guarantee that there is only one firm providing this coverage at any point in time. This simplifies the calculation of the consumer surplus as explained below.

Under these assumptions the firm that brings the new insurance policy to market first will set its price as a monopolist (figure 8-1). Policies will be priced so that marginal revenue equals marginal cost, with the price determined by the demand curve. (It is assumed that the lowest-credible-offer clause is written to preclude the first entrant from price discrimination—only one price will be charged for the new insurance product.) The area under the demand curve represents the total value of the new insurance contract to the insureds. The total cost of the policies sold by the monopolist is the rectangle formed by multiplying the price times the quantity. The difference between the value received and its cost, given by the shaded triangle in figure 8-1, is known as *consumer surplus*. Consumer surplus represents the net value of the transaction to the consumer.

New potential entrants with marginal costs below the monopolist price in figure 8-1 but above the marginal cost of the monopolist will force the monopolist to lower its price (so that it is just below the marginal cost of the new entrant), but they will not drive the first entrant out of the market. A new entrant with marginal costs below the first entrant's marginal cost will drive out the first entrant, capturing all of the initial entrant's business with the meet-the-lowest-credible-offer clause, and sell its policies at a price just below the first entrant's marginal cost. This is illustrated in figure 8-2. This second entrant maximizes profits at the new price, just lower than the first entrant's marginal cost. Not only will all of the first entrant's insureds switch to the new provider, the lowered price will induce additional customers to buy coverage as well. Consumer surplus, given by the triangle above the new price (and below the demand curve), increases.

Figure 8-2 also indicates what happens as other entrants come into the market. Generally, given our assumption of heterogeneous costs, only one insurer will supply the market at any given point in time. As their preparation time elapses, other insurers enter the market only if their marginal

Figure 8-1. *Model of Insurance Innovation: First Entrant Sets Prices as a Monopolist*

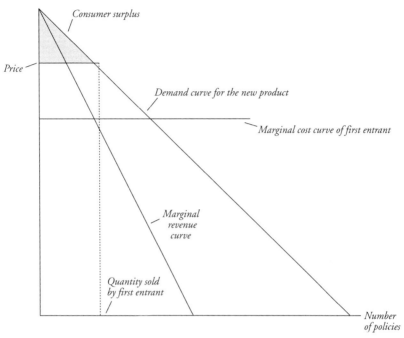

cost is lower than the marginal cost of the current market supplier and if they can make a profit. Each new entrant lowers the price, increases the number of policies, and increases the consumer surplus.

Tables 8-2 and 8-3 represent the simulated market outcomes when there is an innovative insurance product. The upper figure in each pair of values represents the percentage of the total possible consumer surplus captured by the insureds in the market for the new policy. In figure 8-2, if the price were zero, then the value of consumer surplus would be the whole area under the demand curve, and the upper value would be 100 percent. If half of that area were captured as consumer surplus for the whole year, the upper value would be 50 percent. In this model of delayed innovation, consumer surplus increases throughout the year as prices fall with new entrants. Thus the upper figures are actually weighted averages of the consumer surplus over the year—the weights being the fraction of the year that the given level of consumer surplus was in effect. So, for example, if the consumer surplus were 40 percent for half a year and 60 percent for the other half of the year,

Figure 8-2. *Model of Insurance Innovation: First Lower Marginal Cost Insurer Drives Out Monopolist and Sells at a Lower Price*

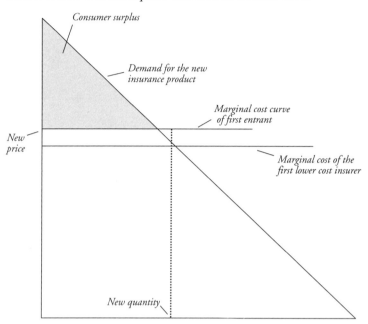

the recorded consumer surplus would be 50 percent. The higher the consumer surplus percentage, the better off the consumer would be.

The lower figure in each pair of values, shown in parentheses, represents the amount of consumer surplus in the presence of form regulation. Form regulation is assumed to increase the time to market by thirty days in these simulations.

One thousand pairs of marginal costs and preparation times were generated using the SAS package software, representing 1,000 firms in the market for a new insurance policy.[8] A program simulated the market outcomes of the model outlined above: lower cost entrants drive out higher cost entrants as the market for the innovation matures and more insurers are able to bring their policies to market. (See appendix 8A for a technical description of the program.)

For this simulation a linear demand curve was chosen with an intercept premium value of $1.5 million and a slope of $50. These parameters

8. SAS Software Version 6, SAS Institute, Cary, North Carolina, 1999.

Table 8-2. *Consumer Surplus for Low-Cost Producers and Impact of Thirty-Day Delay*[a]

Percent

Depreciation of preparation time[b]	Correlation between preparation time and marginal costs of production						
	−.75	−.50	−.25	0	.25	.50	.75
α = 0	94.1	95.2	95.8	96.3	96.5	96.7	96.7
	(86.1)	(87.2)	(87.9)	(88.3)	(88.6)	(88.7)	(88.7)
α = .01	94.4	95.3	95.9	96.3	96.6	96.7	96.7
	(86.9)	(87.7)	(88.2)	(88.6)	(88.7)	(88.9)	(88.8)
α = .1	95.9	96.2	96.4	96.6	96.6	96.7	96.7
	(86.9)	(88.2)	(88.4)	(88.6)	(88.7)	(88.8)	(88.7)
α = .2	96.5	96.6	96.6	96.7	96.8	96.8	96.7
	(88.4)	(88.5)	(88.6)	(88.8)	(88.8)	(88.8)	(88.8)
α = .5	96.9	96.9	96.8	96.9	96.9	96.9	96.8
	(88.8)	(88.8)	(88.8)	(89.0)	(88.9)	(88.9)	(88.8)

Source: Author's calculations using SAS package software.

a. The upper values are the simulated consumer surplus, written as a percent of the total consumer surplus possible in a model where firms have different costs of entry and production. The lower values in parentheses are the consumer surplus in the presence of form regulation, which is assumed to increase time to market by thirty days.

As the correlation between being the first to enter and the lower cost producer increases, the consumer surplus also generally increases. See Appendix 8A for a complete description of the simulation process.

b. Depreciation of preparation time T is determined by the equation $T = T_0^* \exp(-\alpha^* forms)$.

Table 8-3. *Consumer Surplus for High-Cost Producers and Impact of Thirty-Day Delay*[a]

Percent

Depreciation of preparation time[b]	Correlation between preparation time and marginal costs of production						
	−.75	−.50	−.25	0	.25	.50	.75
α = 0	39.6	40.4	41.7	41.6	42.0	42.4	34.7
	(36.1)	(36.9)	(37.5)	(38.1)	(38.5)	(38.9)	(31.8)
α = .01	40.0	40.7	41.2	41.6	42.0	42.4	34.7
	(36.5)	(37.2)	(37.6)	(38.1)	(38.5)	(38.9)	(31.8)
α = .1	42.0	42.0	41.9	41.9	42.4	42.6	34.7
	(38.5)	(38.5)	(38.4)	(38.4)	(38.9)	(39.1)	(31.8)
α = .2	42.4	42.5	42.4	42.2	42.6	42.7	34.7
	(38.9)	(38.9)	(38.9)	(38.7)	(39.1)	(39.1)	(31.8)
α = .5	42.9	42.7	42.6	42.6	42.8	42.8	34.7
	(38.9)	(38.9)	(38.8)	(38.7)	(39.1)	(39.1)	(31.8)

Source: Author's calculations using SAS package software.

a. See footnote to table 8-2 for detailed explanation.

were arbitrarily chosen to give, at the midpoint of the demand curve, a price of $750,000 for each policy with 15,000 policies sold, for a total market value of $11.25 billion. However, because all the simulated outcomes are reported in relative terms below, the results are independent of the particular slope and intercept values chosen for the demand curve. Table 8-2 (simulations for low-cost producers) assumes a mean value for the firm's marginal costs to be $500,000, with a standard deviation of $250,000. Table 8-3 (simulations for high-cost producers) assumes a mean value for the firm's marginal costs to be $1,250,000, with a standard deviation of $250,000.

The new insurance product simulations employed different correlations between preparation times and marginal costs of production. These correlations go from $-.75$ (so that low-cost producers tend to have higher preparation times) to .75 (so that low-cost producers also tend to have the lowest preparation times).

The leftmost column of tables 8-2 and 8-3 displays an alpha parameter that represents learning from others in the market. Each increase in this parameter represents more learned from prior market policies and thus lower preparation time. The model assumes that prior transactions become public knowledge, including the content of those forms previously approved by regulators. Such an assumption squares with the existence of markets in which firms collect and disseminate information about previously approved forms to other insurers. This suggests later entrants learn from earlier entrants, reducing the preparation time of later entrants. This effect would be cumulative—the more forms that are approved, the shorter the subsequent preparation times of future entrants—but likely subject to diminishing returns. To capture this "learning-from-the-market" effect, every time there is another insurer entering the market, the preparation times of potential entrants are shrunk by a factor of $e^{-\alpha \, forms}$ for all potential entrants, where α is rate of shrinkage as listed in the leftmost column of tables 8-2 and 8-3, and *forms* are the number of prior entrants to the market. The numeric value of *forms*, therefore, equals the cumulative number of insurers having sold policies in this market. When α is equal to zero, there is complete depreciation of learning from prior forms filed; in this case no entrant learns anything that would lower the preparation time. When α is equal to .5, there is substantial learning from others: seeing just one previously approved form cuts preparation time to 60 percent of its original value; seeing five previously approved forms cuts preparation time to 8 percent of its original value.

The upper value in the first row and first column of table 8-2 indicates that equilibrium for the low-cost production model is such that 94.1 percent of the potential consumer surplus is captured by the insureds in this model, even though firms with low preparation time tend to be producers with the highest marginal cost and do not learn from prior forms filed (α equals zero). The imposition of a thirty-day waiting period increases the average "total time to contract readiness" from twenty to fifty days, and the consumer surplus falls to 86.1 percent, as indicated in the parenthetical entry in the first row and first column.[9] Form regulation slows the introduction of new contracts, lowering the welfare of the insureds in this model. The entries in table 8-3 are much lower than those in table 8-2 because firms with high production costs charge higher prices upon entry, reducing the consumer surplus available for capture by the commercially insured customers.

Going down any column in table 8-2 or in table 8-3 increases the consumer surplus, as expected. The greater the degree of learning from others, the sooner lower priced contracts enter the market and the better off insurance consumers are. There is a less clear-cut pattern as the correlation between preparation time and marginal costs increases: for low values of α (little learning), consumer surplus tends to increase up to a correlation of .5 and then falls.

Notably in both tables, the relative loss in consumer surplus remains constant. For example, the consumer surplus for low-cost producers with no learning and zero correlation between preparation time and marginal costs falls from 96.3 percent to 88.3 percent once form regulation is in place. This is an 8.3 percentage loss in the original consumer surplus $(0.083 = [96.3 - 88.3]/96.3)$. The percentage loss in consumer surplus for all the scenarios in tables 8-2 and 8-3 falls between 8.3 and 9.3 percent, a considerable reduction in the consumers' surplus from innovation. To achieve an equivalent welfare loss in consumer surplus, state regulators would have to tax the insurance premiums paid by buyers of insurance (that is, state regulators would have to tax the premiums of business firms purchasing insurance) between 4.2 and 4.8 percent whenever buyers purchased an insurance policy (assuming an initial price of $750,000—the middle point of the demand curve).[10]

9. Fifty days reflects the full impact of form regulation: after twenty days of internal preparation of the new contract, there is an additional thirty days spent getting legal approval from the state.

10. This comparison is just in terms of the *insurance buyers' consumer surplus*, ignoring the treatment of tax revenues. (Assume that they are removed and of no benefit to insurance purchasers.) However,

Since changes in the degree of learning and the correlation between the firm's entry time and marginal costs do not affect the relative welfare loss, what does? It is not the marginal costs of production, since the results in terms of relative losses seem to be robust whether high- or low-cost production is assumed. Changes in other parameters of the bivariate distribution of preparation times and marginal costs of production didn't affect the relative welfare loss either in the simulations: whether doubling the standard deviation of marginal costs, the mean of preparation time, or the standard deviation of preparation times, the relative welfare loss still remained in the 8.3–9.3 interval.

As expected, the simulations of market equilibrium suggest that welfare losses grow proportionately with the delay. Raising the regulatory delay from thirty to sixty days increases the welfare loss from about 8.5 percent to approximately 17 percent. Tripling the delay to ninety days increases the welfare loss to about 25 percent. The implicit "sales" tax on insurance premiums (the tax that generates the same welfare loss as the delay) would go from 4.3 percent (for a thirty-day delay) to 8.9 percent (for a sixty-day delay) to 13.4 percent (for a ninety-day delay).[11]

If everyone with any type of "insurance" coverage (including self insurers and ART insureds) paid this tax, and if it could be passed on to the consumers of business products, then this implicit tax would not affect the share of premiums going to traditional insurers, although it still would represent a welfare loss to the economy as a whole. But obviously only traditional insurers are "taxed" through form regulation, so the tax cannot be passed along by competitive insurers to their customers. Self-insurance, captive insurers, and some other forms of ART do not incur this tax. Delays are costly to firms seeking innovative changes to their insurance coverage, so many of these commercial risks will tend to avoid the form-regulation tax by seeking alternative forms of insurance protection, as suggested above in table 8-1.

---

if one views the tax revenues as income transfers and evaluates what the tax would have to be to create the equivalent deadweight loss to *society as a whole* (and not just to the purchasers of insurance), then the premium tax would rise to between 28.8 and 30.5 percent of the premium price (instead of the 4.3 to 4.8 percent premium tax reported in here). Thus, from society's perspective as a whole, the tax equivalent to the deadweight loss from the days delayed is almost seven times greater than the tax increase that comes when just looking at the welfare of buyers of insurance. A similar increase applies to the premium tax reported below for delays greater than 30 days.

11. See previous footnote for why this is an understatement from society's perspective (rather than the insurance buyers' perspective).

Form Regulation and Delays to Market Innovation

When the duration of delays is calculated for one commercial lines insurer, the delays are long and exhibit large interstate variation (table 8-4).[12] "Days delayed" is measured as the time between the filing of a form with an insurance department and its introduction into the market. Even in states with no explicit form filing requirements, the days delayed may be greater than zero for two reasons. First, even where there are no form regulations in a state, there may be rate regulation for some lines of insurance. Thus, in the absence of form regulation, policy approval still may be delayed because of the rate regulation. Second, for the insurer whose data is used in tables 8-4, 8-6, and 8-7, the "approval" date actually represents the date the policy was implemented. Since there appears to be no reason why the difference between formal approval and implementation of the contract *within this insurance company* should vary systemically across states, it does not seem that the relative rankings of the states in table 8-4 will be affected by differences between implementation and approval dates.

The substantial variation in days delayed depends in part on the type of form regulation in each state. Stringency of regulatory systems ranges from state-determined forms (not generally applicable to the commercial insurers analyzed here) to no statutory requirement for filing forms. Table 8-5 shows the continuum from most strict to least strict.

Form regulation may vary by line of insurance and size of the policy, even among commercial insurers.[13] In table 8-4 when two or more lines have differing form regulation, the more stringent is generally recorded in the right-hand column. Moreover, for both statutory and administrative reasons, form regulation in practice does not strictly follow the theoretical continuum just presented. Some states with prior approval regulation, such as Oregon, may approve policy changes more quickly than seemingly less restrictive "prior approval with express deemer" or "file and use" states. In terms of regulatory approval speed, the express deemer provisions may be of little practical consequence: state regulators simply ask for extensions to the deemer, which if refused will likely result in disapproval of the proposed form changes. However, form regulation does seem to make a

12. The insurer agreed to share its forms filing experience on the condition of remaining anonymous.

13. As discussed later, policies with lower premium values (for smaller firms) are subject in some states to more stringent form regulation than policies with higher premium values (for larger firms).

Table 8-4. *Ranking of States by Delayed Approval Index, One Commercial Lines Insurer, 1999* [a]
Days from filing to approval

| | | *Average days delayed by line* | | | | |
States[b]	All lines	CMP[c]	FA	GL	PL	*Type of Forms regulation*
1. Louisiana	222.7	315.0	239.3	304.9	273.2	Prior approval with express deemer
2. New York	163.4	129.8	117.4	223.5	113.9	Prior approval with express deemer
3. Massachusetts	151.3	123.5	142.7	241.4	128.4	Prior approval with express deemer
4. Maine	139.7	154.0	118.3	121.9	185.5	Prior approval with express deemer
5. Nebraska	123.7	164.7	84.0	111.7	128.9	Prior approval with express deemer
6. South Carolina	117.6	121.3	181.9	77.5	118.1	Prior approval
7. Vermont	116.6	46.3	96.0	187.2	121.1	Prior approval with express deemer
8. Connecticut	115.5	111.8	70.1	125.8	150.4	Prior approval
9. Washington	109.0	170.8	104.1	59.9	74.3	Use and file
10. Montana	107.2	113.8	80.0	144.4	88.0	Prior approval with express deemer
11. New Hampshire	104.8	143.5	122.8	92.2	110.1	Prior approval with express deemer[c]
12. Kansas	102.9	127.3	88.5	115.0	105.8	Prior approval with express deemer
13. Texas	94.1	84.1	102.6	108.6	100.0	Prior approval with express deemer
14. New Mexico	92.4	61.9	115.0	78.7	75.5	Prior approval
15. Georgia	91.8	77.5	75.6	63.2	100.3	Prior approval with express deemer
16. Alaska	88.1	55.3	36.6	109.1	111.9	Prior approval with express deemer
17. District of Columbia	87.3	94.2	67.7	64.1	86.4	Form filing only
18. Virginia	83.3	136.6	151.9	115.5	70.1	Prior approval with express deemer
19. Ohio	80.0	100.2	78.1	38.1	72.6	File and use

20. Missouri	79.1	34.0	107.9	92.8	85.7	Use and file[e]
21. Iowa	74.3	60.8	71.2	117.3	73.3	Prior approval with express deemer
22. California	70.5	54.1	133.4	72.7	61.6	Prior approval with express deemer
23. North Dakota	64.2	67.7	52.5	69.6	38.1	Prior approval with express deemer
24. Oklahoma	62.8	87.5	43.9	47.1	75.3	Prior approval with express deemer
25. Arizona	60.3	94.7	29.7	46.2	63.8	Prior approval with express deemer[e]
26. Pennsylvania	59.3	55.3	98.3	10.2	59.4	Prior approval with express deemer[e]
27. North Carolina	58.4	49.3	63.1	55.1	52.1	Prior approval with express deemer
28. Wisconsin	54.2	74.8	67.5	39.7	48.8	Prior approval with express deemer
29. Utah	54.0	36.0	81.2	62.9	47.1	File and use
30. Florida	52.2	39.9	88.3	72.1	46.5	Prior approval with express deemer
31. New Jersey	51.8	25.8	76.0	49.6	38.2	Prior approval with express deemer
32. Mississippi	51.2	37.5	74.4	44.5	58.3	Prior approval with express deemer
33. Arkansas	50.0	43.7	16.4	17.9	54.8	Prior approval with express deemer[e]
34. Hawaii	47.6	40.6	33.8	28.1	30.2	Form filing only
35. Illinois	45.7	71.6	49.7	18.1	51.3	File and use
36. Indiana	44.3	46.1	37.9	30.5	33.4	No form filing
37. Maryland	43.1	33.8	65.9	24.9	39.4	Prior approval with express deemer
38. Colorado	41.4	41.3	64.2	24.6	27.9	No form filing
39. Alabama	36.3	17.2	17.7	17.6	19.0	Prior approval with express deemer
40. Minnesota	36.0	12.3	23.0	29.9	65.1	No form filing
41. Oregon	34.2	28.5	19.6	24.1	45.2	Prior approval
42. Kentucky	32.9	17.5	27.8	23.3	22.5	Prior approval with express deemer
43. Tennessee	30.7	22.0	35.6	25.4	39.1	Use and file
44. Nevada	30.4	14.8	18.6	19.3	20.4	File and use

Table 8-4. *Continued*
Days from filing to approval

	Average days delayed by line					
States[b]	*All lines*	*CMP*[c]	*FA*	*GL*	*PL*	*Type of Forms regulation*
45. Delaware	29.3	26.1	21.2	20.3	24.4	Prior approval with express deemer
46. West Virginia	26.5	18.3	18.7	15.9	27.2	Prior approval with express deemer
47. South Dakota	26.3	30.4	14.4	23.1	20.6	Prior approval with express deemer
48. Rhode Island	24.4	18.3	14.5	33.4	17.8	No form filing
49. Idaho	24.2	15.8	38.9	18.5	17.3	Form filing only
50. Wyoming	22.5	17.3	16.2	18.7	21.9	Prior approval with express deemer
51. Michigan	22.4	19.5	14.2	15.6	16.7	No form filing

Source: Author's calculations based on data from insurer that wished to remain anonymous.

a. Rankings are based on estimated coefficients for state dummy variables from a regression of "days from file to approval" on dummy variables for individual analyst, lines of insurance, and states. Calculations are based on filings from January 1, 1999, to January 1, 2000. The number of filings in each state ranges from a low of 53 in Virginia to a high of 156 in Texas. For example, mean days delayed for Louisiana, the state with the highest number of days delayed, is based on 68 filings.

b. Includes the District of Columbia.

c. Abbreviations: CMP, commercial multiperil; FA, fire and allied; GL, general liability; PL, professional liability.

d. American Insurance Association (1999); National Association of Insurance Commissioners (1999).

e. Indicates fewer filing restrictions for large commercial policies.

Table 8-5. *Stringency of Form Regulation*[a]

Degree of stringency	Form regulation	Description
1	State-adopted forms	State regulator specifies form.
2	Prior approval	Regulator must approve forms prior to their use.
3	Prior approval with express deemer	Regulator must approve forms, but if the forms are not disapproved by the end of statutory waiting period, then they will automatically be *deemed* to be in compliance.
4	File and use	Forms must be filed with the regulator before the proposed effective date.
5	Use and file	Forms may be used but must be filed within a certain number of days after the effective policy date.
6	Form filing only	Forms must be filed, but the statutes do not specify that they be filed before the effective date. (The laws are silent on what happens after the effective policy date, and there is no express deemer provision).
7	No form filing	There is no statutory provision that requires insurers to submit forms.

Source: American Insurance Association (1999).
a. Ranking: 1, most stringent; 7, least stringent.

difference: in table 8-4 a comparison of days delayed with the type of regulation indicates that the correlation between prior approval state regulation and days delayed is positive, whereas the days delayed falls as the likelihood of being a no-form-filing state increases.

The relative rankings of states by days delayed varies substantially. For example, days delayed listed in the second column of table 8-4 have an (unweighted) mean variation of 71.2 days, with a standard deviation of 42.1 days. The range of these values reflects the large variance: the average delay of 223 days for top-ranked Louisiana is ten times greater than Michigan's average of 22 days delayed. Fifteen states have days delayed exceeding ninety days; even the median is almost sixty days. If form regulation has potentially important welfare ramifications, as suggested in the preceding section, then this variation suggests significant differences in regulatory efficiency across states.

Moreover, the correlation across lines of insurance in days delayed before form approval is relatively large. For the commercial insurer whose data is presented in table 8-4, the correlation between lines of insurance lies between 74 and 94 percent, with the least amount of correlation between the commercial multiperil and general liability lines of insurance. Thus the number of days delayed appears to be related more to the state where the form approval is sought than to the line of insurance for which the form approval is sought.

To examine whether rate regulation has an impact on days delayed once controls are made for states' economic circumstances, two types of regressions have been performed. In the first, shown in table 8-6, days delayed are regressed on form indexes (using the classifications from table 8-5). In the second, days delayed are regressed on prior approval dummy variables, which equal one if prior approval for form changes is required (using stringency levels 1, 2, and 3 from table 8-5). If more stringent regulation increases the time to market, then the estimated sign of the *form index* coefficient in table 8-6 should be negative, and the estimated sign on the *prior approval* coefficient in table 8-7 should be positive.

There are three classifications of insurance for which there are consistent measures of regulation. One classification is for property-casualty insurance in general so that the regulation applies to smaller, noncommercial risks as well as to larger risks in states with regulations that do not differentiate between commercial and noncommercial risks. There is another form index for large business firms that has the same regulatory value as the general property-casualty index in states that do not differentiate commercial risks from other risks, but it has higher values in those states that subject large commercial insurance policies to less stringent form regulation. Arkansas, for example, has prior approval with express deemer for smaller insurance policies (so the general form index equals three), whereas it was no form filing for larger insurance policies affecting commercial insureds (so the commercial form index equals seven).

Finally, there is a third classification of regulation for workers' compensation insurance. States with monopoly state funds in workers' compensation—Nevada, North Dakota, Ohio, Washington, West Virginia, and Wyoming—are excluded from the analysis since form regulation is not defined for these states. Including such states and assigning them an index

Table 8-6. *Form Regulation and Time to Approval, Regression on Form Indexes*[a]

Independent variables and constant	No controls	Demographic controls only	Demographic and rate controls
		Dependent variable[b]	
Constant	4.796	4.389	4.522
	(19.28)	(6.80)	(6.80)
Property-casualty form index	−0.203	−0.226	−0.216
	(3.51)	(4.40)	(3.26)
Property-casualty commercial form index	0.022	0.017	0.009
	(0.43)	(0.35)	(0.15)
Workers' compensation form index	0.002	−0.007	−0.010
	(0.05)	(0.18)	(0.23)
Property-casualty rate index	...[c]	...	0.003
			(0.04)
Property-casualty commercial rate index	...	...	0.007
			(0.16)
Workers' compensation rate index	...	...	−0.041
			(0.74)
South	...	−0.224	−0.217
		(1.27)	(1.26)
Population	...	1.77E-9[d]	3.08E-9
		(0.18)	(0.33)
Unemployment rate	...	0.009	0.008
		(0.12)	(0.12)
Personal income	...	2.03E-5	1.83E-5
		(1.22)	(1.08)
R^2	0.238	0.311	0.315

Source: Author's calculations.

a. Form regulation is measured by the index values shown in table 8-5, where the lower valued numbers indicate more stringent regulation. Absolute t statistics are in parentheses and are based on heteroskedastic-robust standard errors. States with monopoly funds for workers' compensation are excluded; therefore sample size is forty-five.

b. Log(time to approval).

c. Respective variable was not included in this specification.

d. $E-X = 10^{-x}$.

Table 8-7. *Form Regulation and Time to Approval, Regression on Prior Approval Dummy Variables*[a]

Independent variables and constant	Dependent variable[b]		
	No controls	Demographic controls only	Demographic and rate controls
Constant	3.818	3.214	3.174
	(20.13)	(5.17)	(5.32)
Property-casualty form dummy	0.689	0.752	0.903
	(3.20)	(3.78)	(5.58)
Property-casualty commercial form dummy	−0.016	0.033	−0.175
	(0.07)	(0.16)	(0.79)
Workers' compensation form dummy	−0.210	−0.191	−0.115
	(1.17)	(1.12)	(0.66)
Property-casualty rate dummy	...[c]	...	−0.601
			(3.81)
Property-casualty commercial rate dummy	...	...	0.453
			(2.18)
Workers' compensation rate dummy	...	...	0.087
			(0.53)
South	...	−0.260	−0.230
		(1.54)	(1.39)
Population	...	−2.49E-10[d]	3.14E-9
		(0.03)	(0.31)
Unemployment rate	...	0.034	0.060
		(0.53)	(0.79)
Personal income	...	1.65E-5	1.26E-5
		(1.01)	(0.77)
R^2	0.219	0.293	0.350

Source: Author's calculations using stringency levels 1, 2, and 3 from table 8-5.

a. Form regulation is measured by dummy variables that equal one when the respective regulation requires prior approval (or approval with express deemer) from the state and that equal zero when there is less stringent regulation. Absolute *t* statistics are in parentheses and are based on heteroskedastic-robust standard errors. States with monopoly funds for workers' compensation are excluded; therefore sample size is forty-five.

b. Log(time to approval).

c. Respective variable was not included in this specification.

d. $E - X = 10^{-x}$.

value of one has virtually no impact on the estimated results reported in tables 8-6 and 8-7 (nor on the results reported later in tables 8-10 and 8-11). As a result of the exclusion of monopoly state funds, all regressions in tables 8-6 and 8-7 (as well as in tables 8-10 and 8-11) are based on a forty-five observations.

The results in table 8-6 and table 8-7 indicate that more stringent property-casualty form regulation (the property-casualty form index variable) significantly increases time to market, whether the effect of the regulation is measured as an index value or as a dummy variable for prior approval. The estimates using the form indexes given in table 8-6 show that a unit increase in the form regulation index (going, for example, from a "file and use" to a "prior approval with express deemer" type regulation) results in at least a 20 percent increase in the days delayed. At the sample means, this would increase days delayed by about fifteen days. The estimated change in days delayed between states with prior approval and those without is even larger: prior approval states have time-to-market regulatory delays that are about 90 percent longer (table 8-7, far right column) than states without prior approval.

Interestingly enough, when there was an increase in stringency for large commercial insurance policies form regulation (the property-casualty commercial form index), the days delayed declined; however, the change was statistically insignificant and quantitatively small. Also, the estimated impact of regulatory stringency for workers' compensation insurance was relatively small, statistically insignificant, and unstable in sign.

Control variables in tables 8-6 and 8-7 were of two types: controls for rate regulation and controls for state economic variables. The controls for rate regulation were necessary because there could have been delays associated with the rate regulation for policies that also had changes in the form. The controls for rate regulation had the expected sign: more rate regulation generally increased the days delayed. The one exception was the prior approval rate dummy variable in the far right column: where prior approval of rates tended to be more stringent, there were fewer days delayed in approving forms. Though this might suggest that rate and form regulation are substitutes, this is not supported by the results presented later on (see tables 8-10 and 8-11).

The state economic variables used as controls do not indicate any systematic variation in days delayed due to such factors. The variable "south" equals one for states from the South (as defined by the Bureau of

the Census) and equals zero otherwise. State population, state unemployment rate, and average personal income in the state were included as measures of insurance demand.

Comparative Analysis: Minnesota versus New York

While the cross-section evidence in tables 8-6 and 8-7 indicates that
regulatory stringency does make a significant difference in days delayed,
unmeasured state differences—correlated with the regulatory stringency—
may be clouding the interpretation of the results, either because the choice
of regulation is endogenous or because of other, unmeasured factors that
might increase both regulatory stringency and days delayed (for example,
the quality of insurers offering products in particular states). Therefore, to
get another measure of whether a change in regime affects days delayed, a
difference-in-differences estimator is provided.

To understand the idea of difference-in-differences estimation, consider how you would check the following statement: "Butler male children are unusually tall relative to Butler female children." Suppose there
are both many male and female children, and you take all their height
measurements at age sixteen so that you have a consistent basis for comparison. The analogy here is simple: height is days delayed, height of Butler male children is days delayed before the change to no form filing, and
height of Butler female children is days delayed after the change to no
form filing (that is, after the deregulation). Then one test of the statement
that "Butler male children are unusually tall relative to Butler female children" is to simply difference their heights. This would be the difference
estimate.

However, the problem with the difference estimate in heights lies with
the part of the statement "*are unusually tall relative to.*" That is, girls are
usually shorter than boys, just as general, nationwide trends may decrease
the days delayed in New York at the same time that they reduce the days
delayed in Minnesota. So a better estimate of the proposition that "Butler
male children are unusually tall relative to Butler female children" is a
comparison of the gender differences in height within the Butler household to the gender differences in height in all other households. This is the
difference-in-differences estimate. For example, if the gender height difference between Butler males and Butler females is six inches, while the gender difference in most families is only two inches, then the statement is

true. On the other hand, if the Butler differential is six inches and the gender differential in everyone else's family is five and a half inches, then the Butler differential doesn't seem so *unusual.*

Analogously, if days delayed fell by 80 percent in Minnesota between 1994 and 1995 (the difference in a state that went to deregulation) and days delayed fell by 75 percent in New York between 1994 and 1995 (the difference in a state that didn't deregulate), then the correct estimate of the impact of form deregulation is probably not 80 percent. New York fell 75 percent even without deregulation, presumably because of other general trends that could have been affecting both states. In these circumstances, as with the heights, a better measure is the difference in differences: 80 percent minus 75 percent, or about 5 percent. Thus difference-in-differences estimates can be used to control for trends common to both states.

Therefore the comparison is the percentage change in days delayed in Minnesota before and after a change in stringency (the difference), relative to the percentage change in days delayed in New York over the same period (the difference in differences). Minnesota form regulation changed on January 25, 1995, when the state went from prior approval with express deemer to elimination of filing requirements for most commercial forms. Table 8-8 shows that Minnesota's change in regulatory stringency lowered days delayed by 65 percent between 1994 and 1995; during the same period, New York days delayed fell by 20 percent for all commercial lines, using differences in logarithms. Since there was no change in stringency for New York form regulation during this period, this state's decrease in days delayed may be an effect of general trends operating in the absence of any change in form regulation. Subtracting this overall "trend" change from the Minnesota-specific change provides an estimate of the impact of the regime change after accounting for other trends: 65 percent minus 20 percent, or about a 45 percent decline in days delayed in Minnesota due to changes in its law.

Year to year volatility in days delayed is an obvious problem with the data shown in table 8-8. Hence form regulation effects are better measured by comparing the three-year average before the change with the three-year average after the change. The percent decline in days delayed due to Minnesota's law change, *based on three-year averages* by lines of business, is shown in table 8-9. The difference-in-differences estimates, once we exclude the outlier value of 428.3 days (for New York's multiperil lines in 1994), range from 16.4 to 84 percent, with the overall difference-in-differences estimate of 54.6 percent falling right in the middle of the

Table 8-8. *Time from Forms Filed to Forms Approved, Minnesota versus New York, One Commercial Lines Insurer, 1988–98*[a]
Number of days

Year	All commercial lines		Commercial multiperil		Fire and allied lines		General liability		Professional liability	
	Minn.	N.Y.	Minn.	N.Y.	Minn	N.Y.	Minn.	N.Y.	Minn.	N.Y.
1988	43.6	78.7	61.0	63.5	13.4	86.8	44.3	113.8	51.2	123.4
1989	58.6	113.0	88.6	99.8	39.9	52.6	104.7	180.6	60.8	75.6
1990	69.3	197.2	95.6	178.3	77.7	134.1	62.5	75.7	56.7	1242.7
1991	80.8	183.7	230.9	243.3	58.8	61.1	88.0	181.7	72.1	1145.0
1992	50.8	146.4	76.9	206.6	35.5	36.0	48.7	182.3	41.9	182.3
1993	78.1	121.2	64.0	116.8	65.4	76.7	67.4	185.9	128.4	37.5
1994	56.4	180.8	58.7	428.3	76.5	178.1	68.8	156.4	49.7	196.5
1995	29.2	147.8	38.0	156.7	43.0	33.3	25.3	108.4	40.4	230.6
1996	36.6	103.4	26.9	66.4	53.8	97.6	37.1	160.8	26.4	89.1
1997	24.1	124.3	38.8	73.7	11.7	86.1	16.8	147.7	31.0	108.7
1998	25.4	132.7	13.0	136.0	20.7	115.9	16.0	127.9	78.9	110.4

Source: See footnote to table 8-4.

a. Averages for 1999 were omitted because of sample selection: claims filed in 1999 were less likely to have been approved by the time this sample was drawn, especially for New York (whose approvals were taking longer than those for Minnesota). This was reflected in a smaller number of forms in the 1999 sample year: 68 for Minnesota (versus 144 in 1998) and 53 for New York (versus 127 for 1998)

Table 8-9. *Decline in Days Delayed Based on Three-Year Averages,*
1992–97
Percent

Line of insurance	Minn. difference[a]	N.Y. difference	Minn. difference – N.Y. difference
Overall	72.3	17.7	54.6
Multiperil	65.5	92.9 (49.1)[b]	−66.1(16.4)[b]
Fire	49.2	29.3	19.9
General liability	84.7	23.0	61.8
Professional liability	81.1	−2.9	83.9

Source: Author's calculations from data in table 8-8.
a. In-state difference based on average from 1992 to 1994 minus average from 1995 to 1997.
b. Numbers in parentheses are calculated without the outlier value of 428.3 days from 1994.

values. This is slightly smaller than the estimates in the property-casualty form dummy row of table 8-7 but is within two standard deviations of the estimated impacts given there. It provides further evidence that form regulation significantly prolongs time to market.[14]

14. As an alternative to estimating the effect of the law change, a regression was performed with all the individual claims approval data used in calculating the means shown in table 8-8. The natural logarithm of days delayed was regressed on four dummy variables—analysts who filed the form, lines of insurance, state location, and each year in the sample (1999 observations were deleted for reasons explained in the footnote to table 8-8)—and on a state post-change interaction term. This last interaction variable estimated the effect of the law change on days delayed, holding constant the state, year, line of business, and analyst effects. The estimated impact of the law was to reduce days delayed by 66 percent in Minnesota, other things being constant. The corresponding t statistic was 5.5, a statistically significant difference.

Regressions were also done for each line of insurance separately, holding state, year, and filing analyst constant. The resulting reduction in Minnesota days delayed (relative to New York) was 87.4 percent for commercial multiperil (t statistic, 2.52), 82.3 percent for fire and allied lines (t statistic, 2.10), 101.1 percent for general liability (t statistic, 2.94), and −15.6 percent for professional liability (t statistic, 0.54). Only the last regression was insignificant (and of the wrong sign), possibly because that was the only line of insurance (other than crop damage) that did not undergo form deregulation. All professional liability in Minnesota written for individuals (such as doctors) must still have prior approval of the state for forms.

One final note is that while dummy variables for year and line of insurance were highly significant, those for different analysts filing the forms were considerably less significant: the F statistic was 3.2, with 25 and 1,731 degrees of freedom. Of the twenty-five dummy variables for analysts (representing the twenty-six analysts who filed forms in New York or Minnesota over the ten-year period), only three had t statistic values greater than two (2.08, 2.03, and 2.16), and only one other analyst dummy was significant at the 10 percent level (with a t statistic of 1.68). This suggests that there is not much of an analyst effect in terms of days delayed, that is, days delayed did not depend on who was filing the form approval requests, at least in this company.

Aggregate Benefits and Costs of Form Regulation

The model just discussed focuses on how regulation can delay the introduction of innovative insurance products and hence lower consumer welfare. It is a model most appropriate for commercial insurance, a market in which both buyers and sellers are relatively sophisticated. In such markets information asymmetry and legal formalities will not be significant factors hampering optimal risk-sharing arrangements through insurance contracts.

Not only does economic theory suggest that a competitive commercial insurance market benefits insurance consumers, most businesses purchasing commercial insurance also report that they are better off in a competitive environment. In a survey of 1,206 businesses with annual sales between $5 million and $100 million, the Insurance Research Council reports that 80 percent of these firms believe that commercial insurers are moderately or very competitive.[15] They also believe that such competition confers benefits: most firms feel they could negotiate a lower insurance premium under competition than under state regulation, and the majority report that their insurers understand their insurance needs and the coverage that firms are offered. Less than half, however, report satisfaction with how quickly insurers respond to quotes, perhaps in part because of form regulation.

For less informed consumers and those not well versed in insurance contracts (that is, many noncommercial policyholders), form regulation may limit fraud and consumer abuse. Regulation may ensure that contract language for homeowners', auto, and life insurance is readily understood by both the insureds and their agents and that potentially vague or fraudulent contract terms are avoided. To the extent that it serves this function—minimizing fraud potential for the less sophisticated consumer and providing a sort of warranty of the contract language—form regulation may increase the demand for insurance in the noncommercial lines. Since noncommercial premiums are at least as large as commercial premiums, the warranty effects may offset the delay effects in the overall market if the former effects are important for the noncommercial market.[16]

Thus, in the noncommercial markets, the impact of form regulation is ambiguous. To the extent that its warranty function is more important, insurance will increase with regulation so that increases in the form index

15. Insurance Research Council (2000).
16. NAIC (2000a and b).

will decrease insurance output. On the other hand, to the extent that the delayed time-to-market impact is more important, demand for noncommercial insurance will fall with regulation so that increases in the form index will increase insurance output (have a positive coefficient).

Workers' compensation form regulation may also have an ambiguous sign. Most larger buyers either self-insure or have insurance policies with large deductibles. This suggests that much of the form regulation for workers' compensation insurance will affect small and medium-size buyers who are not likely to be very sophisticated about insurance contract language. Hence one could expect the workers' compensation form regulation index to be ambiguous a priori, just as it was for the general property-casualty index.

Despite the ambiguous effect of form regulation on noncommercial risks, the model described above predicts that less stringent regulation for commercial insurers should increase the quantity-demanded for insurance both on a per capita and a relative basis. The quantity of insurance at the state level can be measured by the insurance gross state product (GSP), where insurance GSP is a measure of value added and is the sum of three components: compensation of employees, indirect business tax and non-tax liability, and property-type income (such as corporate profits, rental income, and net interest). GSP for the state is the sum of the GSP originating in all industries in the state. Included as alternative dependent variables are the insurance GSP per capita and the insurance GSP relative to state gross domestic product.

As form regulation decreases in the commercial market, insurance prices will fall (for new insurance products), and a larger number of policies will be sold. That is, there will be a change in the quantity-demanded of insurance. To the extent that commercial insureds move into the ART market because of regulatory delays, deregulation will increase the demand for insurance as well; thus more insurance will be sold because the demand curve will shift out. This is in addition to the increased quantity-demanded effect as buyers purchase more because of the lowered price. Whether the quantity of insurance demanded increases because of falling prices or because of an outward shift of the demand curve, the form index variable will have a positive coefficient both in regressions of per capita insurance GSP on the form regulation index and in regressions relative to insurance GSP on the form regulation index.

The descriptive statistics for the estimation are given in table 8-10. Form regulations for commercial insurers are only slightly less lax than

Table 8-10. *Descriptive Statistics and Data Sources, 1999*

Variables	Mean	Standard deviation	Minimum	Maximum
Dependent[a]				
ln(*ins GSP/pop*)	−7.35	0.46	−8.14	−5.83
ln(*ins GSP/st GSP*)	−3.82	0.40	−4.91	−2.64
ln(*agent$/pop*)	−7.71	0.54	−8.52	−6.29
ln(*agent$/agent #*)	−2.34	0.38	−2.98	−1.33
Form and rate regulation[b]				
PC form index	3.68	1.50	2.00	7.00
PC commercial form index	4.18	1.85	2.00	7.00
WC form index	3.09	1.29	1.00	7.00
PC rate index	3.80	1.06	2.00	8.00
PC commercial rate index	4.60	1.97	2.00	8.00
WC rate index	3.13	0.81	2.00	7.00
State control[c]				
South	0.33	0.48	0	1.00
Population (in millions)	5.58	6.18	0.52	33.15
Unemployment rate (percent)	4.13	1.11	2.20	6.50
Personal income (in thousands of dollars)	27.63	4.46	20.9	39.86

Source: Author's calculations. Information on insurance agent employment is from Dun and Bradstreet (1999) databases, using SIC codes 63 and 64. Gross state product (GSP), overall and for insurance insurers and agents, for 1999 is from the Bureau of Economic Analysis (BEA), as are the state population values for that year. See BEA, "Regional Accounts Data: Gross State Product Data" (*www.bea.doc.gov/bea/regional/gsp* [October 2001]), and "Regional Accounts Data: Annual State Personal Income" (*www.bea.doc.gov/bea/regional/spi* [October 2001]).

a. GSP is a measure of value added, calculated from three components: compensation to employees, indirect business tax and nontax liability, and property-type income (including corporate profits, business transfers, rental income, and net interest). Ratios are defined as follows: ln(*ins GSP/pop*) = log(*insurance GSP in state/state population*); ln(*ins GSP/st GSP*) = log(*insurance GSP in state/total GSP in state*); ln(*agent$/pop*) = log(*total agent income in state/state population*); ln(*agent$/agent #*) = log(*total agent income in state/number of agents in state*).

b. All insurance regulation indexes were constructed as described in the text from the American Insurance Association (1999). *All property-casualty (PC) index variables used the lower value from table 8-5 and were regulation varied by line, except for standard state-adopted policies (used almost exclusively for standard fire insurance), whose values were ignored because of their limited application to the issues addressed here.* PC form index = degree of form regulation in general for property-casualty insurance within the state. PC commercial form index = degree of form regulation for commercial insurers within the state. WC form index = degree of form regulation for workers' compensation insurers in the state. PC rate index = property-casualty rate regulation within the state. PC commercial rate index = property-casualty rate regulation for commercial insurers. WC rate index = rate regulation for workers' compensation insurers.

c. South = one if the state is in the South Census Region. Population = 1999 state population (from BEA website). Unemployment rate taken from Bureau of Labor Statistics, "Current Labor Statistics, July 1999" (*www.bls.gov/opub/mlr/2000/10/cls0010.pdf* [October 2001]). Personal income taken from BEA website for 1999.

they are for noncommercial insurers (with respective mean values of 4.18 and 3.68). Not only is the general property and casualty market still heavily regulated, the commercial end of the market (populated with many large businesses buying from many insurers) is heavily regulated as well. When rate regulation is tabulated in the same manner as form regulation was earlier, the resultant sample means show that there is less rate regulation than there is form regulation. Means for the control variables indicate that about a third of our sample comes from the South Census Region of the United States, that the average unemployment rate was about 4 percent, and that the average level of personal income was $27,625.

The results of our GSP regressions are given in table 8-11. Per capita insurance output is lower in the South, other things being equal. The other control variables in the last four rows of table 8-11, which capture factors that affect the demand for insurance, have the expected signs if the demand for insurance tends to increase with consumer income, that is, if insurance is a normal good.[17] The demand for insurance increases as personal income increases and falls as the unemployment rate increases. Demand is also higher in states with larger populations (perhaps a density effect, since the dependent variable is measured on a per capita basis).

The pattern of effects in table 8-11 indicates that the warranty function of form regulation dominates for the general property-casualty and workers' compensation markets, but the days-delayed effect is stronger for the commercial insurance market. The magnitude and level of statistical significance further suggests that the effect of form regulation on the demand for insurance is greater than the impact of rate regulation (see the values on the far right when both form and rate regulation variables are included in the model). Although these tables employ the form index as the measure of regulatory stringency, results using the corresponding prior approval dummy variables were virtually identical and therefore are not reported here. These results, both from table 8-11 and from using the prior approval dummy variables, were also robust to the inclusion of states with monopoly workers' compensation systems, as well as robust to the exclusion of the personal income variable.

The form index coefficient values of -0.07 and -0.084 in the middle columns indicate that as form regulation increases by one category (say from file and use to prior approval with express deemer), insurance out-

17. For empirical evidence that insurance is a normal good, see Browne, Chung, and Frees (2000) and Browne and Hoyt (2000).

Table 8-11. *Regressions for Form Regulation and Gross State Product: Overall and for Insurance, 1999*[a]

	Dependent variables: natural logarithms of					
	No controls		Demographic controls		Demographic and rate controls	
Independent variables and constant.	$\dfrac{ins\ GSP}{pop}$	$\dfrac{ins\ GSP}{st\ GSP}$	$\dfrac{ins\ GSP}{pop}$	$\dfrac{ins\ GSP}{st\ GSP}$	$\dfrac{ins\ GSP}{pop}$	$\dfrac{ins\ GSP}{st\ GSP}$
Constant	−7.333	−3.646	−8.755	−3.601	−8.943	−3.833
	(28.90)	(18.59)	(30.75)	(9.77)	(25.61)	(9.53)
Property-casualty form index	−0.011	−0.058	−0.070	−0.084	−0.050	−0.053
	(.20)	(1.17)	(2.72)	(2.78)	(1.51)	(1.31)
Property-casualty commercial form index	0.032	0.061	0.048	0.061	0.021	0.021
	(0.60)	(1.41)	(1.95)	(2.48)	(0.58)	(0.49)
Workers' compensation form index	−.036	−.070	−.053	−.076	−.055	−.078
	(.92)	(2.27)	(2.38)	(3.05)	(2.45)	(3.09)
Property-casualty rate index	...[b]	...	...	...	.017	.014
					(.54)	(.36)
Property-casualty commercial rate index	...	...	...	...	.024	.037
					(.84)	(1.06)

Workers' compensation rate index	...	...	...	...	.013	.015
					(.50)	(.50)
South	...	...	−.094	−.108	−.089	−.103
			(1.17)	(1.35)	(1.09)	(1.26)
Population	...	...	3.87E-9[c]	1.29E-8	2.62E-9	1.14E-8
			(.78)	(1.81)	(.58)	(1.75)
Unemployment rate	...	...	−.127	−.195	−.121	−.187
			(3.52)	(4.66)	(3.27)	(4.54)
Personal income	...	...	7.81E-5	3.03E-5	7.79E-5	3.01E-5
			(8.99)	(2.66)	(8.61)	(2.63)
R^2	.017	.088	.754	.584	.765	.609

Source: Author's calculations based on data from table 8-10.

a. *st GSP* is the state's gross state product (GSP), derived as the sum of individual industries' GSP in each state. Each industry's GSP is its value added: gross output (sales or receipts and other operating income, commodity taxes, and inventory change) minus its intermediate inputs (consumption of goods and services purchased from other industries). *ins GSP* is the insurance sector's gross state product, measured accordingly. States with monopoly funds for workers' compensation are excluded; therefore sample size is forty-five states. Absolute *t* statistics are shown in parentheses and are based on heteroskedastic-robust standard errors.

b. Respective variable was not included in this specification.

c. $E - X = 10^{-x}$.

put increases by 7 percent per capita and by roughly 8.4 percent more than gross state product. The estimated effects are statistically significant. These estimates are consistent with the hypothesis that form regulation provides a warranty for small risks, and they suggest that contract-warranting mechanisms are quite valuable. The same seems to be true for workers' compensation insurance, as indicated by the significant negative coefficients -0.053 and -0.076 in the fourth row of table 8-11.

The form index coefficient values for large commercial regulation indicate that for each unit increase in form deregulation, insurance output per capita will increase by 4.8 percent and insurance output will increase by 6.1 percent more than the rest of the state output. That is, whether the insurance effect is measured either on a per capita basis, as in the $\ln(ins\ GSP/pop)$ regression, or on a basis relative to the rest of state output, as in the $\ln(ins\ GSP/st\ GSP)$ regression, the results are consistent with the model discussed earlier. Where regulation for commercial insurers is less stringent, more insurance is sold (and, presumably, relatively less risk is financed by the ART market).

White tests reject the assumption that the errors are homoskedastic; hence the t tests in table 8-11 are calculated using heteroskedasticity-consistent, robust standard errors.[18] Normal F tests show the index variables as jointly significant (at the 7 and 3 percent levels), but these values are suspect because of the heteroskedasticity. Heteroskedastically robust F tests, which are strictly valid only for large samples, behaved poorly in this small sample of forty-five observations.[19]

The results in the two columns on the far right of table 8-11 include both form and rate regulation variables. Again, heteroskedasticity-consistent F tests of the joint significance of the form and rate regulation variables behaved poorly in this small sample. Normal F tests, which are subject to bias because of the heteroskedasticity, have lower p values for the form regulation variables (they are more significant) than they do for the rate regulation variables: the former have a p value of .14 under the joint test of significance in the $\ln(ins\ GSP/pop)$ regression; the latter have a p-value of .67 in the same regression. The form regulation variables are jointly significant in the $\ln(ins\ GSP/st\ GSP)$ regression with a p value of .06, while the rate regulation variables have a p value of .54 in the same regression.

The problem with including both the form and rate regulation vari-

18. Wooldridge (2000).

19. For discussion on heteroskedasticity and F tests, see Wooldridge (2000, p. 254) and Davidson and McKinnon (1993, p. 401)

ables in the same specification is that they are highly correlated across states, making it difficult to disentangle their effects in a regression model. This is known as the collinearity problem and is evidenced by high values of the variance inflation factors (VIF). VIF measures were computed for each independent variable in the regression to measure the degree of collinearity between that variable and the other independent variables. Some rate and form variables had relatively high VIFs in tables 8-11 and 8-12: the VIF was 3.5 for the property-casualty form index, 4.9 for the property-casualty commercial form index, and 3.3 for the property-casualty commercial rate index. For these reasons the middle two columns of tables 8-11 and 8-12 are probably the better empirical specifications.

The results suggest that insurance agents should be in favor of measures that would eliminate, or at least reduce, form regulation for commercial insurers. Yet some appear to oppose reduced form regulation for commercial insurers since it likely would result in more different—and more complex—insurance contracts. Reduced regulation may indeed have that effect, but it seems that the greater the degree of form regulation, the greater the flight out of traditional insurance products and into the ART market. In the long run, this flight could be more detrimental to insurance agents since the derived demand for their services would shrink along with the insurance market. To test the hypothesis that agents are better off with commercial form deregulation, agent income per state population and agent income per agent (average agent income) were regressed on the same variables used in table 8-11. If commercial form deregulation increases the demand for insurance, then it ought to increase the derived demand for insurance agents. That is, under this model's specifications, the form regulation index for commercial insurers should be positive and statistically significant. The results of these regressions are shown in table 8-12.

While the signs of the effects are robust and consistent with the results in table 8-11 (and roughly of the same magnitude), they are not always statistically significant. Commercial form deregulation has a significantly positive impact on average agent income but an insignificantly positive impact on the ratio of total agent income per statewide population. As in table 8-11, the state control variables in table 8-12 had the predicted signs, and except for the South dummy variable, these signs were generally the same as those in table 8-11. Though these results are somewhat mixed, they suggest that it is not in the agents' long-run interest to oppose form deregulation for commercial insurers.

If all states were to completely deregulate with respect to forms, so that

Table 8-12. *Regressions for Form Regulation and Insurance Agents, 1999*[a]

	Dependent variables: natural logarithms of					
	No controls		Demographic controls		Demographic and rate controls	
Independent variables and constant	$\dfrac{agent\ \$}{pop}$	$\dfrac{agent\ \$}{agent\ \#}$	$\dfrac{agent\ \$}{pop}$	$\dfrac{agent\ \$}{agent\ \#}$	$\dfrac{agent\ \$}{pop}$	$\dfrac{agent\ \$}{agent\ \#}$
Constant	−7.678	−2.360	−8.841	−3.230	−8.938	−3.383
	(28.93)	(12.66)	(22.96)	(7.67)	(16.54)	(7.77)
Property-casualty form index	0.006	−0.004	−0.043	−0.033	−0.017	−0.023
	(0.09)	(0.07)	(0.97)	(0.73)	(0.31)	(0.39)
Property-casualty commercial form index	0.018	0.041	0.038	0.056	0.003	0.038
	(0.28)	(0.97)	(1.26)	(2.00)	(0.06)	(0.72)
Workers' compensation form index	−0.043	−0.047	−0.058	−0.057	−0.049	−0.045
	(0.86)	(1.36)	(1.05)	(1.41)	(0.85)	(1.11)
Property-casualty rate index	...[b]	...	...	...	−0.073	−0.089
					(1.17)	(1.52)

Property-casualty commercial rate index	...	...	...	...	0.040 (1.11)	0.025 (0.65)
Workers' compensation rate index	...	...	...	...	0.046 (0.52)	0.084 (1.36)
South	...	...	0.026 (0.16)	0.042 (0.35)	0.008 (0.05)	0.015 (0.14)
Population	...	...	4.74E-9 c (0.53)	2.87E-9 (0.35)	3.98E-9 (0.41)	1.29E-9 (0.16)
Unemployment rate	...	...	-0.170 (3.48)	-0.071 (1.77)	-0.173 (3.45)	-0.076 (1.89)
Personal income	...	...	7.17E-5 (5.35)	4.37E-5 (3.42)	7.5E-5 (5.00)	4.93E-5 (3.82)
R^2	0.012	0.048	0.494	0.342	0.510	0.402

Source: Author's calculations based on data from table 8-10.

a. *agent $/pop* is insurance agent income per capita (state population); *agent $/agent #* is total agent income in the state divided by the number of insurance agents (the average agent income). States with monopoly funds for workers' compensation are excluded; therefore samples size is forty-five states. Absolute *t* statistics are shown in parentheses and are based on heteroskedastic-robust standard errors.

b. Blanks indicate respective variable was not included in this specification.

c. $E - X = 10^{-x}$.

the mean value of the commercial form index rose from 4.18 to 7, the implied increase in insurance per capita would be 13.6 percent. If this increase were applied to the 1997 (Conning) values in table 8-1 (assuming, for the moment, that these numbers apply to the commercial market only), the complete deregulation of forms would increase traditional insurer market share by $18.3 billion. And if this increase were at the expense of the ART market, it would return market share of traditional insurers back to the 1980 level, that is, market share would rise from about 66 to 75 percent. Since the data in table 8-1 include noncommercial insurers as well, the preceding suppositions will substantially overstate the absolute gains in market share for commercial insurers, but they may also understate the relative percentage gains of the commercial insurers (relative to their market share that has been eroded by the ART market). Hence the estimated effects of form regulation on commercial insurers are substantial, while the potential harm to insurance agents from form deregulation in the commercial market seems to be minimal.

Conclusions

The commercial insurance market does not seem to be fraught with imperfections: there are many informed buyers and sellers in this market and little evidence of significant externalities. When knowledgeable buyers and sellers in such markets are free to form contracts over risk allocations, the resulting outcomes will be Pareto optimal. Government restrictions on such contracts will only tend to reduce economic output and consumer well being. This analysis has focused on one potential aspect of form regulation: the impact of such restrictions on market innovation and, in particular, the prediction that such delays may lead to a considerable reduction in consumer surplus and hence flight of capital from traditional commercial insurers to the ART market.

The empirical results are generally consistent with these predictions. Commercial form deregulation is associated with an increase in insurance output, whether measured on a per capita basis or relative to the statewide gross state product (table 8-11). Other bits of empirical evidence seem generally consistent with this explanation. The state controls for demand factors generally have the expected sign in the regression: increases in personal income lead to increases in the demand for insurance, and increases in the unemployment rate lead to decreases in the demand for insurance.

In addition, if form deregulation for commercial insurance increases the demand or quantity-demanded for insurance, it also ought to increase the derived demand for insurance agents. It apparently does (table 8-12).

It is important to note that form regulation results not only in an "approval tax," as discussed earlier in this chapter, but also in another category of tax that may be even larger: the "never approved" tax. Discussions with industry underwriters suggest that several states will not approve certain types of forms or form provisions (such as "defense-within-limits" terms). This stifles innovation at least as much as the approval tax and drives business into the ART market. It is to be hoped that future research will examine both types of taxes, with more data than was available for this research project.

The results presented here also indicate that form regulation increases insurance output in the noncommercial market and for workers' compensation insurance. This suggests that the commercial and noncommercial markets are very different. One possible explanation for the differential market response is that noncommercial risks are not well informed about the nature of insurance contracts (and the legal language they contain) and look to form regulation as a kind of warranty. If this result continues to hold in further studies, it would suggest a large demand for warranties of noncommercial contracts. It is not an argument, however, that the government ought to be the institution offering those warranties, for if there were such a demand, warranties would quite likely evolve in the absence of form regulation.

References

American Insurance Association. 1999. *State Rate and Form Law Guide.* Washington, D.C.

Browne, Mark J., and Robert E. Hoyt. 2000. "The Demand for Flood Insurance: Empirical Evidence." *Journal of Risk and Uncertainty* 20 (3): 291–306.

Browne, Mark J., JaeWook Chung, and Edward W. Frees. 2000. "International Property-Liability Insurance Consumption." *Journal of Risk and Insurance* 67 (1): 73–90.

Conning Company. 1999. *Alternative Markets: An Ever-Evolving Mosaic 1999.* Hartford, Conn.

Davidson, Russell, and James G. MacKinnon. 1993. *Estimation and Inference in Econometrics.* New York: Oxford University Press.

Dun and Bradstreet. 1999. *Dun and Bradstreet Marketplace Data File,* CD-ROM, 1999 edition. Waltham, Mass.: iMarket.

Hartwig, Robert P. 2000. "ART 101: A Primer on Alternative Risk Transfer." *John Liner Review* 14 (1): 7–16.

Insurance Research Council. 2000. *Business Attitude Monitor 2000: Commercial Lines Deregulation, Satisfaction with Insurance.* Malvern, Pa.

Mas-Colell, Andreu, Michael D. Whinston, and Jerry R. Green. 1995. *Microeconomic Theory.* New York: Oxford University Press.

National Association of Insurance Commissioners. 1999. "Rate Filing Methods for Property/Casualty Insurance, Workers' Compensation, Title." In *Compendium of State Laws on Insurance Topics*, PC-10 NAIC Chart. Kansas City, Mo.

————. 2000a. *1998 Life Insurance Industry Aggregates.*

————. 2000b. *1998 Property/Casualty Insurance Industry Aggregates.*

Swiss Re. 1999. "Alternative Risk Transfer (ART) for Corporations: A Passing Fashion or Risk Management for the 21st Century?" Sigma publication 2. (www.swissre.com [August 2001]).

Wooldridge, Jeffrey M. 2000. *Introductory Econometrics: A Modern Approach.* Cincinnati: South-Western College Publishing.

Appendix 8A. Simulating Surplus for Tables 8-2 and 8-3

The program to simulate the consumer surplus in tables 8-2 and 8-3 was written in SAS. The program consists of the following steps:

1. The means and standard deviations for production costs and time preparation costs are entered into the model, as well as the correlation between them. The simulation assumes that all insurers differ in the marginal costs of producing an insurance contract and in the number of days it takes to prepare a contract before it can be brought to market. Because all firms differ (and they are myopic Bertrand players), there will only be one producer in the market at any given point in time.

Let "prodmean, prodsd" be the mean and standard deviation specified for the marginal costs and producing the new insurance policy, and "prepmean, prepsd" be the mean and standard deviation specified for the preparation time required before the new insurance policy is ready for market. The correlation between these variates is defined by the correlation value chosen, "corr." Results for different correlations are given in tables 8-2 and 8-3. Prepmean = 20, prepsd = 10, and prodsd = 250,000 in both tables. Prodmean = 500,000 for the low-cost producers (table 8-2), and prodmean = 1,250,000 for the high-cost producers (table 8-3).

2. The alpha parameter is also set, where the degree of learning from others who have previously filed forms in the market is given by a reduction in preparation time whose factor is $e^{-\alpha\,forms}$. Also, for these simulations the same linear demand curve is used throughtout:

policy price = 1.5 million − 50 *quantity of policies.*

The means and standard deviations for the production costs are set so that the "high costs" simulation is mostly on the elastic proportion of the demand curve (above the midpoint), and the "low costs" simulation is mostly on the inelastic portion of the demand curve (below the midpoint).

3. SAS built-in functions are used to randomly generate normal variates with means zero and variance one (denote these variates as "U1, U2"). Then a bivariate distribution of preparation times for 1,000 firms is generated using these formulas:

$$production\ costs = prodmean + prodsd*U1$$
$$preparation\ time = prepmean + prepsd*corr*U1$$
$$+ prepsd*[1 - corr**2)**.5]*U2$$

4. The 1,000 firms are then sorted, from the shortest preparation time to the longest preparation time.

5. If the generated preparation time or the production cost is negative, that observation is deleted. Production costs greater than the assumed intercept of the demand curve (greater that 1.5 million) are also deleted (since such firms would never be observed).

6. The first entrant would be the firm with the shortest preparation time. The price and quantity of policies sold is determined assuming that the first entrant would be pricing its policies as a monopolist. Consumer surplus is calculated for the fraction of the year that hte first entrant remains the only supplier.

7. Subsequent potential entrants have their preparation time lowered in accordance with the learning-from-other factor as discussed in step 2.

8. If a potential entrant has marginal costs lower than the monopolist's price but higher than the monopolist's marginal cost, the monopolist lowers its price to an epsilon amount less than the potential entrant to keep it out of the market.

9. The first lower marginal cost producer (the first insurer with marginal costs below the first entrant's marginal costs) will enter and price its insurance policy just an epsilon amount less than the monopolist, and take all of its business (because of the assumed "match the lowest price available" clause in the insurance contracts). However, the first lower marginal cost producer only enters if it projects it will make a positive profit. Those preparation costs up to the time that the monopolist enters are taken as sunk and ignored, but "future" preparation times until the contract is ready are counted as costs.

10. Subsequent entry is based on repeated application of step 9: the next lower marginal cost producer will replace the previous lowest by pricing its insurance policies just an epsilon amount less than the previous lowest cost producer, as long as it can enter and make a positive profit. Again, sunk costs do not matter, but future expected preparation costs do.

11. When the last lowest cost producer enters, its contribution to consumer surplus is tallied for the remainder of the year. Consumer surplus is calculated as the percent of the maximum consumer surplus that is attainable for the whole year.

GEORGES DIONNE

9 | *Insurance Regulation in Other Industrial Countries*

As a result of worldwide changes, markets are becoming more integrated across countries, and as a consequence, traditional forms of regulation must be adapted to this new reality. The foundations of any regulatory revisions, however, must be carefully considered so that participants in the different markets are protected against undue risks. It is now a well-documented fact that the liberalization of financial markets has made doing business more risky. In the banking industry, for example, new risk management mechanisms are being used to regulate the credit and market risks facing banks in many countries so as to protect depositors and governments (lenders of last resort), who want to see banks stay in business. Regulation of capital is often justified by information problems (moral hazard and adverse selection) generated by fixed-rate deposit insurance, which may tempt managers to take greater risks than they would otherwise.[1] Credit-risk regulations are also designed to handle similar information problems arising between banks and entrepreneurs. More specifically, credit rating and monitoring policies are set up to protect banks and evaluate the amount of capital they need. Banks that develop effective internal credit-risk models will require less capital.

Comments by Jean Côté, David Cummins, Claude Dussault, Rémi Moreau, Pierre Picard, René Pollet, Jean Pinquet, and Harold Skipper were very useful. I thank Claire Boisvert and Sybil Denis for their collaboration in the preparation of the final version.

1. Crouhy, Dan, and Mark (2000).

Information problems also play a large role in insurance markets, and the regulations governing these markets are in part designed to take such problems into account.[2] Automobile liability insurance regulation is mainly designed to deal with moral hazard and maintain standard road-safety incentives. In the absence of liability insurance regulation, appropriate rate-setting schemes are necessary to provide similar incentives for road safety.[3] Tight control of premium rates may be justified to protect policyholders and minimize the differences between insurers when search costs are high. In many countries, especially in those where insurance is compulsory, standard rating practices are often implemented to protect consumers by regulating and standardizing the effects of moral hazard and adverse selection. However, major differences have been observed among countries and states. In France, for example, insurers now have complete freedom to set basic rates and classification variables, but they are obliged to apply the same bonus-malus system to all policyholders. In Belgium and Germany, until just recently, activities involving rating, the bonus-malus system, and contract wording were tightly regulated, whereas such activities have not been regulated in the United Kingdom for many years.[4]

Classification variables are usually the tools used to reduce adverse selection, whereas bonus-malus (or merit-rating) schemes are introduced because risk categories lack homogeneity or fairness and because such categories do not really take moral hazard into account.[5] Recent research findings also highlight the role *commitment* plays in bolstering incentives when faced with moral hazard in a bonus-malus scheme.[6] It is not clear whether the commercially motivated, across-the-board deregulation now being proposed in Europe would be the most beneficial solution for those markets where some sort of commitment is implemented by regulation.

In the economic literature on multiperiod contracting, the notion of commitment to the contract by the principal or the insurer plays a significant role on incentives. There is a range of commitment levels; at baseline, the agent or the insured does not have to commit to the contract. However, different assumptions must be considered for the insurer. Under full commitment the insurer fully commits to a long-term contract whatever the nature of the results in each period. In other words, the terms of

---

2. Skipper and Klein (2000); Klein (2000).
3. See the recent survey on liability insurance by Harrington and Danzon (2000).
4. Lemaire (1997).
5. Dionne and Vanasse (1997).
6. Chiappori and others (1994); Dionne and others (2001).

the insurance contract or the bonus-malus scheme cannot be renegotiated at a particular date. At another level there is commitment and renegotiation, where the parties agree to sign long-term contracts but can alter, ex post, the initial contract whenever it is mutually advantageous to them both. Since these renegotiations can be anticipated ex ante, the optimal relationship is restricted to renegotiation-proof contracts.[7] Finally, under noncommitment the relationship between the insurer and the insured is governed by a series of short-term contracts in which a bonus-malus scheme has no value since the insureds would derive no benefit from this additional incentive scheme.[8]

In fact, the efficiency of competitive markets depends on many characteristics. First and foremost, these markets must be transparent to all their participants (a characteristic difficult to achieve when there are information problems). Another important characteristic often neglected by academics and regulators is the parties' degree of commitment to the contract. For example, Dionne and Doherty have shown that some form of commitment will increase efficiency in situations where there is adverse selection in multiperiod contracting.[9] However, commitment is not observed in many unregulated competitive markets, especially when moral hazard is present. Parties to the contract are usually highly motivated to re-negotiate the initial contract at the end of the first period, particularly when consumers can easily move from one insurer to another. Under these conditions regulation can generate a certain form of commitment that may benefit all the participants in the market. Regulation does, in fact, impose some form of commitment on the industry, and recently this aspect has been discussed as a way of reducing insurance fraud or ex post moral hazard.[10]

In this chapter the effects of information and commitment are analyzed for two automobile insurance markets: that of the province of Quebec, Canada, and that of France. In 1978 and 1992, the Quebec market underwent radical changes. Since 1978 a pure no-fault system has been used for bodily injuries, run by a public monopoly. Property damages are administered by the private sector, which is not strongly regulated. Loss reserving is monitored, but premium rating and the bonus-malus system

---

7. For an application to automobile insurance under adverse selection, see Dionne and Doherty (1994).

8. Dionne and Fluet (2000).

9. Dionne and Doherty (1994). They established that a significant number of efficient insurers in California use highballing that involves some form of commitment.

10. Picard (2000).

are free of regulation. However, in the interest of maintaining competition, each insurer must publish and file a rate manual with the inspector general's office, which must, in turn, produce a detailed report on insurance rates each March.

It will be shown that the private market in Quebec deals very efficiently with adverse selection, since there is none in the portfolio of the insurer studied here. Because the great majority of insurers in this province use the same variables, the same results likely apply to the whole market. Although moral hazard in the private market was not explored, this study does show that under full commitment the public monopoly has built up a bonus-malus system that effectively reduces its moral hazard risk.

In France, where automobile insurance is managed by the private insurance industry, basic insurance rates are not regulated, but the bonus-malus scheme is. Regulation of this kind constitutes a form of commitment on the part of the industry, one that should reduce moral hazard effectively. This type of bonus-malus, regulated by a law, implies that each insurer must apply the same formulas for premiums for the same kinds of driving history according to ex ante rules that cannot be renegotiated—whatever the behavior or experience of the insureds—in order to keep or increase market share. Indeed, the findings presented here show that the bonus-malus coefficient is significant in explaining both individual risks and individual choices of insurance coverage. They also demonstrate that insurers in France are successful in eliminating residual adverse selection. Thus, in a competitive environment, adverse selection does not seem to require tight regulation, but regulated commitment does appear to help control moral hazard in both Quebec and France.

It is not clear whether the European Commission has accurately accounted for these kinds of information problems in proposing its transitional rules for a unified European insurance market. At least, no such considerations have been well documented.[11] This state of affairs can be explained by the fact that, until just recently, relatively few empirical studies have been conducted to measure the impact of information problems.[12]

A final component of this study focuses on Japan. A review of that country's regulatory history and system reveals that insurance deregulation has been a major concern of the Japanese government in recent years.

11. Picard (2000).

12. See the recent survey by Chiappori and Salanié (2000a) on the econometrics of information problems.

Automobile Insurance Regime in Quebec

In December 1977 the Quebec government adopted the Automobile Insurance Act, which established the new no-fault insurance plan for bodily injuries. In academic circles this plan is called a "pure" no-fault plan since it provides for no legal action, no matter what the nature of the bodily injuries.[13] Since March 1978 the plan has been administered by the Quebec Automobile Insurance Board (henceforth referred to as the SAAQ: Société de l'Assurance Automobile du Québec), a public monopoly that collects its revenues from car registration fees, drivers' licenses, and investments. The objective of the public plan is to compensate insureds for any real economic loss caused by an automobile accident, up to the maximums provided for in the Automobile Insurance Act. Health and hospital costs are covered by the other public plans in Canada.

Property damages are administered and paid for by the private insurance sector. The 1978 reform made liability insurance compulsory but kept the right to compensation for vehicular damages under the traditional liability regime. A minimum of $50,000 in liability insurance is compulsory; however, the minimum increases for certain types of vehicles. Also in 1978 private insurers began awarding direct compensation to victims of property damage, according to the Agreement on Direct Compensation between insurers. The owner whose car has been damaged through no fault of his own cannot pursue the responsible party and that party's insurer but rather his own insurer.

Solvency regulation in Canada is managed by both the federal and provincial governments. Other forms of regulation are administered by the provinces. The federal Office of the Superintendent of Financial Institution is concerned with solvency of insurance companies registered under federal statutes and those incorporated outside Canada. The provincial authority is responsible for regulating the solvency of provincial incorporated insurers. Of the 134 insurers having business in Quebec in 1999, 59 were registered at the federal level and 24 at the provincial level (18 in Quebec and 6 from other provinces), while 51 were foreign.[14]

On the whole, residents of Quebec are pleased with the current plan. Various studies have shown that the reform has achieved its objectives: increased protection of victims, reduction of management costs, substan-

---

13. See Devlin (1992), Rousseau-Houle (1998), and Gauvin (1998). For discussion of the Ontario insurance scheme, see Brown (1998).

14. Inspecteur Général des Institutions Financières (1999).

tial decrease in insurance premiums, and a significantly shorter wait to be compensated for bodily injuries or property damage. In 1990 adjustments were made to certain forms of compensation. In 1992 the rate-setting scheme for bodily injuries was modified to include a bonus-malus system based on demerit points obtained from drivers' violations of the road safety code, so that this scheme would be more equitable and offer greater safety incentives.

Over the past twenty-two years, the role of the SAAQ has been expanded in several ways. It now is responsible for traffic safety; controlling access to the road network; and regulating road transport of people and goods. It is also authorized to pay for the rehabilitation of accident victims.

It would be useful to cite a few statistics at this point. For example, in 1997 automobile owners contributed $87 to the public plan versus $84 in 1978.[15] Also in 1997 the SAAQ's $123 million surplus was passed on to vehicle owners through reduced insurance costs.[16] The average annual premium of licensed drivers was $14 in 1978 versus $20 in 1992. The rate-fixing regime has been criticized as too uniform; but even though the 1992 reform does not provide a clearly distinct category for drivers who accumulate fewer than four demerit points, it does offer the advantage of being easily understood.

It should be remembered that Quebec's traffic safety record improved considerably during the period in question, and the SAAQ, as overseer of traffic safety, was part and parcel of this improvement. This benefited not only the SAAQ but also the private sector, since most prevention programs do not distinguish between the types of accidents avoided. It must be emphasized that the SAAQ reimburses the public health and hospitalization systems for bodily injury treatment as well as the workers' compensation regime for road accidents that involve drivers at work.

Since the reform there has been a radical decrease in administration fees, which dropped from an average of 36.3 percent of total claims in 1978 to 16 percent in 1992 and 12 percent in 1996. As many have suggested, economies of scale do seem to have a significant effect on administration fees in insurance.

The reform was designed to respond to a number of criticisms generated by the previous plan. The primary source of dissatisfaction was linked to that plan's operating costs. In 1974, 36.1 percent of all premiums were

15. Belleau (1998).
16. Gagnon (1998); Société de l'Assurance Automobile du Québec (2000).

for operating costs under the fault-based automobile insurance system. Moreover, 14 percent of premiums were being used to settle claims while 13.8 percent were used to design and sell insurance contracts (actuarial, research, and marketing costs). These two elements are key to any understanding of the 1978 reform.

Another criticism was linked to the hike in insurance premiums. During the 1961–71 period, premiums increased on average 6.1 percent annually, whereas the consumer price index increased by an average of only 4 percent a year (40 percent over the entire period). The culprit was compensation, which climbed from an average of $416 in 1961 to $885 in 1972. But not all victims profited equally from these increases: those with the financial means to hire good lawyers came out ahead.

A third source of dissatisfaction was the number of uncompensated victims. In fact, the Gauvin committee (which sketched the broad outline of the new plan) estimated that 28 percent of victims with bodily injuries received no compensation at all before 1978. Approximately 40 percent of victims' losses were never compensated. What is more, compensation regulations were often applied haphazardly: small losses were underpaid and large losses were overpaid, a clear indication of the role lawyers played in making the settlements.

The pre-1978 plan also was slow to compensate victims: 42 percent of claims for bodily injuries were settled a year after the accident, and the average wait for a court date was 725 days. By the late 1980s, 32 percent of compensation claims were handled within a month, compared to only 5 percent under the previous system of compensation.[17]

Analysis of Insurance Rating System

One criticism of the 1978 plan concerned the way insurance rates were set. In 1978 the private sector was still basing its rates on risk categories and driving records. With this dual approach, insurers could tailor premiums to individual risks (to address equity and adverse selection) and encourage drivers to be prudent (to address moral hazard).[18] There is no regulation of private sector insurance pricing; however, insurers must make their rate manuals available to the Inspecteur Général des Institutions Financières (General Inspector of Financial Institutions) each year and within ten days after a significant modification.

17. Fluet and Lefebvre (1990).
18. Crocker and Snow (2000); Winter (2000).

The private sector uses a traditional classification system for pricing property damage and collision insurance, based on demographic characteristics, profession, group characteristics (such as union or employer), automobile use (vehicle driven to work or not, for business or farm purposes, and kilometers), territory, type of car, and past experience. The primary demographic variables are age, sex, and marital status. For pleasure vehicles, pricing is based on territory, driver's class, past experience, and car group. For other vehicles, driver classes are not used, but the category of the vehicle is important. Driving experience is measured by the number of years of accident-free driving since the last accident. Some insurers use accidents at fault, others use all accidents.

Insurance premiums increase with the number of past accidents. However, the rate varies from one insurer to another. For example, if an individual was responsible for three accidents in the previous three years, the premium is increased by about 30 percent and for each additional accident, by 10 percent. Convictions for driving violations are also used. For example, four convictions for speeding and other types of traffic violations increase the premium by about 25 percent and for each additional conviction, by 15 percent. The application of these rules is not uniform across insurers, however.

In an analysis of eight bonus-malus systems around the world, Lemaire has shown that the Quebec system ranks among the lowest in terms of "efficiency."[19] However, it performs better with regard to the "relatively stationary average level" index, which determines the relative position of the average policyholder in the portfolio. A low value indicates a high concentration of policies in the high-discount bonus-malus classes. A high value suggests a better spread among the risk classes.

In the same study, Lemaire also describes how the Belgian third-party a posteriori rate scheme was set up in 1971: the rate scheme was a bonus-malus structure prescribed by the government, but the insurance was supplied by the private sector. This could be an efficient way to reach the desired social level of road safety because it implies the industry's strong commitment to the pricing scheme. The same kind of system operates in France (see subsequent discussion); however, there is strong competition in ex ante pricing in France, whereas in Belgium this aspect was regulated until the 1990s.

The rating classes used by insurers in Quebec screen very efficiently for adverse selection. In fact, a study by Dionne, Gouriéroux, and Vanasse

19. Lemaire (1985).

found no residual adverse selection in the portfolio of an insurer from which they obtained all the data for a given year.[20] Like any other participant in that market, this insurer used many classification variables to obtain homogeneous classes of risk; thus there was no asymmetry in information between insurer and policyholder when a contract was signed.[21] (The details of this type of analysis are presented in the next section where the same methodology is applied to a sample of drivers in France.)

In practical terms there is strong competition and no regulation of pricing activities for property damages in Quebec. In 1994 the twenty biggest insurers represented 78.5 percent of the automobile insurance market while about 50 percent of the market was controlled by four insurers. Because of the annual obligation to submit a new rates manual to the office of the inspector general, an insurer that finds a new combination of rating variables will hold a market advantage for one year at most. In this way strong competition is maintained.

The 1978 public insurance plan for bodily injuries computed its rate uniformly, totally independent of individual risks and incentives.[22] In other words, each permit holder paid the same amount to be insured. In December 1992 the SAAQ introduced a new rate-setting scheme based on the accumulation of demerit points; table 9-1 shows the relationship between demerit points accumulated over a two-year period and the amount of insurance licensed drivers paid. It was thought that such a system would improve traffic safety because it would encourage individuals to drive more carefully. The Quebec public insurer has found this rate-setting scheme easy to apply since it is responsible not only for bodily injuries but for traffic safety as well. Thus it has had full access to information on traffic violations, revocations of drivers' licenses, and accidents involving injuries and deaths, as well as information on any accidents with property damage that required an accident report.

In 1987 Boyer and Dionne had already shown that, when inserted into a probit model, the number of demerit points accumulated over a two-year period was a significant predictor of the accident rate for the current year.[23] They also found that the number of suspensions accumulated during the year before license renewal was significantly related to the num-

20. Dionne, Gouriéroux, and Vanasse (2001).
21. Puelz and Snow (1994) obtained contrary evidence for the United States. For a discussion see Dionne, Gouriéroux and Vanasse (2001) and Chiappori and Salanié (2000a and b).
22. Boyer and Dionne (1987).
23. Boyer and Dionne (1987).

Table 9-1. *Variation in Biennial Insurance Payments, 1992*
Units as indicated

Demerit points[a]	Insurance payments (dollars)	Distribution of permit holders (percent)
0–3	40	90
4–7	90	
8–11	164	
12–14	276	10
15+	398	

Source: Dionne and others (2001).
a. Number of demerit points accumulated during previous two years.

ber of accidents occurring the year after renewal. These findings have been confirmed by subsequent studies. Specifically, it has been shown that the results were robust to various econometric models, including those using count data methods.[24]

These preliminary results that link past demerit points to current accidents are interesting because they can be used to test the validity of establishing a rate scheme based on past experience: if the demerit points accumulated do not provide sufficient statistical grounds for evaluating current prevention activities, they cannot be used as rate-setting variables. However, these findings cannot be used as a basis for *predicting* the effect demerit points will have on traffic safety. In other words, they are not sufficient to conclusively identify the presence of moral hazard. There is, in fact, no indication from these preliminary results that any particular policy of rate-setting will change the behavior of licensed drivers. Therefore additional research into this relationship has been done, and its results are presented here.

One objective of introducing a bonus-malus system was to encourage individuals to be more prudent. When the insurer has no control over safe driving, insurance tends to lessen the precautions policyholders will take to prevent an accident. As a rule, insurance coverage reduces the private benefits of prevention and protection without modifying their cost. The policyholder is thus less motivated to take precautions, and this increases the frequency (and seriousness) of accidents.[25]

There are several ways of dealing with the distortion this type of moral

24. Dionne and Vanasse (1997).
25. Winter (2000), Picard (1996).

hazard introduces into insurance mechanisms. The first has to do with how insurance contracts are actually drawn up.[26] The policyholder might be persuaded to exercise greater caution if the insurer offers only partial coverage (for example, via deductibles). Because this incorporates some degree of uncertainty into the coverage, the insured has more reasons to be cautious than under a contract covering all risks. Thus a driver that poses a moral hazard risk is presented with a trade-off: improve driving safety or pay more out of pocket for damage.

Another way the insurer can reduce the impact of moral hazard is by acquiring information on the policyholder's behavior with regard to prevention. This information may be acquired ex ante (prior to the signing of the contract) or ex post (from the investigation of accidents or traffic violations). However, because such information is costly and imperfect in both cases, it is still justifiable to offer only partial coverage. In addition, insurers can use information about a policyholder's preventative behavior to push for safer driving habits by offering contracts with premiums adjusted to the number of past accidents or accumulated traffic violations.

The bonus-malus system is an a posteriori complement to the a priori fixing of insurance rates. On the one hand, it corrects the flaws of risk categories based on imperfect criteria. Specifically, it allows the insurer to make the risk categories more homogeneous since a priori categorization of risks mitigates the inefficiencies caused by adverse selection and imperfect information. On the other hand, the bonus-malus system motivates drivers to exercise caution and reduces the distortions associated with moral hazard.

The bonus-malus system is also often used for reasons of equity, so that each policyholder pays a premium corresponding to his or her own risk level. Adding this argument to those arising from problems with information, the SAAQ decided in 1992 to reintroduce a bonus-malus system into its pricing scheme for bodily injuries. Note that in computing its premiums, the SAAQ uses demerit points associated with traffic violations rather than information associated with accidents.[27]

Effect of the New Rate-Setting Scheme on Accidents

In 1997 Dionne and Vanasse analyzed the effect of the new rate-setting scheme on accidents.[28] Overall the number of persons killed on Quebec

---

26. See the synthesis in Winter (2000).

27. We must also add that the promotion of highway safety is also based on education driving access standards and monitoring.

28. Dionne and Vanasse (1997).

roads decreased from more than 2,000 a year in the early 1970s to 752 a year in 2000, even though the number of vehicles had more than doubled from 2 million in 1970 to 4.4 million in 1997. From 1980 to 1992, the number of fatalities per kilometer decreased by 58 percent in Quebec compared to 50 percent in Germany and 48 percent in the United States.[29]

The reform's incentive component can be evaluated by comparing the accumulated accidents and violations of the road safety code before and after the 1992 reform. However, there are several methodological problems that stand in the way. The first is isolating what effect the change in regulation might have had on the behavior of drivers. Though the sample used is representative of all licensed drivers in Quebec before and after the reform, several observations (not necessarily all simultaneously because this can be an incomplete panel data set) may be influenced in various ways by other factors and regulations over the period studied. For example, the regulation for new drivers modified in 1991 affected their behavior during their first two years of driving: after 1991 new drivers received a probationary license that was revocable after only ten (rather than the usual fifteen) demerit points were accumulated. Thus new drivers may have been more careful after 1991. However, the new regulation was less restrictive for becoming a new driver, so the net effect is ambiguous. This example illustrates the need to control for the various forms of private and public insurance regulations applied during the period studied. Another example is the increase in the limit for a license suspension from twelve to fifteen points for all drivers. In fact, the study had to take into account all major regulatory changes as well as the aggregate exposure-to-risk factors that shape the motorist's environment.

The economic situation opens up another dimension. The unemployment rate can, for example, have a negative impact on the accident rates of new male drivers, and higher gas consumption can positively affect the accident rate for all drivers. These relationships indicate that the economic situation also influences the accident rate and thus also has to be accounted for, even though the database is only a sample.

The exogenous nature of the 1992 change in regulation is also open to question. Using a dummy variable to measure a change in regulation poses no methodological problem if this change is exogenous to the participants in the market. Since the study used individual data on policyholders whose market shares were very small, it could be assumed that for them the 1992 change was perfectly exogenous.

---

29. Gagnon (1998).

The test performed is similar to a laboratory experiment if the legal and economic environment can be carefully controlled. With the 1992 change, the public insurance plan switched from a pricing scheme that offered no incentives for prudent driving to an incentive scheme that used demerit points to set insurance rates, while still offering the same types of coverage. This 1992 change in the rate-setting scheme can be shown to have a significant effect on traffic safety if, and only if, there is for each period a reduction in accidents and violations accumulated—two variables thought to be accurate measurements of individual risks. In addition, such a test requires that the temporal evolution of accidents and violations be carefully tracked to account for the effect of general, concurrent trends.

This was the nature of the 1997 study done by Dionne and Vanasse, and it produced empirical evidence that the new rate-setting scheme did encourage motorists to drive more carefully: the new scheme actually reduced the number of traffic accidents and violations. Such results also confirmed the hypothesis that safety code violations are a good measure of nonobservable driver behavior, that is, that violations are an appropriate reflection of the way drivers behave.[30]

Subsequently, additional tests have been performed to isolate the incentive component of the findings and to confirm that there actually was a reduction of moral hazard.[31] The results showed that traffic violations have declined more quickly than accidents since 1992, a result that seems to reinforce the interpretation suggesting a reduction of moral hazard. But this outcome may also be explained by the significant increase in the cost of fines after 1991, so that drivers may be more likely than before to contest a ticket or police officers may be less motivated to issue one. Given that the new rate-setting scheme increases the total cost of a violation, it is possible that the drop in violations with convictions (the only data available from the SAAQ) may be due to the fact that tickets are more frequently (and successfully) contested. This factor does not compromise the positive impact of the new regulation on traffic safety because accidents really have declined; however, it does make the interpretation of the findings more difficult.

The results presented in table 9-2 were obtained by constructing a panel data set with intertemporal individual data covering the period from January 1, 1983, to December 31, 1996.[32] The panel was incomplete because individuals entered or left the panel when they entered or left the market. A

30. Note: the age of the drivers was controlled in this study.
31. Dionne and others (2001).
32. Dionne and others (2001).

first sample of 40,000 licensed drivers was randomly selected on April 1, 1983. Then, to maintain an age structure that included a sufficient number of young drivers, a new random sample of young drivers was added each year. For each driver data was available from four sources: information on the individual's characteristics from the driving permit for the current year, and information on accidents, demerit points, and suspensions during the current year and the two previous years, when possible.[33]

Table 9-2 clearly shows that traditional rating variables such as age, sex, experience, risk exposure, and territory are very significant in explaining an individual's risk. Therefore they must be used for risk classification at the beginning of the contract period. Table 9-2 also indicates that the past experience variables corresponding to the classes of demerit points (see table 9-1) are also highly significant in explaining an individual's accident rate.

However, most important to this discussion is the observation from table 9-2 that the law*trend variable has a negative coefficient. The coefficient of the trend variable indicates that accidents have decreased by about 5 percent a year since 1984 and that the interaction variable (law*trend) has accelerated this decrease in the trend. Similar results were obtained for demerit points.

Two interpretations are possible. The first, related to adverse selection, is that the new pricing scheme has eliminated bad risks from the market.[34] However, this interpretation does not seem very plausible because insurance is compulsory in this market. Since demerit points are a direct measure of drivers' traffic violations, the results appear to be more strongly related to a reduction in ex ante moral hazard.[35]

Automobile Insurance Regime in France

Since July 1994 the European Union has tried to implement a single insurance market for its fifteen current members. The goal of integrating financial services, including insurance, has been to reduce anticompetitive restrictions. One change made in 1994 was the regulation of solvency at the European Union level. The country of domicile is assigned the authority to verify an insurer's solvency throughout its entire area of activity, but

33. For details see Dionne and others (2001).
34. Dionne, Doherty, and Fombaron (2000).
35. For further tests of the moral hazard interpretation, see Dionne and others (2001).

these solvency certificates must then be recognized by all participating nations. Taxation, contract law, and technical reserves are still controlled by the individual nations. (See appendix 9B for more details.)

Car owners may choose between two types of insurance in France: third-party insurance, which is compulsory, or comprehensive insurance that includes third-party insurance.[36] Third-party insurance covers property damage and bodily injury to a third party when the driver is at fault (totally or in part). Comprehensive insurance includes third-party insurance but also covers damage to the insured's car when the policyholder is at fault. Both coverages are usually taken from the same insurer. About 53 percent of vehicles are covered by comprehensive insurance. There also is noncompulsory coverage available for theft or fire (vandalism) and for injuries to a driver who is at fault (only 50 percent of drivers choose the protection for injuries). In 1996, 73 percent of accident victims were drivers, of which 42.4 percent were fully compensated by third-party liability, and 12.1 percent were partially compensated. The remainder (45.5 percent or 60,000 individuals) received compensation only if they were covered.[37]

Deductibles are not legally available for third-party insurance, but they can be offered for collision insurance. Because insurers are obligated to completely indemnify third parties, such deductibles are a way to reduce claim payments to the policyholder and reduce costs. Deductibles can be fixed, proportional, or mixed (partly fixed and partly proportional), and they vary from one guarantee to another.

Insurance premiums are based on different factors. First, ex ante premiums are set according to vehicle, geographic, and driver characteristics. There are no regulations governing this aspect of pricing. Premiums are then adjusted by a bonus-malus coefficient that takes into account the driver's liability for previous accidents. This multiplicative bonus-malus scheme is standardized from one insurer to the next by a law. In that sense the scheme's incentive pricing has the industry's full commitment. This situation is very instrumental in obtaining the desired incentives to offset moral hazard.

Many methods can be used to estimate the individual's expected number of accidents. During the first stage, models can be estimated to identify significant risk classification variables, determine rate classes, and calculate premiums. This would be the a priori model.

36. Richaudeau (1998, 1999); Comité Européen des Assurances (1996); Commission Consultative de l'Assurance (1991); Grun-Réhomme (2000); Pinquet (1999); Pollet (2000), Rosenwald (2000).
37. Richaudeau (1998).

Table 9-2. *Number of Accidents, Quebec, 1983–96*[a]

Independent variables	Coefficient	t statistic
Intercept	−0.86841	−3.855
Gender (male = 1)	0.67986	42.215
Age in years		
16	0.15155	1.926
17–19	Reference group	
20–24	−0.14283	−2.976
25–34	−0.46517	−7.329
35–54	−0.66377	−9.979
55–64	−0.76985	−10.767
65+	−0.83142	−11.195
Place of residence		
Bas St. Laurent	−0.02468	−0.559
Saguenay Lac Saint-Jean	0.25058	7.094
Québec	0.21620	8.183
Mauricie Bois-Francs	0.15031	5.254
Estrie	0.14333	3.999
Montréal	Reference group	
Outaouais	0.22433	6.175
Abitibi-Témiscamingue	0.18037	3.980
Côte-Nord	0.32926	6.056
Nord-du-Québec	0.03641	0.285
Gaspé, Iles-de-la-Madeleine	−0.04439	−0.701
Chaudière-Appalaches	0.04407	1.377
Laval	−0.03561	−0.980
Lanaudière	0.10201	3.217
Laurentides	0.10567	3.482
Montérégie	0.11066	4.992
Driving license class		
1: Heavy truck	−0.00805	−0.171
2: Bus with more than 24 passengers	0.21586	3.956
3: Truck less than 4500 kg	−0.01185	−0.202
4a: Emergency vehicle	0.16025	1.810
4b: Bus with less than 24 passengers	−0.67748	−7.285
4c: Taxi	0.93323	16.266
5: Car	Reference group	
6a: Motorcycle without restriction	−0.00287	−0.134
6b: Motorcycle 400 cc and less	0.34558	2.898
6c: Motorcycle 125 cc and less	0.22673	1.017
6d: Moped	−0.62757	−2.651

Table 9-2. *Continued*

Independent variables	Coefficient	t statistic
Experience		
Less than 1 year	−0.04006	−0.522
1–3 years	0.04610	1.040
3–5 years	Reference group	
5–10 years	−0.09693	−3.393
10+ years	−0.18378	−5.262
Number of day-years		
1983	0.00339	15.900
1984	0.00224	18.763
1985	0.00339	16.126
1986	0.00222	14.124
1987	0.00305	14.909
1988	0.00226	11.750
1989	0.00249	12.113
1990	0.00218	9.676
1991	0.00255	12.933
1992	0.00209	8.827
1993	0.00235	12.074
1994	0.00247	9.763
1995	0.00225	15.369
1996	0.00237	9.142
Unemployment rate	−0.00901	−1.865
Aggregate gas sold	0.31184	3.725
January 1990	−0.02102	−0.372
New drivers (1991)	0.18259	2.755
Driving license suspensions	0.27839	6.682
Accumulated demerit points		
0–3	Reference group	
4–7	0.38363	8.246
8–12	0.35130	3.838
12–14	0.87341	5.169
15+	0.67115	2.235
Trend	−0.04992	−2.299
Law*trend	−0.01644	−3.020
Parameter a (beta distribution)	73.37666	11.195
Parameter b (beta distribution)	2.07713	33.490
Summary statistics		
Log-likelihood	−101,772	
Number of individuals	42,863	
Number of observations	295,600	

Source: Author's calculations based on unpublished data from Société de l'Assurance Automobile du Québec.

a. Maximum likelihood negative binomial with random effects, using the number of accidents as the dependent variable. See appendix 9A for explanation of the variables.

However, the classes obtained are usually not homogeneous and may generate a ratemaking structure that is unfair to the insured driver. Moreover, risk classification does not take moral hazard into account. To reduce the discrepancy between an individual's premium and risk as well as increase incentives for road safety, the individual's past record is considered under a bonus-malus system. This represents the a posteriori model.

The French bonus-malus system was defined by law in 1976; the actual regulated system has been compulsory since 1991. As already mentioned, this is a multiplicative system: the initial coefficient is equal to one and is increased by 25 percent after an accident with full liability (12.5 percent otherwise). For drivers with no such accidents, the coefficient decreases by 5 percent. The total premium is the product of the premium determined by risk classification multiplied by the bonus-malus coefficient. However, the coefficient cannot be lower than 0.5 or higher than 3.5. After two years without an accident, the coefficient cannot be higher than one. Thirteen accident-free years are required to obtain the maximum bonus. In addition, since 1991 the first accident does not count for those who stay at 0.5 for more than three years. More severe penalties are possible for accidents associated with risky behavior (for example, driving with a suspended license or under the influence of alcohol).[38]

One important characteristic of this bonus-malus scheme is that it is transferable from one insurer to another. Moreover, the new insurer can use any a priori pricing for its clients before applying the bonus-malus coefficient. In that sense there is competition among insurers even though they have to apply the same bonus-malus rules to their policyholders. It is on the basis of this competition and transparency that French insurers try to convince the European Community that their bonus-malus system should not be eliminated.[39]

One significant advantage of this bonus-malus system is its simplicity. It is easily understood by the insureds, and they are pleased with the actual system. In fact, it facilitates switching from one insurer to another and guarantees the sort of commitment needed from insurers to obtain the desired incentive for reducing moral hazard. Insurers also like the present system: it is a source of reliable information on individual risk that would be difficult to acquire otherwise, and it allows for more technical competi-

---

38. For more details, see Richaudeau (1998).
39. Picard (2000); Organization for Economic Cooperation and Development (1999).

tion on costs. Finally, the regulation is fair and transparent: two extremely desirable ingredients.[40]

Efficiency of the Pricing System

This section presents preliminary results obtained from a sample of consumers covered by different insurers. Drawn from a paper by Dahchour and Dionne, these results emphasize the information value of the bonus-malus scheme and demonstrate the efficiency of the pricing system in eliminating residual adverse selection.[41]

The first objective was to see whether risk categories retained any residual adverse selection once the risks had been classified. In other words, it entailed determining whether the information asymmetry existing when the contract was signed could be adequately accounted for by what the insurer already knew about the driver's profile, or whether the driver's choice of coverage or deductible added anything to the assessment of risks. This research applied the methodology of Dionne, Gouriéroux, and Vanasse to panel data.[42]

The Dionne-Gouriéroux-Vanasse adverse selection model is designed to verify whether the ex ante risk categorization efficiently eliminates residual adverse selection in insurers' portfolios. It tests whether insureds' decisions on insurance contract parameters reveal any information on individual risk, as has been suggested by Rothschild and Stiglitz.[43] In this study the choice between comprehensive coverage and third-party insurance is examined: it is usually claimed that bad risks buy more insurance coverage than good risks. (The same has also been claimed regarding choice of deductible for collision insurance.)

Estimations were based on a probit model using panel data from 1995 through 1997 from the Parc Automobile de la Sofres survey, which contains responses to numerous questions on road safety and automobile insurance coverage that are used for research by INRETS: Institut National de Recherche sur les Transports et leur Sécurité (the National Institute for Transport and Safety Research).[44] The model uses four types of variables:

40. Skipper and Klein (2000).
41. Dahchour and Dionne (2001).
42. Dionne, Gouriéroux, Vanasse (2001). See also Chiappori and Salanié (2000b) for an analysis of the French automobile insurance market. They obtained similar conclusions on adverse selection by using a different methodology and a different source of data.
43. Rothschild and Stiglitz (1976).
44. INRETS, Arcueil, France.

—driver characteristics: age, gender, number of accidents;
—vehicle characteristics: year, group (classified by horsepower), kilo-
    metrage;
—automobile insurance contracts: bonus-malus coefficient, choice of
    insurance coverage;
—usage: casual versus work.

For a single-period analysis, the test consists of verifying whether an individual's accidents during the contractual period are significant in explaining the insured's choice of contract.[45] If the answer is positive, it means that the risk categorization system does not provide insurers with all the private information they need on an individual's risks and that possible residual adverse selection will be present in the portfolio.[46] If the answer is negative, it means that asymmetries in information between insurer and insured do not exist at the time a contract is arranged. This procedure has to be applied properly in order to eliminate conclusions that may stem from misspecification of the econometric model. Therefore it is appropriate to include in the model the expected number of accidents, a variable usually computed using the estimated parameters for accident distribution. Note that this process does not reveal any private information since any insurer can use observable variables to compute the individual's expected number of accidents. If this variable is statistically significant, it means that the specification has not been sufficiently elaborated and additional variables must be added to the model. If it is not significant, then it confirms that the explanatory variables generate a risk classification accurate enough to provide full information on individual characteristics prior to signing the contract.

The use of panel data also allows the monitoring of information contributed by the bonus-malus clause. To fit the model to this task, Dahchour and Dionne took into account certain characteristics of the French automobile insurance market:

—When the driver is at fault in an accident, it is public information to a certain extent since rival companies will learn of it from the information the subscriber is obliged to provide when purchasing an insurance contract or changing insurers.

45. Dionne, Gouriéroux, and Vanasse (2001).
46. On risk classification, see Crocker and Snow (2000).

—Information on former purchases of contracts (type of coverage and premiums paid) is quite public.

—There is one insurer for all coverage (exclusivity of contract purchased).

—High-risk subscribers are subsidized by low-risk subscribers: artificial inflation of insurance premiums is most often cited as one of the perverse effects of the French bonus-malus system. New drivers are most affected by such inflation.

—As a result of the bonus-malus scheme, there is commitment on the part of the insurer (or the industry).[47]

The single and regulated bonus-malus clause establishes a kind of dynamic link between the policyholder and the insurance company: the insurer commits only to the formula for the bonus-malus coefficient as long as the driver does not change insurance companies. Thus the industry offers commitment on the bonus-malus but none on the basic insurance premium if the driver leaves one insurer for another.

Insurance policies contain no clauses obliging drivers to stay with the same company beyond the period covered by the contract. This being so, the premise of noncommitment by the policyholder is maintained, even though satisfied clients tend to stay with their company for as long as possible. However, a commitment by the insured is not necessary to obtain the desired incentive effect.

The test uses individual panel data in a two-step estimation.[48] The first step estimates the accident distribution for each period to compute the expected number of accidents; the second step estimates the likelihood of choosing comprehensive coverage over third-party coverage. In the second step, the expected number of accidents obtained from the first estimation is included in the list of explanatory variables. This type of estimation is known to give convergent estimators in the second step.

A very limited specification of the model is presented in table 9-3, which shows that the number of accidents (NBACC) variable has a positive and significant coefficient. This means that bad risks choose the higher insu-

47. Dahchour and Dionne (2001).

48. Use of individual panel data offers several advantages over aggregate data. It eliminates biases linked to aggregation and thereby produces more sharply defined estimators. Individual panel data also measure certain variables more accurately. Finally, use of individual panel data allows for individual heterogeneity, making it possible to go beyond the notion of the representative agent and thus favoring the search for better econometric modeling.

Table 9-3. *Choice of Insurance Coverage, France, 1995–97*[a]

Independent variables	Coefficient	Standard deviation	t statistic[b]	p value
Constant	4.1469	620.9680	0.0067	.9947
NBACC	0.1787	0.0651	2.7460	.0060
T	−0.2941	0.0450	−6.5375	<.0000
ρ	0.952	6.3974	0.1540	.8776
Summary statistics				
Probability log		−8,272.13		
Number of observations		16,399		
Number of individuals		11,506		

Source: Author's calculations based on data from INRETS, Parc Automobile de la Sofres survey.

a. Random effects probit model used; the dependent variable is choice of insurance coverage. NBACC is the number of accidents during the contract; T is the time variable; ρ is the time correlation measure. A coefficient is statistically significant from zero at a degree of confidence higher than 95 percent when $p < .05$.

b. Student's *t* statistic.

rance coverage, as predicted by the models of Rothschild and Stiglitz and of Wilson.[49] However, this result also can be explained by a specification error.

In table 9-4 the expected number of accidents (variable ENBACC) is added to the model and is significant.[50] However, the coefficient of the accident variable is no longer significant, which means that there is no residual asymmetrical information (or residual adverse selection) between the contracting parties at the beginning of the contract period or when risk classification is done.

The ENBACC variable remains significant in table 9-5, even after introduction of the classification variables (not shown here) and the bonus-malus variable for the estimation. This proves that some nonlinearities linked to insurance rates still have not been taken into account. Their elimination is a matter of finding the right crossovers between classification variables.

Nevertheless, the results here suggest that the policyholder has no informational advantage over the insurer, a conclusion recently reached by a similar study with a different data set.[51] As for the bonus-malus variable,

49. Rothschild and Stiglitz (1976) or Wilson (1977).

50. The expected number of accidents was obtained from the estimated parameters of the negative model shown in Appendix 9C.

51. Dionne, Gouriéroux, and Vanasse (2001).

Table 9-4. *Choice of Insurance Coverage with ENBACC Variable, France,* *1995–97*[a]

Independent variables	Coefficient	Standard deviation	t statistic[b]	p value
Constant	1.1227	0.1368	8.2050	<.0000
NBACC	0.0793	0.0712	1.1130	<.2658
ENBACC	8.3124	0.3390	24.5230	<.0000
T	−0.1345	0.0410	−3.2760	.0011
ρ	0.9644	0.0027	359.8860	<.0000
Summary statistics				
Probability log		−8,137.47		
Number of observations		16,399		
Number of individuals		11,506		

Source: See table 9-3.

a. Random effects probit model used; the dependent variable is the choice of insurance coverage with ENBACC (expected number of accidents) variable, obtained from appendix 9C. NBACC is the number of accidents during the contract; T is the time variable; ρ is the time correlation measure.

b. Student's *t* statistic.

Table 9-5. *Choice of Insurance Coverage with ENBACC and Bonus-Malus Variables, France, 1995–97*[a]

Independent variables	Coefficient	Standard deviation	t statistic[b]	p value
Constant	0.8815	0.6063	1.4538	.1460
NBACC	0.0944	0.0688	1.3732	.1697
ENBACC	6.9177	0.4548	15.2118	.0000
Bonus-malus	−3.7286	0.1517	−24.5783	.0000
T	0.0903	0.0361	2.4993	.0124
ρ	0.8953	0.0065	138.1420	<.0000
Summary statistics				
Probability Log		−6,697.21		
Number of observations		16,399		
Number of individuals		11,506		

Source: See table 9-3.

a. Random effects probit model used; the dependent variable is the choice of insurance coverage with ENBACC and bonus-malus variables. See footnote to table 9-4 for explanation of abbreviations. Note: this regression was done with twenty-nine additional control variables. See Dahchour and Dionne (2001) for details.

b. Student's *t* statistic.

its coefficient is significant in table 9-5 (and in appendix 9C). The negative coefficient in the insurance choice equation shown in table 9-5 confirms the prediction made previously: the bad past experience of a policyholder is a signal for a bad driver. In table 9-5 the bonus-malus variable acts like a price variable: policyholders choosing comprehensive coverage pay a lower premium because their bonus-malus coefficient is low, while the contrary is true for those choosing third-party liability insurance only. In appendix 9C the bonus-malus variable has a positive and significant coefficient, thus confirming that it also is a reliable source of information on the type of risk involved. This conclusion is reflected in the coefficient of the ENBACC variable in table 9-5, which was positive and significant.

Automobile Insurance in Japan

There are two types of automobile insurance coverage in Japan: voluntary automobile insurance and compulsory automobile liability insurance (CALI), which covers bodily injury.[52] CALI had its origin in the Automobile Liability Security Law enacted on December 1, 1955, which was intended to provide financial security to traffic accident victims and to control the premium rates. CALI policies were marketed starting in February 1956.

Before the Automobile Liability Security Law, tort liability procedures for automobile accidents had been based mainly on the civil code, under which victims could only claim damages if they succeeded in proving that the other party was at fault. By replacing the legal concept of "responsibility for negligence" with "responsibility for no-fault," the Automobile Liability Security Law sought to strengthen victims' rights. Under this rule damages could be claimed if the victims or their heirs could prove that injury or death was caused by a traffic accident.

Under the law a driver is responsible for a tort liability claim unless he or she is able to prove three points: the driver was not negligent in operating the vehicle; there was negligence on the part of the victim or a third party; and there were neither structural defects in nor malfunctioning of the driver's vehicle. The limits of insurer liability are legally stipulated for death, different grades of permanent disability, and other bodily injuries. These limits of liability are applicable for each victim, but there is no total

52. Information in this section comes from the Marine and Fire Insurance Association of Japan, "Non-Life Insurance in Japan" (www.sonpo.or.jp/english/english.html [December 2000]).

limit per occurrence. After payment of a claim, the limits of an insurer's liability remain unchanged for the remainder of the policy period. In the case of a fatal accident, however, the insurance company requires the policyholder to pay an additional surcharge premium on a pro rata basis for the remaining period of the policy.

The limits of insurer liability have been increased periodically to reflect prevailing economic and social conditions. In 1999 these limits were 30 million yen for death; 30 million to 0.75 million yen for the first through fourteenth grades of permanent disability, respectively; and 1.2 million yen for bodily injury.

The premium portfolio of all CALI contracts (except for policies for motorcycles with 125 cubic centimeters or less in displacement) is reinsured en bloc with the government on a 60 percent quota share basis. The remaining 40 percent is placed in a private CALI pool and is shared by all non-life insurance companies providing CALI coverage. Since the acceptance of all CALI risks is obligatory, the purpose of this pooling arrangement is to prevent adverse economic impacts to any one insurer and to distribute bad risks equitably among all insurers.

In 1964 the Automobile Insurance Rating Organization was established under the Law Concerning Non-Life Insurance Rating Organizations. The organization is a neutral, independent body, assigned the task of calculating reference pure risk premium rates for voluntary automobile insurance and also calculating a standard premium rate for CALI. It maintains survey offices at major cities throughout the nation for settlement of CALI claims, and its membership includes thirty-four domestic and eighteen foreign companies.

Two or more non-life insurance companies may, with the approval of the Financial Reconstruction Commission, establish a rating organization, which calculates reference risk premium rates and standard premium rates for member firms. These rating organizations are supervised by the commission, which has the authority to suspend their activities. The rating organization also notifies the commission of new rates and alterations to existing rates. Within thirty days of notification, the commission examines the new rates and has the opportunity to raise objections to the application.

For a while the number of deaths from traffic accidents declined steadily, from a peak of 16,765 in 1970 to 8,466 in 1979. However, after 1979 the trend reversed, with the number of deaths exceeding 10,000 in 1988. After 1993 the annual number of deaths began to decline again, with fatalities dropping below the 10,000 level from 1997 through 1999.

In 1998 the number of traffic accidents involving bodily injury reached 803,878, with 9,211 people killed and 990,675 people injured. The number of traffic accidents in Japan had fluctuated until 1991, but since then the total has increased each year; the 1998 figure for accidents is the highest on record, and the number of people injured is also the highest in twenty-eight years. Consequently, the Japanese are faced with a severe traffic accident problem.

Recent Regulatory Changes

As a result of the Big Bang—the push for financial reform in 1996— a number of changes have occurred in the regulatory environment of Japanese non-life insurance. Some changes have affected data collection, and others have involved restructuring.

IMPROVEMENT OF LOSS SURVEY METHOD FOR CALI   One of the changes affected the aforementioned Automobile Insurance Rating Organization, whose loss surveys are used by non-life insurance companies in deciding the ultimate amount of claims payment under CALI. In April 1998 this organization established a board of examiners and a board of reexaminers to determine the degree of permanent disability and, in fatal accidents, the negligence of victims involved. These boards improved the organization's examination structure so that the loss survey could become even more just and fair, as well as objective and transparent. Non-life insurance companies have not only cooperated with the organization in implementing these changes, but they have also taken their own measures to help improve the loss surveys, thus making every effort to offer a fine-tuned response to victims and other claimants.

FINANCIAL SYSTEM REFORM BILL OF JUNE 1998   On March 13, 1998, the Financial System Reform Bill was submitted to the Diet, passed on June 5, and published on June 15, 1998. It amended en bloc twenty-four finance-related laws, such as the Insurance Business Law, the Law Concerning Non-Life Insurance Rating Organizations, the Securities and Exchange Law, and the Banking Law. Thus a framework was established for sweeping reform of Japanese financial systems. Except for a few sections, the Reform Bill was enforced on December 1, 1998.

STRUCTURAL CHANGES IN THE MINISTRY OF FINANCE   On June 22, 1998, the Financial Supervisory Agency was established to inspect and supervise financial institutions, including insurance companies. These functions were transferred from the Ministry of Finance and included the authority to issue orders to improve or suspend the business operations of financial institutions. In addition, the agency was made separate and independent from the Ministry of Finance to ensure transparency, fairness, and equity in financial administration. Because of these changes, the primary focus of the Ministry of Finance shifted to policy planning, research relating to the overall financial system, and establishment and repeal of finance-related laws and regulations.

As a result of the creation of the Financial Supervisory Agency, there were now two insurance advisory councils. The first was the Financial Council, which reported to the Minister of Finance. It was established as part of the June 1998 reorganization and was created by combining three former councils: the Financial System Research Council, the Insurance Council, and the Securities and Exchange Council. The second was the Compulsory Automobile Liability Insurance Council, which reported to the Commissioner of the Financial Supervisory Agency. The CALI Council had already been established under the Automobile Liability Security Law of 1955. It had thirteen members and was exclusively responsible for matters related to CALI. As advisory organs to the administrative bodies, these councils, at the request of the minister or the commissioner, were to discuss possible ways and means to improve the financial system, including the business affairs and administration of the insurance industry and matters related to CALI.

In the most recent reforms (July 2000), the Financial Services Agency was established to take over the inspection and supervision responsibilities of the Financial Supervisory Agency. The new agency has been placed under the Prime Minister's Office.

MOVES TOWARD DEREGULATION   As an integral part of its deregulation requests to the government, Keidanren (the Japan Federation of Economic Organizations) requested the abolition of the government reinsurance scheme for CALI in October 1998. In the same month privatization of the CALI system was also being considered during discussions on the reform of the central ministries. As a result of these circumstances, the CALI Ad Hoc Committee was established in December 1998 to review the CALI system as a whole.

One fundamental position of the committee supports maintaining the current compulsory nature of the insurance, the obligation of insurance companies to provide CALI contracts, and the no-loss and no-profit principle. At present, the CALI system as a whole is being deliberated at the round table of the CALI Council, with particular focus on protecting traffic accident victims, streamlining administrative procedures, and reviewing the government reinsurance scheme.

Separately from the CALI Council deliberations, the Ministry of Transport in February 1999 established its own round table on the future direction of the CALI system. These discussions concluded at the end of September 1999, and their results were reported to the round table of the CALI Council held on October 7, 1999.

In June 2000 the CALI Council submitted a report on the new direction for the CALI system. The non-life insurance industry has welcomed this report, which calls for future deliberations on the CALI system as a whole and consideration of the abolition of the CALI government reinsurance scheme in the near future.

Even in the moves toward deregulation, the Insurance Business Law states that insurance companies should be inspected by a supervisory authority in order to ensure appropriate business operation and to protect policyholders. However, insurance premium rates are now liberalized in the sense that the obligation for the members of the rating organizations to use premium rates calculated by the rating organizations is abolished.

Conclusion

The first part of this chapter reviewed how the automobile insurance market works in Quebec. This market is characterized by a dual organizational structure: a public monopoly offering compensation for bodily injuries in a pure no-fault system, and a competitive private sector offering compensation for property damages under a liability system that includes a direct compensation agreement designed to reduce insurance costs. In other words, subrogation between insurers is not permitted.

The public monopoly, regulated by the government, reinvests a large fraction of its benefits back into the market in order to reduce the cost of premiums. In fact, a good driver with no demerit points will pay only $50 for this insurance for two years of protection when renewing his or her license and about $117 a year for vehicle registration. Underwriting and marketing costs are very low by definition in such a public monopoly scheme, and large economies of scale seem to account for its very low administrative costs.

The private sector is not regulated. Both ex ante and ex post pricing rules operate under free competition, and the insurers' rate manuals must be publicly accessible. Since 1991 all accidents are reported to a central file that is available, as public information, to any insurer. The solvency of insurers is regulated by both levels of government according to where insurers are registered.

Information on traffic violations has been used as an incentive for traffic safety in Quebec. Since 1992 the SAAQ has been using demerit points accumulated over two years to set the public insurance rate for bodily injuries over the next two years. Those who commit various traffic violations accumulate demerit points and see their insurance premiums rise. It has been judged preferable to base this bonus-malus system on demerit points rather than accidents: the public insurance plan is a no-fault regime, which implies that information about violations will measure deviant driving practice more accurately than information about accidents.

Results of studies show that implementation of the new rate-setting scheme has reduced the number of accidents. Complementary studies are under way to clarify whether this outcome is attributable to drivers' increased commitment to prevention or to elimination of bad risks. Recent findings seem to support the first interpretation and thus lead to the conclusion that the new rate-setting scheme has encouraged drivers to be more prudent. It must be emphasized that by making the bonus-malus scheme part of a law that precludes renegotiation of the initial contract in subsequent periods, the public insurer has created an environment of full commitment in which its scheme can function efficiently to maximize road safety.

In the second section of this chapter the workings of the automobile insurance market in Europe were examined, with particular focus on France. The insurance business is now deregulated in many European countries. In France, insurance is provided by the private sector; the basic pricing of insurance is not regulated, but a common bonus-malus scheme is administrated by the industry. Moreover, commitment by insurers is guaranteed by law, and the bonus-malus score is transferable between insurers. Despite these advantages, the European Commission is considering recommending the abolition of the bonus-malus scheme because it may limit competition in the French automobile insurance market. Strong commitment is necessary to maintain an efficient bonus-malus scheme when insurers do not control driving activities. Under competition it is very difficult to achieve such a commitment without using a law or regulation. Consequently, if the European Commission convinces the French government to eliminate its current bonus-malus scheme, it would be necessary to find a substitute for the present mechanism in order to maintain the same incentives for road safety.

Moreover, as widely documented, it is not at all clear that the actual bonus-malus scheme limits competition in the French automobile insurance market.[53] In fact, it offers many advantages to consumers such as a simple pricing scheme based on past experience and ease of movement between insurers and between cars. Moreover, this form of regulation is transparent.

An analysis of the French market demonstrated that the variables used by the insurance industry screen very efficiently for the adverse selection problem: there was no residual adverse selection in the sample studied. Moreover, the bonus-malus variable was significant in explaining both the individual distribution of accidents and the individual choice of insurance coverage. Thus the bonus-malus system is a valuable source of information that can be used to create appropriate incentives in this market.

In Japan, the automobile insurance regime has been tightly regulated until recently. However, since 1998 there have been discussions about the possibility of deregulating the whole industry as well the compulsory automobile liability insurance program. In general, the environment of non-life insurance companies is changing rapidly in Japan with the steady progression of deregulation and liberalization. For example, insurance rates are no longer regulated: the obligation to use premium rates calculated by the rating organization was abolished in July 1998. Nonetheless, in order to protect policyholders' interests, three new regulatory measures have been introduced in recent years: a solvency margin ratio, an early warning measure based on the solvency margin ratio, and a policyholder's protection corporation to deal with the possible insolvency of insurers.

References

Belleau, Claude. 1998. *L'Assurance Automobile sans Égard à la Responsabilité: Histoire et Bilan de l'Expérience Québécoise.* Sainte-Foy: Publications du Québec.

Boyer, Marcel, and Georges Dionne. 1987. "Description and Analysis of the Quebec Automobile Insurance Plan." *Canadian Public Policy* 13 (2): 181–95.

Brown, Craig. 1998. "No-Fault Automobile Insurance in Ontario: A Long and Complicated Story." *Assurances* 66 (3): 399–422.

53. See Picard (2000) for a review.

Chiappori, Pierre-André, and Bernard Salanié. 2000a. "Testing Contract Theory: A Survey of Some Recent Work." Mimeo, University of Chicago, 39 pages.

_____. 2000b. "Testing for Asymmetric Information in Insurance Markets." *Journal of Political Economy* 108 (February): 56–78.

Chiappori, Pierre-André, and others. 1994. "Repeated Moral Hazard: The Role of Memory Commitment and the Access to Credit Markets." *European Economic Review* 38 (October): 1526–53.

Comité Européen des Assurances. 1996. *Procès-Verbal de la Réunion du 14 Juin 1996.* Paris.

Commission Consultative de l'Assurance. 1991. *Rapport sur le Bonus-Malus en Assurance Automobile.* Paris.

Crocker, Keith, and Arthur Snow. 2000. "The Theory of Risk Classification." In *Handbook of Insurance,* edited by Georges Dionne, 245–76. Boston: Kluwer Academic Publishers.

Crouhy, Michel, Galai Dan, and Robert Mark. 2000. *Risk Management.* McGraw-Hill.

Dahchour, Maki, and Georges Dionne. 2001. "Automobile Insurance Rates and Adverse Selection: A Study on Panel Data." Working Paper 01-06. Center for Research in Transportation, University of Montreal and Risk Management Chair, HEC-Montreal.

Devlin, Rose-Anne. 1992. "Liability versus No-Fault Automobile Insurance Regimes: An Analysis of the Experience in Quebec." In *Contributions to Insurance Economics,* edited by Georges Dionne, 499–520. Boston: Kluwer Academic Publishers.

Dionne, Georges, and Neil Doherty. 1994. "Adverse Selection, Commitment and Renegotiation with Application to Insurance Markets." *Journal of Political Economy* 102 (April): 209–35.

Dionne, Georges, Neil Doherty, and Nathalie Fombaron. 2000. "Adverse Selection in Insurance Markets." In *Handbook of Insurance,* edited by Georges Dionne, 185–244. Boston: Kluwer Academic Publishers.

Dionne, Georges, and Claude Fluet. 2000. "Full Pooling in Multi-Period Contracting with Adverse Selection and Non-Commitment." *Review of Economic Design* 5 (1): 1–21.

Dionne, Georges, Christian Gouriéroux, and Charles Vanasse. 2001. "Testing for Evidence of Adverse Selection in the Automobile Insurance Market: A Comment." *Journal of Political Economy* 109 (April): 444–53.

Dionne, Georges, and Charles Vanasse. 1997. "Une Évaluation Empirique de la Nouvelle Tarification au Québec." In *Économétrie Appliquée,* edited by C. Gouriéroux and C. Montmarquette, 47–80. Paris: Economica.

Dionne, Georges, and others. 2001. "The Role of Memory in Long-Term Contracting with Moral Hazard: Empirical Evidence in Automobile Insurance." Working Paper 01-05. Risk Management Chair, HEC-Montreal.

Fluet, Claude, and Pierre Lefebvre. 1990. "L'Évolution du Prix Réel de l'Assurance Automobile au Québec depuis la Réforme de 1978." *Canadian Public Policy* 16 (4): 374–86.

Gagnon, Jean-Yves. 1998. "The Société de l'Assurance Automobile du Québec—An Integrated Model of Action to Insure and Protect People from Risks Inherent in Use of the Road." In *Automobile Insurance: Road Safety, New Drivers, Risks, Insurance Fraud and Regulation,* edited by G. Dionne and C. Laberge-Nadeau, 183–190. Boston: Kluwer Academic Publishers.

Gauvin, Jean-Louis. 1998. "La Réforme de l'Assurance Automobile au Québec : Vingt Ans Après." *Assurances* 66 (3): 389–98.

Grun-Réhomme, Michel. 2000. "Prévision du Risque de Tarification: le Rôle du Bonus-Malus Français." *Assurances* 68 (1): 21–30.

Harrington, Scott, and Patricia Danzon. 2000. "The Economics of Liability Insurance." In *Handbook of Insurance*, edited by Georges Dionne, 277–313. Boston: Kluwer Academic Publishers.

Inspecteur Général des Institutions Financières. 1999. *Rapport Annuel sur les Assurances*. Quebec.

Klein, Robert W. 2000. "Insurance Regulation in Transition." *Journal of Risk and Insurance* 62 (3): 363–404.

Lemaire, Jean. 1985. *Automobile Insurance: Actuarial Models*. Boston: Kluwer Academic Publishers.

_____. 1997. *Insurance Regulation in Europe and the United States*. Huebner Foundation Monograph 16. University of Pennsylvania.

Organization for Economic Cooperation and Development. 1999. *Liberalisation of International Insurance Operations*. Paris.

Picard, Pierre. 1996. "Auditing Claims in Insurance Market Fraud: The Credibility Issue." *Journal of Public Economics* 63 (1): 27–56.

_____. 2000. "Les Nouveaux Enjeux de la Régulation des Marchés d'Assurances." Paper presented at Les Conférences Jules Dupuit, ENA, Paris, October.

Pinquet, Jean. 1999. "Une Analyse des Systèmes Bonus-Malus en Assurance Automobile." *Assurances* 67 (2): 241–49.

Pollet, René. 2000. "Cours de l'ENASS." Course notes.

Puelz, Robert, and Arthur Snow. 1994. "Evidence on Adverse Selection: Equilibrium Signaling and Cross Subsidization in the Insurance Market." *Journal of Political Economy* 102 (April): 236–57.

Richaudeau, Didier. 1998. "Le Marché de l'Assurance Automobile en France." *Assurances* 66 (3): 423–58.

_____. 1999. "Automobile Insurance Contracts and Risk of Accident: An Empirical Test Using French Individual Data." *Geneva Papers on Risk and Insurance Theory* 24 (1): 99–114.

Rosenwald, Guillaume. 2000. "Devenirs du Bonus-Malus." Paper presented at the conference of the Société Française de Statistique, November 29.

Rothschild, Michael, and Joseph Stiglitz. 1976. "Equilibrium in Competitive Insurance Markets: An Essay on the Economics of Imperfect Information." *Quarterly Journal of Economics* 90 (November): 629–49.

Rousseau-Houle, Thérèse. 1998. "Le Régime Québécois de l'Assurance Automobile, Vingt Ans Après." *Assurances* 66 (3): 367–88.

Skipper, Harold D., and Robert W. Klein. 2000. "Insurance Regulation in the Public Interest: The Path Towards Solvent, Competitive Markets." *Geneva Papers on Risk and Insurance: Issues and Practice* 25 (4): 482–504.

Société de l'Assurance Automobile du Québec. 2000. *An Integrated Road Safety Model, Unique in the World*. Quebec.

Wilson, Charles A. 1977. "A Model of Insurance Markets with Incomplete Information." *Journal of Economic Theory* 16 (December): 167–207.

Winter, Ralph. 2000. "Optimal Insurance under Moral Hazard." In *Handbook of Insurance*, edited by Georges Dionne, 155–84. Boston: Kluwer Academic Publishers.

Appendix 9A. Description of Variables Shown in Table 9-2

Driving License Variables

Gender: Dummy variable equal to one for a male.

Age at the beginning of each period: Seven classes of age ranging from 16 to 65 years old, with the 17-to-19 class as the reference group.

Place of residence: Sixteen administrative regions in Quebec, with Montreal as the reference group.

Driving license class: Eleven driving classes that define the type of vehicle the individual is allowed to drive, with category 5-car as the reference group.

Experience: Number of years since the first driving license, with 3-to-5 year class as the reference group.

Variables for Regulatory Changes and Pricing

January 1990: Dummy variable equal to one after the introduction of a new regulation for all drivers in Quebec that increased the number of points from 12 to 15 before a driving license suspension.

New drivers (1991): Dummy variable equal to one after the introduction of a probationary license for new drivers in Quebec.

Law: Dummy variable equal to one for those who renew their driving license in periods after application of the new pricing scheme that uses memory (after December 1, 1992).

Cyclical and Risk Exposure Variables

Number of days: Total number of days the driving license is valid during a year. This variable screens for two effects: individual risk exposure and aggregate characteristics of the year.

Unemploymet rate: Percent annual unemployment rate according to sex, age group, and periods. Less economic activity should generate fewer accidents and fewer demerit points. Statistics Canada, "Labour Force Information," SDDS 3701 STC [71-001] (www.statcan.ca [October 2001]).

Aggregate gas sold: Tens of millions of liters sold each year in Quebec according to periods. A positive sign is predicted in both regressions. Statistics Canada, SDDS 2150 STC [45-004] (www.statcan.ca [October 2001]).

Trend: Time variable that takes into account possible reductions in the distributions of both accidents and demerit points for reasons that are not controlled by the variables in the model.

Law*trend: An interaction variable isolates the effect of the change in law from the time trend. If the trend variable is significant in the regression, this law*trend variable will indicate how the new pricing scheme, with its use of memory, affects the time trend variable.

Past Experience Variables

Demerit points accumulated: This variable tests the predictive power of the demerit points accumulated in period $t - 1$ on the distribution of accidents in period t.

Driving license suspensions: The number of driving license suspensions accumulated due to a driver's criminal offenses during period $t - 1$ is used as an explanatory variable for accidents in period t. Most of the suspensions are alcohol related.

Appendix 9B. Insurance Regulation in Europe

Since July 1, 1994, a single insurance market has been in effect in the European Union, permitting free movement of services and capital among member states. In particular, it allows insurers to sell their products without anticompetitive restrictions. Prior approval of contracts (products) and premium rates has been banned. Solvency regulation also operates at the European Union level, but contract law and regulation of technical reserves remain under national control.

The following table presents an overview of the arrangements for premium rates, guaranty funds, and bonus-malus schemes in a sample of countries.

Table 9B-1. *Insurance Regulation in Europe, 1997*

Country	Premium rate regulation	Guaranty funds	Bonus-malus regulation
Belgium	No	Yes	No
Finland	No	Yes	Yes
France	No	Yes	Yes
Germany	No	Yes	No
Italy	No	Yes	No
Spain	No	No	No
Sweden	No	No	No
United Kingdom	No	Yes	No

Appendix 9C

Table 9C-1. *Expected Number of Accidents, France, 1995–97*[a]

	Coefficient	Standard deviation	t statistic	p value
Constant	1.1207	0.5426	2.0655	0.0389
Gender and age of driver				
Male	−0.1822	0.0540	−3.3724	.0007
A1820[b]	0.0076	0.2672	0.0285	.9773
A2124		Reference group		
A2534	−0.1101	0.1255	−0.8771	.3805
A3544	−0.0992	0.1422	−0.6979	.4853
A4554	−0.2394	0.1464	−1.6359	.1019
A5564	−0.3246	0.1606	−2.0209	.0433
A65plus	−0.2206	0.1780	−1.2395	.2152
Experience				
Exp01[c]	0.2704	0.2867	0.9429	.3457
Exp23		Reference group		
Exp410	−0.0979	0.2106	−0.4647	.6421
Exp11plu	−0.2323	0.2190	−1.0607	.2888
Bonus-malus	0.9174	0.1262	7.2679	.0000
Parameter a (beta distribution)	40.6622	13.7181	2.9641	.0030
Parameter b (beta distribution)	1.3800	0.2143	6.4387	.0000
Summary statistics				
Probability log		−7,895.85		
Number of observations		16,399		
Number of individuals		11,506		

Source: See table 9-3.

a. Estimation of random effects negative binomial model, using the total number of accidents as the dependent variable. Note: this regression was done with sixty additional control variables. See Dahchour and Dionne (2000) for details.

b. A xy is age between x and y years.

c. Exp xy is experience between x and y years.

Contributors

David Appel
Milliman and Robertson,
  New York

Richard J. Butler
Brigham Young University

J. David Cummins
Wharton School, University
  of Pennsylvania

Stephen D'Arcy
University of Illinois, Urbana-
  Champaign

Richard Derrig
Automobile Insurers Bureau
  of Massachusetts

Georges Dionne
École des Hautes Études
  Commerciales,
  Montreal

Martin F. Grace
Center for RMI Research, Georgia
  State University

Scott E. Harrington
Darla Moore School of Business,
  University of South Carolina

Dwight M. Jaffee
Haas School of Business,
  University of California,
  Berkeley

Robert W. Klein
Center for RMI Research, Georgia
  State University

Richard D. Phillips
Center for RMI Research, Georgia
  State University

Laureen Regan
Temple University

Thomas Russell
Leavey School of Business,
    Santa Clara University

Sharon Tennyson
Cornell University

Mary A. Weiss
Temple University

John D. Worrall
Rutgers University

Index

Accident rates: California, 217–21, 243–44; and economic factors, 372; France, 375, 380–82, 396; Japan, 385–86; Massachusetts, 51; Quebec, 371–74, 376–77, 389, 393–94; South Carolina, 170

Adverse selection: France, 21, 364, 379; Quebec, 21, 364, 369, 374

Aetna, 113

Alaska automobile insurance, rating by Conning Company, 260

Alliance of American Insurers, 278

Allstate, 9, 113, 115, 126, 161, 257

Alternative risk transfer (ART) market, 18, 321–23, 332, 356, 357

American Risk and Insurance Association (ARIA), 84

AMGRO, 112

Antitrust law: California, 201; federal, 6, 253–55; Illinois, 257; New Jersey, 130

ARIA (American Risk and Insurance Association), 84

Assessments on insurers: New Jersey, 112; South Carolina, 158

Assigned risk pool. See Residual market

Atlantic Employers, 118

Auto theft in New Jersey, 126–27, 131

Automobile insurance, history of, 252–156

Automobile Insurance Plans Service Office, 273

Automobile Insurers Bureau, 7, 12, 126

Banking industry: alternative commercial insurance offered by, 323; authorized to offer insurance, 19, 201, 324; and credit risk, 361; deregulation, 1, 16, 18–19, 22

Belgium, 362, 368

Bertie, Marjorie M., 81

Bodily injury liability (BIL): California, 138-39, 245; Illinois, 276; Massachusetts, 37, 52, 65–76, 138; Michigan, 138; New Jersey, 86–87, 106, 110, 127–29, 138; Quebec, 367; South Carolina, 169, 171–89. See also Loss costs

Bonus-malus system, 362; France, 364, 378, 381, 389–90; Quebec, 364, 366, 368, 370–71, 389

Boston fire, 250–51

Boyer, Marcel, 369

Bureau insurers, 8–9, 251. See also Antitrust law

Business firms. See Form regulation in commercial insurance

CALI. See compulsory automobile liability insurance

California automobile insurance, 3,
195–247; accident rates and incurred
losses, 217–21, 243–44; assigned risk
pool, 208–09; banks authorized to sell,
201; comparison to other states,
210–15, 237–38, 243, 244–45;
complaints received by Department of
Insurance, 230–31; cross-subsidies,
246; decline in premiums and incurred
losses, explanations for, 14, 226–31,
237–45; driving under the influence,
222, 233; earned premiums, 216; entry
and exit of insurers, 201, 204–07;
excess claims, 138–39; fatalities, 219;
fraud, 223–26, 231, 245; fundamental
factors in creating proximate
determinants, 216; "good driver"
incentives, 199, 201, 222–23, 231,
242–43; history of Proposition *103*,
10–11; Insurance Department website,
19, 201, 225, 230; lawsuits against
insurers, 196; Low Cost Automobile
Insurance Program, 209; lower quality
insurance, 230–31; predictions of
Proposition *103*'s effect, 201–04;
premium rollback and freeze, 197–98,
202–04, 210, 226, 245; premium
structure and Proposition *103*, 222–23,
237–42; pricing and profitability,
210–15, 227–30, 231, 241; prior
approval of rates, 198–99, 204, 228,
239; proximate determinants of
premiums, 216–17, 242–45; rate-
setting formula, 199; regulatory
framework of Proposition *103*, 196,
197–201, 232; regulatory lag
hypothesis, 204, 228–30; residual
market, 14, 208–09, 245; roadway
safety improvements, 222; seat belts
and safe driving experience, 221–22,
224–25, 231, 233; state website
offering information, 19; third-party
lawsuits, 226–27, 233; zip codes used
for rating, 199
California electricity deregulation, 232
California workers' compensation, 246
Camden Fire Insurance Co., 127
Canada. *See* Quebec automobile insurance

Caps: Massachusetts, 31, 144–45; New
Jersey, 92–93, 144
Captive insurance, 322, 332
Capture theory, 265, 279, 287
Cardinale, Gerald, 111, 129
Chen, X., 126
Chicago: fire, 250–51; rates within,
257–58. *See also* Illinois automobile
insurance
Chicago theory, 7
Claim costs. *See* Loss costs
Clayton Act, 253
Collisions. *See* Accident rates; Fatalities
Collusion. *See* Antitrust law
Commercial insurance. *See* Alternative risk
transfer (ART) market; Form regulation
in commercial insurance
Commitment levels and international
regulation, 21, 362–63; France, 21,
364, 381, 389; Quebec, 21, 364
Competition, 264; alternative risk
transfer (ART) market, 321–23, 356,
357; and bureau insurers, 9;
commercial insurance benefits from,
346–56; France market, 389;
Massachusetts market, 55–65, 78;
Quebec market, 364, 369; states using
competitive ratings, 313–14. *See also*
Deregulation; Open competition in
Illinois
Compulsory automobile liability
insurance: Japan, 384–88; New Jersey,
82; Quebec, 365; South Carolina, 150,
192
Computer Services Corp., 112
Conning Company rankings, 259, 260,
269, 270, 273, 279
Consumer attitudes toward insurers: and
capture theory, 265; dissatisfaction over
rates, 4; France, 378; influence of, 10;
Massachusetts, 28, 41–42; New Jersey,
103; Quebec, 365. *See also* Interest
group theory
Consumer protection aspect of form
regulation, 346
Consumer surplus, 326–31, 359–60
Contract language, 321.
Credit-risk regulations, 361

Cross-subsidies, 4; California, 246; Massachusetts, 12, 26, 33, 36, 50–55, 64; negative effects of, 5, 12; New Jersey, 117; and political movements, 10
Cummins, J. David, 114, 115, 118, 260
Customizing contract language, 321

Dachour, Maki, 380
Deductibles: France, 375; New Jersey, 111; Quebec, 371
Demand for insurance, 349; South Carolina, 189–91
Demerit point system in Quebec, 366, 369–70, 371, 373
Deregulation, 1–24; banking industry, 1, 16, 18–19, 22; benefits from, 2, 5, 11, 15–16, 19; California electricity, 232; commercial insurance benefits from, 346–57; and consumer interest groups, 10; endorsement of, 23; European Union, 1, 364; further research needs, 23, 318–20; history of, 9–10; and interest group theory, 9; international adoption of, 1, 5–6; Japan, 387–88, 390; negatives of, 22, 262; and savings and loan crisis, 22. See also Open competition in Illinois; specific states
Derrig, Richard, 126
Dionne, Georges, 363, 369, 371, 373, 380
Direct writers: Massachusetts, 55–57; New Jersey, 100–01, 116, 117, 136; variable in prior approval rate regulation analysis, 293, 294
Discounts: California, 201; Massachusetts, 29, 61, 78, 140. See also Safe driving incentives
Discriminatory rates, 264, 279
Doherty, Neil, 363
Dowling, Vincent J., Jr., 135
Driving under the influence (DUI): California, 222, 233; South Carolina, 158, 170

Earned premiums in California, 216
Economic theories of regulation, 6–11, 261–67, 280–81; and form regulation, 346
Efficiencies of deregulation, 15–16, 19

Election issue, auto insurance pricing as, 10–11, 111, 132, 144. See also Maximization of political support
Electric Insurance Co., 99
Entry and exit of insurers, 1; California, 201, 204–07; Massachusetts, 53–54, 59–60, 77, 136, 146–47; New Jersey, 84, 91, 108, 112, 113, 116–22, 130, 131, 136, 146–47; and rate suppression, 14–15; South Carolina, 14, 158, 163–64, 193
European Union: elimination of bonus-malus scheme in France, 389–90; overview of insurance regulation, 395; solvency regulation, 374, 395; Third Generation Directives and insurance industry, 19; transitional rules for unified European market, 364; unified insurance market as goal of, 374
Excess profit law: deemed unnecessary, 7, 141; New Jersey, 98–103, 111, 130
Excessive claiming. See Fraud
Exit of insurers. See Entry and exit of insurers

Fatalities: California, 219; Canada and Quebec, 319, 371–72; France, 319; Japan, 385–86; regulated versus unregulated states, 319; South Carolina, 170. See also Accident rates
Federal regulation of insurance, 252–53
Federal Trade Commission Act, 253
File and use system, 259, 290; Massachusetts, 27
Financial Services Modernization Act of 1999. See Gramm-Leach-Bliley Act
Finite risk solutions, 324
Fire insurance, 250–52
Fireman's Fund, 59
Flex-rating system, 290; New Jersey, 92, 111; South Carolina, 152–53
Florio, Jim, 95, 111, 126
Foreign industrialized nations and insurance regulation, 18–19, 361–96; bonus-malus system, 362–63; commitment levels, 362–63; moral hazard, 362. See also France automobile

insurance; Japan automobile insurance; Quebec automobile insurance

Form regulation in commercial insurance, 5, 16–18, 321–60; alternative risk transfer (ART) market, 18, 321–23, 332, 356, 357; benefits and costs of, 346–56; and collinearity problem in analysis, 353; consumer protection aspect of, 346; and consumer surplus, 326–31, 359–60; customizing contract language, 321; delay in innovation, effect of, 5, 324–42; elimination or reduction of, reasons to favor, 353; in European countries, 362; "file and use" states, 333; fraud lowered by, 346; large business firms, 338, 341, 349; Minnesota versus New York, 324, 342–45; and monopolist pricing of first entrant, 17, 326; prior approval regulation states, 16, 333; property-casualty insurance, 338, 341, 349; states and delayed approvals, 17, 18, 333–38; workers' compensation insurance, 338, 341, 349, 352

Foundation for Taxpayer and Consumer Rights, 226, 227, 230

France automobile insurance, 362, 374–84, 389–90; accident rates, 375, 380–82, 396; adverse selection, 21, 364, 379; bonus-malus system, 364, 378, 381, 389–90; commitment levels, 21, 364, 381, 389; deductibles, 375; fatalities, 319; moral hazard, 364; positive effects of regulation in, 21; premiums, 375, 378; pricing system, 379–84; rating system, 368, 389; types of, 375

Fraud, 138; California, 138–39, 223–26, 231, 245; and form regulation in commercial insurance, 346; Massachusetts, 21, 37–38, 52, 74; need for regulation to prevent, 20–21; New Jersey, 82, 86, 125–27, 131; South Carolina, 175–76, 186–89

Freifelder, Len, 113

Garamendi, John, 197, 202
GEICO, 108, 122

General Accident Insurance Co. of America, 121–22

Germany automobile insurance, 362

"Good driver" incentives. See Safe driving incentives

Gouriéroux, Christian, 368, 379

Gramm-Leach-Bliley Act, 1, 18, 324

GSA Insurance Co., 89–90

Hamm, William, 227

Harleysville-Garden State, 99

Harrington, Scott, 159, 202, 203, 208, 228, 269

Hartford Group, 99

Herfindahl-Hirschman indices and concentration ratios: California, 202–03; Illinois, 261; New Jersey, 114–15; South Carolina, 161

History of insurance in United States, 249–56

Home State Insurance, 118, 119

Illinois automobile insurance, 3, 248–84; analysis of, 267–81; antitrust concerns, 257; Chicago coverage, 257–58; comparison to regulated states, 267–81; economics of regulation, 261–67; Herfindahl indices and concentration ratios, 261; history of rate regulation, 256–58; insolvency of insurers, 279; loss ratio, 263–67, 269; open competition, 131, 257–58; prior approval rate regulation, 256–57; prior approval states compared to, 272–73; rating by Conning Company, 260; research on state open competition, 258–61; residual market, 263–65, 273, 275; unfair discrimination, 264; uninsureds, 264–65, 275–76; unique position as sole state without rate regulatory law, 258, 260, 267; urban versus rural population, 274–75, 276

Incentives: cross-subsidies' effect on, 12, 50–51; Massachusetts, 50–55; Quebec, 389; South Carolina, 156. See also Safe driving incentives

Independent agents in New Jersey, 100–01

Independent insurers, 8

Inefficiency overcome by deregulation, 15–16

INRETS. *See* National Institute for Transport and Safety Research

Insolvency of insurance companies, 250–51, 265, 266, 278; Illinois, 279

Insurance Company of North America, 249

Insurance Research Council of New Jersey, 96, 87, 125, 127, 276

Insurance Services Office (ISO), 257

Interest group theory, 7–10, 17

Interest rates and insurance pricing, 11

International regulation, 18–19, 361–96; bonus-malus system, 362–63; commitment levels, 362–63; moral hazard, 362. *See also* France automobile insurance; Japan automobile insurance; Quebec automobile insurance

Interstate commerce and insurance regulation, 252–55

Jaffe, Sanford, 110

Japan automobile insurance, 19, 364, 384–88, 390; Automobile Insurance Rating Organization, 385; Automobile Liability Security Law, 384, 387; compulsory automobile liability insurance (CALI), 384–88; deregulation of, 387–88, 390; fatality and accident statistics, 385–86; Financial System Reform Bill (June *1998*), 386; government agencies dealing with, 386–87; Law Concerning Non-Life Insurance Rating Organizations, 385, 386; loss survey method, 386; Ministry of Finance structural changes, 386–87; no-fault system, 384; pooling of risk, 385; rating organizations, 385; reform after *1996*, 386–88; tort liability claims, 384–85; types of, 384

Joint pricing, history of, 251–54. *See also* Antitrust law

Joint Underwriting Association (JUA): New Jersey, 82, 101, 108–10, 111, 123–24; South Carolina, 159, 168, 191

Joskow, Paul, 262

Justice, Department of, study on state regulation, 258

Kansas regulation of rate making, 251

Klein, Robert, 202

Lascher, Edward L., 84

Lawsuits against California insurers, 226–27, 233

Leibenstein, Harvey, 226

Lemaire, Jean, 368

Lesniak, Raymond J., 109

Liberty Mutual Fire Insurance Co., 99

Liebenstein, Harvey, 226

Loss costs: Massachusetts, 54, 65–76; and regulation of insurance pricing, 11; South Carolina, 164, 170–71, 170–91; variable in prior approval rate regulation analysis, 293, 294

Loss ratio volatility, 296–97, 306–07, 310, 315

Loss ratios: Illinois, 263–67, 269; methodology and data to analyze, 288–98, 316–18; New Jersey, 101–03; and prior approval rate regulation, 288–309, 296–309, 315, 318; South Carolina, 164, 170–71

Louisiana and delay in form approval, 17, 337

Low, Harry, 199

Market concentration: New Jersey, 114–15; South Carolina, 159–62. *See also* Competition; Entry and exit of insurers; Herfindahl-Hirschman indices and concentration ratios

Market disruption theory, 266–67, 269, 281

Maryland Casualty, 90

Massachusetts automobile insurance, 3, 25–80; accident rates, 51; caps, 31, 144–45; Commonwealth Automobile Reinsurers (CAR) for undesirable policies, 36–37, 50, 53, 54, 62–65; comparison to New Jersey, 135–47; comparison to other states, 41–42, 54–58, 66–76, 140–41; competitive rate setting, 27–29, 41, 145; consumer interest as factor in rate setting, 28, 41–42; cross-subsidies in rates, 12, 26, 33, 36, 50–55, 64; determination of regulated rates, 31–36; direct writers, 55–57, 136–37; discounted rates, 29, 61, 78, 140; entry of insurers, 59–60, 78; excess claims, 138; exit of insurers, 53–54, 59–60, 77, 136, 146–47; file and use system, 27; fraud, 21, 37–38, 52; goals of, 25–26; higher costs due to regulation, 54–55; history of regulatory system, 26–29; incentive effects, 50–55; insurer return on equity (ROE), 42–50; loss costs and premiums, 54, 65–76; mandatory offer rule, 27; market structure and competition, 55–65, 78; need for deregulation, 143–47; negatives of current regulatory system, 26; no-fault system, 27, 37, 52, 138; policy cancellation restrictions, 51; preference for regional insurers, 57–59; rate increases, 139–40; rate setting, 27–36, 38–50, 137; rate suppression's effect on insurers, 13, 53–54, 144; rating classes, 29–30; reforms, 37–38, 73–74, 78, 139, 143–47; regulatory process, 29–31, 77; repair costs, 139; residual market, 14, 32, 36, 52–53, 62–65, 78, 275; Safe Driver Insurance Program (SDIP), 29; safe driving incentives, 61, 78; single-state writers, 15, 59, 61, 136–37; territory definitions, 29–31, 32; underwriting results, 38–42, 141–43; uninsureds, 26; universal coverage guaranteed, 26, 36, 62

Massachusetts history of insurance, 249
Massachusetts Insurance Fraud Bureau (MIFB), 21, 37, 74
McCarran-Ferguson Act, 7, 255–56
McGreevey, Jim, 91
Merritt committee of New York Senate and Assembly, 251, 252
Metropolitan, 118
Michigan automobile insurance: delay in form approval, 17, 18, 337; excess claims, 138; rating by Conning Company, 260

MIFB (Massachusetts Insurance Fraud Bureau), 21, 37, 74
Minnesota versus New York, form regulation in commercial insurance, 324, 342–45
Missouri's suit to reduce rates (1922), 254–55
Monopolies. See Antitrust law
Moradi-Shalal v. Fireman's Fund (1988), 196, 225, 226–27, 233
Moral hazard: foreign countries' regulation of, 362; France, 364; Quebec, 364, 370–71. See also Accident rates
Multiline-multiyear products, 323

National Association of Insurance Commissioners (NAIC), 9, 256, 263
National Board of Fire Underwriters, 251
National Convention of Insurance Commissioners (NCIC), 251, 252
National Institute for Transport and Safety Research (INRETS: Institut National de Recherche sur les Transports et leur Sécurité), 379
Nationwide, 108, 120, 161
New England Fidelity, 61
New Jersey automobile insurance, 3, 81–134; antitrust exemptions for industry, 130; assessments on insurers, 112; auto theft, 126–27, 131; Automobile Insurance Cost Reduction Act (AICRA), 83, 85–87, 92, 95, 110, 125; caps, 92–93, 144; "Clifford formula," 83, 104; comparison to Massachusetts, 135–47; comparison to other states, 81–83, 101, 122–23, 129; concentration in New Jersey market, 114–15; consumer attitudes toward insurers, 103; demographics, 82; direct writers, 100–01, 116, 117, 136; entry of insurers, 116–22, 131; excess claims, 138; excess profit law, 98–103, 111, 130; exit of insurers, 84, 91, 108, 112, 113, 116–22, 130, 131, 136, 146–47; expedited filing rule, 92; Fair Automobile Insurance Reform Act of 1990 (FAIR Act), 111–14, 118, 120; flex-rating scheme, 92, 111; fraud, 82,

86, 125–27, 131; high claims costs, 127–29; history of regulatory system, 82, 105; Insurance Department's outreach, 96, 130; Joint Underwriting Association (JUA) period, 82, 101, 108–10, 111, 123–24; loss ratios, 101–03; Market Transition Facility (MTF) period, 82, 101, 111–14, 120, 123–24; minimal coverage, 86; named-driver exclusion, 86; need for deregulation, 130, 143–47; New Jersey–only subsidiaries to handle, 120–21; no-fault system, 82, 84, 104–08, 130, 138; private passenger automobile rate regulation, 87–103; Public Advocate Office eliminated, 91; qualified persons who can seek rate review hearings, 91; rate cases, 88–91; rate suppression, 13, 117; reforms, 130–32, 143–47; regulatory process, 87–88, 129; "Remand Case," 83, 104; residual market, 108, 122–25; residual market equalization charge (RMEC), 108–09; rollback of 15 percent, 85–87, 132; strict prior approval rate regulation, 84, 87, 114; territories and rates, 86, 131; tier rating system, 94–98; tort claims, 84, 85, 86, 138; underwriting results, 141–43; uninsureds, 85, 124–25, 131; Urban Enterprise Zone (UEZ) plan, 85, 93–94

New Jersey Economic Development Authority, 113

New Jersey Manufacturers, 115

New Jersey Re-Insurance, 88

New York: history of insurance, 249–50, 256; versus Minnesota, form regulation in commercial insurance, 324, 342–45; website offering information, 19

Niehaus, Gregory, 228

No-fault system: Massachusetts, 27, 37, 52, 138; New Jersey, 82, 84, 104–08, 130, 138; Quebec, 363

North Carolina automobile insurance, 156, 163, 296

North Dakota automobile insurance, rating by Conning Company, 260

Older drivers (after age 65) in South Carolina, 185, 186

Parc Automobile de la Sofres survey, 379

Paul, Samuel, 252–53

Paul v. Virginia (*1869*), 6, 253, 254, 255

PDL. *See* Property damage liability

Peltzman, Sam, 265

Pennsylvania Contributorship for the Insurance of Houses from Loss by Fire, 249

Pennsylvania history of insurance, 249

Personal injury protection (PIP), 293–94; Massachusetts, 37, 52; New Jersey, 86–87, 106–08, 110, 112, 127–29

Pilgrim Insurance Co., 59

Policy Management Services Corp., 112

Political entrepreneurship theory of regulation, 10

Political issue. *See* Election issue, auto insurance pricing as

Political support, 265, 269, 281

Powers, Michael, 84

Premiums: California premium rollback and freeze, 197–98, 202–04, 210, 226, 245; California premium structure, 222–23, 237–42; France, 375, 378; Massachusetts loss costs and, 65–76; Quebec, 366, 367, 368, 388. *See also* Cross-subsidies; Rate setting

Price deregulation. *See* Deregulation

Pricing. *See* Cross-subsidies; Rate setting

Prior approval rate regulation, 3, 232, 259, 285–320; California, 198–99, 204, 228, 239; and capture theory, 287; conceptual framework of, 287–88; control variables affecting, 292–94; empirical results for analysis of loss ratios, 298–309; and expenditure growth rates, 297–98, 307–09, 310, 315; and form regulation in commercial insurance, 16, 333; further research needs, 318–20; history of, 7; Illinois, 256–57, 272–73; interaction variables affecting, 294–95; and interest group theory, 8–9; least squares estimate, 298–309; and loss ratio volatility, 296–97, 306–07, 310, 315;

and loss ratios, 288–309, 315, 318;
Massachusetts, 292; methodology and
data to analyze loss ratios, 288–98,
316–18; New Jersey, 84, 87, 114, 292;
and rate suppression hypothesis, 4, 287;
and regulatory lag hypothesis, 287–88;
and residual market share analysis,
295–96, 305–06, 310, 315; South
Carolina, 153, 191, 292; states using,
292, 313–14
Pritchett, S. Travis, 159
Product Liability Risk Retention Act of
1981, 322
Productivity benefits from deregulation,
15–16
Profit margins: analysis of, 262–63;
California, 210–15, 227–30, 231, 241.
See also Excess profit law
Profitability: California, 210–15, 216;
South Carolina, 164–67. *See also*
Excess profit law; Profit margins
Progressive, 108, 120, 122, 161
Property damage liability (PDL):
California, 138–39, 245;
Massachusetts, 66–76, 138; Michigan,
138; New Jersey, 86–87, 106, 110,
127–29, 138; South Carolina, 173–89
Provident Washington Co., 122
Prudential Group, 89, 115
Prudential Property and Casualty Co. of
New Jersey, 121

Quebec automobile insurance, 363–74,
388–89; accident statistics, 371–74,
376–77, 389, 393–94; administration
fees, 366; adverse selection, 364, 369,
374; Agreement on Direct
Compensation, 365; Automobile
Insurance Act, adoption of, 365;
bonus-malus system, 363–64, 366,
368, 370–71, 389; commitment levels,
21, 364; competition in market, 364,
369; compulsory liability insurance,
365; consumer attitudes toward, 365;
criticisms of, 366–67; delay in
compensating victims, 367; demerit
point scheme, 366, 369–70, 371, 373;
goals of reform, 365–66; lawyers' role

in, 367; moral hazard, 364, 370–71;
no-fault system, 363, 365; operating
costs, 366–67; positive effects of
regulation in, 21; premium increases,
366, 367, 368; private sector rating
system, 368–69, 388–89; public
insurer rating system, 369, 388; rating
system, 367–71; safe driving incentives,
366, 370, 389; solvency regulation,
365; traffic violations, 372–74, 389;
uncompensated victims, 367
Quebec Automobile Insurance Board
(SAAQ: Société de l'Assurance
Automobile du Québec), 365–66, 369,
373

Rate setting: California, 199; European
Union, 395; France, 368, 389; history
of regulation, generally, 249–56; Japan,
385; and market disruption, 266–67,
273; Massachusetts, 27, 31–36, 38–50;
New Jersey, 87–103; objectives of,
263–64; Quebec, 367–74, 389; South
Carolina, 152–56. *See also* Regulation
of prices
Rate suppression, 2, 4, 264–65; effect on
insurers, 14, 281, 287; Massachusetts,
13, 53–54, 144; negative effects of, 5,
12–15; New Jersey, 13, 117; South
Carolina, 13, 177, 181
Rating organizations: bureau insurers,
8–9, 251; Japan, 385; U.S. cartels, 6–7,
253–55
Regional insurers: effect on insurance
rates, 15; Massachusetts, 57–59
Regulation of prices, 3; and interest group
theory, 7–8; need for, 6, 19–21;
negative effects of, 5, 12–15; regulated
states, defined, 269; tested by economic
theories, 261–67, 280–81. *See also*
Deregulation; Rate setting; specific
states
Regulatory lag hypothesis, 204, 228–30,
287–88
Reinsurance, 296; Commonwealth
Automobile Reinsurers (CAR) for
undesirable policies in Massachusetts,
36–37, 50, 53, 54, 62–65; Reinsurance

Facility for residual market in South
Carolina, 148–50, 156–59, 167–69,
183, 184–86, 187, 191. *See also*
Residual market
Rent-a-captive insurers, 322
Research on state open competition,
258–61
Residual market: California, 14, 208–09,
245; factors increasing size of, 5,
13–14; Illinois, 263–65, 273, 275;
Massachusetts, 14, 32, 36, 52–53,
62–65, 78, 275; New Jersey, 108,
122–25, 275; and prior approval rate
regulation, 295–96, 305–06, 310, 315;
rate setting needed after deregulation,
20; South Carolina, 148–49, 156–59,
167–69, 183, 184–86, 187, 191, 275
Risk retention groups (RRGs), 322–23
Roadway safety improvements in
California, 222
Robinson-Patman Act, 253
Rothschild, Michael, 379
Royal Globe Insurance Co. v. *Superior Court*
(*1979*), 226–27
RRGs (risk retention groups), 322–23
Rural versus urban areas: Illinois, 274–75,
276; Massachusetts urban caps, 145;
South Carolina, 175, 183, 185, 187,
189

SAAQ. *See* Quebec Automobile Insurance
Board
Safe driving incentives, 2, 5; California,
199, 201, 222–23, 231, 242–43;
France, 378; Massachusetts, 61, 78;
Quebec, 366, 370, 389; South
Carolina, 156, 177, 183
Safeco, 108, 120
San Francisco fire, 250, 251, 252
Savings and loan crisis and deregulation,
22
Seat belt use in California, 221–22,
224–25, 231, 233
SEAU. *See* Southeastern Underwriters
Association
Self-insurance, 322, 332
Sherman Act, 253

Single-state writers: market exit resulting
in, 15; Massachusetts, 15, 59, 61,
136–37
Solvency regulation, 1, 20; European
Union, 374, 395; Quebec, 365. *See also*
Insolvency of insurance companies
South Carolina automobile insurance, 3,
148–94; accident rates, 170;
assessments against insurers, 158;
availability, 167–70; claim costs,
170–91; comparison to other states,
152, 156, 161, 171–75, 190;
compulsory liability insurance, 150,
192; demand for insurance, 189–91;
entry and exit of insurers, 14, 158,
163–64, 193; fatality rates, 170; flex
rating system, 152–53; "forgiveness
statutes" for traffic violations, 156;
fraud, 175–76, 186–89; history of
regulatory system, 149–51, 191; Joint
Underwriting Association (JUA), 159,
168, 191; legislative reform, 149,
192–93; loss cost inflation, 176–84;
loss costs and loss ratios, 164, 170–71;
market concentration, 159–62; price
level regulation, 152–53; prior approval
rate regulation, 153, 191, 292;
profitability, 164–67; rate setting,
152–56; rate suppression, 13, 177, 181;
recoupment fee for residual losses,
158–59, 192; regulatory process,
149–59, 191; Reinsurance Facility for
residual market, 148–50, 156–59,
167–69, 183, 184–86, 187, 191; rural
versus urban areas, 175, 183, 185, 187,
189; safe driving incentives, 156, 177,
183; territories and ratings, 153–56;
tort claims, 175; uninsureds, 169–70
Southeastern Underwriters Association
(SEUA), 6, 254–55
State Farm, 9, 91, 92, 115, 161, 198, 257
State Farm Indemnity, 99, 121
State National Insurance Co., 122
Stiglitz, Joseph, 379
Stone, James, 28
Strict prior approval. *See* Prior approval
rate regulation
Subrogation, 388

Subsidiaries formed in New Jersey to
    handle auto insurance, 120–21
Suppression of rates. *See* Rate suppression
Surplus lines of insurance, 323

Tennyson, Sharon, 116, 228
Territories and ratings: Massachusetts,
    29–31, 32; New Jersey, 86, 131; South
    Carolina, 153–56
Theft of autos in New Jersey, 126–27, 131
Third-party lawsuits in California,
    226–27, 233
Tier rating system in New Jersey, 94–98
Tort claims: Japan, 384–85; New Jersey,
    84, 85, 86, 138; South Carolina, 175
Traffic violations: Quebec, 372–74, 389;
    South Carolina, 156, 170. *See also* Safe
    driving incentives
Trust Insurance Co., 61
Twin City Fire Insurance, 118

Underwriting: Massachusetts and New
    Jersey, 141–43; Quebec, 388; South
    Carolina, 155. *See also* Joint
    Underwriting Association (JUA)
Unfair discrimination, 264, 279; Illinois,
    264
Uninsureds, 266; Illinois, 264–65,
    275–76; Massachusetts, 26; New Jersey,

85, 124–25, 131; South Carolina,
    169–70
United Kingdom automobile insurance,
    362; bodily injury claims, 320
Universal coverage in Massachusetts, 26,
    36, 62
Urban versus rural population. *See* Rural
    versus urban areas
Use and file system, 290

Vanasse, Charles, 368, 371, 373, 379
Venezian, Emilio, 229
Volatility of loss ratio. *See* Loss ratio
    volatility

Warner Insurance Services, 112
Websites: California, 19, 201, 225, 230;
    New Jersey, 96, 130; New York, 19
Weisberg, H. I., 126
Weiss, Mary, 118, 260
Whitman, Christine Todd, 83, 85, 91,
    114
Workers' compensation insurance, 3;
    California, 246; and form regulation,
    338, 341, 349, 352

Young drivers: Massachusetts, 65, 145;
    South Carolina, 185

JOINT CENTER